ADMINISTRATION OF HIGH SCHOOL ATHLETICS

seventh edition

IRVIN A. KELLER
CHARLES E. FORSYTHE

Prentice-Hall, Inc., Englewood Cliffs, New Jersey 07632

Library of Congress Cataloging in Publication Data

KELLER, IRVIN A.
  Administration of high school athletics.

  Authors' names reversed on 1977 ed.
  Bibliography
  Includes index.
  1. Sports—Organization and administration—United
States.   2. School sports—United States—Management.
3. Athletics—United States—Management.   I. Forsythe,
Charles E. (Charles Edward), 1899–   II. Title.
GV713.K45   1984   373.18′9   83–17636
ISBN 0–13–005728–2

Editorial/production supervision and interior design: Virginia Rubens
Cover design: Wanda Lubelska Design
Manufacturing buyer: Harry P. Baisley

Printed in the United States of America

10 9 8 7 6 5 4 3 2 1

ISBN 0-13-005728-2

Prentice-Hall International, Inc., *London*
Prentice-Hall of Australia Pty. Limited, *Sydney*
Editora Prentice-Hall do Brasil, Ltda., *Rio de Janeiro*
Prentice-Hall Canada Inc., *Toronto*
Prentice-Hall of India Private Limited, *New Delhi*
Prentice-Hall of Japan, Inc., *Tokyo*
Prentice-Hall of Southeast Asia Pte. Ltd., *Singapore*
Whitehall Books Limited, *Wellington, New Zealand*

Contents

PREFACE vii

1 THE INTERSCHOLASTIC ATHLETIC ADMINISTRATOR 1

The First High School Athletic Administrators *1*
Athletic Directors Gain Professional Status *2*
Qualifications for Interscholastic Athletic Administrators *4*
Responsibilities of the Interscholastic Athletic Administrator *5*

2 HISTORY, PHILOSOPHY, AND OBJECTIVES OF HIGH SCHOOL ATHLETICS 8

Stages in the Evolution of High School Athletics *8*
Phases in the Development of Athletic Control *10*
Emergence of a Philosophy of High School Athletics *12*
Objectives of Interscholastic Athletics *16*
Challenges Still Facing the Schools *18*

3 THE NATIONAL FEDERATION OF STATE HIGH SCHOOL ASSOCIATIONS 23

The Origin of the National Federation *23*
The Expanded Scope of the National Federation *24*
Nature of the National Federation *27*
Administration of the National Federation Program *27*
National Federation Philosophy *28*
Accomplishments of the National Federation *29*
National Federation Services *32*
Sanctioning Policies and Procedures *38*
Nonschool-Sponsored Activities *46*
Continuing Eligibility *51*
Guiding Principles *57*
Additional National Federation Activities *60*

4   *STATE HIGH SCHOOL ATHLETIC AND ACTIVITIES ASSOCIATIONS* **67**

Early State Organizations   *67*
Athletic and Activity Associations   *68*
Purposes of State Associations   *68*
Types of State Associations   *71*
Functions of State Associations   *75*
The State High School Association Must Be Supported   *89*

5   *STANDARDS OF ELIGIBILITY FOR INTERSCHOLASTIC ATHLETIC COMPETITION*   **94**

Development of Standards of Eligibility   *94*
Common Eligibility Regulations   *97*
Special Eligibility Regulations   *113*

6   *ATHLETIC CONTEST REGULATIONS AND STANDARDS*   **124**

Purpose of Contest Regulations   *124*
Common Regulations   *125*
Special Contest Administrative Regulations   *144*
Contest Regulations for Junior High School   *148*

7   *ATHLETIC CONTEST MANAGEMENT*   **154**

Importance of Efficient Management   *154*
Before-Game Preparation (Home Contests)   *156*
Game Responsibilities (Home Contests)   *165*
After-Game Responsibilities (Home Contests)   *170*
Preparation for Out-Of-Town Games   *171*
General Management Duties and Policies   *177*
Meet and Tournament Management   *186*

8   *ADMINISTRATION OF THE LOCAL INTERSCHOLASTIC PROGRAM*   **194**

Division of Responsibility in Local High School Athletic
   Administration   *194*
Administrative Organization   *200*
Athletic Leagues and Conferences as Administrative Agencies   *212*
Matters Appropriate for Athletic Council Consideration   *213*
Establishing and Defining High School Athletic Policy   *215*
Implementing Local Athletic Policies   *217*
Evaluation of the High School Athletic Program   *225*

9 ATHLETIC AWARDS 231

General Awards Policies *231*
School and Sport Awards Policies *233*
Problems Schools Face in Regard to Awards and Amateurism *237*

10 ATHLETIC EQUIPMENT 240

The Purchase of Equipment *240*
Issuing Equipment *245*
General Care of Athletic Equipment *250*

11 ATHLETIC FINANCES AND BUDGETS 255

General Athletic Finance Considerations *255*
Financing the Athletic Program *257*
Athletic Budgets *265*
Preparing a Budget for Board of Education Approval *268*
Presenting the Budget *270*

12 PROVIDING FOR THE HEALTH AND SAFETY OF ATHLETES 277

The Safety Program *277*
Athletic Safety Essentials *278*
Safety Suggestions *288*
Safety in Transportation *292*
The Sanitation Program *293*
Medical Supervision of Athletics *295*
Athletic Accident Insurance *297*

13 ATHLETIC FACILITIES—LAYOUT AND MAINTENANCE 308

General and Indoor Facilities *308*
Outdoor Playing Facilities *311*
Maintenance of Athletic Fields *324*
Long-Range Planning *326*
Metric System *328*

14 INTRAMURAL ACTIVITIES 330

Place in the Program *330*
General Intramural Objectives *335*
Administration of Intramural Activities *338*
Suggested Intramural Policies and Practices *346*
Financing Intramurals *347*

15   *JUNIOR HIGH SCHOOL ATHLETICS*   **350**

Development of Athletics in Junior High Schools   *350*
Guiding Principles for Junior High School Athletics   *353*
Major Concerns of Junior High School Athletic Administrators   *358*
Guidelines for Levels of Athletic Competition   *360*

16   *LEGAL ASPECTS OF INTERSCHOLASTIC ACTIVITIES*   **362**

Necessity of Basic Legal Understanding   *362*
Due Process   *368*
Dealing With Unruly Fans   *371*
Discrimination   *372*
Standards of Eligibility and the Law   *374*
National Federation Legal Aid Pact   *378*
Legal Status of State High School Associations   *379*

17   *INTERSCHOLASTIC ACTIVITIES AND THE FUTURE*   **385**

Three Major Problems Facing Athletic Administrators   *385*
Anticipated Developments and Trends   *387*

Appendix A: Directory of State High School Associations   *394*
Appendix B: Metric Conversion Table   *399*
Appendix C: Four-Hundred-Metre Track Diagram   *400*

INDEX   **401**

Preface

Interscholastic athletics, along with other student activities, play an important role in modern secondary education. A tremendous increase in girls' athletics and an expanded scope in both the boys' and girls' programs, together with societal changes, present many new and difficult problems for those responsible for interscholastics in the 18,000 high schools in this country which extend educational athletic opportunities to over 5,000,000 participants.

The administration of high school athletics has become increasingly complex as conditions have changed. In an earlier period, the athletic program was generally administered by the high school principal or superintendent, either of whom quite frequently was a former coach. The demands placed on their positions today leave insufficient time to attend to athletic administrative details and to provide the necessary leadership for the athletic program. Further, today many of those who have been trained for secondary school administration have not had the background in athletics their predecessors had. Consequently, the responsibility for directing athletic programs more often falls to an athletic administrator. When this trend began, it involved primarily the assigning of routine administrative details to some coach on the staff who was given the title of "athletic director" in recognition of his or her extra duties. In contrast, today's director of athletics occupies a position of administrative significance, and he or she must have professional training to be successful in providing the essential leadership for the athletic program, which is less and less being provided by principals and superintendents.

All of these matters, and others, have been taken into consideration in the preparation of the seventh edition of this book. Our original purpose was to aid (1) those in the field responsible for administering high school physical education and athletic programs, (2) coaches needing suggestions and guidance in handling inherent administrative responsibilities, and (3) students planning to become coaches or supervisors and directors of physical education and athletics. This seventh edition of *Administration of High School Athletics* still embraces those original objectives but has been revised to contain new and up-to-date information of importance to those involved in athletic administration, whether they be full-time or part-time athletic directors, or principals assuming the responsibility for administering high school athletics.

A new first chapter traces the evolution of the position of athletic administrator and outlines the responsibilities involved. Succeeding chapters deal with the history and development of athletic activities; the functions of state and national high school associations; local, state, and national policies; standards of eligibility; contest management; equipment; awards; finances and budgets; health and safety of athletes; layout and maintenance of facilities; intramurals; junior high school athletics; legal aspects; and a look to the future of interscholastic athletics. An important feature of the book is that, in addition to discussing athletic administrative responsibilities, we also present practical policies and procedures for implementing them, with emphasis on how to enhance the educational values of interscholastic athletics.

It was my privilege to have been invited to co-author the fifth and sixth editions of *Administration of High School Athletics* with the late Charles E. Forsythe, whose wide experience as a coach, athletic director, high school administrator, and executive secretary of the Michigan High School Athletic Association for many years enabled him to author a highly successful book in its first four editions. This seventh edition will prove to be an excellent text for courses in high school athletic administration and an invaluable guide for athletic administrators directing high school athletic programs.

I wish to express my appreciation to all those school administrators, authors, publishers, and executives of state and national high school associations who so kindly consented to the inclusion of some of their material.

Irvin A. Keller

1

The Interscholastic Athletic Administrator

Athletic games between teams of high school students were played long before there were athletic directors and even before there were high school coaches. In fact, there was little or no direction given these activities. High school students took care of simple administrative details through athletic clubs they formed. Elected officers or other chosen representatives scheduled the games, selected the players, engaged game officials, arranged for scorers and time-keepers, and handled other arrangements. As volunteer coaches began to offer instruction to players, they also started relieving high school players of some of these simple administrative responsiblities.

THE FIRST HIGH SCHOOL ATHLETIC ADMINISTRATORS

Official high school athletic administration developed slowly and gradually. When out of a need to avoid embarrassment and problems resulting from teams being identified with schools in athletic contests initiated by students, superintendents and principals began to assume some administrative duties. In the smallest high schools, in which the superintendent was the only administrative officer, he reluctantly scheduled games, selected officials for the contests, and exercised some supervision over athletic games. Faculty members were frequently appointed to accompany teams and oversee the players. In the larger high schools it was the principal who handled these matters in the early period of interschool competition. It was also not uncommon for the superintendent or principal also to be the coach of the high school team.

As secondary schools grew in size, interscholastic programs expanded. Contests were played in more sports and a larger number of students were involved. Consolidation of school districts resulted in still larger high school units, and the duties of principals and superintendents broadened and became more complex. This made it necessary to delegate responsibilities, and assistant principals and assistant superintendents were assigned the task of directing interscholastic athletics. Hence, in reality the first directors of athletics were superintendents, principals, and assistant principals and assistant superintendents. The increasing complexities of their responsibilities in coping with expanding administrative details of the total secondary education program stimulated the appointment of coaches or other faculty members as part-time athletic directors to schedule athletic contests, engage officials, and handle other routine matters inherent in interscholastic athletic competition. Although they assumed many of the mundane chores of the principals, these part-time directors were still responsible to administrators who continued to give direction to the interscholastic program.

But changing conditions demand modifications in practices. There was a period in the history of secondary school administration when a large number of the superintendents and principals were former coaches with a good deal of know-how in administering athletics. Many had taught physical education and coached high school teams before completing their graduate degrees qualifying them for principalships. However, other individuals who had no athletic experience, not even as players, began to seek graduate degrees in secondary school administration. These persons were not well qualified to administer interscholastic athletics.

In the meantime, teacher training institutions had upgraded the training of physical education teachers and coaches. Courses in the administration of physical education and high school athletics became requirements for those majoring in this area. Coaches with this educational background had better qualifications for athletic administration than did many of the young principals and assistant principals. This situation prompted superintendents and boards of education to give added significance to the position of athletic director. Although in most cases it was still a part-time phase of some faculty member's duties, and he or she was under the supervision of the principal, more and more responsibilities were delegated to the position. Just when the term *athletic director* or *director of athletics* was first used is unknown, but those serving in this capacity proved to be of considerable assistance to busy secondary school administrators, and more schools appointed someone to such a post.

No phase of secondary education has grown more in recent years than has interscholastic athletics. This has been due in part to the increase in girls' interscholastic competition, but boys' athletics have expanded also. Consequently, the responsibilities of athletic directors have grown tremendously.

ATHLETIC DIRECTORS GAIN PROFESSIONAL STATUS

By the 1960s most of the medium-sized and large high schools had athletic directors. Many still devoted only part of their time to athletic administrative matters in keeping with the extent of the interscholastic program in their schools, but in larger high schools several served full-time, except for coaching one or more sports during respective seasons. A sizable number of the school districts with multiple high schools employed a director of athletics for the district who oversaw the work of athletic directors assigned to each high school. This provided for uniform policies and practices and helped prevent friction among high schools in the district.

Athletic directors eventually began to exert increasing influence in the forming of policies and practices in their schools and for athletic conferences to which they held memberships. Principals began to look to them for advice and recommendations on interscholastic matters. Conference meetings provided opportunities for athletic directors to exchange ideas and discuss mutual problems. The benefits realized prompted leaders in several states to initiate regional and state athletic directors associations.

A number of state high school associations gave assistance by sponsoring athletic directors conferences and forming athletic directors advisory committees as a channel for input in state association policies and procedures.

In 1967 the American Association for Health, Physical Education and Recreation sponsored a National Council of Secondary School Athletic Administration. An outgrowth of that meeting was the formation of the National Council of Secondary School Athletic Directors in 1969. However, this organization failed to gain the support of school administrators across the nation.

During the 1970s there were developments which helped to upgrade the professional competencies and status of directors of athletics. In 1971 the National Federation of State High School Associations started sponsoring conferences for athletic directors. At the conference held in 1976 a constitution was drafted for a National Interscholastic Athletic Administrators Association (NIAAA), which was adopted at the 1977 National Federation Conference for Directors of Athletics.[1] (*Note:* Footnotes are at the end of each chapter.) The use of the term *Athletic Administrator* is significant. It better describes the role and status of the position than does *Director of Athletics* or *Athletic Director*.[2]

The NIAAA is a professional organization of individuals with responsibilities in high school athletic administration. The association is administered by an executive committee of ten members and is composed of one member from each of the association's eight geographical sections, a representative of the National Federation of Athletic Directors Advisory Committee, and a representative of the National Federation staff. The objectives stated in the NIAAA Constitution include:

To Promote the professional growth and image of interscholastic administrators;

To Promote the development and prestige of state athletic administration organizations which will contribute, in cooperation with their state high school associations, to the interscholastic programs of each state;

> To PROVIDE an efficient system for exchange of ideas between the National Federation of State High School Associations and state athletic directors organizations and individual interscholastic administrators; and
>
> To PRESERVE the educational nature of interscholastics and the place of these programs in the curricula of schools.[3]

The annual meeting of the NIAAA held in conjunction with the National Conference of High School Directors of Athletics sponsored by the National Federation of State High School Associations provides an excellent exchange of ideas and is a source of valuable information for all athletic administrators.

A quarterly, *Interscholastic Athletic Administration*, is published by the National Federation and is a most valuable publication for athletic administrators in all sizes of high schools. Subscriptions can be ordered by contacting:

> Interscholastic Athletic Administration
> c/o National Federation of State High School Associations
> P.O. Box 20626
> Kansas City, Missouri 64195

A study of the developments of the 1970s clearly reveals that athletic administrators have acquired professional status in the secondary educational program. Whether the individual is a part-time or full-time director of athletics in a small, medium-size, or large high school, he or she will be found to be much better qualified than was the case a few decades ago when routine athletic administrative tasks were simply assigned as extra duties to a coach given the title of athletic director. Today a very large number have completed masters degrees and some have even received doctorates. Their educational background combined with practical experience enables them to provide better leadership in high school athletics.

QUALIFICATIONS FOR INTERSCHOLASTIC ATHLETIC ADMINISTRATORS

Standards have been established by teacher training institutions and state departments of education for the certification of teachers in various fields, for principals, and for superintendents. Several colleges and universities have formulated standards for the certification of coaches, but few, if any, have outlined standards for certifying high school athletic administrators. This does not mean that those now serving in that capacity are not qualified. Many have majored in physical education at the undergraduate level, and most have had coaching experience, which is invaluable in carrying out the duties of an athletic director. A large number have regularly attended athletic directors' conferences, workshops, and NIAAA meetings, from which much practical knowledge of significant value in athletic administration was acquired.

If one examines the qualifications of successful directors of athletics, whether acquired through formal education or informally, the following will be among those noted:

Personal qualities.   He or she will be a person of high integrity, with a personality which enables him or her to work effectively with school administrators, boards of education, coaches, other members of the faculty, athletes, other students, the school community, members of the news media, and representatives of other schools.

Philosophy.   The respected high school athletic administrator has a clear understanding of the philosophy of secondary education and the philosophy of physical education and interscholastic athletics.

Objectives.   He or she knows the most important values physical education and interscholastic athletics have for boys and girls and is cognizant of the most worthwhile objectives to be achieved through these activities.

Knowledge.   In addition to understanding the philosophy and objectives of high school athletics, the director of athletics possesses a broad knowledge of interscholastic athletic administrative policies and the procedures necessary to carry out the responsibilities of the position.

Experience.   Nearly all, if not all, athletic administrators will have a background of both teaching and coaching experiences. Some will have served first as assistant athletic directors or assistant high school principals.

The above are only general qualifications for athletic administrators. The responsibilities outlined below list specific areas of preparation essential for success in the position.

RESPONSIBILITIES OF THE INTERSCHOLASTIC ATHLETIC ADMINISTRATOR

The job of today's high school athletic administrator is a complex one involving numerous details. Although the director will often find it necessary to delegate many responsibilities, he or she is still the person held accountable by the school administration and board of education for seeing that the job is done properly. The details of these responsibilities will be discussed in later chapters; only the areas of responsibility are enumerated below:

1. *Leadership*
2. *Formulation of athletic administration policies and procedures*
3. *Selection and assignment of coaches*
4. *Supervision of the coaching staff*

5. *Establishing eligibility standards and verifying the eligibility of athletes*
6. *Budgeting and financial administration*
7. *Scheduling of athletic contests*
8. *Management of athletic contests*
9. *Administration of tournaments*
10. *Providing for the health and safety of athletes and their medical supervision*
11. *Purchase of athletic equipment*
12. *Care and maintenance of athletic equipment*
13. *Transportation of teams*
14. *Supervision of intramural activities*
15. *Public relations*
16. *Contracting game officials*
17. *Athletic awards*
18. *Avoiding legal liability*
19. *Record keeping*

SUMMARY

Superintendents and principals were the first official school representatives to assume responsibility for administering interschool athletic contests. As high schools grew in size, they eventually found that they could not find time to attend to the details of such a program without neglecting other important duties. Simple routine responsibilities were delegated to coaches or others on the faculty. In time, such persons were designated as *athletic directors*.

From this humble beginning the position developed into one of professional status in the 1970s. State and national athletic administrators' associations were formed, which are working to improve the educational values of interscholastic activities.

The responsibilities of athletic administrators have increased in keeping with the growth in boys' and girls' athletic competition, and their efforts have been of valuable assistance to secondary school administrators and boards of education.

QUESTIONS AND TOPICS FOR STUDY AND DISCUSSION

1. Why were there no directors of athletics when interschool athletics were initiated?
2. What were the circumstances which caused superintendents and principals to assume responsibility for the supervision and administration of athletic contests?

3. Why did school administrators delegate responsibility for administering school athletics to others?

4. What is the National Interscholastic Athletic Administrators Association? When was it formed?

5. Discuss the objectives of the NIAAA. Do you think they are significant? Why?

6. If you were a superintendent of schools in the process of selecting a director of athletics, what qualifications would you look for in applicants for the position?

7. Enumerate areas of responsibility athletic directors must assume. Select five you think most crucial to success and give your reasons.

8. Do you think the position of athletic administrator will increase or decrease in importance in the future? Why?

NOTES

1. John Youngblood, "NIAAA's New Organizational Structure," *Interscholastic Athletic Administration*, 7, no. 2 (Winter 1980), 19.

2. Dick Hill, "Job Description for Athletic Administrators," *Interscholastic Athletic Administration*, 6, no. 3 (Spring 1980), 25–26.

3. NIAAA Constitution.

BIBLIOGRAPHY

ANDERSON, GERALD "CHIC," and WILLIAM B. THIEL. "Ten Principles of Administration for the Athletic Director." *Interscholastic Athletic Administration*, 7, no. 1 (Fall 1980), 8, 28.

HILL, DICK. "Job Analysis for Athletic Administrators." *Interscholastic Athletic Administration*, 6, no. 3 (Spring 1980), 25–26.

KANABY, ROBERT F. "Athletic Revolution: A Tale of Two Cities." *Interscholastic Athletic Administration*, 8, no. 2 (Winter 1981), 5–7 and 26–27.

NATIONAL FEDERATION OF STATE HIGH SCHOOL ASSOCIATIONS. "From the 1970s into the 1980s." *Interscholastic Athletic Administration*, 6, no 4 (Summer 1980), 5–12.

YOUNGBLOOD, JOHN. "NIAAA's New Organizational Structure." *Interscholastic Athletic Administration*, 7, no. 2 (Winter 1980), 19.

History, Philosophy, and Objectives of High School Athletics

High school athletics today are considered a significant phase of the secondary school educational program. Coaches, athletic directors, and school administrators proclaim the educational values of their athletic programs with pride. However, school officials cannot take credit for the introduction of these activities into the school program. In fact, they were initiated by students themselves. Athletic contests were started by groups of students as social events in the colleges following the Civil War. Athletic clubs were formed patterned after independent athletic clubs to which many of the elite in society belonged during that era. Imitating their older brothers and friends, high school students began to form *athletic associations* around 1900. They elected their own managers, scheduled their own games, and played any teams available. As the interest in competition grew, it was not uncommon for persons outsde the school to be recruited to play on the teams. Disputes and brawls occasionally occurred. The development from this dubious beginning which culminated in the program of interscholastics as we know it today is an interesting story.

STAGES IN THE EVOLUTION OF HIGH SCHOOL ATHLETICS

Most school activities, including athletics, have gone through similar stages in their development. Observers have differed on the dates assigned to these periods, which were not simultaneous from state to state. However, four distinct periods can be recognized in regard to the position school administrators and boards of education have taken.

The Period of Opposition

Although not sponsored by the schools, the teams representing the student athletic associations eventually came to be identified with their schools and began to embarrass them. School officials found themselves forced to take positions on the recruiting of outsiders to play on the teams, controversies that arose, and volunteer coaching by individuals who had no training as teachers and whose tactics were questionable. Some of the practices borrowed from professional and other nonschool athletics were considered detrimental to the cause of education. It was only natural that under these conditions the athletic associations were discouraged and opposed. Some attempts were made to abolish them, but these efforts were futile. Because of the enthusiasm that had developed for athletic contests among high school youth and the realization that they would be continued outside the schools' jurisdiction if outlawed, the majority of school administrators came to the conclusion that the only feasible alternative would be to assume control over them, thereby inaugurating the second period.

The Period of Toleration

Out of necessity, rather than because of any established school athletic philosophy, steps were taken to make these athletic games more respectable. Faculty members were appointed to chaperone the teams. These persons had little or no knowledge of the game and their chief responsibilities were to supervise the conduct of the players and to prevent controversies.

Sometimes faculty members with some knowledge of the game were allowed to coach the team. It was also not uncommon for coaches to be members of the team. A former superintendent in Missouri liked to relate his first experiences as a high school coach. It was understood when he was employed that he would not only coach but also play on the basketball team. He served in this dual capacity for two years before other schools began to object. The game he remembered best was the one in which he not only coached and played the entire game, but also officiated the last half. He concluded it was his officiating that was the main cause of the "big fight" that followed the game.

Situations such as this caused schools to begin to adopt a few "controls" to prevent abuses. The first on record was the requirement that all players must be bona fide students. Other controls pertaining to players, eventually known as "eligibility rules," were to follow. Still later, standards for coaches were established, generally requiring that coaches must be members of the faculty. Although the attitude that prevailed during this period was still the notion that it was better to exercise minimal control and to tolerate these athletic activities, nevertheless some improvement was noted.

The Period of Recognition and Capitalization

School officials began to recognize, with the help of the controls just described, that some desirable educational outcomes could result from properly planned and properly administered interschool athletic contests. Some noted that they provided learning experiences which supplemented the curricular offerings of the schools. During this period principals and coaches began to formulate specific educational objectives for the interscholastic program. After more standards were adopted to guide it, many schools began to capitalize on the educational values of athletic activities and to consider them as an integral part of the total secondary school education program. This is clearly evidenced by the attempts to extend athletic experiences to all students through mandatory physical education.

The Period of Exploitation

When a school activity reaches a certain point in popularity, it enters the fourth period, during which attempts are made to exploit it. So it was with school athletics. Noting the attractiveness of interscholastic games, nonschool organizations and individuals began to promote events involving high school athletes and the interscholastic athletic program. The primary interests of these promoters were generally in gaining recognition, advertising, and raising funds. Although this kind of activity is potentially present even now, the collective efforts of schools at the state and national levels have been effective in eliminating much of this type of exploitation of high school athletes and school athletic programs.

PHASES IN THE DEVELOPMENT OF ATHLETIC CONTROL

It is evident from an analysis of the periods in the history of school athletics that a corresponding development was taking place in the area of control of these activities. That these functions were called *controls* is both interesting and revealing. Obviously, the term was applied because of the necessity to control or eliminate abuses that became prevalent.

The First Phase

Individual schools first attempted to establish some controls over the athletic contests in which students participated by appointing faculty chaperones and sponsors and by unilaterally adopting a few rules. However, the activities they sponsored in this manner and the policies they followed were to a large extent influenced by local community pressures. Policies in effect in a school against which another competed affected that school's own standards and policies. Public and private high schools and preparatory institutions developed different ideas as to the functions of their athletic programs. These differences caused leading school administrators to realize that they could not cope individually with all the problems.

The Second Phase

After enough schools concluded that attempts by individual schools to control the abuses noted in athletic practices were not sufficient, they began to organize themselves into associations, leagues, and conferences. A few simple *agreements* were adopted and all the schools belonging to such a group pledged to abide by them. Constitutions were adopted containing a set of regulations to guide these organizations. This practice had many advantages and most schools today belong to some conference or league. However, the fact that different leagues had different standards, policies, and regulations limited their influence in establishing any general athletic standards such as exist today.

The Third Phase

As interest in athletics developed and broadened in scope, it was only natural that contests would be arranged among schools which did not all belong to the same local league. As improved means of travel broadened the range of competition, it became apparent that different leagues and conferences had different standards for their athletic teams. These differences involved scholastic regulations, age and previous play limitations, amateur standing, transfer and time of enrollment, and other criteria. If schools were to compete under uniform regulations, some form of organization larger than local units was imperative. The result of this need was the formation of statewide associations. Most of these were voluntary organizations, but they set up minimum standards to which their member schools had to adhere if they were to retain membership. As has been widely recognized, the development of high school athletics to their present high plane has been largely due to the outstanding pioneer work done by school leaders who were instrumental in the formation of statewide organizations for the supervision and control of interscholastic athletic activities.

The Fourth Phase

In the same way in which it was realized that benefits would result from local groups' organizing into state groups, it was apparent that a national organization could serve a useful function. Thus the National Federation of State High School Athletic Associations was formed in 1920. As its name implies, this body is an organization of state high school associations rather than of individual schools. It has done much to raise athletic standards in various sections of the country as well as to promote greater uniformity in athletic regulations. Its organization and functions are described in detail in Chapter 3.

EMERGENCE OF A PHILOSOPHY
OF HIGH SCHOOL ATHLETICS

In essence, athletic activities were forced upon the schools. As we have seen, they were initiated by student groups, because of student interest. Community interest and pressures grew steadily until athletics were finally officially permitted and tolerated. The only evident reason for this recognition was that it appeared better to exercise some control and sponsorship over them than to have students participating in athletic events managed by groups outside the jurisdiction of the schools. In the beginning there were no general beliefs regarding the educational values of athletic programs for youth or the contributions such activities could make to the educational programs of the schools. This vacuum resulted in the copying of athletic practices from professional athletics and other nonschool athletic programs, which were based on philosophies which conflicted with educational philosophy. Recruiting of players, monetary and merchandise awards, championships, and all-star games are examples.

After it was recognized that through established controls educational values could be provided, educators began looking for answers to questions such as why athletics were part of the school program and what they were trying to achieve through them. Thus was born an interscholastc athletic philosophy which formed the basis for the formulation of objectives to be attained. It is highly important that high school coaches and those responsible for administering school athletic activities thoroughly understand the philosophy which evolved and which has given these activities an educational sense of direction. It is further necessary that they understand how this philosophy differs from other athletic philosophies.

Professional Athletic Philosophy

The philosophy of professional athletics is clear. It is essentially a business philosophy. The owners are engaged in an enterprise to make a profit. Playing is a vocation for the athletes. Together, owners and players produce a product for sale in the form of entertainment. The principal ingredient is competition. The product doesn't sell wthout a winning team. Recruiting the best players is necessary to produce that team. Championships and all-star games are sponsored to attract additional gate receipts. The spectator accepts this philosophy and supports it by his or her attendance.

Amateur Athletic Philosophy

The fundamental principle of the philosophy of amateur athletics is that the amateur shall engage in athletic activities for reasons other than material gain. Awards must be symbolic, or within prescribed amateur athletic award codes. There are various types of amateur athletic programs, of which school athletics are one. However, they are sponsored for different purposes. Some are offered primarily for the benefit of the participant, while others are promoted to benefit the sponsor as much as, or more than, the athletes. Thus, although school athletics are amateur, *not all amateur athletics are identical with school athletics in their objectives*.

High School Athletic Philosophy

In the beginning the absence of a philosophy of school athletics resulted in interscholastic athletic activities being patterned after professional and general amateur practices. It is true that much was imitated from collegiate athletics, but colleges originally were also influenced by professional athletic philosophy. In time, high school coaches and administrators began to consider seriously the *why* of their programs. The need to clarify their beliefs was eventually realized, and some began to adopt official statements of athletic philosophy for their schools. A number of high schools today publish such statements in athletic handbooks which serve as guides for their interscholastic programs. The following is an example of a statement of the general beliefs on which interschool athletic activities are based:

> The philosophy of athletics at Parkway is such that athletics is considered an integral part of the school's program of education which provides experiences that will help boys and girls physically, mentally, and emotionally. The element of competition and winning, though it exists, is controlled to the point that it does not determine the nature of the program and is kept on the "readiness" level of secondary youth. This is considered to be educationally and psychologically sound because of the training it offers for living in a competitive society. Students are stimulated to want to win and excel, but the principles of good sportsmanship prevail at all times to enhance the educational values of contests.
>
> We believe that participation in athletics, both as a player and as a student spectator, is an integral part of the student's educational experiences. Such participation is a privilege that carries with it responsibilities to the school, to the team, to the student body, to the community, and to the student himself. In his play and in his conduct, he is representing all of these groups. Such experiences contribute to the knowledge, skill, and emotional patterns that he possesses, thereby making him a better person and citizen.[1]

NATIONAL FEDERATION STATEMENT OF PHILOSOPHY

The purpose of the National Federation of State High School Associations is to coordinate the efforts of its member state associations toward the ultimate objectives of interscholastic activities. It shall provide a means for state high school associations to cooperate in order to enhance and protect their interscholastic programs. In order to accomplish this, the National Federation is guided by a philosophy consistent with the accepted purposes of secondary education. Member state associations' programs must be administered in accordance with the following basic beliefs:

Interscholastic athletics shall be an integral part of the total secondary school educational program that has as its purpose to provide educational experiences not otherwise provided in the curriculum, which will develop learning outcomes in the areas of knowledge, skills, and emotional patterns and will contribute to the development of better citizens. Emphasis shall be upon teaching "through" athletics in addition to teaching the "skills" of athletics.

Interschool athletics shall be primarily for the benefit of the high school students who participate directly and vicariously in them. The interscholastic athletic program shall exist mainly for the value which it has for students and not for the benefit of the sponsoring institutions. The activities and contests involved shall be psychologically sound by being tailored to the physical, mental, and emotional maturity levels of the youth participating in them.

Any district and/or state athletic meet competition to determine a so-called champion shall provide opportunities for schools to demonstrate and to evaluate the best taught in their programs with the best taught in other schools and in other areas of the state.

Participating in interscholastic actvities is a privilege to be granted to those students who meet the minimum standards of eligibility adopted cooperatively by the schools through their state associations and those additional standards established by each school for its own students.

The state high school associations and the National Federation shall be concerned with the development of those standards, policies, and regulations essential to assist their member schools in the implementation of their philosophy of interscholastic athletics. Interschool activities shall be kept in proper perspective and must supplement the academic program of the schools.

Nonschool activities sponsored primarily for the benefit of the participants in accordance with a philosophy compatible with the school philosophy of interscholastics may have values for youth. When they do not interfere with the academic and interscholastic programs and do not result in exploitation of youth, they shall be considered as a worthwhile supplement to interschool activities.

The welfare of the schools demands a united front in sports direction policies and the high school associations provide opportunity for this unity. They must be kept strong.[2]

It is evident from present-day school athletic philosophy that emphasis is being placed upon educating youth *through* athletics as well as upon teaching athletic skills. Educators are in general agreement that when athletics fail to be educational, they cannot be justified as a part of the educational program.

Philosophy of Girls' Interscholastic Athletics

A number of different positions have been taken regarding interscholastic athletics for girls. In the beginning there were attempts to pattern girls' programs after boys' interscholastics. Girls' teams scheduled games and competed in invitational, conference, and state tournaments in several states. Basketball was one of the most popular sports. Coaching and athletic administrative responsibilities were generally handled by men.

The same type of competitive spirit surrounded girls' games as surrounded boys' interschool games. Professional women physical educators expressed opposition toward this type of competition for girls, for in their opinion it offered athletic opportunities for a limited number of girls and neglected the great majority. A philosophy was developed that provided for broader participation and less attention to interscholastics for girls. Many expressed themselves as being against any type of interschool program for girls similar to that for boys.

School administrators accepted this philosophy, and many schools discontinued interscholastic competition for girls except for a few culminating activities. Steps were taken through state high school associations to ban championships for girls, and some associations considered abolishing all interschool contests for girls. As late as 1961, nine states prohibited interschool games for girls.[3] Large and small high schools were frequently divided on these issues. The latter generally did not have enough girls enrolled for a balanced girls' intramural program and, therefore, continued sponsoring girls' interscholastic athletics. However, there was a definite trend toward less interscholastic competition for girls of the same type as was being provided boys.

During the 1960s interest in girls' interscholastic contests among women physical educational leaders revived. The opinion was expressed that athletically talented girls needed more competitive experiences than those provided in the intramural program and those offered in play days and sports days. This was made evident in speeches given by Dr. Katherine Ley, representing the Division for Girls' and Women's Sports of the American Federation for Health, Physical Education, and Recreation, at the annual meetings of the National Federation of State High School Athletic Associations in 1963[4] and 1965.[5]

Title IX of the Education Amendments of 1971 (see pages 372–373) has had an impact on attitudes toward girls' interscholastic competition. In essence, it requires schools to provide athletic opportunities for girls comparable to those for boys. Court decisions in cases of sexual discrimination in athletics profoundly affected the number of interschool athletic contests for girls.

Figures released by the National Federation of State High School Associations well illustrate the effects of these developments. In 1971, 294,015 female participants in interscholastic athletics were reported. This number increased to 1,853,789 in 1981, an increase of over 500 percent during this ten-year period.[6] The point of view of the National Federation relating to girls' athletics is found in Chapter 3.

All state high school associations now sponsor district and state tournaments in some sports, with basketball, track and field, and volleyball being the most popular.[7] Iowa has a separate state association for girls' athletics,

Iowa Girls' High School Athletic Union, which has sponsored girls' inter-scholastics for many years. Several state associations have women on their executive staffs directing girls' programs.

It is apparent that the philosophy guiding girls' athletics today is essentially the same as that for boys' athletics. There is general agreement that the interschool athletic program shall supplement and enrich the physical education program by affording opportunities for the more talented high school athletes of both sexes to test their skills against those of the better athletes of other schools. Contemporary interscholastic philosophy is emphasizing the development of the individual person, contributing to society's needs, and developing human values through athletic competition.[8]

Practically all athletic administrators support providing equal but separate interscholastic opportunities for boys and girls. In some instances when schools did not offer interschool competition for girls, suit was brought in court to allow them to play on boys' teams. The courts have generally ruled in favor of girls in such cases on the basis of discrimination because of sex (see Chapter 16). The principle of separate but equal programs for boys and girls is a sound one if the primary purpose is to supply more girls the opportunity to participate. If a school has separate programs for each sex and allows a girl(s) to compete on the boys' teams just because she is more talented than other girls, there will eventually be these results:

1. Boys will have to be permitted to compete on the girls' teams, if they so desire, to avoid the issue of discriminating against boys.
2. If there are mixed teams, fewer girls will then get the opportunity to compete, because of the physical differences between the sexes at the senior high school level.
3. The girls' program will deteriorate to a "second rate" program when the better girl athletes compete on the boys' teams.

OBJECTIVES OF INTERSCHOLASTIC ATHLETICS

The keen urge of competition has had its effects upon the interscholastic program from the beginning. Until the establishment of controls began to reveal that playing games could have educational values, winning the game was the only noticeable goal. Soon, however, coaches and school administrators were stimulated, probably by criticisms of interscholastic sports, to begin to formulate some objectives, other than just winning, as justification for these activities. Objectives for the participating athlete occupied first attention. As school athletics became better accepted as a phase of the educational program, statements of aims began to give consideration to the student body and to the community as well. An examination of present-day codes of objectives generally reveals that they are stated in terms of desirable learning outcomes that are not limited to the athletes.

If an athletic program is to be maximally worthwhile, the principal, athletic director, and coaches must accept the responsibility for getting across to the athletes, the student body, and the community the objectives the school is trying to attain through the athletic program. The following list includes learning outcomes that schools are attempting to achieve and is followed by a broader statement of the general aims of an athletic program.

1. An understanding of why the school offers a program of athletics
2. A knowledge of the values that athletics have for the individual and for society
3. An understanding of the rules essential to playing the game and to being intelligent fans
4. The ability to think both as an individual and as a member of a group
5. Faith in democratic processes
6. Realization of the values of group ideals
7. Improved motor skills
8. Better health and physical fitness
9. An appreciation of wholesome recreation and entertainment
10. The desire to succeed and to excel
11. Higher moral and ethical standards
12. Self-discipline and emotional maturity
13. Social competence
14. A realization of the values of conforming to rules
15. Respect for the rights of others and for authority
16. High ideals of fairness in all human relationships

It is sometimes thought that when emphasis is placed on the achievement of these ultimate educational objectives of athletes there is a de-emphasis upon "winning." Such thinking is entirely unfounded. Winning, involving the spirit of competition, is an immediate objective in all athletic contests, but is not an end in itself. If it were, it could only be "half" realized. Fifty percent of the teams that take part in athletic games must lose. The desire to win can and should be used to stimulate the achievement of the ultimate objectives.

The attainment of these goals will enhance the education of boys and girls and contribute toward the development of better citizens for a democratic society. They will not, however, be achieved by chance. It is only by helping a student to clearly understand what the objectives are and by carefully directing him or her in appropriate, well-planned learning situations that he or she will master such aims. This is the great responsibility and stimulating challenge that faces all who really believe in high school athletics.[9]

There are objectives others may have which are related to the inter-scholastic program and may influence its direction. These might include such personal objectives of the coach as the desire to produce a winning team, to gain individual recognition as a *winning coach*, to develop star athletes colleges will want to recruit, to gain support for a particular sport, and others. The board of education and school administrator(s) may also have goals of their own. An athletic program which will gain community support is one. Some administrators consider a *winning team* an asset in influencing patrons to support school tax levies and/or bonds. Others look to the athletic program as an aid in fostering school and community spirit. Revenue producing may be another goal, especially from such sports as football and basketball, from which income may exceed expenses and provide financial help for other sports and different phases of the school's student activities program.

When kept in proper perspective, such objectives can contribute to a better overall interscholastic program. However, caution should be exercised to make certain they don't prevail over the attainment of the most worthwhile, long-range objectives of school athletics or supplant the inherent values of such activities for students. Interscholastic athletics are primarily *for students*, and any goals sought by others must not adversely affect the educational outcomes and benefits such experiences offer high school students.

CHALLENGES STILL FACING THE SCHOOLS

The fact that athletics now have an established place in the secondary school program under an accepted philosophy and have purposes consistent wth the general objectives of education should not be interpreted to mean that there are no prevalent problems facing the schools in controlling athletic programs. Various developments are creating influences which may conflict with the philosophy of interscholastic athletics and detract from their educational values unless we have strong leadership from school athletic administrators. It is not difficult to note why schools must be alert to present-day influences that can affect their programs.

Exposure through television has stimulated greater public interest in athletic activities, and particularly in professional athletics. Athletic events are televised primarily for entertainment purposes. Television rights provide a source of income of considerable magnitude to the participating teams and organizations. The *show* is planned for public consumption. Enthusiastic citizens are sometimes prone to want to see their high school emulate what they see on television without regard to the effects this might have upon the primary learning goals for high school students.

Collegiate athletics have become a tremendous entertainment program, as evidenced by attendance at games and the number viewing intercollegiate contests on television. Millions are now paid by TV networks for these television rights, and national telecasts are a major medium of advertising for many major companies. Rising costs have made it important for athletic departments to have a winning team to avoid financial difficulties, and more games are scheduled and bowl games played to increase revenues. Recruiting of high school players has become more intense. College athletic scholarships have increased in value, and more high school athletes and their parents are aware of this. The scholarship provides both honor and opportunity to the athlete, and it is a financial asset to the parents. Consequently, youths are more and more being pushed, even at the junior high school level, to try to "win a college scholarship." Some are even sent by their parents to summer athletic camps with the hope that this will help them attain this objective.

Summer athletic programs sponsored by nonschool organizations have grown rapidly in recent years. These programs have capitalized on the high school interscholastic program by offering competition to high school athletes in popular school sports, despite the fact that this practice often conflicts with high school eligibility standards. An increase in specialization, once a source of much criticism, has resulted. No longer does the star high school trackman "drop his spikes" at the close of the high school season and enjoy a typical summer sport such as baseball, tennis, golf, or swimming. Instead, the athlete is invited to partcipate in summer track meets. The individual is led to believe that there is less chance of receiving a college athletic scholarship if he or she does not specialize. The same development is taking place in other sports, sometimes involving national championships for youths from ages eight to eighteen. This tendency toward extending a particular sport season for the individual high school athlete is a matter of increasing concern to high school athletic leaders.

Furthermore, athletic competition for youth is employed as an advertising medium. National championship contests are being promoted for youths of high school and pre-high school age by advertising companies backed by business organizations primarily for advertising purposes. The use of school facilities is frequently sought for these contests, which often are in conflict with the principles of interscholastic sports. There are even international meets for high school teams and for individual athletes (see Chapter 17), which have caused conflict with the athletes' academic programs.

The women's movement and civil rights legislation have presented further challenges in school athletics. Litigation through the courts has made it clear that comparable opportunities must be provided for boys and girls. Problems related to sharing of facilities, scheduling, and staffing have resulted. Chapter 16 will discuss the more recent developments in girls' athletics and related court actions.

One need not conclude that these and similar developments are necessarily evil. The purpose of discussing them in this chapter is to illustrate that they have a potential adverse effect upon the high school athletic program. If they interfere with the purposes of the interscholastic program, school representatives can be expected to raise objections and to look toward ways of protecting the high school athletic program. It therefore would seem wise to give careful attention to ways and means of better implementing the philosophy and objectives of interscholastics that have evolved as part of the tradition of school athletics.

SUMMARY

Athletic activities were initiated in high schools by students who formed their own athletic associations, selected their team managers, and scheduled contests with other teams.

The history of high school athletics consists of four stages or periods. These were the periods of opposition, toleration, recognition and capitalization, and exploitation.

After school officials determined that it would be impossible to *outlaw* athletic activities sponsored by students, they began to exercise controls to eliminate what they noted as evils. There were four phases in the development of these controls. The first was by unilateral action of individual schools. Second, conferences (or leagues) were formed, with member schools agreeing to abide by certain common rules and regulations. Third, state high school associations were formed to provide for more statewide uniformity. Finally, a national organization, the National Federation of State High School Athletic Associations, was formed to foster more interstate uniformity in athletic regulations. The developments during these phases and the rules and regulations adopted *grew out of necessity* to protect the welfare of high school students.

A philosophy of interscholastic athletics emerged after these activities were recognized by school officials. The philosophy which guides high schools today is that interscholastic athletics are an important part of the total secondary education program which provides experiences to help students grow physically, mentally, and morally.

The fundamental objectives of interscholastic athletics are educational in nature. All other objectives are secondary and should not conflict with the educational objectives of interscholastic activities.

QUESTIONS AND TOPICS FOR STUDY AND DISCUSSION

1. Give characteristics of each of the four phases in the development of school athletics.

2. Discuss the control phases through which interscholastics have passed.

3. Why did the formulation of a philosophy for school athletics follow rather than precede the initiation of interscholastics? Discuss the effects this has had on school athletics.

4. Enumerate and give examples of the three areas of learning outcome inherent in the Parkway High School statement of objectives for its interscholastic program.

5. Explain why it is important that coaches, players, students, and the community understand the school's philosophy of athletics.

6. How does the philosophy of interscholastic athletics differ from the philosophy of professional athletics? From other types of amateur athletics?

7. Formulate a plan for making the public aware of the philosophy and objectives of interscholastic athletics.

8. Why should players be taught "how to lose" as well as to want to win?

9. Give reasons why beginning high school coaches may not fully understand the philosophy and objectives of interscholastic athletics.

10. Do you think collegiate athletics are affecting the interscholastic athletic program? Explain.

11. Discuss some nonschool athletic contest promotions which may be in conflict with the philosophy of school athletics.

12. Enumerate ways in which the increase in girls' athletic competition is affecting the interscholastic program.

NOTES

1. *Handbook for Interscholastics*, Parkway School District, Chesterfield, Mo., 1969, p. 1.

2. National Federation of State High School Associations, *1980–81 Handbook* (Kansas City, Mo.: National Federation, 1981), pp. 14–15.

3. National Federation of State High School Associations, *1960–61 Handbook* (Kansas City, Mo.: National Federation, 1961), p. 59.

4. Katherine Ley, "Girls' Interscholastics," *National Federation Press* (Kansas City, Mo.: National Federation, July 1963).

5. Katherine Ley, "Increasing Opportunities for Girls' Sports," *National Federation Press* (Kansas City, Mo.: National Federation, July 1965).

6. National Federation of State High School Associations, *National Interscholastic Coach*, 1, no. 2 (October 1981), p. 2.

7. National Federation of State High School Associations, *1982–83 Handbook*, pp. 77–78.

8. American Alliance for Health, Physical Education and Recreation, "Development of Human Values Through Sports," *Proceedings of National Conference* (Washington, D.C., 1974).

9. *Clarification of the Philosophy and Objectives of Secondary School Athletics* (Missouri State High School Activities Association, 1967), pp. 7–8.

BIBLIOGRAPHY

BROYLES, J. FRANK, and ROBERT D. HAY. "Objectives of High School Athletic Programs." *Interscholastic Athletic Administration*, 3, no. 2 (Spring 1977), 26–28.

DANNEHL, WAYNE E., and JACK E. RAZOR. "The Values of Athletics—A Critical Inquiry." *NASSP Bulletin*, September 1971, 59–65.

GALLON, ARTHUR J. *Coaching Ideas and Ideals*, pp. 25–31. Boston: Houghton Mifflin, 1974.

LINDHOLM, KARL. "Coaching As Teaching: Seeking Balance." *Phi Delta Kappan*, 60, no. 10 (June 1979), 734–36.

MCINTYRE, DOROTHY E. "A Philosophy of Girls' Sports," in *Contemporary Philosophies of Physical Education and Athletics*, pp. 133–47. Columbus, Ohio: Charles E. Merrill, 1973.

MONTGOMERY, JAMES A. *The Development of the Interscholastic Movement in the United States, 1890–1894*, pp. 31–32. Ann Arbor, Mich.: University Microfilms, 1962.

NATIONAL FEDERATION OF STATE HIGH SCHOOL ASSOCIATIONS. *1980–81 Handbook*. Kansas City, Mo.: National Federation.

RESICK, MATTHEW C., and CARL E. ERICKSON. *Intercollegiate and Interscholastic Athletics for Men and Women*, pp. 1–11. Reading, Mass.: Addison-Wesley, 1975.

RYAN, ALLAN J. "Philosophy of Athletics at the Junior High School Level." in *Contemporary Philosophies of Physical Education and Athletics*, pp. 92–113. Columbus, Ohio: Charles E. Merrill, 1973.

SEATON, DON CASH, IRENE A. CLAYTON, HOWARD C. LEIBEE, and LLOYD L. MESSERSMITH. *Physical Education Handbook*, pp. 7–9 and 12–19. Englewood Cliffs, N.J.: Prentice-Hall, Inc., 1974.

"Sports Participation Survey Indicates Overall Increase." *National Interscholastic Coach*, 1, no. 2 (October 1981), 1–2.

TUCKETT, GLEN. "Athletic Values: More Than Winning," *Interscholastic Athletic Administration*, 8, no. 3 (Spring 1982), 22–23 and 29.

3

The National Federation of State High School Associations

All athletic administrators should be thoroughly familiar with the educational organizations which have functions in the area of interscholastic athletics. Of primary importance in this field, because of the services it offers, is the National Federation of State High School Associations.

THE ORIGIN OF THE NATIONAL FEDERATION

Inception and Organization

By 1920 state high school associations had been formed in 29 states. They proved to be both desirable and necessary in keeping interscholastic athletics in proper perspective within the total school program and in making them educationally worthwhile. Many problems were resolved for the schools in each state by the establishment of minimum uniform standards to which each member of the state association was obligated to comply by virtue of its membership. Some problems persisted with which state associations could not cope individually. The most difficult included:

1. Friction which arose as the result of interstate competition between schools along state borders in natural geographical areas for interschool competition. Differences in eligibility rules and in other areas caused concern for these schools and their state associations.
2. National and interstate promotions of athletic championships by colleges, clubs, and nonschool promoters. Leaders of state associations realized that because of the interstate and national character of these and other problems, a broader organization was much in need.

With the formation of the original Midwest Federation of State High School Athletic Associations in 1920, there came into being the first cooperative effort of state associations to control high school athletics. The original organization of four states was the forerunner of the National Federation of State High School Athletic Associations.

ORIGIN AND GROWTH

The national organization had its beginning in a meeting at Chicago on May 14, 1920. L. W. Smith, secretary of the Illinois High School Athletic Association, issued invitations to neighboring states, and state association representatives came from Illinois, Indiana, Iowa, Michigan and Wisconsin. The primary purpose of the meeting was to discuss problems which had resulted from high school contests which were organized by colleges and universities or by other clubs or promoters. In many cases little attention was paid to the eligibility rules of the high school associations or to other high school group regulations, and chaotic conditions had developed. At this first meeting it was decided that the welfare of the high schools required [that] a more active part in the control of such athletic activities be exercised by the high school men through the state associations, and this control necessitated the formation of a national organization. A constitution and by-laws were adopted and the group decided on the name "Midwest Federation of State High School Athletic Associations." Principal George Edward Marshall, Davenport, Iowa, was elected President and Principal L. W. Smith of Joliet, Illinois, was elected Secretary-Treasurer.

In 1921, four states, Illinois, Iowa, Michigan and Wisconsin continued their interest and became charter members through formal ratification of the constitution. Largely due to their efforts, the national organization grew during the early years.

In 1922 the Chicago annual meeting was attended by representatives from 11 states, and the name of the National Federation was adopted. A number of college and university representatives who attended the meeting expressed sympathy for and interest in the efforts to introduce a high degree of order in the regulation of interscholastic contests.

Since that time the National Federation has had a healthy growth to its present nationwide membership. By 1940 a national office with a full-time executive staff became necessary and such office was established in September of that year.

The legislative body is the National Council made up of one representative from each member state association. Such representative must be an officer or a member of his state board of control. The executive body is the Executive Committee of eight state board of control members from the eight territorial sections outlined in the constitution.[1]

THE EXPANDED SCOPE OF THE NATIONAL FEDERATION

As high school administrators began to experience difficulties in regulating nonathletic activities similar to the problems they had faced in athletics, the schools turned to their state high school associations for assistance. In a few

FIGURE 3-1   Territorial sections (*National Federation*)[2]

states these organizations had been founded to supervise both athletic and nonathletic activities, but most of them were strictly athletic associations in the beginning. Because of their success in developing controls and standards which kept athletic activities in proper educational perspective, the scope of many state high school athletic associations was expanded to include nonathletic activities also. By 1970 twenty-nine state associations had responsibilities for both athletic and nonathletic activities.

These associations began to feel the same need for uniform standards as had their member schools and turned to the National Federation for help. The National Council voted in 1970 to delete the word *athletic* from its name and so became the National Federation of State High School Associations, with expanded responsibilities in nonathletic activities. In 1978 the Federation made an addition to its administrative staff by employing a person to deal solely with the administration of nonathletic activities, and in the same year also appointed a National Federation Speech Committee. In 1979 it expanded to include a Music Committee and it also started hosting the national debate topic selection committee. These expanded services are providing much help to state high school associations and their member schools.

Because this book concerns only the administration of high school athletics, we shall not discuss the administration of nonathletic activities.

All state high school associations are members of the National Federation. The years of their affiliation are as follows:

Alabama (1924)	Kentucky (1941)	North Dakota (1923)
Alaska (1954)	Louisiana (1925)	Ohio (1924)
Arizona (1925)	Maine (1939)	Oklahoma (1924)
Arkansas (1924)	Maryland (1946)	Oregon (1931)
California (1940)	Massachusetts (1944)	Pennsylvania (1925)
Colorado (1924)	*Michigan (1920)	Rhode Island (1952)
Connecticut (1926)	Minnesota (1923)	South Carolina (1947)
Delaware (1945)	Mississippi (1924)	South Dakota (1923)
†District of Columbia (1958)	Missouri (1926)	Tennessee (1927)
Florida (1926)	Montana (1934)	Texas (1969)
Georgia (1929)	Nebraska (1924)	Utah (1927)
Hawaii (1957)	Nevada (1939)	Vermont (1945)
Idaho (1928)	New Hampshire (1945)	Virginia (1948)
*Illinois (1920)	New Jersey (1942)	Washington (1936)
Indiana (1924)	New Mexico (1932)	West Virginia (1925)
*Iowa (1920)	New York (1926)	*Wisconsin (1920)
Kansas (1923)	North Carolina (1949)	Wyoming (1936)[3]

* Charter Members
† Washington, D.C. is an allied member of the National Federation.

In addition to the member state associations, there are also Canadian and international affiliate members, which include:

Canadian Federation of Provincial School Athletic Associations (1967):
  Alberta Schools' Athletic Association (1968)
  British Columbia Federation of School Athletic Associations (1969)
  Manitoba Secondary Schools Athletic Association (1962)
  New Brunswick Interscholastic Athletic Association (1943)
  Newfoundland-Labrador High School Athletic Federation (1972)
  Nova Scotia School Athletic Federation (1952)
  Ontario Federation of School Athletic Associations (1953)
  Prince Edward Island Interscholastic Athletic Association (1964)
  Saskatchewan High Schools Athletic Associations (1953)
  Okinawa Secondary School Athletic Association (1978)
  Philippine Secondary Schools Athletic Association (1974)
  SPG Interscholastic Activities Association (Guam) (1980)
  St. Thomas–St. John Interscholastic Athletic Association (Virgin Islands) (1981)[4]

Affiliate members participate in meetings of the National Federation without voting privileges. They receive the same services as do all state high school associations.

NATURE OF THE NATIONAL FEDERATION

As its constitution provides, the National Federation of State High School Associations is a *federation* of state high school athletic and/or activities associations. Membership is voluntary. Because it is a federation, it can only recommend standards and policies for consideration by individual state associations. No state high school association is mandated to adopt a particular recommendation. Unlike our federal constitution, the constitution of the National Federation contains no provision that supersedes the authority of a state high school association. There are both advantages and disadvantages in this situation. It allows for some flexibility, which permits individual state associations to formulate regulations tailored to meet local conditions. On the other hand, there can be a lack of uniformity from state to state in such matters as eligibility, the number of contests permitted, season limitations, and so on. This situation can lead to ambiguity about the reasonableness of a standard or regulation adopted by a particular state association.

It is unlikely that the nature of the National Federation will be changed in the foreseeable future. The cooperative leadership provided through the years by its executive staff and state high school association representatives has aided in its becoming one of the nation's most highly respected educational organizations.

**ADMINISTRATION OF THE NATIONAL
FEDERATION PROGRAM**

The program of the National Federation is administered by the Executive Committee elected by the National Council. Its members are executive officers and members of the governing boards of their respective state high school associations. They receive only expenses for their services.

The Executive Committee is empowered to employ an executive director and a headquarters staff to carry out its responsibilities. The National Federation office is located near the Kansas City International Airport.

In its history, only five individuals have served as executive officers:

Executive Secretaries

1920–27	L. W. Smith, Illinois (deceased)
1927–40	C. W. Whitten, Illinois (deceased)
1940–58	H. V. Porter, Illinois (deceased)
1958–77	Clifford B. Fagan, Wisconsin
1977–	Brice B. Durbin (title changed to Executive Director)

In addition to the Executive Director, the headquarters staff consists of some nine administrative officers plus other employees comprising a total staff of over 30 persons.

Advisory committees are appointed for each of the following activities: baseball, basketball, field hockey, football, boys' gymnastics, girls' gymnastics, ice hockey, music, soccer, speech, swimming and diving, track and field, volleyball, and wrestling. The members of these committees provide a valuable service to the administrators responsible for the various activities and furnish input from the *grassroots level* of activities. Each committee is generally comprised of one representative from each of the National Federation's eight sections. Although they serve only in an advisory capacity, their contributions range from recommended rules changes to suggested policies to guide the activity concerned.

This blend of efforts in the administration of the National Federation provides one of the most wholesome youth programs in the world, *interscholastics*, which is a significant phase of modern secondary education.

NATIONAL FEDERATION PHILOSOPHY

The basic beliefs that guide the activities of the National Federation are well established, and the National Federation Articles of Incorporation set forth its primary objectives:

- To formulate and carry into effect policies and plans for improving high school athletic conditions.
- To make continuing studies of the relationship of sports to the overall program of high schools.
- To develop, promulgate and make uniform suitable rules and interpretations governing high school athletic contests and meets and to provide programs and training for the administration thereof.
- To develop, promulgate and make uniform suitable rules and interpretations governing eligibility to participate in high school athletics, athletic safety and protection and other matters relating to high school athletics and participants therein.
- To secure proper adherence to the eligibility rules of state high school athletic associations in interstate contests and meets and to sanction such meets.
- To cooperate with other athletic organizations in the writing of rules and in approving national or other records.
- To provide information concerning all facets of high school athletics and, in connection therewith, to prepare, publish, issue or sponsor all types of written, filmed, recorded or audio-visual material in high school athletics or related subjects.
- To engage, generally, in not for profit activities of an educational or athletic nature.

ACCOMPLISHMENTS OF THE NATIONAL FEDERATION

The assertion by the National Federation that it represents the largest closely knit body of amateur athletes in the world bears weight when it is considered that it has grown from a charter membership of four states in 1920 to include all 50 state associations and the District of Columbia in the United States and affiliated members including the Canadian Federation and Provincial School Athletic Associations. It represents some 18,000 high schools and approximately 9,000,000 secondary school students.

These associations and the affiliated members have worked cooperatively thorugh the National Federation, just as the high schools have worked cooperatively through their state associations. The accomplishments have been tremendous and have elevated interscholastic activities to a status that commands universal respect. Despite its being a federation with power only to make recommendations, its recommendations have been of immeasurable value to state associations and their member high schools as a basis for establishing standards which have provided more wholesome and educational interscholastic activities for the millions of high school students who have participated and are participating in them. The contributions of the National Federation will be realized from the discussion which follows.

RECOMMENDED MINIMUM ATHLETIC ELIGIBILITY REQUIREMENTS

It is recommended (not required) that state associations adopt eligibility standards at least as restrictive as those contained in this section. Due to increased interstate competition and more numerous nonschool sponsored athletic programs for high school age students, the need for more uniformity in eligibility standards between states is increasingly apparent.

In 1979 a campaign was started by the National Council to encourage state associations to adopt standards at least as restrictive as the minimum eligibility standards recommended by the National Federation. This move is particularly important in avoiding friction among schools engaging in interstate competition, and some progress has been made. Minimum eligibility requirements should be reevaluated periodically to insure they serve their purpose of protecting both the high school participants and the interscholastic program. Each of the standards recommended below was developed out of necessity to accomplish these purposes.

Age:

A student who becomes 19 before September 1 shall be ineligible for interscholastic competition. A student who becomes 19 on or after September 1 shall remain eligible for the entire school year.

Enrollment/Attendance:

A. *Enrollment:* To be eligible for participation in interscholastic activities a student shall be enrolled by the fifteenth calendar day of the credit grading period (quarter, trimester, semester, or annual). Enrollment shall be continuous after a student has officially enrolled in a school until the student is officially withdrawn.   B. *Attendance:* The student shall attend school according to the officially adopted attendance plan of that school unless the principal of the school authorizes an excused absence. Unless excused, a student not attending the first day of a credit grading period shall be ineligible to participate in interscholastic contests until the fifteenth calendar day after that student's first day of attendance.

Maximum Participation:

A student may have the privilege to participate in the interscholastic program for four consecutive years (eight consecutive semesters or equivalent) after entering the ninth grade of a four-year high school or three consecutive (six consecutive semesters or equivalent) after entering the tenth grade of a three-year high school. By state high school association adoption, exceptions may be permitted to the requirement of consecutive years of participation.

Attendance of fifteen days or participation in an interscholastic contest shall count as a credit grading period of eligibility.

A student may have the privilege to participate in the same interscholastic sport for four seasons after entering the ninth grade in a four-year high school or three seasons after entering the tenth grade of a three-year high school.

Amateur/Awards:

A student who represents a school in an interscholastic sport shall be an amateur in that sport. An amateur athlete is one who engages in athletic competition solely for the physical, mental, social and pleasure benefits derived therefrom. An athlete forfeits amateur status by:

1. competing for money or other monetary compensation (allowable travel, meals and lodging expenses may be accepted);
2. receiving any award or prize of monetary value which has not been approved by his/her state association;
3. capitalizing on athletic fame by receiving money or gifts of monetary value (scholarships to institutions of higher learning are specifically exempted);
4. signing a professional playing contract in that sport. Accepting a nominal, standard fee or salary for instructing, supervising or officiating in an organized youth sports program or recreation playground or camp activities shall not jeopardize amateur status. "Organized youth sports program" includes both school and nonschool programs. Compensation for giving private lessons is permissible if approved by the state association.

A high school student who loses amateur status may apply to his/her state high school association for reinstatement in the interscholastic program after a waiting period to be determined by that state association.

Only awards of no intrinsic value and approved by his/her state high school association may be accepted by a high school student-athlete as a result of participation in school or nonschool competition in a sport recognized by that state association.

Transfer/Residency:

A student-athlete who transfers enrollment with a corresponding change of residence of parents (or other persons with whom the student has resided for a period of time approved by the state high school association) shall be eligible at the new school as soon as properly certified. A student-athlete who transfers enrollment without a corresponding move into the new school district by his/her parents (or other persons with whom the student has resided for a period of time approved by the state association) shall be required to be in attendance in the new school for one year from the date of enrollment in order to establish athletic eligibility. By state association adoption, the requirement of one year attendance for a student-athlete may be waived but not shortened. School attendance zones are established by either the state association or the appropriate governmental unit.

Academic:

A student-athlete is required to do passing work in the equivalent of at least 15 periods (three subjects with full credit toward graduation) per week. Failure to earn passing marks in three full credit subjects during a credit grading period or the equivalent shall render a student-athlete ineligible for the following grading period. The record at the end of the credit grading period shall be final and scholastic deficiencies may not be removed for the purpose of meeting minimum eligibility requirements, but they may be made up during the intervening credit grading period if approved by that school's state association.

Medical Examination:

Prior to the first year of participation in interscholastic athletics, a student shall undergo a medical examination and be approved for interscholastic athletic competition by the examining medical authority. Prior to each subsequent year of participation, a student shall furnish a statement signed by a medical authority, which provides clearance for continued athletic participation.

Nonschool Participation:

Participation in organized nonschool sports competition while a student is a member of a school team in that sport shall cause a student-athlete to become ineligible for a period of time to be determined by the state association of his/her school. However, a student may participate as an individual without loss of eligibility:

(a) as a member of a **National Team**, which is defined as one selected by the national governing body of the sport on a national qualification basis either through a defined selective process or actual tryouts for the purpose of international competition which requires the entries to officially represent their respective nations, although it is not necessary there be team scoring by nation, or

(b) in an **Olympic Development Program**, which is defined as one funded by the **United States Olympic Committee** and conducted or authorized by the national governing body of the sport involved,

Provided in both (a) and (b):

(1) participation, if during the school year, is approved by the student's high school principal, and the state high school association is notified in writing by the principal at least 30 days prior to the start of the program; and

(2) the student makes prior arrangement to complete missed academic lessons, assignments and tests before the last day of classes of the credit grading period in which that student's absence occurs; and

(3) the student misses no state high school association-sponsored athletic event involving a team in that sport.

Recruiting/Undue Influence:

Transfer from one high school to another for athletic purposes because of undue influence by anyone connected directly or indirectly with the school shall cause a student to forfeit eligibility for at least one year from the date of enrollment.

Parental Permission:

Prior to each year of interscholastic athletic participation, a student shall furnish a statement signed by the student's parents (or other persons with whom the student has resided for a period of time approved by the state high school association), which grants permission for the student to participate in interscholastic athletics.

Assumed Name:

Participating under an assumed name in any interscholastic contest shall make the student-athlete ineligible for a period of time to be determined by his or her state high school association.[5]

NATIONAL FEDERATION SERVICES

The founders of the National Federation envisioned its primary service to be assistance in (1) controlling interstate competition and (2) preventing exploitation of high school athletes and interscholastic athletics by promoters of athletic events to which high school teams and individual athletes were invited. Without this service it would have been impossible for individual state high school associations to adequately protect their interscholastic programs. The support that was forthcoming prompted state high school association executives to request additional services from the National Federation in order to increase the value of athletic competition for high school students. The result has been a continuous expansion of services, which are now numerous.

National Federation Press

Communication is important to the success of any organization. Each year a multitude of news releases, announcements, bulletins, pamphlets, and other publications are distributed to the editors of state and national publications, directors of the broadcast media, state high school association offices, and various other organizations and individuals. State associations are privileged to reprint in their publications and mailings to member schools information from the *National Federation Press* without special permission other than giving proper credit to the source. This procedure enables communications from the National Federation to reach thousands of high school administrators, coaches, and officials, as well as the general public.[6]

Other publications of the National Federation will be noted in appropriate sections of this chapter.

National Interscholastic Records

The need to recognize outstanding athletic performances of high school students on a national basis stimulated the National Council in 1925 to have the National Federation develop a plan for verifying and keeping records of the best athletic achievements in high school sports. It was only logical that the organization through which state high school associations cooperated in directing and protecting interscholastic programs should be the keeper of these records; however, implementation was slow.

Honor rolls listing outstanding performances in track and field were started soon after 1925, and records in this sport have been maintained since that time. Official swimming records were published for the first time in 1973. In 1978 records in twelve additional sports were compiled and published in a National High School Sports Record Book. The 1982 edition contains records in baseball, basketball, cross country, field hockey, football, golf, gymnastics, ice hockey, soccer, softball, swimming and diving, tennis, track and field, volleyball, and wrestling.[7]

In addition to recognizing those individuals who have achieved excellence, these records stimulate other boys and girls to strive to reach their highest potential in athletic achievement. The *National High School Sports*

Record Book published by the National Federation is of interest to both athletes and followers of interscholastic athletics.

Rules Writing[8]

This activity began as an experiment when, for various reasons, it was found impossible to effect the organization of a joint committee to write football rules for National Collegiate Athletic Association colleges and National Federation high schools of this country. Some high schools felt that because of the extent to which football is played in secondary schools, it was only just that there should be active high school members on the above national football rules-making body. This cooperative effort did not materialize, however, and in 1930 the Executive Committee was authorized to proceed with preparation of playing rules in football for use in such states as desired them. This was the beginning of an effort to write rules that are more appropriate for high school students. The football rules now being used are formulated by a committee comprised of one member representing each of the member state associations that use the *National Federation Football Rules*. A questionnaire distributed to high school coaches and officials throughout the United States each year provides the basis from which changes are made.

The National Federation published its first edition of the *Interscholastic Basketball Rules* in 1936–37. *Track and Field Rules* made its first appearance in 1942 and the *Baseball Rules Book* in 1945. Since that time the rules publication program has been expanded to include rules books in field hockey; boys' gymnastics; girls' gymnastics; ice hockey; soccer; softball; swimming, diving and water polo; track and field; volleyball; and wrestling. The number of rules books published has grown from some 2,000 copies in 1930 to approximately 3,000,000 in 1982.

The principal motives behind the rules writing program of the National Federation are the desire to ensure that the rules are more appropriate for high school age students, that they provide the basis for more interesting games, and that they better protect the health and safety of athletes.

Except on the football rules committee, in which each state association using the rules is represented, one member is generally appointed from each of the Federation's eight sections to serve on the rules committee for each sport. State associations are not required to use National Federation rules unless they have a member on the rules committee, but virtually all now use them.

Supplementary books and teaching aids are also published. *Casebooks* detail play situations with practical applications of both rules and decisions. *Officials' manuals* in baseball, basketball, football, girls' gymnastics, and wrestling are of particular help to individuals entering the field of officiating. *Handbooks* in football and basketball are helpful to players, coaches, and officials. Cartoons and diagrams are employed in *Rules Simplified and Illus-*

trated in basketball and football to illustrate play situations which might otherwise be difficult to explain. *Meeting folders* are printed for basketball, football, and wrestling to present rules changes and are especially useful at rules interpretation meetings. *Early Season Questions* containing interpretations of the rules in actual play situations in all sports are distributed each year, and *Rules Examinations* are developed for all sports to assist officials in rules study and as a guide to state associations in registering officials.

To reduce the cost of rules publications to high schools, the National Federation has its own printing office. Over 5,000,000 copies of various rules books, bulletins, pamphlets, and so on are printed and distributed each year.

Audio-Visual Aids[9]

A private corporation, Official Sports Film Service, formed to produce rules interpretation films in 1946 in cooperation with the National Federation, was purchased by the latter in 1968 and incorporated as Official Sports Films, Inc. This corporation was dissolved in 1974 and the organization is now a department of the National Federation.

Rules films in baseball, basketball, football, soccer, swimming and diving, track and field, volleyball, and wrestling are produced. They provide players, coaches, officials, and spectators a means of gaining a more thorough knowledge and appreciation of game rules.

Video cassettes of movie titles were added in 1979 and have expanded the audience for National Federation film projects.

Other teaching aids produced include overhead projection materials with suggested scripts in basketball, football, and girls' gymnastics. These materials help supplement verbal presentations at rules clinics.

Athletic Experimental Studies

Many of the improvements in game rules and athletic equipment have been accomplished through experimentation. For example, experiments with mouthpieces and facemasks led to the requirement that these must be worn to better protect the face and teeth of football players. State high school associations may receive approval for using experimental modifications of game rules, which are studied under laboratory conditions on the playing field or gym floor. State associations authorized to conduct such experiments file written reports with the appropriate rules committee for review and consideration. Many games rules have been improved through this procedure coordinated through the National Federation.

Athletic Insurance

One of the more recent service projects of the National Federation, initiated in 1980, was the formation of a trust fund for providing student athletic insurance at rates generally more economical than those charged by commercial companies. The National Federation Student Protection Trust is administered by Doug Ruedlinger, Inc. The trustee is the United Bank of Missouri, Kansas City, Missouri, and the underwriter is Sentry Insurance of Stevens Point, Wisconsin.[10]

Both school-time and 24-hour coverage is offered for student activities, including all interscholastic sports, and is available to all state high school associations which desire it for their member schools.

An important feature of the program is the gathering of data on injuries in high school sports, which is used to identify injury problem areas. This information is considered by rules makers, coaches, officials, and manufacturers as the basis for providing for greater safety for high school students. (See also page 300.)

Athletic Safety And Protection

From the time of its inception, the National Federation has given attention to the health and safety of athletes. An Athletic Equipment Committee was appointed to work toward standardizing the quality and pricing of athletic equipment for the high school market. Growing concern regarding the safety of protective equipment prompted the National Federation in 1970, in cooperation with other organizations, to form the National Operating Committee for Standards of Athletic Equipment (see pages 280–281). This committee (NOCSAE) investigates and tests protective equipment for all high school sports and has established a standard for evaluating the protective qualities of football helmets.

Success in improving the safety of football helmets resulted in the National Federation's adoption of the following resolution in 1977:

> WHEREAS the National Operating Committee for Standards of Athletic Equipment conducted fair and complete testing of football helmets, established a performance standard for football helmets, succeeded in having the two major rule-making bodies for amateur football adopt the standard; and
>
> WHEREAS this experience has proven that the National Operating Committee for Standards of Athletic Equipment has the constituency and facilities to improve other protective equipment used in amateur athletics in the United States;
>
> NOW THEREFORE, BE IT RESOLVED the National Council of the National Federation of State High School Associations, which conducts the nation's largest athletic program, urges the National Operating Committee for Standards of Athletic Equipment become the central agency in the United States for the study of protective athletic equipment and that NOCSAE use its authority for vigorous expanded testing and, where necessary, standard-setting for athletic equipment;
>
> BE IT RESOLVED that the National Council urges rules committees of all organizations to adopt applicable NOCSAE standards at the earliest possible opportuntiy.[11]

The continuous efforts of the National Federation to protect the health and safety of athletes is of inestimable benefit to high school students.

Professional Interscholastic Athletic Organizations

Since 1971 the National Federation has provided informational and support services to athletic directors (see pages 3–4). In January 1981 the National Council voted to extend similar services to interscholastic coaches and officials. It approved the establishment of the *National Federation Interscholastic Coaches Association* (NFICA) and the *National Federation Interscholastic Officials Association* (NFIOA). Each of these organizations has its own constitution and is governed by its own board of directors comprised of eight members, one from each of the geographical districts designated by the National Federation.

The objectives of the NFICA and NFIOA are essentially the same in that they provide for

1. professional growth of the individual;
2. enhancing the image of coaches and officials;
3. services to members;
4. promoting and developing prestige and respect for their respective organizations;
5. establishing channels of communication between coaches and officials, state high school associations, and the National Federation; and
6. promotion and preservation of the nature of interscholastic athletics.[12]

Included in the services provided through membership in the NFICA and NFIOA at no extra cost are

1. ten issues per year of a National Federation publication (*National Interscholastic Coach* for coaches and *National Interscholastic Official* for officials)
2. films, audio-visual productions, and other aids in rules interpretation
3. comprehensive group insurance which includes personal liability, accidental death, and medical protection
4. conferences and clinics for professional development
5. additional benefits in the form of recognition and awards for those performing outstanding services and discount privileges on numerous items and services

Coordinating the efforts of the NIAAA, NFICA, and the NFIOA through the parent National Federation and its member state high school associations is important in maintaining and improving the values of interscholastic athletics.

In addition, the executive director of the National Federation meets with directors of other national educational associations in the *Educational Leadership Consortium*. These meetings provide a means of working with such organizations as the National School Boards Association, the American Association of School Administrators, the National Association of Secondary School Principals, and others. Channels of communication are opened which enhance mutual respect for the associations participating, appreciation of responsibilities, and the fostering of educational leadership. It is important that the National Federation work closely with these organizations sharing interests in education.

SANCTIONING POLICIES AND PROCEDURES

High schools offer interscholastic activities because they provide unique educational opportunities to their students. Standards have been established by individual schools and through state high school associations to insure that the athletic programs of member schools are kept in proper perspective within the total educational programs, and schools which violate these standards subject themselves to disciplinary action. However, there are nonschool organizations which desire to invite school teams and individual athletes to participate in competitive events they sponsor. To prevent exploitation of both the interscholastic program and the athletes themselves, high schools have formulated policies and criteria to consider in approving events, commonly referred to as *sanctioning*. Teams and/or athletes who participate in an unsanctioned meet may lose the privilege of competing with other school teams. There are those who look upon sanctioning procedures as being restrictive, but without them the educational goals of interscholastics would lose their significance.

Sanctioning is administered on three levels:

1. The local board of education will have policies and criteria for approving or disapproving events pertaining solely to the school community.
2. Through their state associations, high schools have collectively established standards and procedures for sanctioning events within the state to which school teams might be invited.
3. Those of an interstate or international nature are sanctioned through the National Federation of State High School Associations.

Purposes of the National Federation Sanctioning Program

There are three general purposes of sanctioning by the National Federation:

1. The primary purpose is to protect the welfare of high school students by insuring that events will be sponsored by authorities who understand the needs of young people and conduct events in accord with sound educational philosophy. Standards established to implement this philosophy assure fairness and equity for high school participants.
2. The second purpose is to protect the interscholastic programs of member schools. Many events simply duplicate opportunities offered in the school program, which tends toward exploitation of both the athletes and interscholastic athletics.

3. Third, sanctioning eliminates the abuses of excessive competition. Extensive travel and an overloaded schedule interfere with the academic work of students and detract from the educational objectives of interscholastics.[13]

The policy of sanctioning meets has resulted in the elimination of numerous undesirable meets and tournaments and has guaranteed to competing schools that only bona fide schools that are members in good standing of their respective state associations will be competing. It also insures that accepted regulations regarding competition will be followed.

Interstate Events

Dual and telegraphic or telephonic interstate contests are not required to be sanctioned by the National Federation, although there is a policy to guide member state high school associations, which provides that

Each participating school shall follow the contest rules of the state association of which it is a member or rules which have been approved by that association for interstate competition.[14]

The above policy applies only to contest rules, not to eligibility rules or other standards. No school can violate the regulations of its own state high school association.

Interstate meets and tournaments. Events involving schools from more than three states must be sanctioned. The school or organization desiring to host such a meet or tournament must first secure approval from its state high school association, through which it then makes application to the National Federation. The National Federation then forwards the proposal to the other state associations involved for their consideration. If any one of them does not sanction the event, schools from that state cannot be invited. Figure 3–2 outlines the conditions which must be met in order for such an event to be sanctioned.

Area and national championships. One of the earliest accomplishments of the National Federation was the elimination of national high school championships. Colleges and universities were hosting district and state tournaments to which high school teams were invited to qualify for a national high school tournament. On February 26, 1934, the National Council voted to instruct the Executive Committee to refuse to sanction any meet or tournament on a national level, and none have been approved since that time for the participation of high school teams. It is the position of high school administrators and state high school associations that the competition provided through the schools' interscholastic programs adequately meets the needs of high school students and that prolonging sports seasons by post-season con-

National Federation of State High School Associations

11724 Plaza Circle, P.O. Box 20626, Kansas City, MO 64195

Application For Sanction Of Interstate Athletic Event

NOTE: Applications are to be initiated by the host school not later than 30 DAYS PRIOR TO THE DATE of the meet or tournament.

Date: _____

On behalf of _____
　　　　　　　　　(School or Organization Sponsoring the Meet)　　　　　　(Street)　　　　(City)　　　(State)

I hereby apply for sanction of the following event: _____
　　　　　　　　　　　　　　　　　　　　　　　　　　　　　　(Name of Meet)

in _____ to be held on _____, 19_____,
　　　　　(Sport)　　　　　　　　　　　　　　　　　(Month - Date)

to be held at _____
　　　　　　　　(Facility)　　　　　　　　　　　　　　(City)　　　　(State)

The meet will be managed by _____
　　　　　　　　　　　　　　(Name of School conducting Meet)　　　　(City)　　　(State)

Manager: _____ Position: _____

We desire to invite schools from the following states only: _____
_____

The maximum number of schools which will compete is: _____

Maximum value of awards, if any: _____Entry fees, if any: _____

NOTE: It is recommended that invitations to schools not be issued until meet is approved for the participation of such schools.

Contest Conditions include the following:
1. Each school guarantees its membership and good standing in its own state high school association and also guarantees that participation in this event shall not violate any rule of that association or of the National Federation. The sanction is void if such membership has been terminated or if participation is found to be contrary to the state or national rules.
2. Each participant shall be eligible under rules of his or her home state association.
3. Awards shall be limited to such as are permitted by the most restrictive state high school association from which competitors enter.
4. If a school fails to fulfill its contract obligation, that school shall make amends in accordance with terms fixed by the National Federation Executive Committee after consultation with the high school association executive officers of the states involved.
5. No entry shall be accepted for any competitor from any state or section of a state not included in the list of states for which sanction is granted.

Signed: _____ Official Position: _____

(After completing the above form, send it to the high school association executive officer of the state in which the meet is to be held.)

APPROVAL OF HOST STATE ASSOCIATION

Date: _____

I recommend that this meet be (SANCTIONED) (NOT SANCTIONED).

Signature of State Executive: _____ State: _____

(If you sanction the Event, send copies of this form to the executive officer of the high school association in each state named in the application. If the event is not sanctioned, return the form to the applicant.)

ENDORSEMENT OF INVITED STATES

Date: _____

We ☐ ENDORSE　☐ DO NOT ENDORSE the above event for　☐ Any of our schools;
　　　　　　　　　　　　　　　　　　　　　　　　　　☐ Schools within _____ miles; or
　　　　　　　　　　　　　　　　　　　　　　　　　　☐ (Specify) _____.

We ☐ REQUIRE　☐ DO NOT REQUIRE that our schools send eligibility lists for contest direct to our state office for approval before they are forwarded to the meet manager.

Comment: _____

Signed: _____ State: _____

OFFICIAL ACTION OF NATIONAL FEDERATION

Kansas City, Mo. _____, 19_____

This meet is hereby sanctioned for the states of _____
_____
_____

DO NOT INVITE schools from _____
nor any other state not included in the above sanctioned list.

By_____　　　　　THE EXECUTIVE COMMITTEE
　　　(Authorized Signature)　　　　　　　　　OF THE NATIONAL FEDERATION

(These blanks may be obtained from any state high school association office.)

FIGURE 3–2　Application for sanction of interstate athletic event (National Federation)

tests conflicts with both the academic responsibilities of athletes and other interscholastic sports seasons. This same policy has been applied to interstate championships since 1969.

However, several nonschool organizations conduct area and national championships for high school age students, particularly during summer months, without National Federation or state high school association approval. Although entire teams do not participate, some high school athletes compete in these events without loss of eligibility because such state high school association eligibility regulations as *limited team participation* do not apply during the time school is not in session.

A notable increase in the number of various nonschool-sponsored national meets has been a matter of serious concern to interscholastic administrators. Some have thought that high school athletes would be better protected if such events were sponsored by the National Federation of State High School Associations. This possibility was studied from 1977 to 1979, but by vote of the National Council on July 7, 1979, it was resolved that they not be conducted.

International Competition

The increase in high school competition at the national level has been influenced in part by a growing awareness of international competition. Prior to 1950 international competition had little influence on interscholastic athletics. During the 1950s, however, it became clear that European countries were training athletes for international athletic competition, a movement that has continued to grow. Sports boarding schools have been established in some countries to which athletically talented youth are sent for training for international competition, particularly in the Olympic Games. Many of the most successful athletes in the Soviet Union and East Germany are state subsidized throughout their competitive lives.[15] Victory in the Olympic Games is looked upon as an achievement that significantly enhances national prestige.[16]

Amateur athletic policies in foreign countries have had an impact on sports competition in the United States. It became clear that the Soviet Union and other European countries were attempting to support their ideological goals by exploiting those athletes who could achieve prominence in international competition as objects of political prestige and propaganda. The United States Olympic Committee responded in 1966 by establishing its own Olympic Development Committee. Instead of following the European pattern of establishing sports schools, the primary thrust of the Committee has been to stimulate U. S. amateur athletic organizations to sponsor developmental programs *within* the various schools, colleges, and sports-governing bodies.[17] Thus, high school and college athletic programs have become the base from which talented athletes are chosen to be groomed for Olympic competition.

To upgrade its developmental program the U. S. Olympic Committee resolved to initiate national training centers. The first were established at Colorado Springs and Squaw Valley. Outstanding athletes are selected to receive training under coaches with recognized expertise in their respective sports. Since 1978 national sports festivals have been held which have attracted many superior high school and college performers. Because they are generally held during the summer, they have caused no serious conflict with the interscholastic program. These training centers are considered a significant phase of the Olympic Development Committee's program. One significant obstacle to the Committee's efforts is the fact that many of the most talented American collegiate athletes turn professional and are no longer eligible for amateur competition.

Two types of organizations recognized by the U. S. Olympic Committee which sponsor international competition are the national sports-governing bodies and the various sports federations. These organizations, such as the U. S. Track and Field Federation and the U. S. Gymnastic Federation, receive some financial support from the Olympic Committee and contribute to the development of athletes for the Olympic and Pan-American Games.

Athletic administrators have different opinions regarding the developmental program of the Olympic Committee. If the events sponsored, including those sponsored by the national sports-governing bodies and sports federations, conflict with a student's academic program or with high school sports seasons, they will generally object. On the other hand, many believe the high schools should support programs which help develop athletes to represent the United States in the Olympics and Pan-American Games, and the National Federation recommends its membership support the Olympic movement.[18]

Policy pertaining to national teams.   The use of the term *national team* frequently leads to confusion and abuse in cases of team sponsorship by an organization other than those referred to above. To guide state high school associations and their member schools, the National Federation Competition Committee has defined a national team as

> . . .one selected by the national governing body of the sport on a national qualification basis either through a defined selective process or actual tryouts for the purpose of international competition which requires the entries to officially represent the respective nations, although it is not necessary there be team scoring by nation.[19]

The National Federation recommends students be permitted to compete on national teams so defined without loss of eligibility, provided the high school principal receives a request for approval at least 30 days in advance of the competition, that prior arrangements be made to complete academic assignments and tests, and that no school-sponsored or state high school association-sponsored event in that sport is missed.[20]

This same policy is recommended for events included in the Olympic Development Program. However, abuse has arisen from nonschool organizations designating events they sponsor as *olympic development* contests. The official definition adopted in 1977 by the National Federation for an Olympic Development Program is

> . . . one which is funded by the United States Olympic Committee and conducted or authorized by the national governing body of the sport involved.[21]

Other types of international competition. There are several other types of international competition which are sponsored by nonschool agencies and often conflict with the interscholastic program. Some have values for high school students, while others are primarily for the benefit of the sponsor. Tourist agencies are frequently among the promoters.

One type, *cultural exchange programs*, involves athletic competition tours by high school teams. Some foreign teams are not entirely composed of high school students. A few of these cultural exchange projects are legitimate in that they are well planned and offer cultural advantages to the participants, but others are of little cultural or educational significance.

An International School Sport Federation is centered in Europe, and memberships are held by athletic organizations in some 25 different countries. There are also provisions for associate memberships, which may be held by individuals who have no official connection with a high school. The World School Games are sponsored by the federation for the avowed purpose of "developing the sporting activities of boys and girls going to school."[22] Some teams from the United States have competed in this event.

The National Federation recognizes that legitimate international athletic competition can foster international understanding and good will but that these events are also subject to abuse and can cause serious conflicts with the interscholastic athletic programs of state high school associations.[23]

Criteria for National Federation evaluation. In general, under state high school regulations, member schools cannot compete in international athletic competition unless it is sanctioned by the National Federation. This policy, to which virtually all state associations subscribe, has helped prevent conflict with both the academic work of students and interscholastic athletic activities. If a high school desires to participate in an international competition, it must make application for sanction to the National Federation through its own high school association. Figures 3–3 and 3–4 constitute the form used for this purpose. Item 12 of Figure 3–4 contains the standards and conditions which must be met for approval.

In addition to the standards spelled out on the application form, the following criteria are used to evaluate the international competition before it is sanctioned:

1. Competition in the United States shall be sponsored by a high school, or state high school association-sponsored nonschool organization.

National Federation of State High School Associations
11724 Plaza Circle, P.O. Box 20626, Kansas City, Missouri 64195

Application for Sanction of International Athletic Competition

NOTE: Submit in **duplicate** at least 60 DAYS PRIOR TO THE EVENT to the National Federation of State High School Associations.

1. Name of state high school association processing this application: _____

2. Nature of competition: ☐ Single Game; ☐ Tour; or ☐ Tournament   **Sport:** _____

3. a) **Single Game** specifics:
Date	Site	Team (school, city, country)	vs.	Team (school, city, country)

   b) **Tour** specifics:
Date	Site	Team (school, city, country)	vs.	Team (school, city, country)
   1.
   2.
   3.
   4.
   5.
   6.
   7.
   8.

   c) **Tournament** specifics:
   Date: _____
   Site: (facility, city, country): _____
   Teams (list below):
	School	City	Country
   1.
   2.
   3.
   4.
   5.
   6.
   7.
   8.

   (Use additional sheet if necessary)

4. Anticipated gross receipts: _____

5. Anticipated expenses: _____

6. Purpose for which net receipts will be used: _____
   _____

7. Are the following benefits provided to all participants?
   Transportation: _____ Yes _____ No   Type of Transportation: _____
   Board and Room: _____ Yes _____ No

8. Does management make all arrangements to pay board and room or does it provide cash to players for these expenses? _____
   If cash is provided for board and room, how much is allowed for each day per participant? $_____
   In addition to board and room, please indicate the per diem allowance to each participant for incidental expenses:
   $ _____

9. Does the management provide travel accident and athletic medical insurance to the participants?
   _____ Yes _____ No   Insurance Carrier: _____
   Amount of principal sum provided for travel accident: $_____
   Please explain medical (injury) insurance provided: _____
   _____

FIGURE 3–3 Application for sanction of international athletic competition (National Federation)

10. Are participants provided any other benefits or awards in cash, clothing or merchandise, in addition to those described above?

_____ Yes _____ No   If yes, please describe such benefits: _____

_____

11. On an attached sheet, please provide a **roster** of the participants representing each school (U.S. and foreign), identifying them by their **name**, their **school**, their **year in school** (9-10-11-12) and their **age.**

12. Please answer the following questions:

a) Each U.S. school is in good standing in its own state high school association and guarantees that participation in this event will not violate any standard of that association or of the National Federation.   Yes _____ No _____

b) Each U.S. high school participant is eligible under the rules of his or her home state association.   Yes _____ No _____

c) Foreign competitors qualify as amateurs and, if students, comply with the eligibility standards prevalent in the host state concerning age, year in school, etc.   Yes _____ No _____

d) Competition will be administered under those playing rules and other requirements approved by the National Federation.   Yes _____ No _____

e) The program of competition will not conflict with either the academic or interscholastic regulations adopted by the state high school associations or with the athletic or scholastic programs of the schools.   Yes _____ No _____

f) The sponsoring agency will provide suitable chaperons for the participants.   Yes _____ No _____

g) A complete financial report involving all phases of the competition will be filed with the National Federation and the involved state associations within 30 days following final competition.   Yes _____ No _____

h) Fees of national governing bodies have been collected.   Yes _____ No _____

13. Any other information concerning the event:

Attest:

State High School Association Executive Officer: _____   Date: _____

(signature)

(If the event is to involve one or more schools from other states, the host state association officer should send a copy of this form to the executive officer of each of the other high school associations involved.)

ENDORSEMENT OF OTHER INVITED STATES

Date: _____

We ☐ ENDORSE   ☐ DO NOT ENDORSE   ☐ HAVE NO JURISDICTION OVER the event

for ☐ Any of our schools;   ☐ Schools within _____ miles; or ☐ (Specify) _____

Comment: _____

Signed: _____ State: _____ _____

OFFICIAL ACTION OF NATIONAL FEDERATION

The event is: Kansas City, Mo. _____, 19_____

SANCTIONED for the states of _____

_____

NOT SANCTIONED for the states of _____

ON BEHALF OF THE EXECUTIVE COMMITTEE
OF THE NATIONAL FEDERATION

By _____

(Authorized Signature)

(These blanks may be obtained from any state high school association office.)

FIGURE 3–4   Reverse of application for sanction of international athletic competition (National Federation)

2. Each school shall guarantee its membership is in good standing in its own state association and that participation will not violate any standard of that state association or the National Federation.
3. There shall be no conflict with either the academic or interscholastic regulations adopted by the involved association or with the scholastic or athletic programs of the school unless approved by state association and the school administration.
4. Competition shall be administered by qualified officials under the domestic or international playing rules and safety requirements approved for that competition by the National Federation and the state association(s) involved.
5. Appropriate provisions shall be made for the validation of records which may be established during the competition.
6. Entries shall be limited to competitors and/or schools from the states for which sanction has been granted.
7. Each participant representing a United States high school shall be eligible under the rules of its state association.
8. Foreign competitors shall qualify as amateurs and, if students, comply with the eligibility standards prevalent in the host state(s) concerning age, year in school, etc.
9. Advance travel arrangements shall be approved by the involved state association(s).
10. Proper medical supervision shall be available for participants.
11. United States teams shall be chaperoned by state association-approved individuals.
12. A complete report, including a detailed financial statement, involving all phases of the competition shall be filed with the National Federation and the involved state association(s) within thirty (30) days following final competition.[24]

The report to be filed provides significant information for studying and evaluating the international competition as well as for considering any future requests for sanction of that event. Figures 3–5 and 3–6 detail the data to be included in the report.

NONSCHOOL-SPONSORED ACTIVITIES

The position of the National Federation and its member state high school associations regarding athletic competition promoted and conducted by various nonschool organizations and individuals who have no connection with either high schools, the Olympic Development Program, or sports federations is very clear from the statement included in the National Federation Handbook:

Nonschool programs will continue to increase because of the (a) great interest in athletics and in sports; (b) emphasis on physical fitness; and (c) present affluence of society. Interscholastic authorities not only acknowledge the

National Federation of State High School Associations
11724 Plaza Circle, P.O. Box 20626, Kansas City, Missouri 64195

International Athletic Competition Report Form

NOTE: Submit in **duplicate** at least 30 DAYS FOLLOWING THE EVENT to the National Federation of State High School Associations.

1. Name of state high school association processing this application: _____

2. Nature of competition: ☐ Single Game; ☐ Tour; or ☐ Tournament   **Sport:** _____

3. a) **Single Game** specifics:

Date	**Site**	**Team** (school, city, country)	**vs.**	**Team** (school, city, country)

b) **Tour** specifics:

Date	**Site**	**Team** (school, city, country)	**vs.**	**Team** (school, city, country)
1.				
2.				
3.				
4.				
5.				
6.				
7.				
8.				

c) **Tournament** specifics:

Date: _____
Site: (facility, city, country): _____
Teams (list below):

	School	**City**	**Country**
1.			
2.			
3.			
4.			
5.			
6.			
7.			
8.			

(Use additional sheet if necessary)

4. Gross receipts: _____

5. Expenses: _____

6. Summary and analysis of off-field/court activities (school visits, media interviews, receptions, other host country entertainment, etc.):
_____
_____
_____
_____

— Answer 7 thru 14 if competition was outside of U.S. —

7. Comment on adequacy of sports facilities: _____
_____
_____

8. Description of unusual health conditions encountered and comment on adequacy of medical care obtained locally: _____
_____
_____

FIGURE 3–5   International athletic competition report form (National Federation)

9. Description of any ''cultural shock'' problems and how they were dealt with: _____
_____
_____
_____
_____

10. Recommendations to improve organization of future tours to same area and suggestions which may be helpful to leaders of such tours:
_____
_____
_____
_____

11. Assessment of tour from standpoint of its having furthered international goodwill and the education of the participants (provide suggestions for improvement in this direction): _____
_____
_____
_____
_____

12. Was there any stop-over where your group was provided with unsatisfactory transportation? _____
_____
_____
_____
_____

13. Was there any stop-over where accommodation was unsatisfactory? If so, what was the problem? _____
_____
_____
_____
_____

14. Were there any areas where the officiating was unsatisfactory? _____
_____
_____
_____

15. Attach if available:
    (a) press clippings/translations
    (b) photographs
    (c) reports or stories by team members

Chief State High School Association Executive Officer: _____
                                                        (signature)

Date: _____

(These forms may be obtained from any state high school association office)

FIGURE 3–6   Reverse of international athletic competition report form
              (National Federation)

worthwhileness of competitions arranged by other agencies, but also concur that they can make valuable contributions. However, all too frequently there is considerable disregard for protection of the athlete's future high school eligibility and for existing school-sponsored athletic programs. Sometimes the athletes are given awards that violate state association standards. There is a need for a greater cooperation in this area. This matter was discussed in a fall conference of executive officers held in Ohio in October of 1966. It was pointed out that certain individual awards had violated the amateur rules of various state associations and had nevertheless been within the presenting organization's amateur rule. A case in point was the definition of an amateur by the United States Golf Association as, "one who has not accepted more than $200 worth of merchandise." The acceptance of any merchandise prize violates the traditional amateur rule and that of most all state associations. The executive officers in attendance at that meeting agreed that the presentation of awards by nonschool groups as defined by the following standards would not be objectionable:

1. Nonschool groups may present awards which are in agreement with school awards.
2. There should be a reasonable limit on the cost of awards.
3. All awards should be symbolic in nature.

A report of this October meeting was presented to the Mid-Winter Meeting of the Executive Officers held in Des Moines, Iowa, on January 5, 1967. At that time the executive officers voted to adopt the foregoing criteria as a basis for judging the appropriateness of awards. In addition, the executive officers voted to request the National Federation to appoint a committee to meet with nonschool groups sponsoring athletic activities for high school age youngsters in order to review the types and quantities of awards to be presented by the various groups. It was understood the committee so appointed would use the foregoing criteria as a means for determining whether the awards should be approved.

The increased activity of nonschool-connected groups in sponsoring athletic events is of considerable concern to State High School Associations and to the National Federation because in most instances they duplicate the comprehensive, well-functioning interscholastic program. Those promoting these events concentrate on soliciting high school athletes who have distinguished themselves during competition sponsored by schools. For the most part, the purposes of the nonschool program are to bring attention to the promoter of the organization sponsoring the competition while providing other individuals opportunities to scout talents of the competitors. Such programs have been termed "developmental," which is a misnomer. They are, instead, "selection" programs designed to advance the most expert performers to the next higher level of competition. There is no attempt made to develop talents in these programs.

Competitors are attracted to these programs because they are highly publicized and offer the promise of more glamorous competition at both the national and international levels. This selection process conducted by nonschool organizations is detrimental to the interscholastic program because promoters believe interscholastic athletics is only a training ground for nonschool programs. It is true, nonschool competition thrives because of healthy well-organized school programs, but the interscholastic athletic program is not subservient to any other athletic program. Its purpose is to educate boys and girls through athletic competition. All connected with the program must oppose the present trend of serving the interest of the promoters rather than the interest of the student.[25]

Recommended Criteria to Evaluate Nonschool Competition

Competitive activities are sponsored and promoted by nonschool organizations at the local, state, and national levels. School officials frequently receive requests for approval of events held within the school community or the district. This approval is often sought to give the event more significance and status for attracting participants. Although the National Federation leaves local and state matters to state high school associations and their member schools, it does have criteria which are recommended to them for evaluating nonschool competition involving high school students. Here is an excerpt from the National Federation's guidelines:

Nonschool competition shall be evaluated by applying these criteria in total context. An individual criterion or a single factor within a criterion may or may not determine whether the competition shall be endorsed.

1. *Is the primary purpose of the activity to benefit the participants?*
   a. Will it benefit the participants more than the sponsor?
   b. Does it provide an activity not otherwise available to the students involved?
   c. Will the program develop abilities and skills rather than capitalizing on those students already highly skilled and served in other programs?

2. *Will it contribute to the mental, physical, and emotional welfare of youth?*
   a. Is the activity psychologically sound in regard to the physical, mental, and emotional maturity level of the participants?
   b. Is the individual participating because of his own desire or because of outside pressure?
   c. Will it be conducted under standards appropriate for the age level of the youth concerned?

3. *Will it interfere with the academic program of the school?*
   a. Will it cause a loss of academic work?
   b. Will the time for competition, practice, etc., interfere with the home study of the students?

4. *Will it interfere with the interscholastic program of the school?*
   a. Does it conflict with the philosophy and objectives of the interscholastic program?
   b. Will any standards of eligibility for interscholastic activities be violated?
   c. Does it involve students who are simultaneously participating in a similar school activity?
   d. Will it compete for the time the student devotes to other interscholastic activities?
   e. Will it exploit the interscholastic program?[26]

CONTINUING ELIGIBILITY

Protecting the eligibility of high school players for future participation has been an ongoing issue facing coaches and athletic directors. The National Federation's *Handbook* contains sections which explain the nature of these problems and the accomplishments and steps taken by that organization to help protect the future eligibility of high school athletes. This information is important for all directors of athletics.

Administrative bodies at both the state and national levels have responsibility for protecting students' future eligibility. To accomplish this, the National Federation has worked closely with other national organizations in adopting standards which insure high school athletes will not be enticed to participate in programs which would cause them to jeopardize their future eligibility.

In 1944, the National Federation negotiated an agreement with Professional Baseball designated to insure a friendly working relationship between the two groups and to stimulate a healthy interest in high school baseball. It prohibits any major or minor league club from signing a high school student while still eligible for participation in high school athletics. Professional Baseball has, without exception, continuously honored this agreement. It has the support of the owners as well as the commissioner's office.

In addition, representatives of the National Federation and collegiate athletic associations have discussed standards for recruiting. In order to explain the restrictions which colleges have voluntarily agreed to place upon themselves, those associations have published summaries of their rules and regulations governing eligibility, financial aid, and recruiting.

COLLEGE RECRUITING

The evils which result from the bidding by college alumni groups for the services of the high school athletes and the adulation that accompanies the ostentatious banqueting and transporting of such athletes is familiar to high school administrators. As early as 1937 the National Federation recognized the problems being created by solicitation pressures placed on high school athletes in an attempt to strengthen college teams. In that year a resolution was adopted pointing out the detrimental effects of such solicitation on the athlete, upon the high school student body, and upon the public confidence in educational integrity. The National Federation urged the cooperation of all institutions of higher learning in attempting to eliminate all types of solicitation of boys of outstanding athletic ability which differ in manner or form from the ethical practices used by such institutions in attracting all students.

In recent years there has been an attempt by some individuals to establish agencies which would sell information on athletes to different colleges for the purpose of recruiting these individual boys for college scholarships. This matter was brought to the attention of the Executive Committee of the National Federation, and after a thorough consideration of abuses which had developed as a result of the so-called athletic talent clearing houses, scouting service or athletic placement agency, it was the Committee's unanimous decision that the National Federation and member state associations should attempt to establish with high school coaches an arrangement whereby the coaches would refuse to assist in any illegal or unethical recruiting practice. The procedures and purposes of such organizations are not in the best interest of high school athletics nor do they consider the best interest of the individual high school athlete.

Illicit recruiting practices are recognized as one of the major problems in competitive athletics. High pressure tactics can only erode the objectives of the educationally oriented athletic program. Secondary schools must accept some responsibility for exposing violations in recruiting standards. Abuses can be eliminated only through cooperative action.

NCAA legislation requires college representatives to obtain permission of the high school principal or his representative before contacting a prospective student-athlete in the school building. The NCAA is in no position to enforce this regulation, but it must be done at the local secondary school level. If school administrators wish to eliminate the practice of college recruiters contacting students in the halls and locker rooms of their schools, they can by reporting college representatives who circumvent the regulation and by disciplining high school coaches who contribute to these violations. Contact between recruiters and athletes on the school premises may be made only when the chief school official approves it or overlooks it.

An opportune time for college coaches to contact prospective student-athletes is during state level competition at sites at which some of the best teams and athletes are brought together. The NCAA recruiting standards are explicit and emphatic prohibiting college recruiters from contacting the athlete until after he has completed competition in the meet in progress and is released by the appropriate school authority, in most cases the coach. There is to be no contact before the competition or while traveling to the site of competition. There is to be no contact between competition at the site, even if there is a day in which the athlete does not compete. There is to be no contact after competition is concluded unless the coach dismisses the athlete from his charge. These regulations cannot be enforced from the NCAA office unless the violations are reported by high school authorities. By reporting such violations, school administrators are accepting the responsibility which the NCAA has appropriately left to those who have the authority for protecting their high school programs.

Loss of school time by students visiting college campuses at the expense of the college institution has become a major problem for school administrators relative to collegiate recruiting. Again, however, this is a problem which can be solved by local administrators who accept the responsibility to hold athletes to the same attendance standards as nonathletes. NCAA recruiting legislation limits student athletes to accepting six paid visitations to college institutions. However, NCAA recruiting legislation quite properly has no limit to the number of school days a student-athlete may miss. Loss of school time can only be controlled by the local school administrator.

State high school associations are in a position to assume leadership in eliminating recruiting abuses and by informing principals, athletic directors, and coaches of NCAA recruiting regulations. Urging high school administrators to report recruiters who ignore these standards would result in the NCAA reprimanding the recruiting institutions. This would deter the recruiter who intimidates the high school coach. It is also necessary to urge school administrators to discipline high school coaches who encourage and contribute to violations. Other school organizations and educational associations should be urged to encourage their members to report violations and thus eliminate improper recruiting practices.

A Guide for the College-Bound Student-Athlete is the title of a pamphlet published by the National Collegiate Athletic Association, which is a summary of rules and regulations governing recruiting, eligibility, and financial aid. Presented in an easy-to-read manner, the guidelines relate primarily to the recruitment and eligibility of student-athletes as well as to the permissible financial aid they may receive. Every high school administrator and athletic director should have a copy for his use in counseling athletes who plan to compete in college.[27]

Athletic administrators and high school coaches should have copies of this pamphlet, which can be obtained by writing the NCAA, P. O. Box 1906, Shawnees Mission, Kansas 66222.

The recruiting regulations of the Association of Intercollegiate Athletics for Women and those of the National Junior College Athletic Association are not the same as those of the NCAA. Information regarding recruiting legislation of the A.I.A.W. is available from the Association of Intercollegiate Athletics for Women, 1201 16th Street, N.W., Washington, D. C. 20036. Regulations of the N.J.C.A.A. can be obtained by writing to that organization at P. O. Box 1586, Hutchinson, Kansas.

AGREEMENT WITH PROFESSIONAL BASEBALL

An agreement between Professional Baseball and the National Federation has been in effect since 1944. This followed a conference on September 15, 1943, of President George M. Trautman and the Federation Executive Secretary who were representing their respective organizations on the National Physical Fitness Committee. A Joint Baseball Committee made up of Commissioner K. M. Landis, Warren Giles, George M. Trautman, Jack Zellers, Albert Willis, Lyle T. Quinn, R. E. Rawlins and H. V. Porter drew up a statement designed to insure a friendly working relationship between the two groups and to stimulate a healthy interest in high school baseball. This was approved by Commissioner Landis in Chicago on July 18, 1944, and adopted by the Major and Minor Baseball Leagues in December of that year.

The original agreement was slightly revised and expanded at subsequent meetings but the essentials have been retained through the administrations of Commissioner A. B. Chandler, Commissioner Ford Frick, Commissioner William D. Eckert and current Commissioner Bowie K. Kuhn.

At the Professional Baseball meeting in December 1950 it was voted to rescind the agreement but with the knowledge that the rescinding action would not shorten the term of the agreement which did not expire until January 1, 1952. The matter received nationwide attention and many sports writers and national organizations joined forces with the high schools in an attempt to secure a satisfactory agreement to go into effect when the old one expired. In states such as New York and Washington, bills were introduced in the state legislature to prevent the signing of high school boys to a professional contract. The bill in Washington became a law. The bill in New York was vetoed by Governor Dewey with the understanding that the high schools and Professional Baseball would probably agree on a new regulation before the old one expired.

At the baseball meeting in December 1951, a new regulation was adopted for the year 1952, and has been in effect since that time. Item 4 about tryouts was revised in 1953, and Item 2 in 1955.

Major-Minor League Rule 3(h)

(H) High School Players.

1. No student of a high school shall be signed to a contract by a Major or Minor League club during the period the student is eligible for participation in high school athletics. In any instance where such eligibility has expired prior to the student's graduation from high school (a) because of the student's age; or (b) because he has completed the maximum number of semesters of attendance, he may thereafter be signed to a contract which does not obligate him to report for service prior to graduation of the class with which he originally entered high school, i.e., until eight semesters after his original entry into the ninth grade.

2. A student who drops out of high school prior to expiration of his athletic eligibility and continues to remain out for at least one year may thereafter be signed to a contract for immediate service provided his withdrawal from high school was not suggested, procured or otherwise influenced by the club contracting with him, or by any official or employee of such club or of any of its affiliates.

3. Nothing herein shall be construed as prohibiting any Major or Minor League club, its officers, agents, or employees from talking to any high school student at any time concerning a career in professional baseball and discussing the merits of his contracting, when eligible therefor, with any particular club.

4. "Tryouts" to which students may be invited may be conducted during the school year, provided that (1) no student shall be permitted to participate in any such tryout unless the Principal of his high school, if not employed by a Major or Minor League club, shall have approved such participation in writing, and (2) provided further that any such tryout must be limited to not more than five high school students.

5. Any contract made in violation of this rule shall be declared null and void and the offending club (and any club owned by or affiliated with such club) shall be prohibited from signing such player for a period of three years from the date of declaration of voidance of such contract. In addition, such club shall be fined $500, by the Commissioner in the case of a Major League club, or by the President of the National Association in the case of a Minor League club, and the official, scout, or employee of the offending club who

participated in the violation shall be subject to such penalty as the Commissioner or the President of the National Association, as the case may be, shall impose.

6. This rule shall apply to all high school students in the fifty (50) states of the United States of America, and shall not apply to high school students attending high schools outside the said fifty states of the United States of America.[28]

BOWL, CHARITY AND ALL-STAR GAMES

(The position of the National Federation in regard to these kinds of contests is still firmly in accord with an excerpt from Minutes of the 1948 National Council Meeting of the National Federation.)

"Many problems arise in connection with various promotions in which attempts are made to use the high school athletic program and the high school athlete's prestige in the sponsoring of post-season contests, all-star contests, and games or tournaments for the raising of funds for various charities, clubs or other organizations.

"Evils grow up in connection with this type of contest and untenable situations would arise if this type of promotion were permitted without limitation. Such contest divides the allegiance of high school students, tends to undermine respect for the athlete's own high school coach, and encourages the type of adulation which gives the high school athlete an exaggerated notion of the importance of his individual athletic prowess as compared with the importance of his entire school activity program. The high schools have consistently refused to be drawn into promotions of the all-star and post-season variety. If the schoolmen thought there were any values in this type of contest, they could easily provide them through the regular school channels. This has not been done on any sectional or nationwide basis because the high school authorities do not believe such contests are desirable. The athletes to whom these appeals are made have already had a sufficient amount of football or basketball for the season. If they have not, the schools could easily provide for additional competition. There is no good reason why any university, club, or other organization or individual should attempt to circumvent the school policies or regulations concerning length of season and number of permissible games, by setting up a promotion in which the prestige built up in high school play should be exploited for the purpose of interesting a group of athletes in a given university or for the purpose of raising funds for an organization. If this type of promotion were permitted to develop without limitation, the school program would be disrupted to the point where the entire high school athletic program would be in disrepute with all educational accrediting agencies."

As an example of attempts to take pressures off the individual school, here is one of the State Association by-laws: "No post-season festivals, meets, contests, or tournaments shall be permitted during the school year by members of this Association unless special authorization is given by the Board of Control or the Delegate Assembly.

"No member school or official representative of a member school shall participate, either directly or indirectly, in the promotion, management, supervision, player selection, coaching or officiating of an all-star contest or any other contest involving high school students during the school year unless the entire proceeds of said contest shall revert to the schools or association of schools involved."

A joint statement addressing the proliferation of all-star events during the school year was issued in 1978 by the National Federation, National Collegiate Athletic Association, National Association of Intercollegiate and National Junior College Athletic Association. The text is as follows:

"The National Federation of State High School Associations, the National Junior College Athletic Association, the National Association of Intercollegiate Athletics and the National Collegiate Athletic Association have prepared this statement to express the concern of each organization in regard to recent proliferation of high school all-star games scheduled during the academic year.

"Participation in these all-star contests has resulted in significant loss of class time for the students involved, creating situations in which the student-athlete may not meet reasonable attendance standards during his senior year in high school. As a result, these all-star games may interfere with the academic pursuits of the student-athletes, and could affect their academic eligibility to participate as college freshmen in intercollegiate athletics. Further, in some instances, these all-star games serve primarily to benefit the promoters of the contests.

"Therefore, this statement has been adopted to encourage high school administrators to uphold reasonable academic and attendance standards for all students, regardless of their athletic interests.

"The inordinate loss of class time due to participation in high school all-star games is a problem which high school administrators can help to solve by enforcing attendance requirements. Such action is consistent with the objective of maintaining athletics as an integral part of the high school educational program.

"Accordingly, the NFSHSA, the NJCAA, the NAIA, and the NCAA urge the support of high school administrators in discouraging participation in high school all-star games scheduled during the academic year. With this support the exploitation of high school students by promoters of such competition can be curtailed."

On August 1, 1980, a new regulation of the NCAA took effect which should help discourage high school students from "touring" all-star events. The NCAA regulation limits any athlete who hopes to compete at an NCAA institution to a maximum of two all-star events in basketball and football from the time he completes high school eligibility (not graduation) until he enrolls in an NCAA institution, and it prohibits any participation in unapproved all-star events during that period.

The rule is as follows:

"The student-athlete shall be denied the first year of intercollegiate athletic competition if following completion of high school eligibility in the student-athlete's sport and before enrollment in college, the student-athlete was a member of a squad which engaged in an intrastate all-star football or basketball contest that was not specifically approved by the appropriate state high school athletic association or an interstate all-star football or basketball contest that was not specifically approved by the NCAA Council, or the student-athlete participated in more than two approved all-star football contests or two approved all-star basketball contests."[29]

High school athletes will have no opportunity to know and understand the regulations of intercollegiate athletic organizations or how to protect their future without the help of their athletic administrators and coaches. The athletic director should assume the responsibility of seeing that student-athletes are fully informed of college recruiting standards before they complete high school eligibility in their respective sports. Any coach or athletic administrator who fails to assume this responsibility is negligent in caring for the best interests of high school students.

GUIDING PRINCIPLES

In considering problems such as those referred to above, the National Federation at various times has developed statements of principles to guide the deliberations of its membership, as well as high school principals and directors of athletics. Among them are some which can be of much value to athletic administrators in planning their programs.

At its annual meeting in January 1947, a joint committee of the Federation and the American Association for Health, Physical Education, and Recreation prepared a set of Cardinal Athletic Principles which contain significant guidelines for giving direction to interscholastic athletic programs.

CARDINAL ATHLETIC PRINCIPLES

Schools provide opportunity for each individual to develop himself to the limit of his capacity in the skills, appreciations, and health concepts which engender personal satisfaction and civic usefulness. A good school program includes the means for exploring many fields of activity. One such field is that which involves athletic performance. Participation in and appreciation of the skills in a sports contest is a part of enjoyable living. Ability to recognize degrees of proficiency in these skills is one important attribute of the well balanced individual. The perfectly timed and coordinated activities by which an individual, or a team, strives to achieve a definite objective is an exemplification of cooperation and efficiency. A good school program provides a mixture of benevolent restrictions and freedom; of mental growth and physical development; of liberties and restraints. Developing and maintaining a physically fit nation is one of its important aims.

For developing endurance, strength, alertness, and coordination, contests and conditioning exercises have been made a part of the school program. Nature wisely insured a degree of physical development and social adjustment by endowing the individual with a desire to play. Around this desire, as a nucleus, can be built a complete program of beneficial exercises in which healthful and satisfying habits and attitudes are stressed.

To be of maximum effectiveness, the athletic program will:

1. Be closely coordinated with the general instruction program and properly articulated with other departments of the school.
2. Be such that the number of students accommodated and the educational aims achieved justify the use of tax funds for its support and also justify use of other sources of income, provided the time and attention which is given to the collection of such funds is not such as to interfere with the efficiency of the athletic program or of any other department of the school.
3. Be based on the spirit of nonprofessionalism so that participation is regarded as a privilege to be won by training and proficiency and to be valued highly enough to eliminate any need for excessive use of adulatory demonstrations or of expensive prizes or awards.
4. Confine the school athletic activity to events which are sponsored and supervised by the proper school authorities so that exploitation or improper use of prestige built up by school teams or members of such teams may be avoided.
5. Be planned so as to result in opportunity for many individuals to explore a wide variety of sports and in reasonable season limits for each sport.
6. Be controlled so as to avoid the elements of professionalism and commercialism which tend to grow up in connection with widely publicized "bowl" contests, barnstorming trips, and interstate or intersectional contests which require excessive travel expense or loss of school time or which are bracketed with educational travel claims in an attempt to justify privileges for a few at the expense of decreased opportunity for many.
7. Be kept free from the type of contest which involves a gathering of so-called all-stars from different schools to participate in contests which may be used as a gathering place for representatives of certain colleges or professional organizations who are interested in soliciting athletic talent.
8. Include training in conduct and game ethics to reach all nonparticipating students and community followers of the school teams in order to insure a proper understanding and appreciation of the sports skills and of the need for adherence to principles of fair play and right prejudices.
9. Encourage a balanced program of intramural activity in grades below the ninth to make it unnecessary to sponsor contests of a championship nature in these grades.
10. Engender respect for the local, state, and national rules and policies under which the school program is conducted.[30]

GUIDELINES FOR LEVELS OF ATHLETIC COMPETITION

It is apparent that there always will be competition sponsored by nonschool organizations, by individuals who are interested in using athletics for selfish purposes, and also by advertising agencies, which are anxious to use school-age youngsters to further the interests of individual companies. There are also indications that there will be additional competition provided by schools and school groups. Very often pressures have been brought to bear which force schools into providing competition at levels which are not best suited to the ages of the youngsters. In other words, some school administrators have yielded to the pressure from outside groups to establish competitive programs which are detrimental to the best interests of the youngster. In order to provide school administrators with guidelines which could be followed in establishing school athletic programs and also to provide nonschool organizations with guidelines which would aid them in determining the type of competition which was best suited to a particular age group youngster, the National Council at its meeting in French Lick, Indiana, in June of 1966, adopted the following resolution on "Guidelines for Levels of Athletic Competition":

WHEREAS, the schools are greatly increasing the opportunity for participation in school athletic activities to all of their students and to enhance the physical fitness of these youth, and

WHEREAS, there is an increasing number of nonschool organizations sponsoring athletic activities for high school age youth and for those below high school age, and

WHEREAS, many of these organizations seek to use high school facilities, and seek the cooperation of high school staffs to administer their programs, and

WHEREAS, many of the programs sponsored by nonschool organizations are in conflict with the philosophy and principles applied in school athletics, and

WHEREAS, the schools are committed to the philosophy that appropriate levels of competition that are psychologically sound for different age levels are essential to the proper physical, mental, and emotional development of youth, and

WHEREAS, the National Federation of State High School Athletic Associations and its member state associations represent a predominant majority of all the high schools of the United States whose administrators and staffs have given much professional study to appropriate levels of athletic activities based on the physical, mental, and emotional readiness of different age groups of youth, therefore,

BE IT RESOLVED, that the National Federation of State High School Athletic Associations and its member state associations urge nonschool organizations to conduct their programs in accordance with the following levels of competition:

1. Competition for children below junior high school age (under 12 years of age) shall be only intra-community in nature
2. Competition for junior high school age youth (12–14 years of age) shall be intracommunity or intercommunity in nature corresponding to a county area with no district or state championship
3. Competition for high school age youth (over 14 years of age) shall not extend beyond a state championship level

4. There shall be no all-star contests for any of these age levels
5. Any national competition shall be limited to those youth who have graduated from high school, and

   BE IT FURTHER RESOLVED, that the National Federation of State High School Athletic associations and its member state associations cooperate with non-school organizations which sponsor programs that apply the principles inherent in this resolution when these programs do not interfere with the academic and interscholastic programs of the schools.[31]

ADDITIONAL NATIONAL FEDERATION ACTIVITIES

The National Federation engages in many activities related to interscholastics in addition to those already discussed. Its numerous committees each perform functions which benefit high school athletics. A few of the more important programs are described below.

Rules Interpretation Meetings

Each year rules interpretations meetings are sponsored by the National Federation in each sport to which state high school associations send official representatives. These representatives then conduct similar meetings in their respective states for game officials. Emphasis is placed on recent changes in the rules. This service promotes more uniform application of game rules and greater consistency in officiating, which is of particular importance in interstate play.

Sports Participation Surveys

Data is gathered through state high school associations and compiled into annual reports which reveal the numbers of boys and girls participating in each sport in the programs of each state association. Similarly, tables and charts reveal the number of schools offering each sport, as well as which state associations sponsor district and state meets and tournaments in specific sports. The reports are permanently recorded in the National Federation *Handbook* and are used in studies involving comparisons, trends, and so on.

National Federation Awards

The Federation believes in honoring those who make outstanding contributions to interscholastics. In December 1949 the Helms Athletic Foundation presented a plaque to the organization which reads: *"Awarded to National Federation of State High School Athletic Associations in Recognition of Noteworthy Contributions to High School Athletics, December 29, 1949."*[32] Thereafter, individuals were nominated each year by the National Federation as recipients of the Helms Athletic Foundation Award certificate until 1976 when the award was replaced by action of the National Council.

Award of Merit. The National Federation's most prestigious award is its *Award of Merit*, which was initiated in 1976 to replace the Helms award. It is considered the highest honor award in interscholastics and given for outstanding leadership at the national level.

Other awards. Since 1950 certificates of recognition for outstanding service to interscholastic athletics have been presented at the National Federation's annual banquet to those making noteworthy contributions at the state, regional, and national levels.

Awards are also conferred annually on individuals who have made outstanding contributions as members of rules committees or for other activities in the various sports included in the Federation program.

Special awards in the form of National Federation citations are presented at appropriate functions sponsored by state high school associations honoring those who have performed outstanding services.

An up-to-date record of all present and past recipients of the various awards is contained in the National Federation *Handbook*.

National High School Sports Hall of Fame

The National Council instituted a *National High School Sports Hall of Fame* in 1981, which is housed in the National Federation headquarters in Kansas City. Inductees may include high school players, teams, coaches, game officials, athletic administrators, and others who meet specified qualifications and are accepted.

National High School Activities Week

In 1980 a week was set aside by unanimous vote of the National Federation membership to accord national recognition to high school activities. A joint resolution was passed by the United States Congress proclaiming *Activities Week* in 1982. During this week in October the Federation's total membership participates in projects devised by the state high school associations and their member schools. Various nonschool organizations also participate in National High School Activities Week. Emphasis is placed on promoting public awareness of the values of student activities.

Legal Aid Pact

A synopsis is compiled and maintained by the National Federation of all court rulings in the area of interscholastics. It is provided to all state high school associations as a ready reference for their attorneys when legal challenges are faced. This has proved to be an invaluable service. In addition, the Federation sponsors an annual conference for state association attorneys each year.

SUMMARY

The need for more uniform regulations in interstate competition prompted the leaders of four state high school associations to form a National Federation of State High School Athletic Associations in 1921. This organization is a federation of state high school associations whose authority does not supersede the authority of individual state associations. All 50 state high school associations and affiliates in Canada, Okinawa, the Philippine Islands, and Guam now hold membership in the Federation.

The United States membership is divided into eight geographical sections, with one member from each section elected to the Executive Committee, which is the administrative body. An executive director and office staff is employed to handle administrative details. The legislative body is the National Council, comprised of one representative from each of the 50 state associations.

The scope of the National Federation was expanded in 1970 to include nonathletic activities.

The recommended minimum eligibility standards of the National Federation have resulted in more uniform eligibility standards at the state level.

Among the many services extended to member state associations are:

1. A *National Federation Press*
2. Keeping of national records
3. Rules writing and the publishing of rules books
4. Supplying audio-visual aids
5. Conducting experimental studies of athletic activities
6. Providing available athletic insurance
7. Improving safety standards for athletes
8. Services extended to the professional organizations of high school athletic administrators, coaches, and game officials

Policies and procedures applied by the National Federation help to keep interscholastic athletics in proper perspective. Sanctioning policies are applied in interstate, national, and international competition. High school teams and individual athletes cannot compete in events requiring sanction without loss of eligibility.

Nonschool-sponsored athletic competition has presented problems to the National Federation from the time of its inception. Criteria have been developed to evaluate proposed competition sponsored by outside agencies.

In cooperation with the National Federation, intercollegiate athletic associations have established standards for continuing eligibility in college, which have helped alleviate problems inherent in the recruiting of high school athletes for collegiate competition and in controlling participation in all-star games.

An agreement with professional baseball provides that no major or minor league club may sign a high school baseball player before he completes his eligibility for high school athletics.

The Cardinal Athletic Principles adopted by the National Federation have helped schools give direction to their interscholastic programs.

Some of the various other activities of the National Federation which provide benefits are:

1. Conducting rules interpretation meetings
2. Sports participation surveys
3. Sponsoring an awards program
4. Sponsoring a National High School Sports Hall of Fame
5. Promoting National High School Activities Week
6. Compiling a Legal Aid Pact for state associations

The National Federation is a monument to those early pioneers in athletic administration who realized the need for a national organization to give aid and direction to state high school associations in providing more wholesome and more educational experiences through interscholastic athletics.

QUESTIONS AND TOPICS FOR STUDY AND DISCUSSION

1. What is the National Federation of State High School Associations? Trace its history up to the time of the change made in its name in 1970.
2. Explain the part each of the following play in the administration of the National Federation program: National Council, Executive Committee, Executive Director, and advisory committees.
3. Discuss the objectives of the National Federation. Why is it called a *federation*?
4. Of what value are the National Federation's *Recommended Minimum Athletic Eligibility Requirements* to state high school associations and their member schools?
5. How have the rules writing activities of the National Federation improved interscholastic sports?
6. Explain some of the results of experimental studies conducted by state high school associations.

7. What is the National Federation Student Protection Trust? Of what value is it to both high schools and athletes?

8. In what ways has the National Federation promoted greater safety in athletics?

9. What values can you give for the NFICA and the NFIOA being affiliated with the National Federation? What services are provided them?

10. What are the three general purposes of the sanctioning policies of the National Federation? Do they benefit or interfere with the interscholastic program of high schools? How?

11. Discuss the position of the National Federation regarding area and national championships for high school teams. Do you agree with it? Why?

12. Why has interest in international athletic competition increased?

13. Under what conditions does the National Federation recommend students be permitted to compete on national teams without loss of eligibility?

14. Discuss the criteria applied in evaluating international competition for purposes of sanctioning.

15. Give the four general criteria recommended for evaluating nonschool-sponsored athletic contests.

16. What is the significance of the *continuing eligibility* regulations? How does it help protect the interscholastic athletic program?

17. Discuss the National Federation agreement with Professional Baseball.

18. Why do the National Federation and state high school associations oppose bowl, charity, and all-star games? What is your opinion regarding their positions?

19. What use can an individual school make of the Cardinal Athletic Principles?

20. Why do you think an athletic administrator should be well informed of the National Federation's program?

NOTES

1. National Federation of State High School Associations, *1982–83 Handbook* (Kansas City, Mo.: National Federation, 1983), pp. 13–14.

2. Ibid., p. 4.

3. Ibid., pp. 104–13.

4. Ibid., pp. 112–13.

5. Ibid., pp. 47–50.

6. Ibid., p. 16.

7. Ibid., pp. 16–17.

8. Ibid., pp. 20–23.

9. Ibid., p. 24.

10. Ibid., pp. 25–26.

11. Ibid., pp. 26–28.

12. *National Federation Press*, 1, no. 8 (April 1981), 1.

13. This material is a summary of that found in the *1982–83 Handbook* of the National Federation on pp. 29–30.

14. Ibid., p. 32.
15. William Johnson, "Sports Development Programs in the USSR and Selected European Countries," *The Physical Educator*, 23, no. 3 (October 1977), 153–56.
16. Raoul E. L. Mollet, "Current Trends in European Olympic Development," *Proceedings*, National Conference on Olympic Development (Washington, D. C.: American Association for Health, Physical Education, and Recreation, 1966), p. 130.
17. Merritt Stiles, "Introductory Remarks," *Proceedings*, National Conference on Olympic Development (Washington, D. C.: American Association for Health, Physical Education, and Recreation, 1966), p. ix.
18. Irvin A. Keller, *The Interscholastic Coach* (Englewood Cliffs, N. J.: Prentice-Hall, Inc., 1982), pp. 228–29.
19. National Federation, *1982–83 Handbook*, p. 41.
20. Ibid., p. 41.
21. Ibid., p. 43.
22. Keller, *The Interscholastic Coach*, pp. 230–31.
23. National Federation, *1982–83 Handbook*, p. 35.
24. Ibid., pp. 36–37.
25. Ibid., pp. 38–40.
26. Ibid., p. 40.
27. Ibid., pp. 52–54.
28. Ibid., pp. 53–55.
29. Ibid., pp. 57–59.
30. National Federation, *1974–75 Official Handbook*, pp. 9–10.
31. Ibid., pp. 43–45.
32. National Federation, *1982–83 Handbook*, p. 62.

BIBLIOGRAPHY

DURBIN, BRICE B. "National Report." *Interscholastic Athletic Administration*, 7, no. 4 (Summer 1981), 3.

DUTCHER, JIM, and FRANK IBBOTSON. "Do Administrators Have a Responsibility to Control National High School Championships?" *Interscholastic Athletic Administration*, 7, no. 4 (Summer 1981), 21–22.

JOHNSON, WILLIAM. "Sports Development Programs in the USSR and Selected European Countries." *The Physical Educator*, 34, no. 3 (October 1977), 163–66.

KELLER, IRVIN A. *The Interscholastic Coach*, pp. 226–34. Englewood Cliffs, N. J.: Prentice-Hall, Inc., 1982.

MOLLETT, RAOUL E. L. "Current Trends in European Olympic Development," in *Proceedings*, National Conference on Olympic Development. Washington, D. C.: American Association for Health, Physical Education, and Recreation, 1966, p. ix.

NATIONAL FEDERATION INTERSCHOLASTIC COACHES ASSOCIATION. "Board of Directors Defines NFICA Goals and Priorities." *National Interscholastic Coach*, 1, no. 1 (September 1981), 1, 5.

NATIONAL FEDERATION OF STATE HIGH SCHOOL ASSOCIATIONS. *1982–83 Handbook*. Kansas City, Mo.: National Federation, 1983.

NATIONAL FEDERATION OF STATE HIGH SCHOOL ASSOCIATIONS. "Officials and Coaches Organizations Established." *National Federation Press*, 1, no. 8 (April 1981), 1–2.

NATIONAL FEDERATION OF STATE HIGH SCHOOL ASSOCIATIONS. "Combined Efforts Key National Activities Week." *National Federation Press*, 3, no. 2 (October 1982), 1, 7, 8.

SHANNON, THOMAS A. "Administration: A School Board Perspective of Assessing Leadership." *Interscholastic Athletic Administration*, 9, no. 1 (Fall 1982), 8–11 and 28.

STILES, MERRITT. "Introductory Remarks," in *Proceedings:* National Conference on Olympic Development. Washington, D. C.: American Association for Health, Physical Education, and Recreation, 1966, p. ix.

4

State High School
Athletic and Activity Associations

After high school administrative officers experienced some success in reducing the abuses noted in interschool athletic competition by forming area leagues or conferences (see page 11), it was evident to leaders in several states that greater unformity in regulations and more equity in competition could be accomplished by forming statewide school athletic associations. Their foresight and efforts in forming such organizations resulted in the development and maintenance of high standards in the administrative control of interscholastic athletics, which has enabled high schools to keep these activities in proper educational perspective. All athletic administrators must thoroughly understand the standards and regulations of their state high school association.

EARLY STATE ORGANIZATIONS

There is some question as to which was the first statewide organization for the control of interscholastic athletics. Certainly Wisconsin was early on the list, since a committee was appointed in 1895 in that state to formulate rules to govern interschool athletic contests. Also in 1895 a state field day was held in Michigan in which schools competed under what were considered more or less uniform rules, and a committee of the state teachers' association was appointed at that time to further the organization of the Michigan Interscholastic Athletic Association. Illinois apparently formed its state association that same year, and Indiana set up its organization in 1903. It is apparent, therefore, that the beginnings of statewide athletic associations were made in most states either in the years immediately preceding 1900 or within the next few years thereafter. Some of the organizations were not very strong for a number of years, but with the growth in high school enrollments and the increase in amount and scope of athletic competition, there were associations in all but a few states by 1926.

ATHLETIC AND ACTIVITY ASSOCIATIONS

There are athletic or activity associations in all 50 states at the present time, although not all state organizations use the word *athletic* in their names. Some 29 of them embrace activities other than those pertaining to athletics. During the 1940s and early 1950s there was a strong tendency, especially in the Midwest, to form activities associations to include music, forensic, dramatic, commercial, academic, and other activities as well as athletics. The names of state associations other than those strictly athletic in nature follow:

Alaska High School Activities Association
Arizona Interscholastic Association
Arkansas Activities Association
Colorado High School Activities Association
Florida High School Activities Association
Georgia High School Association
Idaho High School Activities Association
Illinois High School Association
Kansas State High School Activities Association, Inc.
Maine Secondary Schools Principals Association
Minnesota State High School League
Mississippi High School Activities Association
Missouri State High School Activities Association
Montana High School Association

Nebraska School Activities Association
Nevada Interscholastic Activities Association
New Mexico Activities Association
North Dakota High School Activities Association
Oklahoma Secondary School Activities Association
Oregon School Activities Association
South Carolina High School League
South Dakota High School Activities Association
Texas University Interscholastic League
Utah High School Activities Association
Vermont Headmasters' Association
Virginia High School League
Washington Interscholastic Activities Association
West Virginia Secondary School Activities Commission
Wyoming High School Activities Association[1]

The remainder of the state associations, including those in Canada, are strictly athletic in nature and are called either interscholastic athletic or high school athletic associations, leagues, or conferences.

PURPOSES OF STATE ASSOCIATIONS

The purposes of state high school associations are stated in their constitutions, which illustrate why these organizations were founded and what they are expected to accomplish. Typical purposes and objectives of both athletic and activities types of associations appear in the following samples.

New Jersey State Interscholastic Athletic Association

- To foster and develop amateur athletics among the secondary schools of the state.

- To equalize athletic opportunities by standardizing rules of eligibility for individuals, and by classifying for competitive purposes the institutions which are members of the Association.
- To supplement the physical education program of the secondary schools of New Jersey by making a practical application of the theories of physical activity.
- To promote uniformity in the arrangement and control of contests.
- To protect the mutual interests of the members of the Association through the cultivation of ideals of clean sport in their relation to the development of character.

Missouri State High School Activities Association

Section 1. The Missouri State High School Activities Association is a voluntary, nonprofit, educational association of junior and senior high schools. Through it they work cooperatively in adopting standards for supervising and regulating those interscholastic activities and contests that may be delegated by the member schools to the jurisdiction of the Association.

Section 2. Stated more specifically, the general objectives of the Association include:

a. To insure that interscholastic activities shall supplement the curricular program of the school to provide opportunities for youth to acquire worthwhile knowledge, skills, and emotional patterns.

b. To promote the educational values inherent in interscholastic activities which will contribute to the accepted aims of education.

c. To develop standards for the approval and direction of interscholastic activities and contests.

d. To formulate minimum, uniform, and equitable standards of eligibility that must be met by students to attain the privilege of representing their schools in interscholastic activities.

e. To develop standards to be met by schools participating in interscholastic activities under the sponsorship of the Association.

f. To avoid interference with the educational program of the school and to prevent exploitation of high school youth and the programs of member schools by special interest groups.

g. To foster a cooperative spirit and good sportsmanship on the part of school representatives, school patrons, and students.

h. To provide means of evaluating and controllng local, state, and national contests affecting secondary schools initiated by firms, organizations, and institutions outside organized educational agencies.

i. To develop standards of officiating and adjudicating to ensure greater statewide consistency and quality.

Pennsylvania Interscholastic Athletic Association

Health. To organize, develop, and direct an interscholastic athletic program which will promote, protect, and conserve the health and physical welfare of all participants.

Education. To formulate and maintain policies that will safeguard the educational values of interscholastic athletics and cultivate high ideals of good sportsmanship.

Competition. To promote uniformity of standards in all interscholastic athletic competition.

Connecticut Interscholastic Athletic Conference

To provide a central, voluntary, nonprofit organization through which the public secondary schools of the state may cooperate for the following ends:

- To develop intelligent recognition of the place of athletics and sports in the education of our youth.
- To establish and unify policies of administration in interscholastic athletics and sports.
- To offer a system that will provide for equitable competition.
- To encourage the organization of recreational athletics and play for all students as an integral part of the educational program.
- To assist member schools in securing competent officials.
- To organize a force of opinion to keep interscholastic athletics within proper bounds, that will expressly encourage all that is honorable, sportsmanlike, and gentlemanly in all branches of athletics and sports.

Kansas State High School Activities Association

This corporation is organized NOT for profit and it is organized and shall be operated exclusively for the following educational purposes:

1. Administering a program of interscholastic activities, festivals, clinics, and contests among its member schools.
2. Elevating the standards of good sportsmanship and encouraging the growth in good citizenship, not only of junior and senior high school boys and girls but also of adults and all others who come into contact with school activities.
3. Protecting member schools from exploitation by special interest groups.
4. Encouraging pride in scholastic achievement as a fundamental basis for a well balanced activity program.
5. Serving the best interests of all member schools by influencing the proper type of legislation or any other desirable means.

New Brunswick (Canada) Interscholastic Athletic Association

- To foster and develop amateur athletics among the Public High Schools and Private Secondary Schools of the Province.
- To equalize athletic opportunities by standardizing rules of eligibility for individuals, and classifying for competitive purposes, the institutions which are members of the Association.
- To promote uniformity in the arrangement and control of contests.

- To protect the mutual interests of the members of the Association through the cultivation of ideals of clean sport in their relation to the development of character.

Each high school should formulate and publish objectives of its interscholastic athletic program. Athletic administrators can benefit by carefully reviewing objectives of state high school associations and their own state association's statement of purpose.

TYPES OF STATE ASSOCIATIONS

Although state athletic and activities associations function similarly in most respects, they fall into three general classifications in regard to administrative control. The great majority are voluntary associations through which their member schools cooperatively regulate interschool contests and activities. The second type is affiliated with a state education department. A third consists of those administered through institutions of higher learning.

Voluntary State Associations

State associations in this classification are the most numerous. Membership is voluntary but is usually dependent upon member schools meeting specified requirements regarding the financial support of the school, its plan of organization, the status of its coaches, and the payment of annual dues. Usually such organizations limit their competition to member schools. There are well-established regulations for the administration of athletic contests and the eligibility of contestants. In most states, membership is open to public secondary schools accredited by state departments of education. Some states also allow private and parochial schools to join, provided that they meet the standards for membership. Generally there are elected boards of control, delegate assemblies, or legislative councils whose members are representative of geographical sections and often of schools of different sizes. In most cases there are the usual officers—president, vice president, secretary, and treasurer. Often the secretary is the executive officer, although in other states he or she is called commissioner or state director. Typical states with this form of organization, in different sections of the country, are Washington, Colorado, Missouri, Illinois, Wisconsin, Indiana, Connecticut, Florida, Pennsylvania, and Alabama.

There are other state associations almost identical in form of organization to those above except that there are ex officio members on their boards or legislative bodies who are not elected by the schools. The commissioner of education, or as his or her representative, the supervisor of physical and health education, is an ex officio member of the Minnesota Board. California, Ohio, Pennyslvania, Delaware, Maryland, and New Jersey are some of the states in which the state physical and health education director is a member ex officio of the state association executive or legislative body. Members of the state school boards association are now members of the administrative boards of a few associations. Kansas, Minnesota, and South Dakota are states with this provision. Because of the fact that school boards have wide authority under the law in most states, a working relationship with school boards associations can prove valuable to state associations.

State Associations Affiliated with State Departments of Education

In the fall of 1938 New York began a new chapter in the general program of administration of interscholastic athletics in that state. Through action of the New York Board of Regents, there were established what are known as Regulations of the Commissioner of Education Governing Health and Physical Education.[2] These regulations made athletics in New York a definite part of the physical education program. Actually, the state athletic association is a voluntary organization with 11 district divisions. Its general body is a central committee composed of district representatives, with an executive committee of 11 members serving in an executive capacity. The state athletic association has continued to function in furthering its studies of athletics programs, its bulletin publication, its Athletic Protection Fund plan, formation of new rules, and in conducting district tournaments and meets. Since the basic athletic code has been given the force of law by action of the Board of Regents, it is the responsibility of that body, through proper state education department officials, to enforce it.

> It is not the responsibility of any state or local athletic association or league to enforce the Commissioner's Regulations governing athletics as approved by the Board of Regents. It is, of course, the responsibility of athletic associations and leagues to cooperate in seeing that both the spirit and letter of the Regulations are lived up to by the various school districts throughout the state.[3]

The administration of the Michigan Association has been affiliated with the Michigan State Department of Public Instruction since 1924. Its function has been to exercise control over the interscholastic athletic activities of all schools of the state. A change in the state law in 1972 enabled school districts to:

> . . . join any organization, association, or league which has as its object the promotion of sports or the adoption of rules for the conduct of athletic, oratorical, musical, dramatic, or other contests if the organization, association, or league provides in its constitution or by-laws that the superintendent of public instruction or his representative shall be an ex officio member of its governing

body with the same rights and privileges as other members of its governing body.[4]

The policy-making body of the Association is its Representative Council consisting of 14 members elected by the schools of the state and the Superintendent of Public Instruction as an ex officio member. The duties of the Council are:

The Council shall have general control of interscholastic athletic policies.

It shall make rules of eligibility for players.

It shall make regulations for the conduct of interscholastic contests.

It may discipline member schools, contest officials, and athletes for violations of rules and regulations.

It shall provide for the hearing of appeals from decisions of the State Director of Interscholastic Athletics.

It shall exercise all other functions necessary for carrying out the spirit and purpose of this Constitution.[5]

The legislative authority of the Association rests with its member schools. Amendments to its constitution and by-laws are made by them at any annual business meeting of the Association.

The executive director is appointed by the Representative Council. Officers of the Association are elected by the Council and include a president, vice president, and secretary-treasurer.

In summary, the administrative control of the Michigan High School Athletic Association is under its Council of which the Superintendent of Public Instruction is an ex officio member.

The Delaware Secondary School Athletic Association is more directly under the auspices of the Delaware State Board of Education.[6] It functions much the same as the Michigan Association, except that the State Supervisor of Physical Education and Athletics serves as the Executive Secretary-Treasurer of the Delaware Association, and his or her selection must be approved by the State Board of Education instead of being subject to the approval of only the Council as in Michigan. Similarly, amendments to Delaware's constitution and by-laws are subject to the approval of the Delaware State Board of Education, which is not required in Michigan.

Virtually all state high school associations were originally established as voluntary, not for profit, unincorporated organizations, but some are now incorporated under the laws of their respective states (Connecticut, Kansas, Massachusetts, Michigan, Mississippi, New Hampshire, North Carolina, Rhode Island, Vermont and Virginia). The laws differ from state to state regarding the status of voluntary, unincorporated associations, and it is wise to check them carefully. One of the principal factors to consider in determining whether to incorporate is the extent of legal liability of officers and members of governing bodies of a voluntary association in a particular state. An attorney's opinion should be obtained to determine the advantages and disadvantages of incorporation under the laws of an association's state.

The California Interscholastic Federation is unique among the voluntary state high school associations. For administrative purposes it is divided into ten Sections. Each Section has its own Council, which serves as its legislative body—an Executive Committee, officers, and a commissioner. The Sections elect representatives to serve on the State Council of the California Interscholastic Federation. As its name implies, it is a federation through which the Sections cooperate in developing uniform standards and regulations. Its State Council sanctions all state championships and establishes regulations for them.

This plan of organization is well adapted to conditions in California where the geography of the state and distribution of population differs from that of other states. Although its administrative plan differs from that of other state associations, the CIF performs the same functions as do other state high school associations.

University-Directed State Associations

Texas presents a unique example of this type of organization:

> Any public school in Texas below collegiate rank that is under the jurisdiction of and receives apportionment from the Texas Education Agency is eligible for membership. Exceptions: (1) a school whose students are enrolled in that school because of physical, sensory, or emotional disabilities which make it impossible for them to compete effectively with students who do not have such disabilities; (2) a school whose students are enrolled in the school as part of a process of rehabilitation for law violations.[7]

Elementary schools in Texas may become members of the University Interscholastic League and may compete in certain contests sponsored by the League.

The governing body of the league is a state executive committee appointed by the president of the University of Texas. Regional and district committees participate in the management and control of the league. The Texas Interscholastic League covers a larger geographical area and serves more different types of schools than any other state association. During the 1980–81 school year 3,413 schools were registered for participation in league contests in a total of 36 activities. Evidently, the Texas plan represents an organization vastly different from that in most other states.

The South Carolina and Virginia state associations also are affiliated with state institutions of higher learning, the Universities of South Carolina and Virginia respectively. While many of the affairs of their associations are administered by the extension divisions of those universities, they are not handled as completely or as extensively as is the case in Texas.

Although there are administrative differences among state high schoool associations, all such organizations have a common purpose—helping member schools work cooperatively in giving direction to interscholastic activities. Principals generally represent their schools in association matters and have a strong voice in determining those minimum standards and regulations to which all member schools must subscribe. Any individual school may adopt higher standards than those of its state association, but none may adopt lower ones. In essence, a state high school association is an organization which performs functions its members have delegated to it, functions that enable individual schools to perform interscholastically.

FUNCTIONS OF STATE ASSOCIATIONS

Reasons for the existence of state athletic and activity associations are manifold. As new services have been added there have been increased administrative duties. This has been the case not only in activity associations which include other than athletic programs, but also in those limiting their jurisdiction to athletics exclusively.

Activities in Addition to Athletics

Mention has been made previously in this chapter of the fact that a number of state associations include more than athletics in their jurisdiction and functional services. No attempt will be made in this discussion to include all these activities since we are concerned primarily with administration of high school athletics. It will be sufficient to list some of the activities in representative state organizations. Texas is the most inclusive in its program, and according to its constitution it holds contests annually in the following activities:[8]

Baseball, Boys	Music
Basketball, Boys'	Music Theory
Basketball, Girls'	News Writing
Calculator Applications	Number Sense
Choral Singing	Oral Reading
Cross Country, Boys'	One-Act Play
Cross Country, Girls'	Persuasive Speaking
Debate	Picture Memory
Editorial Writing	Poetry Interpretation
Feature Writing	Prose Interpretation
Football, Boys'	Ready Writing
Football, Boys' Six-Man	Science
Golf, Boys'	Shorthand
Golf, Girls'	Softball, Girls'
Headline Writing	Story Telling
Informative Speaking	Spelling and Plain Writing

Swimming, Boys'	Track and Field, Boys'
Swimming, Girls	Track and Field, Girls'
Tennis, Boys'	Typewriting
Tennis, Girls'	Volleyball, Girls'

As compared with this broad range of activities, many state associations remain strictly athletic in nature. Ohio, Michigan, California, Wisconsin, Connecticut, Pennsylvania, New York, Indiana, Iowa, and Alabama are examples of this large group. In Minnesota music, dramatics, and speech activities, in addition to athletics, are under the supervision of the state high school league. Nebraska calls its organization an activities association. It embraces declamatory, debating, music contests, and one-act plays, as well as athletics in its activities. Kansas also is an activities association; and, in addition to athletics, it directs contests in music, debating, speech, and dramatics. The activities of these three state associations, as well as those of Texas, are examples of a type of service rendered to their schools that seems destined to receive attention from other states.

Twenty-nine now have activities associations. The states that have adopted this plan felt that they had the basic machinery set up in their athletic associations whereby they could efficiently handle other activities. This assumption seems logical; and when sectional or state contests in nonathletic activities are desired, such organizations can provide services broader in scope than athletics. Also, if contests are held in activities other than athletics, coordinating them through one central association can help to avoid schedule conflicts and other problems.

State athletic associations perform numerous functions in areas other than those pertaining strictly to eligibility of contestants. Among them are included the following:

Athletic Activities

Regulations for the conduct of contests.   These are discussed in Chapter 6.

Interpretation of playing rules.   This service has resulted in greater uniformity in methods of play and officiating. The National Federation performs an important role in assisting state associations with this function. National rules interpretation meetings are attended by state representatives who take back to their state associations common interpretations. The state associations then brief member schools and game officials on these rulings.

Athletic accident insurance plans.   The Wisconsin Interscholastic Athletic Association under the leadership of Secretary Paul F. Neverman and his board of control was a pioneer in developing a plan whereby member schools could secure insurance coverage for athletic injuries through their state high school association. The Accident Benefit Plan sponsored by the WIAA and initiated in 1930 at first covered only bone fractures but was later revised to include soft tissue injuries and hospitalization. Some 17 other state associations followed in sponsoring accident insurance plans patterned after the Wisconsin plan, but most later entered into contracts with commercial companies, because they felt they should not, or by local state laws could not, become involved in any form of athletic injury insurance business. Only six of them continued administering an insurance program as late as 1981–82.

Many state high school associations have endorsed a group accident insurance plan underwritten by an approved commercial company to make coverage available to their member schools at a reasonable cost.

Kansas was one of the leaders in developing a catastrophe insurance program for members of its state high school association. This type of insurance, usually with a deductible approximately equal to the amount paid in basic accident insurance coverage, provides protection for the more serious accidents. Individual schools cannot afford such a plan, but state associations can, and do, obtain affordable group coverage from commercial companies to cover all students participating in activities sponsored by the association.

A still larger group plan is available to state associations through the National Federation Student Protection Trust inaugurated in 1980 (see pages 35 and 300–301).

Making student accident insurance protection available at affordable costs is a significant service, and virtually all athletes currently competing in high school sports have such coverage.

Registration and classification of athletic officials. Michigan was the first state in the Midwest to establish a plan for registration and classification of athletic officials (1927). Similar plans have been set up in several other states. The feeling generally exists that athletic officials should be included as a definite and necessary part of the athletic program. By implication, the right to license also entails the right to refuse to license, and thus it is possible to dispense with officials who do not meet standards or codes of athletics commonly established.

Registration has brought officials into close contact with state associations. Standards of officiating have been raised through rules-interpretation meetings and through officials' knowledge that their license to officiate depends upon their maintaining established standards. In most state associations licensing fees hardly defray the costs of services rendered. Illinois, Kansas, Wisconsin, Pennsylvania, Minnesota, and Michigan are among the leaders in officials' registration and rating plans. In some states, athletic associations are affiliated with state officials' associations or local boards of officials.

Publications. Most state associations publish monthly or periodic printed bulletins during the school year. In Texas a newspaper type of publication is issued. These carry activity announcements as well as general items pertaining to intramural and interscholastic athletics. A most important feature of such publications is the accounts of executive and legislative meetings concerning eligibility and administrative matters as they pertain to athletics. Decisions in eligibility cases as they are published often perform a double service in that they establish precedents as well as permanent records and provide schools with information regarding interpretations of state association by-laws. Each state also publishes an official handbook containing general interpretations, lists of officials, constitutions, committees, and records of activities. (It is suggested that students write to the association in the state in which they plan to work to obtain a copy of that association's handbook for study. See Appendix A for addresses.) Records, reports, and general eligibility blanks, contracts, and the like are materials furnished by virtually all state associations.

Several states publish special bulletins and pamphlets for specific purposes. Montana provides a pamphlet outlining guides for athletic contest management details. Indiana and other states distribute brochures explaining the functions of their state associations. Missouri publishes such pamphlets as *A Clarification of the Philosophy and Objectives of Secondary School Athletics; Coaches Manual for Teaching Youth through Interscholastic Athletics; Manual for Boards of Education,* and a *Manual for Improving the Education Values of Interscholastic Athletics by Providing for Better Sportsmanship.* These are examples of a few of the many attempts of state associations to provide materials to aid their schools in achieving the most worthwhile objectives of interschool athletics.

Conducting district and state interscholastic competition.   All state high school associations in the 50 states and the District of Columbia conduct state athletic meets and tournaments in those sports in which a sufficient number of high schools participate. These meets are so popular with the public that by now they might be considered a tradition.

The 29 state associations which include nonathletic activities also conduct district and state competition in some of these areas, with the program in Texas being the most extensive.

A tremendous increase in girls' interscholasatic competition in the 1970s and broader offerings in boys' sports has resulted in a similar growth in state high school meets and tournaments. When the number of schools and high school athletes competing in all state high school-sponsored meets and tournaments is taken into account, this vast athletic program is no doubt one of the largest, if not the largest, youth athletic meet program in the world. Its scope can be noted by examining the number of state high school associations conducting boys' and girls' state athletic meets and tournaments shown in Table 4–1 compiled from the 1980–81 National Federation records.[9]

Some educators have questioned the value of state high school cham-

TABLE 4–1. High School Associations Conducting State Meets and Tournaments

Sport	Boys'	Girls'
Archery	0	1
Badminton	0	2
Baseball	44	0
Basketball	51	50
Bowling	3	4
Cross Country	50	45
Decathlon/Pentathlon	6	2
Field Hockey	0	14
Fencing	2	2
Football	43	0
Golf	50	34
Gymnastics	25	34
Ice Hockey	14	0
Indoor Track	11	8
Skiing	11	11
Soccer	25	7
Softball	0	34
Swimming	39	39
Tennis	49	49
Track and Field	51	51
Volleyball	5	43
Wrestling	47	0

pionships. More than 40 years ago, Rogers maintained that state tournaments, as such, have no educational value.[10] Some school administrators have expressed concern regarding an overvaluation of such contests, conflicts with the academic program, and the cost of participating in those that are not self-supporting from admission receipts. Why, then, do state associations sponsor them?

One of the principal reasons is related to the history of state associations. Before their existence, some colleges and organizations outside the high schools had begun to sponsor championships for high school teams. One of the chief motives of school officials who took an early part in the formation of state associations was to eliminate such outside promotions. It became clear to them that state tournaments sponsored and controlled by their own organizations were the most practical way of controlling outside promotions of such events. If state association-sponsored championships were eliminated, it is very probable that others would again attempt to promote championships for high school sports. This is evident from the number of nonschool organizations promoting championships for high school youth, and even for those below high school age, during the summer months; Little League Baseball, for example, includes a national tournament. It is apparent that school administrators and boards of education want to maintain control over any championships in which their students will be representing their schools and that conducting their own through their state associations is the best way to do it. If such championships were undesirable, the state association would be in position to take steps to do away with them.

Some state high school associations have set forth purposes for conducting state tournaments in addition to determining champions. The Missouri Association, for example, includes this statement in all its tournament manuals of instructions and programs:

> There are two primary purposes that justify and cause district and state events to be desirable. They are: to provide opportunity to demonstrate before the public the best knowledge, skills, and emotional patterns taught through a particular sport; to evaluate and compare the best of this teaching of knowledge, skills, and emotional patterns among schools. Unless these purposes are primary, district and state athletic contests cannot be completely justified.[11]

To enhance these purposes, a committee is selected to evaluate the sportsmanship and conduct of players, coaches, cheerleaders, and student and adult followers at the semifinal and final games in the Missouri state high school basketball tournaments. A sportsmanship plaque is presented to the highest rated school in each of the four classes competing. The plaque is presented immediately following the presentation of championship trophies, and high schools in Missouri consider it one of the highest honors to be received.

It is not the purpose of this discussion either to condone or condemn the activity of state athletic associations in conducting tournaments or meets that may or may not lead to state championships. Rather, an attempt has been made to discuss what *is* being done, in the belief that the existence of a tradition of this magnitude justifies some consideration of it. Athletics are in our schools, and with them there is the desire for competition. With competition brought relatively close to home through modern methods of transportation, we have seen it seek new and no longer far-off laurels. Statewide contests have been one of the apparent results of increased public interest developed by the press and radio. The National Federation of State High School Associations has aided states by helping them control the extent of their competition, with the consequent abolition of national championships for high school athletes. If state championships, or variations of them, are to remain, they must be so established and conducted that their purposes, methods, and results are educationally, physically, and financially sound. This is quite an order, and it presents a real challenge to educators themselves.

Establishment of athletic standards. In addition to the establishment of eligibility regulations, state athletic associations have performed valuable services to schools in their states by setting standards for the conduct of athletics.

Although most state associations are the creations of schoolmen, after they are established they become somewhat impersonal agencies. This results in a situation where the state association, through its secretary, commissioner, or director, may advise with schools as a disinterested party and may, as a result, be of aid to them. Schools frequently ask the advice of the state association on matters of athletic policy.

Opinions from the state association officer may be used to improve conditions and raise local standards. An especially fine opportunity is afforded in this respect if the state association is connected or has a close relation with the state education department or its physical, health, or recreation divisions. It is not to be inferred that state associations which do not have, or do not choose to effect, any of these relations do not possess high ethical and administrative standards. Standards often are established by state associations in schedules, sanitation and safety, school-official relations, sportsmanship, relations between schools, scholarship, respect for and proper treatment of officials, the coaching and winning of games, interscholastic–intramural relations, conduct of students, and similar matters.

Several state associations have adopted recommended codes of standards for schools to enhance the educational objectives and values of their interscholastic programs. Michigan's fine set of codes is illustrative:

CODES FOR ADMINISTRATION OF ATHLETICS
(*MICHIGAN*)

Statement of Relationship
In the final analysis the superintendent is responsible for the athletic activities of the school system. His duties will vary according to the size of the school system, ranging from the larger schools, where all duties are delegated, to the smaller schools, where he may be both the administrative and the executive officer. In either case it is his duty to have set up a definite school athletic policy and have a complete understanding of that policy by all concerned.

The principal usually is the official representative of the school and is directly responsible for the general attitude of the student body and the conduct of athletic affairs by the business manager, athletic director, and the coach.

It is the duty of the above named officers to derive from the athletic program a full measure of educational value in developing good sportsmanship on the part of the student body, faculty, parents, and general public. Mutual cooperation is essential in order to carry out properly the work of any or all of these officers.

An Athletic Code for Superintendents and Principals
The Superintendent and Principal are the final authorities responsible for the athletic activities of the school. In realization of this responsibility these guiding principles should prevail:

For the Superintendent
1. I will use all means possible to bring to my community a full realization of the value of athletics as an educational tool in training citizens.

2. I will have a definite understanding with principals and athletic directors concerning the school athletic policy and expect and give mutual support in carrying out that policy.
3. I will judge the success of those in charge of the athletic program by the conduct and attitude of contestants and spectators rather than on the number of games won and lost.

For the Principal

1. I will have a complete understanding of the athletic policy of this school system and of the individual responsibility of all concerned.
2. I will be honest in my certification of contestants and base that certification on complete information concerning the student's athletic and scholastic status. Questionable cases will be referred to the State of Michigan High School Athletic Association Director before the privilege of competition is given.
3. I will give my loyal support to the coach in all his efforts to carry out the state and local athletic policies.
4. I will make every effort to instruct the student body in their responsibilities in making the athletic program a valuable one and point out desirable types of conduct at "home" and "away" games.
5. I will endeavor to foresee possible differences and misunderstandings with other schools and, as far as possible, settle them or provide means of settlement before they materialize.
6. I will insist that any misunderstandings that may arise be settled privately between official representatives of the schools concerned.
7. I will require the passing of a medical examination and parental consent before a student is allowed to compete.
8. I will have a definite understanding with the business manager or athletic director about officials, schedules, finances, care of fields and gymnasiums, handling of spectators, etc., and give him every assstance in carrying out his duties.
9. I will consider it unprofessional to withhold any seemingly authentic information from another school which calls in question the eligibility of any of its players.
10. I will attend as many of the athletic contests in which my school participates as school work will allow.
11. I will commend opposing schools for outstanding examples of fine citizenship.

An Athletic Code for Athletic Directors and Coaches

The Athletic Director, or Business Manager, and Coach are the official representatives of the school in interscholastic athletic activities. In this important capacity these standards should be practiced:

By the Athletic Director

The athletic policy of the school should

1. Be definitely understood with director's responsibility clearly defined

2. Include only those schedules which are educationally and physically sound for the athlete
3. Cooperate with the community in making a character building athletic program
4. Refuse admission to athletic contests to persons who have shown a chronic lack of sportsmanship.

The securing of officials should include

1. Mutual confidence and agreement by both teams
2. Complete support of officials in cases of adverse rulings
3. Definite contractual agreements naming fee, expenses, and time and place of game.

Game preparation involves

1. Provision of programs giving rules changes, names of players and officials, and emphasizing good sportsmanship
2. Proper handling of crowds so there is no encroachment on playing space
3. Maintaining side lines for exclusive use of players, coaches, and officials.

By the Coach

The school may expect

1. Work of the coach to be an integral part of the school system with its educational contribution
2. Mastery of the principles of pedagogy and consequent improvement in teaching as well as coaching
3. Loyalty to superiors in making athletics fit into the general school program
4. Insistence upon high scholarship and enforcement of all rules of eligibility.

The athletes may expect

1. A genuine and up-to-date knowledge of that which the coach proposes to teach
2. Fair, unprejudiced relationship with the students
3. Careful attention to the physical condition of players at the time of each contest
4. Competent and trustworthy officials whose decisions will always be supported.

Sportsmanship includes

1. Teaching athletes to win by use of legitimate means only
2. Counteracting unfounded rumors of questionable practices by opponents.

The influence of the coach necessitates

1. Being the sort of person he/she wants the students under him/her to become
2. Discouragement of gambling, profanity, and obscene language at all times.

An Athletic Code for Officials and Athletes

Competent, impartial Officials and clean, hard-playing Athletes have made a place for interscholastic athletics in the educational program. Sportsmanship and fair play demand these practices:

By the Official

The contest demands

1. A professional relationship calling for the highest type of service
2. Thorough preparation
3. A rested body and an alert mind
4. Reporting for duty at least thirty minutes before time for the game
5. A neat, distinct uniform.

The rules demand

1. Rectifying mistakes in judgment without "evening up"
2. Adherence to right decisions despite disapproval of spectators
3. Control of temper at all times in warning crowds of inflicting penalties for unsportsmanlike conduct
4. Respect for and aid to fellow officials in making decisions
5. That interpretations and announcements be made clear to both teams
6. That plays or players of other teams not be discussed in the presence of prospective opponents.

The financial consideration demands

1. Fees and services should be a matter of explicit agreement
2. Charges should consider the ability of the school to pay and the type of service rendered
3. Willing consent of both original parties to a release before acceptance of a game paying a higher fee.

By the Athlete

The contest demands

1. Fair play at all times
2. A square deal to opponents by players and spectators

3. Playing for the joy of playing and for the success of the team
4. Playing hard to the end
5. Keeping one's head and *playing* the game, not *talking* it
6. Respect for officials and the expectation that they will enforce the rules
7. That an athlete should not quit, cheat, bet, "grandstand," or abuse his body.

The school demands

1. Out-of-school and out-of-town conduct of the highest type
2. Faithful completion of school work as practical evidence of loyalty to school and team
3. Complete observance of training rules as a duty to school, team, and self.

Sportsmanship demands

1. Treatment of visiting team and officials as guests and the extension of every courtesy to them
2. Giving opponents full credit when they win and learning to correct one's own faults through his failures
3. Modesty and consideration when one's team wins
4. An athlete will not "crow" when his team wins or blame the officials when it loses.[12]

State associations are developing procedures to implement better standards of sportsmanship that have been established. The Missouri State High School Activities Association makes use of a Special Report to the High School Principal, which is provided officials in triplicate form. It is used both to commend schools and to call matters that warrant consideration to the attention of the school administrator. Officials are required to file with the principal a report on this form, giving the reason(s) for assessing a penalty for unsportsmanlike conduct when such violation occurs. One carbon each is sent to the superintendent and principal, a third to the Activities Association office as a matter of record. Principals have found that the information provided through this procedure is of significant help as a basis for counseling players (see Fig. 4–1). A similar form is provided schools for reporting to officials weaknesses noted and areas of officiating in need of improvement. A copy is also filed in the association office (see Fig. 4–2).

The judicial function. As has been indicated in the discussion of publications in this chapter, state associations perform a judicial service to member schools. It is necessary that there be a final authority to whom questions may be addressed, controversies presented, and appeals made. The state association is invaluable in this connection. In fact, the ability to render such services has been both the reason most statewide organizations came into being and

SPECIAL REPORT
TO
THE HIGH SCHOOL PRINCIPAL AND THE MSHSAA

This form is to be used to report any matter concerning high school athletic contests that merits the attention of the high school principal. It shall be used to report phases of the athletic program which the school should immediately attempt to improve. It may also be used to report an exceptionally good job of game administration. All instances involving unsportsmanlike conduct on the part of coaches, players, or fans should be reported on this form. Prompt reporting of problems by officials will help to prevent serious incidents.

This form should be filled out in duplicate with the white sheet as the original to be sent to the principal and the yellow sheet as the duplicate to be sent to the MSHSAA Office.

Report for _____ concerning a _____
                (School)   (Sport)

contest between _____ High School and _____
                    (Home School)   (Visiting School)

High School on _____
                    (Date)

Specific matter being reported:

Explanation:

Date _____ Signed _____

                                         Address _____

(This copy to be mailed to the High School Principal)

FIGURE 4–1 Special report to the high school principal and the MSHSAA (Missouri)

SPECIAL REPORT
TO
MSHSAA ATHLETIC OFFICIAL AND MSHSAA OFFICE

This form is to be used to report any matter concerning officiating that merits immediate attention. It shall be used to report errors in applying rules and phases of officiating in which an official should immediately attempt to improve. It may also be used to report an exceptionally good job of officiating. Coaches are requested to use this channel of filing complaints and to refrain from protesting to officials during or following a contest. Prompt reporting to the official would help him to correct errors and improve his competency.

This form should be filled out in duplicate with the pink sheet as the original to be sent to the official and the green sheet as a duplicate to be sent to the MSHSAA Office.

Report for_____who worked a_____
                        (Official)   (Sport)

contest between_____High School and_____
                        (Home School)   (Visiting School)

High School on_____.
                        (Date)

Specific matter being reported:

Explanation or comment:

Date_____   Signed_____

                             High School_____

                             Address_____

(This copy to be mailed to the official)

FIGURE 4–2   Special report to the MSHSAA athletic official and MSHSAA office (Missouri)

the reason they continue to exist. As a result of powers delegated by schools, they have made rules and regulations under which interscholastic athletic programs have been conducted. In most cases, also, they have been faced with the necessity for acting as the administrative body in connection with the enforcement of these judicial regulations.

It is fortunate that associations have acted in this dual capacity because, knowing the background of the rules and regulations, they have been able to enforce them with the original intent in mind. In acting in a judicial capacity, state associations sometimes are faced with the unpleasant task of deciding disputes between schools. Again, a valuable service is performed in this way because an unprejudiced body can decide the case in question on its merits and by application of state association regulations. Hence, the exercise of the so-called judicial function of state associations may be one of their most valuable services.

Extension of services. We noted in Chapter 3 the many services provided by the National Federation of State High School Associations. The state high school associations are the organizations which make these services available to the high schools in their respective states. They not only distribute rules books, audio-visual aids, and other printed matter for use in local high schools, they also reprint significant information contained in the *National Federation Press* in state association publications.

Each high school association extends numerous services of its own to its members in addition to those previously discussed in this chapter. A multitude of printed supplies is furnished each year, including various forms used in administering the interscholastic athletic program. The state high school association is a service organization to its member schools just as the National Federation is for its member state associations.

Protection of the High School Program

The popularity of high school athletics has stimulated many nonschool organizations and individuals to seek to exploit them by promoting contests in which it is desired to have high school teams or individual athletes compete. The primary objectives of such promotions are for the purposes of raising funds, advertising, and seeking recognition for the sponsor. To protect the high school athletic program from such exploitation, state associations have adopted by-laws which regulate the participation of athletes on nonschool teams and which allow schools to compete only in contests approved by the state association. Athletes in most states cannot be eligible to represent their schools if they compete in outside competition during the season they are representing their schools in the same or another sport. Practically no state associations sanction nonschool-sponsored competition for the participation of member schools during the school year.

These types of regulations are sometimes looked upon as being restrictive and harsh, but schools have by experience found them to be necessary to protect the high school program and the high school athlete.

THE STATE HIGH SCHOOL ASSOCIATION
MUST BE SUPPORTED

Each state association will have essentially the same standards and regulations discussed in this book, but it will also have others. The athletic administrator must be thoroughly familar with all the regulations of his/her state association. It must be remembered that (1) they were adopted by vote of the member schools of the association; (2) they are standards of his/her school by virtue of its membership; (3) they provide for fairness and equity in interscholastic competition; and (4) they must be supported. This support must come from the athletic administrator, the coaches, the high school principal, the superintendent of schools, and the board of education.

Sometimes when an athlete fails to meet a standard of eligibility required to participate in interscholastic competition, school officials lead others to think the athlete should be permitted to compete, *BUT he/she cannot because the state high school association has a rule that won't allow the school to let him/her play*. In other words, the impression is left that it would be all right with us, but the state association won't let us. Such hedging causes parents and lay people to believe that the state high school association is a separate entity that forces its will upon the schools of the state. What school officials should make clear in such situations is that there is a rule, or standard, involved which all schools have adopted through the state association, and which all schools have agreed to apply. There are reasons behind each regulation so adopted cooperatively by the schools, which should be explained when it is questioned.

When any interscholastic standard is not satisfactory, there are procedures provided by all state associations for amending it. All high school athletic administrators should make themselves familiar with these procedures, and they should be followed to achieve any change the schools deem advisable. When the schools of a state adhere to and support current regulations and work to make them better through the procedures for amendments, it makes for a stronger state high school association with more benefits to its member schools.

One of the better ways of gaining support for any organization is to make clear what the organization is and what its functions are. The general public usually lacks an adequate understanding of state high school associations and what their purposes are, or what services they render to schools and their students. This situation exists because the public has not been informed. Thousands of boys and girls have competed in district and state high school tournaments without realizing these events would not have been held if it were not for the state high school association. Neither have they understood that the National Federation of State High School Associations supplies the rules books for the games they play. This lack of understanding persists because no one has enlightened them. The most appropriate level to begin imparting knowledge about the high school association, and the National Federation, is with high school students, and particularly with high school athletes. Coaches are frequently derelict in assuming the responsibility for providing athletes with this information, and athletic administrators may also be negligent if they do not make certain their coaches do assume it. If every high school boy and girl athlete acquires a general understanding of the purposes of his/her state high school association by the time he/she graduates, the support and appreciation of these organizations will be greatly enhanced.

Parent-teacher, booster club, service club, and other meetings afford opportunities to inform groups of the objectives of interscholastic athletics, the state high school association, and the National Federation. These groups are interested in hearing about the team's prospects for the coming season and frequently invite coaches and athletic administrators as speakers. Before such a "captive" audience, the administrator can make brief but informative statements about the school's membership in the state association and what services that organization provides.

Sportswriters and sportscasters should also be helped to understand the functions of the state high school association. Unless they realize the reasons for uniform minimum standards adopted through the state association, they may not support the organization—or the individual school—when cases of ineligibility arise or other violations occur.

Many high school associations include statements of information about the purposes of the organization in their state meet and tournament programs. This practice helps inform thousands of spectators about the organization and helps gain support.

The state high school association is the best supporter in the state of the schools' interscholastic programs; the more support member schools develop for it, the more benefits it can provide them.

SUMMARY

State high school associations developed out of a pressing need to establish controls and standards for interscholastic athletics. The first formed were in Michigan, Wisconsin, Illinois, and Indiana. They are now found in all states and the District of Columbia.

Some are athletic associations with jurisdiction solely over athletics, while the majority are activities associations with a variety of nonathletic pursuits.

The constitution and by-laws of all high school associations have a statement of their purposes and objectives that are compatible with the general aims of education.

The administrative control of state associations falls into three general classifications: voluntary associations, associations affiliated with state departments of education, and university-directed associations.

State associations perform many functions for the benefit of member schools, among which some of the most significant are (1) establishment of uniform standards and other regulations; (2) provision of group athletic accident insurance; (3) registration and classification of officials; (4) distribution of rules books and other publications; (5) conduct of district and state meets and tournaments; and (6) formulation of codes to give direction to interscholastic activities.

All high schools should support their state high school association. In the final analysis, state high school athletic and activities associations are organizations through which high schools work cooperatively in establishing and enforcing standards believed to be in the best interests of high school boys and girls. Without them the interscholastic program would collapse.

QUESTIONS AND TOPICS FOR STUDY AND DISCUSSION

1. Review the conditions that existed during the third phase of high school athletics (see page 11) and explain why state high school associations were formed.

2. State and explain what you consider the most important purposes of high school associations.

3. What do you consider the advantages and disadvantages of each of the three types of state association in regard to administrative control? If you were an athletic administrator, which type would you prefer? Why?

4. What are the purposes of rules interpretation meetings sponsored by high school associations?

5. How can state associations provide athletic accident insurance that schools could not individually afford?

6. Why is the registration and classification of game officials of value in interscholastic athletics?

7. Explain some of the types and purposes of publications provided schools by their state association.

8. Give arguments for and against district and state meets and tournaments sponsored by high school associations.

9. What different kinds of athletic standards are established through state high school associations?

10. Give reasons why high schools should support their state association. Explain ways they can help gain support for it.

NOTES

1. National Federation of State High School Associations, *1982–83 Handbook* (Kansas City, Mo.: National Federation, 1983), pp. 104–13.
2. Hiram A. Jones, "Regulations of the Commission of Education Governing Health and Physical Education," *New York Public High School Athletic Association Bulletin*, October 1937, p. 2.
3. Ibid., p. 5.
4. Michigan State High School Athletic Association, Inc., *1979–80 Handbook*, p. 3.
5. Ibid., p. 16.
6. Delaware Secondary School Athletic Association, *1974–75 Official Handbook*, p. 16.
7. University of Texas, Austin, Texas, *University Interscholastic League Constitution and Contest Rules for 1981–82*, p. 13.
8. Ibid., pp. 30–31.
9. National Federation, *1982–83 Handbook*, pp. 75–76.
10. Frederick Rand Rogers, "The Future of Interscholastic Athletics" (New York: Bureau of Publications, Teachers College, Columbia University, 1929).
11. Missouri State High School Activities Association, *1982–83 Football Manual*, p. 2.
12. Michigan High School Athletic Association, Inc., *1979–80 Handbook*, pp. 10–14.

BIBLIOGRAPHY

ALABAMA HIGH SCHOOL ATHLETIC ASSOCIATION. *1981–82 Handbook.**

CALIFORNIA INTERSCHOLASTIC FEDERATION. *1981–82 Constitution and By-Laws*.

COLORADO HIGH SCHOOL ACTIVITIES ASSOCIATION. *1980–81 Handbook*.

CONNECTICUT INTERSCHOLASTIC CONFERENCE. *Constitution and By-Laws*.

DELAWARE SECONDARY SCHOOL ATHLETIC ASSOCIATION. *1980–81 Handbook*.

FLORIDA HIGH SCHOOL ACTIVITIES ASSOCIATION. *1981 By-Laws*.

ILLINOIS HIGH SCHOOL ASSOCIATION. *1981–82 Official Handbook*.

INDIANA HIGH SCHOOL ATHLETIC ASSOCIATION, INC. *1980–81 By-Laws and Articles of Incorporation*.

KANSAS STATE HIGH SCHOOL ACTIVITIES ASSOCIATION. *1981–82 Handbook*.

MICHIGAN HIGH SCHOOL ATHLETIC ASSOCIATION, INC. *1979–80 Handbook*.

MISSOURI STATE HIGH SCHOOL ACTIVITIES ASSOCIATION. *1982–83 Official Handbook*.

NATIONAL FEDERATON OF STATE HIGH SCHOOL ASSOCIATIONS. *1982–83 Handbook*. Kansas City, Mo.: National Federation, 1983.

NEBRASKA SCHOOL ACTIVITIES ASSOCIATION. *Forty-Seventh Annual Yearbook*.

NEW BRUNSWICK (CANADA) INTERSCHOLASTIC ATHLETIC ASSOCIATION. *1974–75 Handbook*.

* Note: addresses of all state high school athletic associations are listed in Appendix A.

NEW JERSEY STATE INTERSCHOLASTIC ATHLETIC ASSOCIATION. *1981–82 Constitution, By-Laws, and Regulations.*

NEW YORK PUBLIC HIGH SCHOOL ATHLETIC ASSOCIATION. *1980–82 Handbook.*

PENNSYLVANIA INTERSCHOLASTIC ATHLETIC ASSOCIATION. *1980–81 PIAA Handbook.*

UNIVERSITY OF TEXAS. *Constitution and Contest Rules of University Interscholastic League for 1981–82.*

VIRGINIA HIGH SCHOOL LEAGUE, INC. *1981–82 Handbook.*

WISCONSIN INTERSCHOLASTIC ATHLETIC ASSOCIATION. *1980–81 WIAA Handbook.*

Standards of Eligibility
For Interscholastic Athletic Competition

In the conduct of any well-organized program of activities there must be generally accepted rules and regulations. Standards of eligibility for contestants in high school athletics fall into this category. Sometimes there seems to be a paradox in the claims of athletics programs and the manner in which they are administered. Frequently it is said that if athletics are defensible from an educational standpoint, especially for the participant, then all students should be allowed to take part in them. Very few schools, if any, have found it possible to provide interscholastic athletic experiences for all students. All of them have some rules which are applied in determining who shall represent them in interschool competition. Why have we built up sets of eligibility rules for contestants? Why have definite methods of procedure for the conduct of athletic contestants, meets, and tournaments been established by state associations all over the country? The fact that they exist is evidence that there must have been some need for them.

DEVELOPMENT OF STANDARDS OF ELIGIBILITY

A brief history of the development of the concept of eligibility will help us to understand better the standards of eligibility we shall discuss later in this chapter.

Evolution of Eligibility Standards

No thought was given to eligibility rules when teams were organized and managed by the students themselves. Dangers to the physical welfare of high school athletes playing on teams with and against outside adults, faculty members, and volunteer player-coaches prompted school officials to adopt some so-called "controls" during the period of toleration referred to in Chapter 2. The first of the controls by which the schools agreed to abide was that only bona fide students were to play on the high school teams. This stopped one abuse, but others still persisted. Hence, one by one, more controls became necessary. After several had been adopted, they began to be referred to as "eligibility rules." Because of the fact that these rules prevented some students from playing, they were sometimes considered as being prohibitive and restrictive in nature. It was many years before a newer concept of "standards of eligibility" was to evolve.

This change appears to have started with a court case. The Oklahoma Supreme Court in 1938 in the *Morrison* v. *Roberts* case ruled, in essence, that an individual has many rights as a citizen and as a high school student, but that he has no *vested right* in athletic eligibility.[1] The Court established the precedent that participation in interschool athletic competition is a privilege rather than a legal right of an athlete. The attainment of this privilege then became dependent upon whether an individual meets the standards set for it. Eligibility standards then became a set of criteria to determine which students with superior physical ability shall be afforded the privilege of representing the school in interscholastic athletics. The Missouri State High School Activities Constitution contains the following definition of eligibility:

> Eligibility to represent a school in interscholastic activities is a privilege to be attained by meeting the standards of eligibility cooperatively set by the member schools through this Association and any additional standards set by a member school for its own students.[2]

Schools have good reason to be concerned about which students shall represent them in interscholastics before the public, for each player on the team represents not only himself, but also the student body and the school community. The public often judges the school by what it sees through the players on the playing field or floor. Standards of eligibility help determine whether a player will creditably represent the school. This concept is compatible with the fundamental theory of representative democracy upon which our society is based. High school students and the public must be educated to this relationship and to the significance of the standards of eligibility if interschool activities are to make any important contributions to the development of better citizens.

The fact that all members and affiliate members of the National Federation of State High School Associations have statewide minimum standards of eligibility is evidence that they are considered necessary and in the best interest of the great majority of high school youth.

General Purposes of State Association
Athletic Eligibility Regulations

Whether they are referred to by individual state associations as rules or as standards, eligibility requirements have several general purposes, among which the following are included:

1. They provide minimum standards for all schools belonging to the association.

2. They establish definite standards which should be known both by students and patrons of the school.

3. They relieve individual schools of possible criticism that the standards of eligibility in their institutions are lower than, or vary from, those in the majority of schools.

4. They provide guidelines for the selection of students afforded the privilege of representing the school in competition with other schools.

5. They stimulate students toward personal improvement by establishing standards they must meet or surpass.

6. They aid in the improvement of relations between schools when both sides know certification of contestants has been made in accordance with common standards.

7. They enable individual school administrators to uphold higher standards when they are established statewide.

8. They help to keep interscholastics in proper perspective within the total school program.

9. They are instrumental in gaining respect and status for the interscholastic athletic program.

10. They provide for great equity in competition.

11. They aid in protecting the interscholastic program and high school youth from exploitation.

It seems reasonable to assume that there are inherent values in interscholastic athletic eligibility regulations. Some educators would open wide the door to athletic competition, justifying this action in the belief that what is good for one is good for all. Others believe that no scholastic requirement (credit hours during preceding or current semester) should be demanded of athletes. It also is maintained that all should be allowed to take part in athletics, not just those who come within the realm of state association eligibility rules.

These assertions, which usually are made in all sincerity, deserve consideration. Athletics are provided for all in some manner in most schools in the form of physical education and intramural activities. These take care of the great mass of students from a competition standpoint. Properly, the interschool athletic program should be the apex of the intramural program. And with the ascendancy in selection should go an ascendancy in responsibility and standards. Two separate organizations—two schools—compete with each other. It is a privilege to engage in such competition, and there should be corresponding responsibilities. Good school citizenship is a requisite for membership on school teams. Scholastic attainment, in accordance with the standards of the school, is another responsibility of the contestant. There should be compliance with sound and tried regulations that have been found necessary to keep interscholastic athletics on their present high level. All in all, then, it does not seem unnecessary, unwise, or unsound educationally to have well-established eligibility regulations for the guidance and protection of the competitor, the school, and the spectator. The courts consistently have upheld the authority of high schools and their state high school associations to establish reasonable standards of eligibility.

COMMON ELIGIBILITY REGULATIONS

Two types of regulations pertaining to athletics will be considered in this and the succeeding chapter. This chapter will deal with those which are quite common and pertain to individual athletes who participate in interscholastic competition. Chapter 6 will concern itself with those regulations which pertain to the administration of the athletic program and the standards for interscholastic contests.

Age

The trend in the upper age limit for contestants has been downward. Whereas, several years ago the upper limit was 20 in a majority of states, now it is 19. New York, one of the first states to do so, established this limit in 1938. New Jersey's rules provide that a student is ineligible upon reaching his or her nineteenth birthday, but may finish the season in a sport whose season began before that birthday. Texas had an 18-year limit for some time, but now has a 19-year age rule. In some states a student becomes ineligible on that birthday; in others he or she may finish the season or semester after having reached the nineteenth or twentieth birthday, as the state rule provides. Still other associations consider a student ineligible whose nineteenth birthday falls on or before an established date, September 1 being the most common. Those who become 19 after that date may compete for the remainder of that school year.

Studies conducted in Michigan and Ohio some years ago indicated that a proportionately small number (between three and five percent) of those eligible, and who participated in athletics, were over 19. Since the majority of today's high school students graduate at ages 17 and 18, the 19-year age limit is a reasonable eligibility standard.

The majority of states consider the 19-year age limit necessary to protect the physical welfare of younger athletes, to provide for more equity among players and schools, to prevent "redshirting" in high school, and because a large number of college and university players are now only 19 years of age and a few college varsity athletes are only 18. If these athletes are sufficiently mature physically to compete on university teams against the toughest athletic competition on the college level, schools have reason to believe they should not be competing on high school teams against less mature individuals. Few, if any, states waive the age rule because of hardship or any other reason. As will be shown in Chapter 16, the courts have upheld the age standard as being reasonable.

Time of Enrollment

In the early days of interschool athletic competition, some athletes who were primarily interested only in playing on the school team would wait to enroll until practice started for a particular sport. They were also inclined to drop out of school at the close of the sport season. The term "athletic bum" was applied to these individuals. To prevent this abuse, a regulation was soon established providing that any student who enrolled after a certain date following the opening of the semester would not be eligible that semester.

Usually the time of enrollment for sports participation during a particular semester is within the first three weeks of the term. If a student enrolls during that period, he is eligible for athletic competition that semester. Oklahoma and New York provide that a participant must have been in regular attendance at least 80 percent of the time. Pennsylvania requires a student to attend a school for a period of 60 days after he has been absent for 20 days or more during a semester. In general, enrollment in schools for a period of from two to three weeks constitutes a semester of attendance in most states. In Illinois a student must be enrolled by the eleventh day of the semester unless late enrollment results from illness or quarantine, in which cases this regulation may be waived under prescribed conditions. Texas requires that a student be in attendance for 30 days prior to a contest or have been enrolled by the first day of the second week of a semester. New Jersey has a similar rule, except that enrollment may be as late as the first Monday in October. Michigan requires that a student must be enrolled in a secondary school by Monday of the fourth week of the semester in order to be eligible during that semester. The general provision in most states is that failure to be enrolled in a secondary school by a prescribed time (six days to three weeks) results in ineligibility during that semester.

Seasons of Competition and Undergraduate Standing

Practically all state associations have regulations which allow participation by students in sports for four seasons in grades nine to twelve, inclusive. In virtually all states, postgraduate students are barred from membership on regular high school teams. In a few states, however, students who have completed the graduation requirements in less than the allowed number of semesters may compete during the full number of semesters for which their regulations provide. Usually they must not have been voted their diplomas by the board of education nor have accepted them and must be enrolled for three one-half units of high school credit.

Number of Semesters of Attendance

Regulations establishing a maximum of eight semesters of enrollment are now generally uniform in all states. Four years, in grades nine to twelve, inclusive, represent the normal period of high school attendance. This is the equivalent of eight semesters of enrollment and, in most cases, takes care of the legitimate time during which a student should be allowed to compete in athletics. It is quite common to require that the last two semesters of attendance be consecutive. In most states a semester of attendance is not charged to a student if he withdraws from school within the period during which he must enroll in order to compete during that semester.

Indiana allows a student to compete during his or her ninth semester if the student entered school at the start of a mid-year term and did not compete in the sport during the first semester of attendance. New York requires that the eight semesters of competition allowed must be consecutive unless there is sufficient evidence to show that failure to attend during a semester was caused by illness or accident, but the player is limited to four seasons of play.

The eight-semester standard is a reasonable one because four years of attendance is the regular amount of time most students spend in high school.

Limited Team Membership

How to cope with out-of-school athletic competition during the school year has been one of the principal problem areas facing high schools and their state associations. Because of conflicts and interference with the academic and interscholastic programs, school administrators have found it necessary to adopt standards through their state associations to avoid chaos. Virtually all states have rules providing that students are not eligible if they compete on outside teams during the season they are representing their schools in the same sport. Some will not permit competition on any other team during a season a student is representing his or her school even though it may be in another sport. The following are among the reasons that limited team membership regulations have been adopted:

1. To avoid interference with the academic programs of the schools. Nonschool organizations frequently desire to sponsor events that cause students to miss class time. Schools attempt to schedule athletic contests to cause as little conflict with the academic program as possible.

2. Interference with the interscholastic program. Participating simultaneously on a school team and a nonschool team results in considerable interference with the interschool athletic program.

3. To protect talented students from undue pressure to compete on outside teams. Students are often solicited and pressured to compete on nonschool teams during the school athletic season.

4. To prevent exploitation of talented athletes by those who want to capitalize on their skills, abilities, and reputations. A number of nonschool organizations are interested in providing activities only for those students who have established a reputation as being outstanding, and do so more for the benefit of the sponsor than for the athlete.

5. To avoid loss of state aid caused by absences from school to participate in nonschool-sponsored activities. Because these activities are not school sponsored, students who participate in them must be recorded absent.

6. To provide opportunities for more youth to participate in athletic activities rather than to limit opportunities to the more talented students. Standards requiring that a student not participate simultaneously in an out-of-school program generally result in two students having opportunities rather than one having the opportunity to compete in two or more programs simultaneously. If athletic participation has values for young people, it should be extended to the greatest possible number. Nonschool competition standards stimulate opportunities being extended to more students.

7. To protect the physical welfare of young persons. Students of junior and senior high school age benefit from physical exercise up to a certain point. Beyond that, it may endanger the health of the student, and this was made clear a few years ago in Missouri when physicians diagnosed the illnesses of some athletes as resulting from playing basketball for the high school and swimming with a nonschool swimming club during the same season. It is important that standards be adopted for the protection of the physical welfare of young athletes.

8. To avoid conflict in coaching philosophy between that of the high school coach and the nonschool coach. Coaching philosophies and techniques differ, and it becomes quite confusing for a junior or senior high school student to be exposed to different coaching philosophies in the same sport during the same season.

9. To discourage athletes from participating in games for which they may not have proper accident insurance protection. A number of nonschool programs do not provide accident insurance protection for the participants and often do not call this fact to their attention.

10. To encourage students not to overemphasize athletic competition in the allocation of their time. Overparticipation sometimes results in a marginal return of investment. For most students, athletic participation will be a leisure-time activity. It should not be overemphasized to the point that it will cause a neglect of the development of other skills important in later life.

During recent years, when more attention appears to have been given to the rights and privileges of the individual as one person rather than to the rights of an individual as a member of a group, there are increasing pressures to allow individuals to do as they please. It is essential, however, to be aware of how what one person is permitted to do affects the opportunities of many others. School officials, therefore, have the responsibility of considering standards that will be in the best interests of the majority of students. Non-school competition standards basically have this as their purpose.

Most states do not prohibit competition on independent teams during the summer months as long as their amateur and award standards are not violated, except that several do not permit such activity in football because of the risk of injury to players who may not be fitted with proper equipment. Some have a limitation on the number of players from the same high school team who may play on the same independent team in the summer. This regulation is to prevent any one team from gaining an advantage over other high school teams by practicing and playing together outside the high school season.

The penalty for violations of the limited team membership rule is in-eligibility, which may last for the remainder of the season up to one year from the date of violation.

The National Federation's Recommended Criteria for Evaluating Non-school Competition are significant in better understanding the reasons why limited team membership standards are necessary (see Chapter 3).

Parental Consent and Physical Examinations

One of the latest eligibility requirements to be adopted, although virtually all states now have it, is that an athlete must have a physical examination and be certified by a physician to be physically fit to participate in interscho-lastic athletics. Among the factors which stimulated the adoption of this regulations were (1) the concern of school officials to protect the physical welfare of athletes; (2) the requirements of athletic insurance plans; and (3) the danger of legal suits based on negligence if a student is allowed to compete without it. Most state association rules provide that certification must be obtained once each year before the athlete participates in his/her first practice. A special form is usually provided by the association to guide the physician in giving the type of examination considered necessary. For the protection of the school and its administrators and coaches, this regulation should be rigidly enforced.

It is further advisable to have a local school regulation related to ill-nesses. Students who have been absent from school because of any serious or extended illness should have the permission of a physician to return to participation in athletics, even though they may have been certified before the illness. This type of regulation or policy helps to avoid charges of negligence in case of injuries following illnesses.

Although not all require parental consent forms, several state associations provide their schools with these forms to be signed by the parent(s) and filed in the school office before the athlete is permitted to participate in practice or competition. High school associations which have their own athletic accident benefit plans require that copies of the consent form be filed in their offices.

There is no doubt that the securing of parental approval is a good public relations gesture, if only because it acquaints the school patron with the athletic policy of the school regarding injuries. Not too much emphasis, however, should be placed on the legal value of such permissions in view of some court decisions involving schools or coaches in cases of athletic injuries. In very few states can local boards of education be held responsible for costs of injuries incurred by students while engaging in any school activity, athletic or otherwise. This does not mean, however, that local school athletic associations, having funds, may not be sued with quite a good possibility of obtaining judgments. Also, if negligence on the part of agents of the board of education—superintendents, principals, coaches, or assistants—can be proved, action is very likely against any or all concerned. This has happened in California and New York. The theory held by the court is that no one has the authority to sign away the rights of a minor as far as opportunity to recover for personal injuries is concerned. In most cases parental consent obviates any misunderstanding and means that the parent is assuming the obligation in case of injury, rather than the school or local athletic association.

Figure 5–1 shows the physician's and parent's certificate found on one side of a form used by Missouri schools and Figure 5–2 is the player's application to participate in interschool athletics. The physician's certificate shown here is similar to that used in several states. Having athletes sign a statement that they understand the standards of eligibility which they are to meet and that they have not violated any of them helps to avoid violations and embarrassment for the school when they occur. It discourages athletes from claiming that they had no knowledge of the eligibility standards.

Too much attention can hardly be paid to the importance of adequate physical examination of athletes or, in fact, of all high school students. Many schools are stressing this matter with excellent results. In some instances tuberculosis tests are required of all athletes as well as complete venereal disease examinations. These are important, and certainly heart and lungs should receive first consideration. Adequate physical examinations do at least three things: (1) they protect the participant; (2) they protect school authorities in case of any unusual occurrence; and (3) they maintain higher and safer standards for athletic competition. Athletes should not be permitted to engage in practice or competition until they have been properly examined and certified physically fit by a physician.

```
PHYSICAL EXAMINATION RECORD

(Patterned after form cooperatively prepared by the National Federation of
State High School Athletic Associations and the Committee on Medical Aspects
of Sports of the AMA.  This form should be on file before a student is per-
mitted to start practice in any sport.)


_____    _____
   (Name of Student - Print)                      (School)
SIGNIFICANT PAST ILLNESS OR INJURY_____HEIGHT_____
                                                      WEIGHT_____
_____
EYES, EARS, NOSE, AND THROAT 20/  20/  _____HEARING  /15   /15
LUNGS_____
HEART_____BLOOD PRESSURE_____
ABDOMEN_____
GENITALIA_____HERNIA_____
MUSCOLO-SKELETAL_____
REFLEXES_____
URINALYSIS_____
BLOOD COUNT, X-RAY (If indicated)        DATE OF LAST IMMUNIZATION
     (To be filed in high school office)  POLIO_____
                                          TETANUS_____
                                          OTHER_____
I certify that I have on this date examined the above student and from the
limited examination above, I could detect no reason for him (or her) not to
participate in supervised activities NOT CROSSED OUT BELOW:
        BASKETBALL       FOOTBALL      SOFTBALL       TRACK
        BASEBALL         GOLF          SPEEDBALL      VOLLEYBALL
        CROSS COUNTRY    GYMNASTICS    SWIMMING       WRESTLING
        FIELD HOCKEY     SOCCER        TENNIS         OTHERS_____
DATE OF EXAMINATION:_____  SIGNED_____
                                             Examining Physician
              PARENT'S OR GUARDIAN'S PERMISSION

I hereby give my consent for the above student to represent his school in inter-
scholastic activities, except those crossed out on the form above by the ex-
amining physician; I also give my consent for him (her) to accompany the team
as a member on its out-of-town trips and will not hold the school responsible
in case of accident or injury.  I also give consent and authorize the school
to obtain, through a physician of its choice, such medical care as is reason-
ably necessary for the welfare of the student, if he (or she) is injured in
the course of school athletic activities.
         Signature of Parents or Guardians_____
                 (both must sign)

                                         _____

Date:_____  Address:_____
                                    (street)            (city or town)
```

FIGURE 5–1   Physical examination and parents' permission (Missouri)

```
┌─────────────────────────────────────────────────────────────────────┐
│                                                                       │
│      APPLICATION TO PARTICIPATE IN INTERSCHOOL ATHLETICS              │
│                                                                       │
│   Name of Student_____    │
│                         (Last)      (First)      (Middle Initial)    │
│                                                                       │
│   Name of School_____        │
│                                                                       │
│   Date:_____Date of Birth:_____         │
│                                                                       │
│   Place of Birth:_____                     │
│                                                                       │
│   This application to represent my high school in interscholastic     │
│   athletics is entirely voluntary on my part and is made with the     │
│   understanding that I have studied and understand the eligibility     │
│   standards that I must meet to represent my school and that I         │
│   have not violated any of them.                                      │
│                                                                       │
│                                                                       │
│               Signature of Student_____             │
│                                   (File in High School Office)        │
│                                                                       │
└─────────────────────────────────────────────────────────────────────┘
```

FIGURE 5–2   Student's application to participate in interschool athletics (Missouri)

Current and Previous Semester Scholarship

As stated earlier in this chapter, the first eligibility rule on record was the requirement that only bona fide students could play on high school teams. Its purpose was to eliminate outsiders from playing on the school team, which included some early high school coaches. However, situations arose that made it necessary to define a "bona fide student." C. W. Whitten in his book, *Interscholastics—A Discussion of Interscholastic Contests,* relates the story of two football players whose eligibility was questioned in Illinois on the premise that they were not bona fide students.[3] Investigation found that they were enrolled in only one subject, spelling, and there was no record that they were passing. There were other instances of "athletic bums" who were enrolled but who dropped out of school following the sport season and before the end of the semester without earning any credit, only to enroll again the next semester or year in time to play on the school team.

Eventually, it was determined that an individual must be enrolled in a prescribed number of subjects to be considered a bona fide student, but this did not completely solve the problem. Some students, as stated above, would drop out at the close of the sport season without earning any high school credits, but would re-enroll the next semester or year and be eligible to compete. Out of this situation evolved the standard that the student also must have earned a prescribed number of credits the preceding semester he or she was in attendance.

Participation in athletics and scholarship are generally thought to be complementary to each other. New York, however, broke away from the tradition some time ago. With the application of the Regulations of the Commissioner of Education, which became effective in September 1938, there is no direct requirement regarding the previous or current semester's scholastic work of a contestant in interschool games.[4] New York, feeling that the time had come when interscholastic athletics should become a definite and integral part of the physical education program of a school, made this conception a reality by the Board of Regents' action. Commenting on the omission of the scholastic requirement in the Regulations, Dr. Jesse Feiring Williams had this to say in its favor at the time:

> The regulations of the Commisssioner of Education are a distinct advance in administrative procedure and I highly commend this forward move in education. I am particularly pleased that the requirement that boys must pass three subjects in order to participate was omitted. If athletics are desirable experiences for boys in school, they should be allowed to gain the advantages of sport, precisely the same way they are allowed to engage in other parts of the school program.[5]

The New York departure from traditional scholastic requirements for interschool competition has points in its favor. It assumes that school standards in that state generally will be uniform. Undoubtedly, New York is one of the best states to employ such a plan because of its central educational control program as administered by the Board of Regents.

Although New York has not had an academic standard for many years, representatives of other high school associations have arguments against the elimination of academic requirements. No one questions the logic that athletics may properly be classed as part of the physical education program. It is difficult, however, to reach the conclusion that scholastic requirements alone should be eliminated because they might interfere with the possibility of a student's competing in athletics, while the commonly accepted rules regarding duration of competition, time of enrollment, transfer, and limitations of competition are retained. The question might logically be asked why these restrictive regulations were not discarded.

The eligibility standards of the Ohio association is typical of the academic standard in most states:

> A student enrolled in grades 9 through 12 to be eligible during any semester must have been in school and received credit during the immediately preceding semester in subjects which count one and one-half units per semester toward graduation unless the student has just been promoted to the ninth grade.[6]

In some states the student must also be currently passing in three such subjects. This requirement has merit in that it stimulates athletes to maintain passing grades, but some athletic administrators have objections to it because of extra work involved and difficulties in administration. Teachers frequently resent having to file weekly grade reports, but this can be alleviated by requesting them to submit at specified times only the names of athletes not doing passing work. Using the previous semester record only is the simplest plan, which is perhaps the reason many principals favor it.

There has been pressure from collegiate athletic associations for state high school associations to raise the academic standard because of the failure of several graduating athletes to meet the academic requirements for a college athletic scholarship. The Kansas association has raised its standard to require a student to have passed four courses of unit weight the last semester in attendance and to be enrolled in four courses during the current semester. Except for special education students, there is no trend toward lowering or eliminating the high school academic eligibility requirement. Merely requiring a student to pass, or be passing, in three subjects is in itself a minimum standard.

State associations' regulations vary regarding the removal of scholastic deficiencies. Some states permit a student to remove them by attending summer school or night school, while others will not.

The establishment of special education programs for slow learners has resulted in exceptions being granted by several high school associations for such students. For example, Virginia allows any special education student to compete

> . . . who made standard progress for his level in a special education program for the handicapped which followed standards set by the Special Education Service of the State Department of Education.[7]

As indicated previously, it seems as though there is a defense for the scholastic as well as the other eligibility requirements established by a large majority of the state associations of this country. True, athletics are activities in which all high school students should have the right to participate. With this right to participate, however, it should be recognized that certain responsibilities obtain. The situation in any athletic contest between schools is somewhat different from that in an activity within the school or class itself. Competition should not be considered as *against* another school but *with* that school. Since the interschool competition should be between teams that are the apex of broad intraschool programs, membership on those teams inevitably will be selective. Therefore, athletic administrators have felt that team members should meet minimum established standards of character, school citizenship, and scholarship as well as of athletic prowess. Also, it is apparent that the establishment of a statewide minimum scholastic requirement has enabled local schools to use this standard to advantage in their own institutions.

Most school administrators also have felt that, with a general regulation requiring successful work in at least three subjects, their schools have been relieved to some extent of doubts on the part of others regarding eligibility of some of their team members. In a great many schools the members of athletic teams must be doing passing work in all their subjects. Experience seems to indicate that scholastic requirements for athletes have done a considerable amount to improve school citizenship and maintain proper morale and attitude toward school subjects. Usually school standards within a local system are sufficiently flexible that no injustices are done. If this is the case, undoubtedly minimum scholastic standards have done a great amount of good in setting up achievement goals that athletes have had to meet in order to play.

Transfer and Undue Influence Rules

In all states students are as eligible in a school to which they transfer as they were in the school they left, provided their parents or legal guardians have moved into the new school district, unless the exercise of undue influence can be proved. Undue influence is an aspect of athletic transfers that has come to the attention of state associations, judging by the adoption of new by-laws dealing with this matter. Iowa has such a rule:

> No student shall be eligible to participate in the contests of this Association if it shall be known that he, or any member of his family, is receiving any remuneration, either directly or indirectly, to influence him or his family to reside in a given school district in order to establish eligibility on the team of said school.[8]

Indiana also has a definite provision relative to undue influence:

> The use of undue influence by any person or persons to secure or to retain a student or to secure or to retain one or both of the parents or guardians of a student as residents may cause the student to be ineligible for high school athletics for a period not to exceed 365 days and may jeopardize the standing of the high school in the Association.
>
> No member school student shall be eligible to participate in any inter-school contest under the rules of the Association, if it shall be shown that they or any member of their family are receiving any remuneration, either directly or indirectly, to influence them or their family to reside in a given school district or territory in order to establish eligibility on the team of said school, and any school permitting such participation shall, upon satisfactory evidence submitted to the Board, be suspended from membership in the Association for a term not to exceed 365 days.[9]

Most states have had sufficient difficulty with problems of recruiting to adopt by-laws concerning it. Before they were adopted, much ill feeling was engendered among schools when an athlete was influenced to transfer schools for athletic reasons. The solicitation of students for athletic purposes is not accepted under the philosophy guiding the interscholastic program.

An examination of the transfer rules of various state associations reveals that the transfer rule, in essence, provides for a period of ineligibility for students who transfer schools. States are divided regarding the period of ineligibility, with some providing for one semester and others for one year. Those that require one year feel that the one semester of ineligibility can be too easily abused. For example, a baseball, football, track or wrestling athlete, or any athlete whose particular sport was in season only during one semester, could transfer to another school after the close of the sport season, attend the semester during which that sport was not in season, and compete the following semester without any loss of eligibility in the sport in which he was interested.

However, provisions are generally made for exceptions to allow for legitimate transfer for other than athletic reasons. The most common is that a student does not lose eligibility if there is a change of residence of parents to the district in which the student transfers enrollment. Also, many state associations have a "hardship rule" under which a student may be granted eligibility in a case beyond his or her control and which does not involve a choice. Missouri provides its Board of Control with authority to grant eligibility to a student from a broken home if it is established that the transfer was made to have a home and in other cases beyond the control of the student or parents.

In the case of a broken home or deceased parent(s), the Board of Control may grant a student eligibility who does not meet the standards of residence when sufficient evidence is provided the Board of Control to show that it was necessary for the student to transfer in order to have a home. The Board of Control is authorized to grant eligibility to a student in a case that is beyond the control of a student or parents, which in the opinion of the Board involves undue hardship or an emergency and does not violate the intent of any of the standards of eligibility. Cases involving any choice on the part of the student or parents shall not be heard under this section.[10]

Transfer and undue influence rules have been designed to prevent the prevalence of "tramp athletes" and proselytizing, and to make student athletic competition incidental to change in parental residence rather than an occasion for such change. Most states have found that the strict interpretation of these rules has been instrumental in the improvement of relations between schools. It has practically eliminated the student who "shops around" for athletic competition, thus reserving the opportunity for team membership to those legitimately entitled to it.

Awards

Theoretically, all amateur sports participation should be for the love of the game and the enjoyment of playing. This is why children play. It is almost an indictment of adults that they have created situations that have made it necessary to establish award policies in schools and colleges and in independent and club competition as well. This came about largely as the result of the desire of well-meaning groups and individuals to honor those to whom they felt honor and recognition were due. However, others sought to gain recognition for themselves by offering awards to popular high school athletes.

Just when schools themselves began to give awards to honor their athletes is not clear, but it soon became evident that this created problems and some friction among them. The award one school gave affected others. Athletes could not understand why those in other schools received more attractive awards than their school offered, and some schools felt compelled to give an award that would be as attractive as those given by other schools. Hence, it is only logical that they realized the need to establish some maximum standards to keep awards more uniform. This realization led to the establishment of award standards through state high school associations. Limits set by state associations vary some, but the general policy has been to allow only those awards that have little or no intrinsic value. Awards that are generally acceptable are medals, ribbons, certificates, plaques, and trophies.

Some state association award standards are more liberal than others. The two following examples will illustrate existing differences; these standards should not, however, be confused with amateur rules, which are discussed in a separate section in this chapter.

Iowa's rule is typical of the more restrictive state association standards:

> A student shall not be allowed to receive for his participation in interscholastic contests any award other than the unattached letter, monogram, or other insignia of the school. In no case shall any award be received from an individual or organization other than a member school of this Association. This shall not prohibit the awarding of a customary medal for specific performances in a sanctioned meet, nor would it prohibit the awarding of medals to members of a team whose school wins a conference championship, i.e., a medal comparable to the medal which the Association provides for state meets. A school not a member of the conference and whose team has achieved excellent performance during the season may make application to the Board of Control for permission to make a similar award.[11]

The Georgia High School Association award standard is an example of those which are more liberal:

> No awards may be made for intramural and interscholastic competition other than customary letters, medals, trophies, and plaques, and only one sweater or one jacket by the school during the pupil's school career.[12]

In concluding this discussion on awards, it may be worthwhile to review the statement included in the Recommended Minimum Eligibility Requirements of the National Federation of State High School Associations (see pages 30–36).

Some high school associations combine award standards and amateur standards into one rule, as the National Federation has done, while others have separate sections in their constitutions and by-laws governing them. All state associations limit the value of awards schools may present their athletes. A problem arises for high school associations and their member schools when nonschool organizations do not comply with these standards. Many such organizations offer awards of greater value than those allowed in interscholastic athletics and still consider the athletes as amateurs. High school athletes frequently desire to compete in such events during the summer, and ineligibility sometimes results. It is often difficult for athletes and their parents to understand why awards standards differ, and they occasionally look upon the high school standards as being unduly stringent.

Amateurism

If we begin to investigate the meaning of amateurism, we are immediately confronted with the ambiguity of the term. There seem to be almost as many definitions of it as there are types of organizations that seek to restrict their competition to what they term amateurs. International sports committees have set up standards that receive most attention during, or immediately proceding, Olympic years. In turn, there are national and sectional organizations that maintain affiliations with international groups; and although their interpretations may vary for their local competition, they are definitely bound to these internationally established precedents. In the United States we are concerned chiefly with rulings on this subject as made by four bodies or groups of bodies: (1) National Amateur Athletic Federation; (2) Amateur Athletic Union of the United States; (3) National Collegiate Athletic Association and its constituent bodies; (4) National Federation of State High School Athletic Associations and its member state associations. The United States Golf Association and the United States Lawn Tennis Association are other organizations with their own standards of awards and definitions of amateurism.

The long-standing definition of an amateur as formulated by the Amateur Athletic Union and the National Collegiate Athletic Association is one of the most general and universally accepted:

> An amateur sportsman is one who engages in sport solely for the pleasure and physical, mental or moral benefits to be derived therefrom and to whom sport is nothing more than an avocation.

This rule probably has been the basis for most of the regulations concerning amateurism which have been formulated throughout the country.

Because of violations and evasions of the spirit of this rule, organizations that sponsor local or sectional competition became more specific in their terminology. As an example, the Western Conference (Big Ten), in essence, declares a college student a professional if he/she participates in an outside game or contest for which admission is charged at the gate or if he/she receives pay for playing after his/her matriculation in the member institution. In most collegiate organizations as well as in the AAU an athlete may not compete with or against a professional in a match, game, or race. A professional, in such instances, is defined as one who is, or has been, paid for his/her athletic services. The United States Golf Association considers a player a professional if he/she caddies for pay after having reached the age of 18 years, but allows winners of its so-called amateur tournaments to accept prizes of considerable intrinsic or commercial value. The Michigan Amateur Athletic Union, a few years ago, awarded winners of its amateur boxing matches merchandise orders for food and clothing and still felt that it was not violating its amateur code. Athletes have often been provided "expenses," which sometimes have been far in excess of actual expenditures.

From these examples it will be seen that variations in general rules pertaining to amateurism are natural and probably inevitable. Even among high school athletic associations there are differences. There are also a great many similarities, however. High schools are pretty much our most cosmopolitan organizations, especially in those states with compulsory attendance laws. School officials have wanted their interschool athletics to be open to all who had average ability to play. They have tried to keep this principle inviolate by ruling out those athletes who, because of their special athletic prowess, could improve themselves by professional competition and at the same time receive pay for their services. Such students, in most cases, are asked to make the choice of remaining amateurs, in accordance with the school or state athletic association definitions, or to participate in what would be nonamateur competition. If they choose the former, their participation would be more nearly on a par with those with whom and against whom they are likely to compete. If they choose the latter, they are merely stepping out of the high school competition and making room for other athletes.

There are varying differences in the wording of high school association amateur rules. Pennsylvania's rule is typical of those which are well detailed:

AMATEUR

Section 1. Loss of Amateur Status

A pupil must be an amateur in order to be eligible to participate in any P.I.A.A. sponsored interscholastic athletic contest. An athlete loses his amateur status for purposes of participation in any P.I.A.A. sponsored interscholastic sport whenever:

(a) He competes in an athletic contest in which prizes are given. *Note:* For purposes of Section 1 the term "prizes" shall include anything which is used primarily as a medium of exchange or a representation of value, such as money, bonds or securities.

(b) He sells or pawns his athletic achievement awards. As used herein, the term "athletic achievement awards" shall mean those awards which are symbolic of personal athletic achievement, such as described in Article X hereof.

(c) He accepts prizes for his athletic ability.

(d) He competes under a false name.

(e) He plays, or has played, on a team any of whose players have received, or are receiving, directly or indirectly, compensation for their athletic services. This rule does not apply to a high school athlete who has participated in summer baseball where no player on his team received any form of compensation for athletic services in that particular game; however, the division of any receipts, whether obtained from admissions, collections, or donations, among the members of the team at any time, shall be construed as a violation of the provisions of this Article.

(f) He receives a consideration for becoming a member of an athletic organization or school.

(g) He signs a contract whereby he agrees to compete in any athletic competition for profit or the promise of profit. It is not a violation for a high school baseball player to attend a professional baseball tryout camp, provided (1) that no expenses are paid him, and (2) his participation is otherwise in conformity with the National Federation Major-Minor league agreement.

(h) He accepts compensation for teaching, training, or coaching in a sport. It is not a violation of this rule for a high school athlete to receive compensation for acting as an instructor in or officiating recreational activities, or for serving as a lifeguard at swimming areas.

Section 2.   How Amateur Status Can Be Regained

A player who has lost his amateur status may be reinstated by the suspending body after a period of one year from the date of suspension, providing that he refrains from all activity prohibited by Section 1 hereof during that year.[13]

Pennsylvania's exemption of playground instruction and supervision is a practice generally accepted elsewhere.

Idaho's rule is an example of those which provide a simple definition of amateurism and the standards for it:

AMATEUR RULE

A student who uses his/her athletic skill or knowledge for gain, who plays with a professional team or who competes for a cash prize shall be ineligible for that sport. (This applies to sports sanctioned by the IHSAA.)

If the athlete competes under an assumed name or signs a professional contract, the athlete shall be ineligible only in the sport in which he or she signs a contract. Ineligibility under this rule is in effect the entire time the athlete is in high school, unless the athlete is reinstated by the IHSAA State Board of Control.

INTERPRETATION

The athlete may work as the following: camp counselor, recreation department employee, tennis club employee or golf shop employee and may coach, teach, or officiate as part of his responsibilities with the aforementioned jobs.[14]

Most high school associations' regulations provide that an athlete is ineligible only in the sport concerned when amateur and/or award standards are violated. Some athletic administrators believe that when a student becomes a professional athlete in any sport, he or she is a professional and should be ineligible for all interscholastic sports, but this position has not prevailed.

It is apparent that high school representatives to the National Federation desire to keep students from using their athletic skills as a means of livelihood or incidental remuneration. Athletics, with their definite place in the educational program, should be kept educational in nature. Also, there are interschool relations to be fostered, and there will be better relations if the students who comprise athletic teams are of the rank and file of high school athletes. For this reason high school associations have said athletes must be amateurs as they have chosen to define the term.

SPECIAL ELIGIBILITY REGULATIONS

The eligibility requirements discussed above—with variations—are common to virtually all high school associations. There are others adopted by some associations which are significant and worthy of consideration. It would be interesting to know all the reasons they were established, but it is safe to assume they evolved from "cases" creating a need for them. After all, that is the way most of our laws, as well as athletic regulations, have been developed.

The fact that some state associations do not have these particular standards does not mean they do not exist in those states. Some are difficult to enforce at the state level and are left to individual schools or conferences.

Conduct or Character Rule

Regulations pertaining to this matter appear almost universal among state associations so they might be classed as a regular rule. The Oklahoma rule is typical:

A student whose conduct or character at school is under discipline or whose conduct or character outside the school is such as to reflect discredit upon the school, shall be ineligible until reinstated by the principal.[15]

Tobacco and liquor rule.   Regulations specifically prohibiting the use of drugs, tobacco, or alcoholic beverages appear in a few states. In others this matter seems to be left to local schools as a disciplinary problem for their settlement. The North Dakota rule is an example of control by state association regulation:

> Use or possession of tobacco, alcohol, other harmful substances, illegal use or possession of narcotics or habit-forming drugs is prohibited. Any cocurricular participant who indulges in any of these harmful practices will be suspended from all game participation or public appearances from the date of infraction for a period of six consecutive school weeks for the first offense and for a period of eighteen consecutive school weeks for any subsequent offense.[16]

Rules pertaining to drugs, tobacco, and liquor are conduct and character standards, which are generally considered among the most important eligibility requirements and consistent with the theory of representative democracy framed by our forefathers. After the "town hall" type assembly became too cumbersome, with an increasing population, and it was resolved that groups of individuals had to be represented by persons chosen for that purpose, specific qualifications were established as standards for the selection of representatives. High moral and ethical character was always emphasized. Athletes on school teams represent more than themselves as members of the team. They represent fellow students, the faculty, and the entire school community. Those who watch them play are inclined to judge all these groups by the attitudes and conduct of the athletes. Hence, it is reasonable that they meet established standards of good conduct. Otherwise, they may reflect discredit upon those whom they represent.

Enforcement of rules of good conduct can present problems for school administrators as the result of our system of justice, which considers an individual innocent until proved guilty. A specific example is when a student is apprehended on a drug or similar charge and is awaiting trial. Can the school consider the student ineligible under these circumstances? If not, and the student is permitted to compete against another school and is later convicted in court, can another school bring charges against the school for playing an ineligible player?

A football coach in Missouri, confronted with this very situation, conceived of a procedure for coping with it. One of his varsity players was apprehended for assaulting a peace officer. His school was threatened with a lawsuit if the athlete was to be ruled ineligible before he was proved guilty in court. The coach advised school officials not to rule on his eligibility under these conditions. He allowed him to dress out with the team, but let him sit on the bench and did not enter him in any games. The player soon dropped from the squad and no suit was brought. Other schools have since followed essentially the same procedure by simply not allowing a player to participate without making a ruling on eligibility.

The logic behind this procedure is that there is really no need to declare a student ineligible to prevent him or her from representing the school. There are many eligible students in every school who are not afforded the privilege of competing on the school team. Each school is privileged to select the players for its team, and there is no law that provides a student with an inherent right to be selected to compete in interschool competition. Therefore, why should a coach select a player whose character and/or conduct is questionable, when there are many other students of high character who also would like to have the opportunity of representing their school as a member of its team, or who would at least be sitting on the bench while the athlete in question was playing? What effect will it have upon the attitudes toward good citizenship among other students if the school does not enforce standards of good conduct in interscholastic athletics?

Perhaps this would not be so much of an issue if schools would assume more responsibility in handling this type of case. Perhaps the reason they do not is because it may seem easier to tell an athlete that he or she is ineligible because "the state association has a rule," not realizing that a court case is more likely when the athlete is declared ineligible. It is fortunate that courts have upheld reasonable good conduct rules, as will be seen in Chapter 16.

There is a significant advantage to the high school association's having a citizenship standard. It gives the athletic director or the principal support when a student is guilty of misconduct. It also makes it much easier to suspend such a student from competition, which any good athletic director or school administrator will want to do. Directors realize that when an athlete whose conduct or character is poor is allowed to play in a game, a good school citizen will be forced to "sit on the bench." It is difficult to impress upon students the importance of good citizenship if a student whose citizenship is poor is allowed the privilege of participation over another whose citizenship is good.

Antifraternity-Membership Rule

In several states there are statutes prohibiting membership by high school students in fraternities, sororities, or other secret organizations. Some state associations have regulations that rule a student ineligible for high school athletics if membership in organizations of this kind is proved. The Colorado association rule is typical:

He shall not be a member of any organization prohibited by law.[17]

There are generally state legal statutes prohibiting high school fraternities and sororities in those states in which the high school association has this type of regulation, which makes the rule easier to enforce and more difficult for an athlete or his/her parents to challenge in court. In other states protected by such statutes, individual school boards have adopted local antifraternity and antisorority rules after experiencing problems stemming from such organizations.

Military Service Rule

Illinois, like most other states, made specific reference to the fact that a student was not to be ruled ineligible because of absence from school for military service.

> Absence of students required by military service to state or nation in the time of any state of national emergency shall not affect students' eligibility.

All-Star Participation

Several high school associations have regulations prohibiting the use of school facilities or the participation of coaches and other school representatives in all-star games. Some associations also apply these rules to athletes. Illinois has such an eligibility provision:

> Students shall not, during their high school career, participate in any all-star competition, either of a team or individual character.[18]

Married Student Rule

Problems sometimes arise regarding residence and transfer of residence standards when a high school student is married and lives outside the home of his/her parents. To cope with such cases a few associations have adopted special regulations, of which the Tennessee rule is an example.

> A male student who is married and who has an athletic record in any sport the previous or current year may not transfer to another school without losing eligibility to participate in all sports for a period of twelve months.[19]

Sometime ago a few states denied eligibility to any married student. However, court decisions prompted the discontinuance of this practice. A regulation such as the Tennessee rule has as its purpose the prevention of abuses. If a change of residence of a married student were considered an exception to the residence and transfer standards, a married student could change schools at will and remain eligible, which would discriminate against unmarried athletes.

Hardship Cases

Several high school associations have a hardship provision in their constitutions and by-laws for exceptions under the residence and transfer standards (see p. 108). Others have a hardship clause authorizing the executive board of the association to waive any eligibility rules except the age standard. The Florida provision is typical:

> The Executive Committee shall have authority to set aside the effect of any eligibility rule except the age limit upon an individual student when in its opinion the rule works an undue hardship upon that student.[20]

Unsportsmanlike Conduct

Several state associations which do not have a citizenship requirement for eligibility do have sportsmanship standards applied during athletic contests. Alabama has this rule:

> A pupil who has been found guilty in an interschool contest of unsportsmanlike conduct, or who has been penalized for a serious offense or rule violation by expulsion from a game or contest because of foul tactics, may be suspended by the District Director or Executive Director from participating for the remainder of the season in that sport. The use of profane language by a player during the process of a game disqualifies him/her for the remainder of the game. Names of disqualified players must be reported to the District Board and Executive Director by the principal of the opposing team and game officials.[21]

Specialized Athletic Camps

Most state associations prohibit high school coaches from instructing their athletes during the summer and from being a member of the coaching staff at a specialized athletic camp attended by any of their players. Missouri has concluded that if athletes are to be permitted to attend specialized camps sponsored by nonschool representatives who charge sufficient fees to make a profit, it is reasonable to allow schools to sponsor their own camps during the summer, but to limit an athlete's attendance to no more than two weeks in any one sport.

> A student shall become ineligible in a sport for 365 days from the date of the last offense if he or she participates in a specialized camp, school, clinic, or other similar program involving coaching and instruction in that sport unless the program and the student's participation meets the following requirements:
>
> a. Any camp sponsored by any individual or organization other than a member school shall be approved by the Board of Control. No camp held during the school year shall be approved.
>
> A camp sponsored by a member school shall be approved by the principal or superintendent who shall be responsible for seeing that there is adherence to all provisions of this section.

b. The camp program does not include any type of competition other than customary practice situations.

c. The fee (tuition) is provided by the student or parents.

d. No school uniforms or player equipment shall be used except helmets.

e. A student's participation in a specialized camp, school, clinic, or other similar program in any one sport shall not be longer than two calendar weeks in any one calendar year. A calendar week is defined as Sunday through Saturday and any part of a week shall count as one calendar week.

f. An athlete shall not receive pay or expenses for working in a specialized summer camp or serving as an instructor or counselor at a camp involving a sport in which he/she participates.

A member school may sponsor its own summer sport(s) camp(s) during the time school is not in session for its students provided the above conditions are met. The school's coach may conduct the camp; school facilities and game equipment may be used; however, no school uniforms or player equipment shall be used. An individual student's participation in a summer sports camp in a particular sport shall be limited to a maximum of two calendar weeks in one calendar year. A student may not participate in both a school camp for two weeks and a nonschool camp for another two weeks.

No sports camp involving a fall season sport shall be attended after July 31.[22]

The Missouri regulations are unique in that they allow member schools to hold camps. One of the principal reasons which prompted adoption of this specific provision was to avoid discrimination against students who could not afford to pay the camp fees, some of which are quite expensive, charged by promoters of nonschool camps.

Other states are divided on the matter of specialized or training camps. Some have no restrictions, while others have very restrictive rules, such as the one in Texas:

Any student who attends a special athletic training camp in football, basketball, or volleyball shall be ineligible for a period of one year from the date he enrolls in the camp in the sport or sports for which he attended the camp. This does not apply to *bona fide* summer camps giving an overall activity program to the participants.[23]

The Texas regulation is not applied to transfer students from other states who may have attended a training camp before enrolling in a Texas school.

A number of athletic administrators look upon specialized athletic camps as a form of exploitation of the interests of students and their parents, many of whom are led to believe such camps greatly enhance a student's chances of receiving a college athletic scholarship. Others consider it none of the schools' business to interfere with what athletes do during the summer as long as other eligibility standards are not violated. That a high school association can adopt and uphold summer camp regulations was well established in a circuit court's ruling upheld by an appeals court supporting the reasonableness of the Missouri State High School Activities Association's summer camp standards (see page 380).

Although there are some who contend that standards of eligibility serve no purpose, the fact that there are many which are essentially the same or similar in all states is ample proof that they are considered necessary by school administrators and athletic leaders. The high regard held for interscholastics can in large measure be attributed to the development of standards for high school athletes.

Courts have upheld that participation in interscholastics is a privilege rather than a legal right of a student. They have further held that schools may form state associations and establish statewide minimum standards through them.

The effectiveness of the state association eligibility standards has been enhanced by the fact that schools have formulated enforcement procedures through their associations, including the authority to assess penalties for violations.

There are always desires for changes in rules. *What will be in the best interest of the great majority of high school youth* must remain the primary guideline for establishing any new standards, amending those in effect, or eliminating some which no longer serve any worthwhile purpose in the interscholastic program.

SUMMARY

This summary of eligibility rules for contestants attempts to show general practices in effect in most states. There may be exceptions in some instances to the general conclusions indicated.

Age.   The upper age limit of 19 years is the most common one, with 39 states having this maximum at present. There is some tendency to establish lower age limits in some states for participation in certain sports.

Time of enrollment.   In general, students must be enrolled at least by the third or fourth week of the semester to qualify for athletic eligibility during a current semester. In some states attendance from 30 to 60 days is required, after a continuous absence of 20 days or more, before a student regains athletic eligibility.

Seasons of competition.   In practically all states there is a limit of four seasons of competition in a sport in grades 9 to 12, inclusive.

Number of semesters of attendance.   Eight semesters of attendance in grades 9 to 12, inclusive, is the common rule.

Limited team membership.   It is an almost universal regulation that a member of a high school team is prohibited membership on a team other than that of the high school in the same sport during the season of the sport concerned.

Parental consent and physical examinations.   Virtually all states require students to pass a physical examination before they may compete in athletic activities. Some require a separate examination for each sport, but in most instances one examination during the school year is sufficient. In several states, consent cards must be signed by parents or guardians before students may participate.

Current and previous semester scholarship.   Almost all states have requirements that students must have received credit in a specified amount of work (usually 15 hours) the preceding semester in order to be eligible. Likewise, virtually all states have regulations requiring a student to do passing work in at least 15 hours during the current semester. New York has removed its previous semester scholastic work requirements.

Transfer and undue influence rules.   In general, a student is eligible in a new school if his/her parents or guardians have moved into the new school district. Usually a semester, but sometimes a full year, of ineligibility follows a transfer by a student from one school to another without an accompanying transfer of parental residence. Undue influence rules, with penalties of ineligibility for students and discipline for schools, have made their appearance in practically all states.

Awards.   The trend in most school districts is to give awards of little or no intrinsic value, such as medals, certificates, and trophies.

Amateurism.   With very few exceptions, high school students may not use their athletic skill or knowledge of athletics for personal gain. Many states do not allow students to compete with, or against, teams any of whose members are paid for their services. Others require only that students themselves not accept pay or a valuable award for playing.

Special rules.   A varying number of state associations in each instance have established regulations dealing with the following:

1. Conduct or character
2. Fraternity or sorority membership
3. Military service

4. All-star participation
5. Married students
6. Hardship cases
7. Unsportsmanlike conduct
8. Specialized athletic camps

Coaches are responsible for teaching the standards of eligibility. Violations of eligibility rules causing students to become ineligible is a source of problems for athletes, their schools, and state associations. The greater number of such cases result from a lack of knowledge of the rules by students and their parents or a misunderstanding of them. When violations occur, athletes and their parents are prone to blame coaches and school officials for not fully informing players of eligibility standards. One of the first responsibilities of coaches is to *teach* and to make certain that all members of their squads have full knowledge of eligibility rules and the reasons for them. The coach must, of course, have a thorough knowledge of the rules as well as the reasons for them.

If coaches will properly assume this responsibility, there will be fewer eligibility problems and less embarrassment for themselves and their schools.

QUESTIONS AND TOPICS FOR STUDY AND DISCUSSION

1. Why did athletic eligibility regulations become necessary?
2. What do you consider some of the most important purposes of eligibility standards? Why?
3. Do you think the academic standard for high school athletic eligibility should be raised or lowered? Why?
4. Select six standards of eligibility which you consider of most significance and give reasons why you think they were established.
5. Why are parental consent and physical examinations for high school athletes important?
6. Why is it said that there are responsibilities as well as privileges connected with representing one's school in interscholastic athletic competition?
7. Discuss the common "transfer rules" in effect in most states. Do you agree with the "undue influence rules"? Why?
8. Should high school athletes be permitted to attend specialized summer athletic camps? Why or why not?
9. Write a brief paragraph giving your philosophy of high school awards and amateur rules.
10. Why is there so much controversy and misunderstanding about amateur and award rules in high schools and colleges?
11. Why are high standards of citizenship important criteria of athletic eligibility?

12. Why should coaches have a thorough understanding of eligibility rules and assume the responsibility for teaching them to players?

13. Explain procedures and techniques coaches might employ to make certain their athletes know and understand eligibility standards.

14. Do you think we could have interscholastic athletics without eligibility standards? Why?

15. What changes in common or special eligibility rules would you recommend? Why?

16. If you were the athletic director of a local high school, would you want to add any eligibility requirements for your student athletes to those already mentioned in this chapter? Explain.

NOTES

1. *Morrison* v. *Roberts,* 183 Okl. 359 Pac. 2d 1023.
2. Missouri State High School Activities Association, *1982–83 Official Handbook,* p. 13.
3. C. W. Whitten, *Interscholastics—A Discussion of Interscholastic Contests* (Illinois High School Association, 1950), p. 3.
4. "Regulations of the Commissioner of Education Governing Health and Physical Education," *New York Public High School Athletic Association Bulletin,* October 1937.
5. J. F. Williams, *New York Public High School Athletic Association Bulletin,* October 1937.
6. Ohio High School Athletic Association, *1981–82 Constitution and By-Laws,* p. 24.
7. Virginia High School League, Inc., *1981–82 Handbook,* p. 58.
8. Iowa High School Athletic Association, *Constitution and By-laws, 1981–82,* p. 10.
9. Indiana High School Athletic Association, Inc., *By-Laws and Articles of Incorporation, 1980–81,* p. 37.
10. Missouri State High School Activities Association, *1982–83 Official Handbook,* p. 21.
11. Iowa High School Athletic Association, *Constitution and By-Laws,* p. 11.
12. Georgia High School Association, *1981–82 Constitution and By-Laws,* p. 40.
13. Pennsylvania Interscholastic Athletic Association, *1980–81 PIAA Handbook,* pp. 7–8.
14. Idaho High School Activities Association, *1981–82 Manual,* p. 24.
15. Oklahoma Secondary School Activities Association, *1981–82 Yearbook,* p. 11.
16. North Dakota High School Activities Association, *1981–82 Constitution and By-Laws,* p. 92.
17. Colorado High School Activities Association, *1980–81 Constitution and By-Laws,* p. 19.
18. Illinois High School Association, *1981–82 Official Handbook,* p. 19.
19. Tennessee Secondary School Athletic Association, *1981–82 Official Handbook,* p. 12.
20. Florida High School Activities Association, *1981–82 By-Laws,* p. 32.
21. Alabama High School Athletic Association, *1981–82 Handbook,* p. 65.
22. Missouri State High School Activities Association, *1982–83 Official Handbook,* p. 22.
23. University Interscholastic League (Texas), *Constitution and Contest Rules for 1981–82,* p. 29.

BIBLIOGRAPHY

ALABAMA HIGH SCHOOL ATHLETIC ASSOCIATION. *1981–82 Handbook,* p. 65.

COLORADO HIGH SCHOOL ACTIVITIES ASSOCIATION. *1980–81 Constitution and By-Laws,* p. 19.

FLORIDA HIGH SCHOOL ACTIVITIES ASSOCIATION. *1981–82 By-Laws,* p. 32.

GEORGIA HIGH SCHOOL ASSOCIATION. *1981–82 Constitution and By-Laws,* p. 40.

IDAHO HIGH SCHOOL ACTIVITIES ASSOCIATION. *1981–82 Manual,* p. 24.

ILLINOIS HIGH SCHOOL ASSOCIATION. *1981–82 Official Handbook,* p. 19.

INDIANA HIGH SCHOOL ATHLETIC ASSOCIATION, INC. *By-Laws and Articles of Incorporation, 1980–81,* p. 37.

IOWA HIGH SCHOOL ATHLETIC ASSOCIATION. *Constitution and By-laws, 1981–82,* pp. 10–11.

MISSOURI STATE HIGH SCHOOL ACTIVITIES ASSOCIATION. *1982–83 Official Handbook,* pp. 13, 21–22.

NATIONAL FEDERATION OF STATE HIGH SCHOOL ASSOCIATIONS. *1982–83 Handbook.* Kansas City, Mo.: National Federation, 1983, pp. 60–62.

NEW YORK STATE PUBLIC HIGH SCHOOL ATHLETIC ASSOCIATION. *Bulletin,* October 1937.

NORTH DAKOTA HIGH SCHOOL ACTIVITIES ASSOCIATION. *1981–82 Constitution and By-Laws,* p. 92.

OHIO HIGH SCHOOL ATHLETIC ASSOCIATION. *1981–82 Constitution and By-Laws,* p. 24.

OKLAHOMA SECONDARY SCHOOL ACTIVITIES ASSOCIATION. *1981–82 Yearbook,* p. 11.

PENNSYLVANIA INTERSCHOLASTIC ATHLETIC ASSOCIATION. *1980–81 PIAA Handbook,* pp. 7–8.

TENNESSEE SECONDARY SCHOOL ATHLETIC ASSOCIATION. *1981–82 Official Handbook,* p. 12.

UNIVERSITY INTERSCHOLASTIC LEAGUE (TEXAS). *Constitution and Contest Rules for 1981–82,* p. 29.

VIRGINIA HIGH SCHOOL LEAGUE, INC. *1981–82 Handbook,* p. 58.

WHITTEN, C. W. *Interscholastics—A Discussion of Interscholastic Contests.* Bloomington: Illinois High School Association, 1950.

Athletic Contest Regulations and Standards

Chapter 5 was concerned with eligibility regulations pertaining to the student contestant. An attempt was made to show reasons for such regulations and to enumerate and illustrate those which were most common among the states as well as some which were rather special in nature. A similar plan will be followed regarding provisions governing contests as they affect schools.

PURPOSE OF CONTEST REGULATIONS

Difference between Contest and Eligibility Regulations

There is a definite distinction between eligibility regulations for contestants and contest regulations which apply to a school. For athletes themselves, the establishment of rules not only serves the school but also presents a code by which students may determine their own eligibility. Contestants should become familiar with these regulations and, in most instances, should be able to see the reasons for their establishment. Usually, athletic eligibility regulations have been set up as the result of experiences of the state associaitons themselves. They are not theoretical, untried, or unworkable ideas that someone has attempted to put into practice. Their worth and value have been proved. Local schools are doing themselves and their students a real service when they acquaint their student bodies and school patrons with these regulations. Following such a policy makes the administration of their programs that much easier.

The philosophies and reasons behind contest regulations are different from those which resulted in ordinary contestant eligibility rules. Two separate schools, two separate organizations, are involved when an athletic contest takes place. Experience has shown that, for mutual harmony, it is necessary to have common unerstandings if a contest is to be successful. In the first place, there is a common set of rules for playing the game. Competent and impartial officials are selected to officiate the contest. It has been found that numerous details also must receive attention before the contest takes place if it is to be the right kind of educational experience. With this purpose in mind, athletic contest regulations as they pertain to high school athletic association rules came into existence.

Contest regulations were adopted to ensure, as far as possible, the fulfillment of certain before-game responsibilities. They have become common codes within their states because they have worked well in most cases. They have not been imposed upon schools in order to display the powers of state associations, as sometimes is charged. Rather, they have been adopted, through educators themselves, as aids to their own schools for the purpose of bringing order out of chaos. Although the degree of success in this accomplishment may be a matter of opinion, the regulations in effect in most states must be agreeable to the majority of schools concerned. Otherwise, they could and undoubtedly would be changed.

COMMON REGULATIONS

In this chapter there will be presented common rules pertaining to the conduct of interschool contests. An attempt has been made to make the illustrations typical and representative of various sections of the country.

Contracts for Athletic Contests

It is an almost universal rule that state associations furnish standard contract forms for the use of member schools. Some states require that arrangements for all games be made on such forms. Many state associations refuse to assume jurisdiction in disputes between schools regarding contract violations unless arrangements for games were executed on standard forms which were properly signed by authorized representatives of the schools concerned. In general, the essential provisions of the various state association contracts for games are similar. Ohio's easily understood contract has provisions for a forfeiture fee, as most state association contracts do, in case there is failure to fulfill contract provisions. In most states contracts may be canceled or their provisions altered only by mutual consent of the contracting schools. Payment of the forfeiture fee by a contracting school when a game is not played is deemed fulfillment of the contract in some states. In others, there must be very good reasons for the cancellation of a contest, even though the forfeiture is paid, unless both schools agree to it. Failure to fulfill contract provisions may result in suspension. In most states the principal of the high school, or a faculty representative authorized by the principal, signs contracts. In many states the contract is between the two schools as such, whereas in others it is in reality an agreement between the principals or other administration

CONTRACT FOR ATHLETIC CONTESTS

HOME SCHOOL COPY

OHIO HIGH SCHOOL ATHLETIC ASSOCIATION

MEMBER NATIONAL FEDERATION OF HIGH SCHOOL ATHLETIC ASSOCIATIONS

_____, Ohio, _____, 19_____

This Contract is drawn under the supervision of the Ohio High School Athletic Association and must be used in arranging games participated in by schools of this Association.

THIS CONTRACT, Subscribed to by the Principals and Faculty Managers of the _____ High School

and of the _____ High School, is made for _____ games of _____ to be played as follows:

One game at _____ on _____ at _____ P. M.

One game at _____ on _____ at _____ P. M.

Do not use term "corresponding dates" — use specific dates.

All games to be played under the following stipulations:

The _____ High School agrees to pay to the _____

the sum of _____ dollars ($_____), and the latter school agrees that this sum shall cover all its claims arising by virtue of this contract, except as provided in Item 1 herein below set forth.

1. If either party hereto fails to fulfill its obligation of any part of this contract, the defaulting party shall pay to the other party the sum of $_____ as damages, which said sum must be accepted by the injured party as complete compensation for any damages it may have suffered, the remainder of the contract shall not be binding on either party, and the breach of said contract shall be reported to the Ohio High School Athletic Association.

2. Postponement cannot result in annulment except by mutual consent.

3. The constitution and rules of the Ohio High School Athletic Association are a part of this contract.

4. The suspension or termination of its membership in the State Association by either of the parties to this contract shall render this contract null and void.

5. It is urged that a suggested list of state approved officials be made on the back of this contract sheet and its duplicate. The principal of the visiting school should scratch the names of those not acceptable and number those acceptable in the order of preference on both the original and duplicate. All officials used in football and basketball games must be registered.

6. Interstate games should be scheduled on National Federation State High School Athletic Association contracts which may be obtained free of charge from the Ohio High School Athletic Association.

7. Unless otherwise specified, this contract shall call for a first team game.

8. This contract must be returned no later than _____ or it will become null and void.

150M—10-69

_____   _____   _____   _____
Principal   Faculty Manager or Athletic Director   Date   School   State

_____   _____   _____   _____
Principal   Faculty Manager or Athletic Director   School   State

FIGURE 6–1 Contract form for athletic contests (Ohio)

officials of the schools concerned. The Ohio contract for athletic contests is quite similar to the type used by most state athletic associations (see Fig. 6–1).

It is desirable to have definite financial stipulations in contracts. Usually, flat guarantees are made, with the result that the visiting school may do as it sees fit in arranging accommodations for its team. This seems to be the best procedure, although the contracts of some state associations provide for definite numbers of players for whom expenses are to be paid by the entertaining school. In some states specific amounts are designated for meals, lodging, and transportation. The provision for listing officials for the game appears on many contracts. This usually is done by the entertaining school, and the visiting school is allowed to cross out the names of listed officials who are not acceptable to it.

Officials should be agreed on well in advance of the date of a contest. Most high school associations' by-laws require the host school to engage officials acceptable to the visiting school. If this is not done, controversies can arise causing friction between schools and adversely affect the sportsmanship of team followers. To expedite the selection of officials, Missouri furnishes a form to accompany contracts for games (see Fig. 6–2). Some associations have a similar form on the back of the contract form.

Following are a few typical provisions of state association by-laws regarding contest contracts:

It is the responsibility of the principal—
To see that all contracts for interscholastic athletic contests in which his school participates are in writing and bear his signature. (*Pennsylvania*)[1]

The Association's "Contract for Athletic Contests" must be used for all interschool athletic contests and must be signed by the Principals of the schools involved. (*Indiana*)[2]

The Principal of the school is responsible to the State Association for all matters pertaining to the athletic relations of his/her school, and all contracts must be signed by the Principal.
All athletic contests between schools shall be regulated by written contract, setting forth the details of time, place, finances, officials, or other agreed upon provisions. (*New Jersey*)[3]

The final management of all interscholastic athletics shall be in the hands of some member or members of the faculty who shall sign all contracts. (*Michigan*)[4]

Because the principal is the chief administrator of the high school, many associations require him/her to sign all contracts. Others permit the principal to delegate this authority to the athletic director or some other member of the faculty. As the duties of the principal have become increasingly complex, this has been the trend, particularly in larger high schools.

It is a good procedure to have the signed contract at all games for reference should any questions about terms or arrangements be raised.

MISSOURI STATE HIGH SCHOOL ACTIVITIES ASSOCIATION

AGREEMENT ON OFFICIALS

DATE MAILED: _____

In compliance with By-Law 8 of the Missouri State High School Activities Association, the following list of officials registered with the

MSHSAA is submitted in duplicate by _____
(Host school)

for the approval of _____
(Visiting school)

It is agreed that the Visiting school may delete the names of any officials on this list who are not approved and that the Host school may secure any officials whose names remain on the list.

It is further agreed that the Visiting school and the Host school will keep this agreement in strictest confidence. The original copy of this form must be signed and returned to the Host school by the Visiting school within ten (10) days after the date given above. Failure by the Visiting school to return this form within ten (10) days will constitute approval by the Visiting school of all officials whose names appear on this list.

This agreement is for contest(s) in the _____
(Name of sport)

to be played on the following date(s) _____
(Date or dates of contests)

OFFICIALS FOR VARSITY CONTEST(S)

OFFICIALS FOR CONTEST(S) OTHER THAN VARSITY

HOST SCHOOL'S APPROVAL	VISITING SCHOOL'S APPROVAL
Signed _____	Signed _____
(Principal or Athletic Administrator)	(Principal or Athletic Administrator)
Signed _____	Signed _____
(Head Coach)	(Head Coach)
School _____	School _____
(Name of host school)	(Name of visiting school)

FIGURE 6–2   Form for agreement on officials (Missouri)

Eligibility List Procedures

Practically all state associations have some procedure whereby lists of players are exchanged between schools prior to athletic contests. These lists document the names of eligible student contestants and varying amounts of data regarding their scholastic and athletic histories. The time for exchange of eligibility lists, or eligibility certificates, as they are called in some states, varies from the filing of one blank at the start or close of the season to an exchange at the time of the contest. In most instances eligibility lists are exchanged between competing schools from within three days to a week prior to the contest.

The most common procedure is that of exchange of a form before either the first game or each game, which gives the complete history of all contestants. Such data usually include birth records; dates of enrollment during the current semester; indication that contestants have passed the required physical examinations; number of semesters enrolled in grades 9 to 12, inclusive; number of subjects carried successfully during the preceding and current semesters; and number of seasons of participation in the sport concerned. In some instances space is provided on such blanks to indicate whether contestants are transfer students from other schools; and, if so, the names of the schools are usually stated. The Athletic Eligibility Certificate of the Kansas State High School Activities Association is used to illustrate this type of blank (see Fig. 6–3).

Several features of this blank are especially desirable, and the forms used by the large majority of states are similar. Attention is called to the brief resume of the eligibility rules for contestants that appears at the top. The next section of the blank provides for listing of pertinent information relative to the contest concerned. The location, date, hour, and officials for the contest may be listed by the entertaining school. Such information is essential, and although much of it may have appeared on the contract blank or in previous correspondence, it is an excellent administrative procedure to call it to the attention of all those concerned immediately preceding the contest.

The use of forms similar to the Kansas sheet has the advantage of furnishing all data on contestants immediately preceding each contest. There has been some objection, however, to the amount of clerical work involved in the preparation of such detailed information on each contestant for each contest. In some instances, also, there has been the feeling that eligibility data would be more valuable if it were in the hands of all schools at the beginning of the season rather than just before a game, with the result that it does not reach some schools until near the end of the season.

Several states use a simpler form and require that it be sent to all schools on the schedule and to the state association office at the beginning of the season. It is understood that all the students on the list remain eligible during the entire season unless a school is notified to the contrary. This procedure has the advantage of furnishing all schools concerned with data on all contestants of a school at the beginning of a season. Questions concerning eligibility of contestants can then be brought up before the contests in most instances, with the effect of decreasing the number of protests after games have been played. Coaches also like to keep copies on file from year to year because of the information it provides about players on opposing teams.

It is felt by some that responsibility for eligibility rests with each indi-

Send one of these blanks to the KSHSAA listing all participants prior to the first contest of each activity season.

Mailed on _____

C

C

KANSAS STATE HIGH SCHOOL ACTIVITIES ASSOCIATION

ACTIVITY ELIGIBILITY CERTIFICATE

THIS APPLIES TO BOTH BOYS AND GIRLS FOR ALL ATHLETIC AND DEBATE ACTIVITIES

We hereby certify the following students are eligible under the rules of the KSHSAA to represent the_____
(name of school) (junior-senior)
High School in all activities listed during the current school year. We further certify that in case additions are made to this list during the season of the activity, the KSHSAA will be notified before the contest. Should any individual on this list become ineligible because of scholastic standing, semesters of attendance, or any other KSHSAA standard, the student will not be allowed to participate during his or her term of ineligibility.

Date of report _____

> $5 penalty if not received prior to first contest of each activity season for each student.

Principal or Superintendent

NAMES OF CONTESTANTS (LIST ALPHABETICALLY)	NUMBER OF SEASONS STUDENT HAS PARTICIPATED IN EACH ACTIVITY, INCLUDING THIS YEAR. ALTER COLUMNS FOR GIRLS SPORTS (BE SURE TO GIVE NUMBER OF SEASONS, NOT CHECK MARKS)										BIRTH			DATE OF PHYSICAL EXAM BY PHYSICIAN FOR PRESENT SEMESTER (ATHLETES ONLY)	DATE FIRST CLASS ATTENDED PRESENT SEMESTER	NO OF FULL AND REGULAR SUBJECTS		TOTAL SEMESTERS ATTENDED INCLUDING PRESENT SEMESTER	PARENTAL CONSENT FORM ON FILE (ATHLETES ONLY) (YES OR NO)
	X COUNTRY	FOOT BALL	DE BATE	SWIM MING	GYM NAS TICS	WREST LING	BAS KET BALL	GOLF	TEN NIS	BASE BALL	TRACK	MO.	DAY	YEAR			PASSED LAST SEMESTER	CARRIED THIS SEMESTER		
EXAMPLE: DOE, JOHN	2		2	(USE NUMBERS—NOT CHECK MARKS)								1	24	'71	1/21	3/23	4	4	4	YES

(OVER)

Listed below are all transfer students who will be participating in the activities listed above:

SCHOOL LAST ATTENDED	DATE OF TRANSFER	SCHOOL LAST ATTENDED	DATE OF TRANSFER

Complete and return to the KSHSAA, BOX 495, TOPEKA, KANSAS 66601, prior to the first contest of each activity season for each student.

FIGURE 6–3 Activity eligibility certificate (Kansas)

vidual school and that no advantage is gained by compiling a great amount of data on contestants, much of which is never used. Oregon's procedure requires only that a list be filed with the state office on a form provided for that purpose. Iowa does not require either an exchange of eligibility lists or that a list be filed with the state association.

Typical of state association by-laws relative to the exchange of eligibility lists, as they apply to each of the plans discussed, the Pennsylvania regulation is:

The principal shall certify to the eligibility of all contestants in accordance with the Constitution and By-Laws of this Association. Such statements, including date of birth, place of birth, date of enrollment for current school year, number of seasons of competition beyond the eighth grade including the present season, number of semesters of attendance in the ninth grade including the present semester, and number of seasons of competition in the ninth grade, shall be presented in writing to the principal of the opponent school or schools at least four days prior to the contest.[5]

Michigan has the following regulation:

Five (5) days prior to the first game in each season, each high school shall submit to all scheduled opponents and to the Association office, a Master Eligibility List (Form-1) of all students eligible for that sport under the provisions of the regulations, including current semester record. Additions to the squad will be certified at once to competing schools in a similar manner on an additional Master Eligibility List. Also, in those sports which carry over into two semesters, an additional Master List is to be submitted at the opening of the second semester to each remaining school on the schedule and to the M.H.S.A.A. (1931)

These lists shall be certified by the superintendent of schools or the principal of the competing high school. Certifications shall be based on complete information concerning the student's age, athletic and scholastic status. Questionable cases shall be referred to the M.H.S.A.A. before the privilege of competition is given. (1931)[6]

Iowa's policy is stated as follows:

The rules and regulations for the Association no longer require the exchange of eligibility lists between member schools. If two member schools desire and agree to exchange eligibility lists, such practice is permissible. The exchange of eligibility lists was merely a means of confirming eligibility of athletes. The Board of Control has the utmost confidence in the administrators of member schools relative to permitting only eligible athletes to participate in interscholastic contests.[7]

There are some advantages and disadvantages to each of the general procedures that have been discussed. Detailed data is desired by coaches in studying the number of upperclassmen on the opponent's team and the number of seasons each has played. Schools are more likely to assume responsibility for checking the eligibility of both their own players and those of their opponents when lists are exchanged. Eligibility lists kept on file in the principal's office make it easier to certify eligibility from year to year. Exchanging lists at the beginning of the season helps to resolve eligibility problems and to avoid protests before games are played. Master lists filed with the state office provide ready information when the eligibility of an athlete is questioned. On the other hand, much time and effort is saved in Iowa's procedure and in using the simpler forms employed by some states. In the final analysis, the schools in each state determine the procedure they think best for that state. Careful attention to the certification of eligibility by the principal, good communication with the coaching staff, and making certain that all athletes understand the standards of eligibility tend to avoid protests.

Records of Transfer Students

The discussion in Chapter 5 indicated that state associations have definite regulations on transfer and undue influence. Several states have prepared blanks that must be executed when a student who transfers from one school to another wishes to compete in athletics at the second school. These forms usually are in addition to the regular scholastic and child-accounting blanks that accompany a transfer student. Transfers are frequently the cause of eligibility problems, and these states apparently have found that requiring a transfer of eligibility application helps to prevent such problems, both for the school to which the student transfers and for the state association.

Missouri requires that a transfer of eligibility form (Fig. 6-4) must be on file in the principal's office before a transfer student can be considered eligible. Several other states use similar forms.

Certification of Athletic Coaches

An early development to improve the educational values of interscholastic athletics was to eliminate volunteer coaches, most of whom were not qualified as teachers. This was accomplished by state high school associations adopting standards which required a coach to be a certified teacher and a full-time member of the school faculty whose salary was paid by the board of education or other governing body in the case of private and parochial schools. The Ohio regulation is typical of this type of rule:

> All coaches shall meet the criteria established by the State Board of Education.
> All coaches shall be approved by the Board of Education or similar governing body in private schools.
> College and University student teachers assigned to a school may assist with coaching duties during their periods of assignment.

MISSOURI STATE HIGH SCHOOL ACTIVITIES ASSOCIATION

Athletic Transfer of Eligibility
(To be filled out by principal of school to which he has transferred.)

Name of Student _____

1. Date Enrolled _____ Parents' residence as of such date _____

2. Present residence of parents _____

   Is this address within the boundaries of your school district? _____

3. Subjects he is carrying _____

4. Total semesters of attendance completed to date in grades 7 and 8 _____. In grades 9-12 _____

   Date _____ Signed _____, Principal

   High School _____ Street Address _____

   Post Office _____ Zip Code _____

(To be filled out by the principal of the school from which he is transferring.) Please give the following information concerning the above student:

Name of student _____
(as listed on your records)

1. Birthdate _____ (Give source of information on birthdate) _____

2. Date enrolled in your school _____ Date of withdrawal _____

3. Total complete semesters of high school (9-12) attendance completed to the time of withdrawal _____

   Total units of credits completed as shown on permanent record _____. Semesters attended in grades 7

   and 8 _____.

4. Credits earned for his last full semester of attendance in your school _____

   If a junior high school student, how many subjects did he fail last semester? _____

5. Residence of parents while he attended your school _____

6. Date of change of residence of parents _____

7. Number of seasons of participation while a student in grades 9-12: (Any part of a game counts as a season of participation.)

   Baseball _____ Football _____ Golf _____ Swimming _____ Softball _____ Basketball _____

   Track _____ Wrestling _____ Tennis _____

8. Would the student have been eligible for athletics if he had remained in your school? _____
   If not, why? _____

9. Is there any reason why he will be ineligible at the above school? _____
   If so, why? _____

   Date _____ Signed _____, Principal-High School _____

   Street Address _____ City-State _____ Zip Code _____

This form is to be filled out by the principal of the new school and sent to the principal of the school from which the student is transferring together with a stamped, self-addressed envelope for return.

FIGURE 6–4 Athletic transfer of eligibility (Missouri)

> The entire salary of the coach shall be paid by the Board of Education or similar governing body in private schools. Bonuses from other athletic association funds or other sources cannot be used to supplement the regular Board of Education salary.[8]

Tennessee's requirement is similar:

> All coaches must be certified teachers and full-time employees of the Board of Education. Coaches must be paid entirely from funds approved by the Board of Education or the governing board of the school.[9]

From an educational as well as an administrative standpoint, it is important that the coach be a regular faculty member, because all coaches should have the school point of view and its educational interests at heart. By and large, there is no question that athletics are much better administered when the coach is a regular part of the school system. There is much less possibility of "downtown influence" if the control and policy making for athletics are administered in the same manner as other phases of a school's educational program.

During the 1960s and 1970s attention was given to further improving the professional competencies of high school coaches. It was noted that although coaches were full-time teachers and knew how to teach the skills inherent in the sports they were coaching, those who were not physical education teachers lacked adequate knowledge about the philosophy of interscholastics, the prevention and care of injuries, the physiology of exercise, and so on. Interest began to stir for raising qualifications for coaching.

Several teacher training institutions started offering voluntary coaching certificates for persons interested in coaching who did not wish to major in physical education. Approximately 15 hours of work in such courses as Administration of High School Athletics, Principles and Problems of Coaching, Theory and Techniques of Coaching, Kinesiological Foundations of Coaching, and Physiological Foundations of Coaching are generally required for the special certificate. Central Missouri State University and Southwest Missouri State University were among the first to initiate such programs in Missouri.

However, conditions also developed during the 1970s which made it impractical to require coaches and assistant coaches to hold physical education degrees or special coaching certificates. Girls' interscholastic athletics increased tremendously and there was a steady growth in the breadth of sports offered boys. Simultaneously, a number of coaches left the profession and fewer teachers were inclined to take on coaching duties. Schools in most states found it impossible to staff their athletic departments with full-time teachers, which left them with one of two alternatives: (1) to drop some sports from their athletic programs, or (2) to allow part-time teachers and nonfaculty individuals to coach. This situation eventually led to a relaxation in high school associations' standards for coaches. By the late 1970s over half of the associations allowed part-time teachers and nonfaculty persons to coach in emergencies.

This slackening of requirements is illustrated by the following clause from Wisconsin's regulations:

> A school may receive emergency relief from the Board of Control for unusual corcumstances to employ other than a certified teacher for coaching, but emergency permission shall not extend beyond one season in the sport involved.[10]

Other associations had somewhat more restrictive regulations for emergencies similar to the Illinois rule:

> Athletic coaches must be regularly certified to teach in the schools of Illinois and be:
>
> (a) regularly employed teachers doing at least two periods of classroom supervision daily in the member school; or
>
> (b) teachers who are employed full-time in any of the elementary or junior high schools in the same attendance area of the member school; or
>
> (c) assistant teachers, resource aides, lay supervisors, or other paraprofessionals who are employed at least half-time per day in the member school; or
>
> (d) teachers who are employed full-time in any elementary district, any of whose territory is a part of the high school district.
>
> (e) If a member school is unable to fill a coaching position under the terms of a, b, c, or d above with personnel acceptable to the Board of Education or governing board, it may, with the approval of the IHSA Board of Directors employ a regularly certified teacher who is not otherwise employed in the member school.
>
> All remuneration for high school coaching must be from the Board of Education of the member school employing the coach.[11]

Generally, approval from the high school association is required in accord with established procedures and for only as long as the emergency exists.

High schools and their state associations realize there are disadvantages to the use of nonfaculty coaches, among which are

1. less administrative control over interscholastic athletics
2. decreased emphasis on the educational values of athletics
3. less rapport among coaches and teachers
4. contractual difficulties
5. internal athletic staff problems
6. less emphasis on sportsmanship
7. lack of coach's loyalty to the administration and the school

Several high school associations sponsor coaching schools, clinics, or workshops which can offer some training for nonfaculty coaches. Coaches' associations do likewise. A school employing a nonfaculty coach should require that person to take advantage of such opportunities.

Although few have tried it, schools might well conduct in-service training programs for coaches in emergency situations. In-service programs for teachers have been conducted by many school districts, and there is no reason why they should not be conducted for coaches. The athletic director could organize a series of meetings for the purpose of instructing nonfaculty coaches in the philosophy and objectives of interscholastic athletics, school policies, caring for the health and safety of athletes, and so forth. It might be advisable for state associations to consider requiring a school to conduct an in-service program when it requests approval of a nonfaculty coach.

There is a precaution schools should exercise before employing a noncertified person as a coach. Some states have laws providing that only certified teachers can instruct or supervise children in the public schools; others legally provide for the use of teachers' aides and paraprofessionals. The high school administrator should check carefully the laws of his/her state to make certain that employment of a nonfaculty coach would not be in violation of state law and thus be the basis for charges of negligence in the event of serious injury to an athlete.

Registration of Officials

It is a general practice of high school associations to require schools to employ officials for team sports who are registered with the association's office. The principal purposes of this requirement are to improve standards of officiating and to foster better relationships between officials and member schools. Usually there is also a procedure for classifying and/or rating officials.

Kentucky's requirements and procedures are typical of those in a number of states:

OFFICIALS MUST REGISTER

Any person who officiates in football, basketball, baseball, or wrestling between member schools of the Association must be registered with the Commissioner and have his or her official card indicating registration.

REQUIREMENTS FOR REGISTRATION

In order for an official to be properly registered he or she must pay a fee in each sport. An official registered in a sport for the first time must be endorsed by four persons who are familiar with his or her ability and shall be required to make an acceptable grade, determined by the Board of Control, on an examination in that sport.

CLINICS

Each registered official shall attend at least one rules interpretation clinic conducted by the K.H.S.A.A. in the sport in which he or she is registered.

CLASSIFICATION OF OFFICIALS

Officials will be classified as Registered, Approved, or Certified. Requirements for these classifications are:

a. Registered.   An official will be classified as Registered as soon as satisfactory references have been received on a completed application, has paid the annual registration fee, and has attained a grade of at least 70 percent on the National Federation Examination, Part I.

b. Approved.   An official will be classified as Approved if he/she has been registered with the K.H.S.A.A. for one year, has attended the clinic, has paid the annual registration fee, and has attained a grade of at least 80 percent on the National Federation Examination, Part II, for the year in which the Approved rating is requested. The Approved classification is given for one year only and must be earned each year.

c. Certified.   An official will be classified as Certified if he/she has been previously classified as Approved, has attended the clinic, has paid the annual registration fee, has been registered with the K.H.S.A.A. for five years and has attained a grade of at least 90 percent on the National Federation Examination, Part II, for the year in which the Certified rating is requested. After having received the Certified rating, the official shall continue to receive this rating each year upon payment of the registration fee and compliance with all other requirements.[12];

The Kentucky regulations further provide that an official's registration may be cancelled for just cause; assignments shall be accepted as prescribed by the local officials' association; contracts for both officials and schools will be protected; and supplies such as rules books will be furnished by the Commissioner.[13]

Some states utilize a rating system instead of classifying officials. Figure 6–5 explains the details of the rating plan employed in Missouri. The reverse side of the worksheet provides additional spaces for keeping records on officials.

Both the classification and the ratings systems benefit schools in their selection of officials and further benefit those officials whose abilities and efforts warrant recognition.

Fees charged for registration vary from state to state, with the association executive board authorized to establish the amount. They range from approximately five dollars per sport to a maximum of around 20 dollars, determined by the number of sports in which an official registers.

It is a common practice for high school associations to furnish contract forms to their member schools for contracting officials. Several associations

MSHSAA WORKSHEET TO RATE OFFICIALS

SPORT_____YEAR _____

1. Each head coach of *BASEBALL, BASKETBALL, FOOTBALL, SOCCER, SOFTBALL, WRESTLING, and VOLLEYBALL* will maintain an ongoing rating for each official working his/her *SENIOR HIGH VARSITY GAMES* (home and away).

   Schools are required to submit their ratings to renew their membership for the succeeding year. It is recommended that you wait until 24 hours after the game, but no longer than 48 hours to rate officials.

2. The roster of officials includes the officials' number. It will be necessary to include this number on the Report Form.

3. The postmark deadline is included with the Report Form. These will be read by Optic Scanning equipment so it is *imperative that the correct officials' number be recorded.* A $5.00 fine will be assessed the school for late filing.

4. It is suggested that one person be assigned by the head coach to be responsible for keeping the game by game record up to date on the worksheet provided. Then transfer the ratings to the data processing report form.

5. The phases of officiating on which the ratings are based are:

   1) Knowledge of the rules.

   2) Attention to mechanics and details of officiating. (Was uniform proper and neat?)

   3) Care in supervising and signaling fouls and violations. Did he "call them as they occurred" regardless of the situation? Were signals given clearly?

   4) Ability to follow the play or match (hustle or effort exerted). When the play speeded up, did the official exert effort to stay in position to observe the action?

   5) Ability to manage players. Extent to which he maintained control of the game or match. Was he courteous, but firm?

   6) Promptness and business-like attitude in matters pertaining to his contract.

   7) Strictness and consistency in his decisions and interpretations. Were decisions influenced by comments of spectators, players or coaches?

   8) Manner in which decisions were made. Was he prompt and sure in his decisions? Were decisions made firmly, but pleasantly?

   9) Poise and self-control.

6. The rating scheme for officials is as follows:

   1. SUPERIOR: Represents an official who will rank among the first 10% of our officials. Good enough to officiate in a state tournament, match or game.

   2. ABOVE AVERAGE: Represents an official who will rank among the top 30% of our officials. Qualified to work in a district or sectional.

   3. AVERAGE: Competent in some phases, but needs improvement.

   4. BELOW AVERAGE: Is not competent in most phases. Needs considerable improvement.

   5. UNSATISFACTORY.

   NOTE: You are reminded that <u>each</u> official you play under during the season must be rated <u>each</u> time he/she officiates one of your games.

Transfer this Information to the Data Processing Report Form which should be mailed immediately after your last contest. Make sure you have listed every official!

Contest Date	Name of Official	Officials No.	Rating (1-5)	Phases That Need Improvement (1-9)

FIGURE 6–5 Worksheet to rate officials (Missouri)

will not hear a protest of any broken agreement unless there is a contract signed by both parties. All contracts should carry a forfeiture clause. The Ohio official's contract form is an excellent example (see Fig. 6–6). The provision under the Official's Certificate making the official an independent contractor instead of an agent is significant and can help to avoid legal liabilities for the school.

Fees paid officials vary from sport to sport, with the highest being paid in football. They are also determined in various ways. Generally, state associations allow schools and officials to negotiate all fees except those paid

HOME SCHOOL COPY

OHIO HIGH SCHOOL ATHLETIC ASSOCIATION
CONTRACT FOR OFFICIALS

.... OHIO .... ,19. ....

The .... High School and. ....
Official's Name and Address
...., an official Rated with the Ohio High School Athletic Association, hereby

enter into the following agreement: The said official agrees to be present and officiate. ....
Name of Sport
games or meets to be played with .... High School

	Date	Hour	Place	Position	Fee and Expenses
1.					
2.					
3.					

NAMES OF OTHER OFFICIALS: _____

1. If either of the contracting parties fails to fulfill the terms of this contract, except by mutual consent, a forfeiture of the fee stated above shall be paid by the offending party to the other party within five (5) days after the date set for the game in this contract. It is understood that there is a moral obligation as well as a contractual obligation to be considered in making and breaking of contracts. Where moral obligations are not mutually adjusted, the OHSAA reserves the right to review the facts and determine what these adjustments should be. Officials must be mutually agreed upon by both schools.

2. The said school will pay the said official the amount stated above for services rendered, provided that the obligation of the school ceases if and when the official ceases to be a Rated official or if the contest is cancelled because of unfavorable weather, epidemics or other emergencies.

3. The obligation of an official ceases if both teams are not present within 30 minutes of the scheduled starting time unless notified that a team will be late. Officials will be paid as per contract.

4. This contact must be returned no later than _____ or it will become null and void.
Date

Principal _____ Date signed _____ , 19 ____

OFFICIAL'S CERTIFICATE

As a licensed official of the Ohio High School Athletic Association, I acknowledge that when I am employed as an official that I am an independent contractor not an agent. I will administer in an unbiased and non-prejudicial manner all contests in accordance with contest rules and interpretation of rules as well as rules and regulations adopted by the OHSAA or its Board of Control. I further agree to be honest in my association with school administrators and the OHSAA and will not be a party to any attempt to establish officiating fees that other officials must follow. I further ˙gree to honor each contract which I sign and will not request a school to void a contract except for illness, injury or a family emergency beyond my control. My conduct on or off the playing surface will be such as to bring credit to myself, the contestants, coaches and the OHSAA. I understand that failure to honor a contract without just cause or violation of the rules of the OHSAA could result in the suspension or termination of my officiating license.

Official _____ Current Rating No. _____ Date signed _____ ,19 ____

Official's Telephone: Home _____ Business _____

NOTE SEND REMINDER NOTICE TO OFFICIALS ONE WEEK PRIOR TO CONTEST

FIGURE 6–6 Contract for officials (Ohio)

district and state tournament officials. There are officials' associations in virtually all states, and many have established base fees for which their members have agreed to officiate. Some take into account the officials' experience or their classification and the sizes of schools, and have a graduated fee schedule. Lesser amounts are charged for junior varsity and junior high school games. On the other hand, some school conferences set their own pay schedules for officials' services. Although some individual schools may also decide what fees they will pay, they are inclined to be in line with what is paid by other schools. There is less chance of friction between officials and schools when fees are determined by mutual agreement between officials' associations and school conferences. When either group establishes them without consulting the other, ill feeling can result.

The Texas association is unique in that, although it does not establish officials' fees, it has a graduated scale of maximum fees which may be paid individual officials based on gross gate receipts.[14]

Most state associations make no distinction in the regulations for women officials. The same standards apply as apply for men officials, and they attend the same rules meetings in sports in which both boys and girls compete.

Because of the expanded girls' interscholastic athletic program, more capable young women athletes should be encouraged to train to become athletic officials.

Faculty Managers at Contests

It is impossible to place too much importance on adequate faculty management of athletics. Usually this need is realized if the coach is a regular member of the faculty. Under no circumstances should athletic contests be arranged or managed by students without the active direction or supervision of adult faculty managers. Likewise, it should be a definite rule in all schools that a member of the faculty be in attendance at all contests either at home or away. This statement may seem unnecessary, but its importance is indicated by the fact that numerous state athletic associations make such a requirement a part of their by-laws. Of course, student managers and student assistants should be given a place in the program, but administrative duties or responsibility should never be delegated to them. In most states the superintendent or principal is charged with the responsibility of local athletic management. This individual may delegate it to faculty members who then assume immediate responsibility. In the final analysis, however, responsibility in all cases goes back to the school administration. Ohio stresses the fact in this by-law:

> The administrative head of the school shall be held ultimately responsible in all matters pertaining to interscholastic activities involving his or her school.
> The administrative head or some faculty member(s) authorized by him, in addition to the coaches, shall be present throughout all football and basketball contests involving his school. In all other sports the coach or a faculty member shall accompany the team.[15]

The person(s) to whom authority is delegated should be provided a clear outline of his/her responsibilities, and students and followers should be informed of who is in charge.

The fact that some states have laws in regard to the legal liability of school representatives makes it important that the school exercise precaution regardless of whether or not its state association has such a rule.

Protests and Forfeitures

Machinery for hearing protests is provided in virtually all states. In most instances, however, it is recommended that contests be played, even under protest; then evidence upon which the protest is based must be presented in writing, usually within a specified time and in a prescribed manner. This procedure is not universally followed but is in effect in many states. There is a growing tendency to look with disfavor upon protests which are made after contests have been played and lost and which undoubtedly would not have been made had the game been won. Likewise, most states are definite in their dealings with schools that remove their teams from the field or court before the natural conclusion of contests in which they are competing. Such a procedure can hardly be justified educationally.

Most states rule that the use of ineligible players by a school automatically results in forfeiture of the game or games in which such players participate. Usually this action results regardless of the circumstances under which the violation occurred. Most associations consider protests under by-laws similar to that of Illinois:

Penalty for violating rules. Any violation of the rules of the Association shall be reported to the Executive Secretary who shall conduct an investigation as hereinafter provided into all alleged violations of the Constitution and By-laws. The findings of the investigation shall be made known to the school (or schools), person (or persons) alleged to have violated these By-laws. The Board of Directors shall have the final authority to impose penalties . . . expulsion or other penalty deemed appropriate by the Board of Directors.

Forfeiture of contest. The use of any ineligible participant in any interscholastic game or contest shall make the forfeiture of the game or contest automatic, and mandatory if won by the offending school. However, if a participant whose name was omitted from the eligibility certificate due to a clerical error is certified in writing by the principal to have been eligible at the time the eligibility list was exchanged for the contest, the Board of Directors and the Executive Secretary shall have discretionary authority to determine whether a penalty is appropriate and the nature and duration of such penalty. Principals who have certified to a clerical error shall submit a report to the Executive Secretary explaining the circumstances of the error.

Protest Procedure. Any school making a protest shall submit in writing a full statement of facts to the Executive Secretary of the Association . . . who shall transmit a copy of the statement to the principal of the school against which a protest has been made or to the principal, parent, or guardian if such protest pertains to an individual.

Each protest must be accompanied by a deposit of $10.00.

The Board of Directors shall have final authority in determining the outcome of properly filed protests. Should the Board of Directors, after due investigation, decide in favor of the school making the protest, the deposit shall be returned. Should the Board of Directors decide against the school making the protest, the deposit shall become a part of the funds of the Association.

Protest against the decision of a game official shall not be reviewed by the Board of Directors.

Principals should file with the Executive Secretary, on forms provided by the IHSA Office, reports of unsatisfactory performance on the part of game officials, which may be due to alleged lack of knowledge of the rules, errors in judgment, or improper conduct.[16]

Many other states have regulations similar to the example presented above.

The fact that there have been several court cases in recent years related to ineligibility makes it advisable that due process procedures be followed in handling rulings on eligibility (see Chapter 16). A school administrator should always afford athletes and their parents a hearing, when requested, before declaring them ineligible. It is best that a written due process policy be approved by the board of education providing for an appeal to that body when a ruling by the principal is not accepted. Publishing the procedural policy is recommended. Likewise, state associations should have a due process procedure through which a case can be appealed to the executive board. Cases are generally against both the school and the state association. Courts take note of whether due process has been provided. On the other hand, if suit is brought and there is an established appeals procedure, courts are not inclined to assume jurisdiction until all administrative steps have been exhausted. Making sure that due process is provided is very important in any situation where there is any possibility of a court case.

Approval of Meets and Tournaments

In addition to sanctioning interstate meets (see pp. 39–41), state associations generally approve and conduct intrastate invitational meets and tournaments among three or more schools in accord with their own regulations. In some states such meets must be approved by the association's executive officer, while in others there has been a trend toward delegating responsibility to the high school principal of the host school for making certain all high school association standards are upheld. Athletic directors must determine which of the two procedures are employed by their own state association before their school hosts an invitational tournament or meet. Those associations which require approval from the state office will provide forms for this purpose.

Limitation in Number of Contests and Duration of Seasons

Action in the direction of limiting the number of contests or the duration of the season by state athletic associations is becoming general. The thought has persisted in a great many schools that the number of games they should schedule is their own business. During the last few years there has been a tendency to establish limits in the number of contests allowed in all sports. More requests have come to state associations to set up season limits in basketball and football than in the others, because of outside pressure for post-season, interstate championship and so-called bowl, charity, and all-star games. To lessen exploitation of athletes and undue emphasis on a particular sport, many states have set a maximum for the number of games that a school may play and have also limited the time during which its contests may occur. In many states these regulations, as they affect basketball, pertain to the regular season and make allowances for state association-sponsored tournament competition. In football especially, the practice period is often defined in relation to the season. The number of basketball games, exclusive of tournament games, varies among the associations from 16 to 24. In football the range is 8 to 11.[17]

Sports Seasons

A large number of state associations have established definite seasons for all sports, which include a beginning practice date, the date of the first allowable game, and the date that terminates the season, which is usually the last regularly scheduled game. The trend toward establishing definite sports seasons stemmed from common problems faced by individual schools in arranging practice and interschool competition schedules following the expansion of the high school sports program. There is a tendency to provide three seasons (fall, winter, and spring) and to assign each boys' and each girls' sport to one of these seasons. This regulation assists individual schools in planning practice and competition schedules for boys' and girls' teams and alleviates conflicts for athletes participating in more than one sport by eliminating most of the overlapping of seasons.

Although the sports seasons may differ somewhat from state to state, Virginia's sports season rule is a good example:

Sports Season Rule

No member school team shall engage in any athletic practice in any sport prior to the following dates:

(1) Fall Sports: August 10
(2) Winter Sports: November 1
(3) Spring Sports: February 10

and no interscholastic contest shall be played prior to the following dates unless specifically excepted in Sections 34 through 50 of this Handbook:

(4) Fall Sports: September 1
(5) Winter Sports: December 1
(6) Spring Sports: March 10

Note: Each school's sports season ends with its last regularly scheduled game or its last League tournament or play-off contest.[18]

Those state associations which have established uniform sports seasons for their member schools have found it helpful in setting dates for state-sponsored boys' and girls' state meets. Some associations are experimenting with holding them simultaneously at the same sites, but most are held separately. Providing comparable seasons and programs for both sexes is made easier by having fixed sports seasons.

National Federation Rules To Be Observed

Virtually all state associations require the use of rules published by the National Federation for all contests in sports for which such rules are available from that organization. This requirement is particularly important in avoiding controversies in interstate competition.

Mutual Agreements To Violate Rules Prohibited

Although it is generally understood by member schools that they must comply with the rules and regulations of their state associations, occasionally two schools will mutually decide to set aside a certain regulation, in the belief that this is acceptable. The constitutions and by-laws of all state associations contain a provision that member schools must adhere to the regulations and standards of the association. Alabama's is specific and provides the penalty for a violation:

> Mutual agreements to violate the rules of the Association shall result in the suspension of all schools concerned.[19]

SPECIAL CONTEST ADMINISTRATIVE REGULATIONS

Some special regulations have been adopted by state associations that are not universal but have been considered necessary in the best interests of the interscholastic program and to the boys and girls participating in it. The following are typical of some adopted by the states mentioned and by others.

Conduct of Players

All states have rules governing sportsmanship of players. Florida's rule pertaining to the conduct of players during games is one of the more specific:

> Unsportsmanlike Conduct: A student who strikes, curses, or threatens an official during a game or at any other time because of resentment over occurrences or decisions during a game, or who fails to maintain a standard of conduct satisfactory to the principal of the school he/she attends and the Florida High School Activities Association, shall be ineligible to participate in interscholastic athletics for a period of six weeks. The Executive Secretary, or the Executive Committee on appeal, may restore his/her eligibility prior to the expiration of the six weeks when in his/their opinion the student has been properly disciplined by the authorities of the school which he/she attends and the student signs a written statement of his/her intention to comply with the sportsmanlike rule in the future.[20]

Conduct of Coaches

A number of states also have regulations that apply to the conduct of coaches and that assess penalties for unsportsmanlike actions. These penalties may also extend to the school which employs such a person to coach. Alabama's regulation is typical:

> A coach proved guilty of immoral or unsportsmanlike conduct may be disqualified by the Central Board of Control. Any school using a disqualified coach shall be subject to suspension from the Association.[21]

Missouri has a specific provision applying to a coach's withdrawal of a team from a game:

> Any school whose coach removes a team from play in protest may be required to appear before the Board at its next meeting to show reason why the school shall not be suspended.[22]

The character of coaches and their conduct at athletic contests have a great influence upon the attitudes and ideals of players and team followers and often "set the tone" for the sportsmanship exhibited at games. The athletic administrator should counsel his/her coaches regarding the significant position they occupy at athletic contests, which can either contribute to or detract from the values of interscholastic games.

Conduct of Team Followers

Several states have rules that make the home school responsible for the conduct of the crowd. Several others insist that a team is responsible for its followers wherever it plays.

Tennessee fixes the responsibility in the following manner:

> Visiting teams shall be accompanied by the principal or someone designated by him or her.
> All games shall be properly supervised and policed to insure a sportsmanlike contest. The host school shall be responsible for providing a sufficient number of policemen to insure orderly conduct on the part of all spectators. If the game is played on a neutral field and neither team is designated as the host team, the competing schools shall share the responsibility of providing sufficient police protection.
> Member schools are responsible for the conduct of their own fans and students at every athletic contest, regardless of where it may be held.
> The coach and principal of each of the schools participating in an athletic contest shall file a report immediately with the state office if there is any unusual incident involving poor sportsmanship, during or following the game, on the part of players, coaches, school administrators, game officials or spectators.[23]

No Sunday or Christmas Day Games

Many state associations have no specific regulation regarding playing games on Sunday, primarily because their schools refrain from scheduling games on this day. A few associations, however, have experienced some problems and have a specific regulation prohibiting Sunday games, while another few have some schools playing them.

Likewise, there are no restrictions in most associations' rules related to holidays. Thanksgiving Day football games at one time were practically a tradition in most communities, but this practice has all but disappeared. A few associations do have a definite regulation prohbiting athletic contests on Christmas Day.

Holidays should be "family days" and schools should avoid interfering with activities in the homes of their students on these days.

Midweek Contests

Steps have been taken by schools, both unilaterally and collectively through their state associations, to avoid unnecessary interference by athletic activities with the academic program of students and with preparation for their class work. Some associations set limits on the number of games which may be played during a calendar week, and all of them encourage member schools to limit the number of midweek contests. The Ohio association has been a leader in this area as evidenced by its regulation:

> Schools engaging in interscholastic contests on a night preceding a day of school should abide by the applicable State Department of Education Minimum Standard.*
>
> *The current standard states: "An activity or preparation for an activity does not ordinarily involve the presence of students after 9:00 P.M. on an evening preceding a school day."[24]

Elimination of Interschool Boxing

A Michigan regulation that became effective in 1938 states:

> There shall be no interscholastic competition in boxing.[25]

This rule was originally adopted and is currently operative in most states because of difficulties that appeared inevitable if such action were not taken. Boxing ceased to be a sport of skill and became one of combat, in which punishment of one of the contestants was necessary in order that the other might win. Difficulties also have been encountered in teaching and officiating the activity and at the same time keeping educational objectives in mind. Many communities have had too keen an interest in boxing as an interschool activity. Michigan was the first state association to specifically eliminate boxing from the interscholastic athletic program and was prompted in its action by the resolution adopted by the Society of State Directors of Physical and Health Education at its Twelfth Annual Meeting held at Atlanta, Georgia, April 19, 1938, and reaffirmed at its St. Louis meeting, April 6–9, 1946, as follows (this was the first resolution of its kind):

> WHEREAS, There seems to be an increasing tendency to promote interscholastic boxing in some communities and on the part of some individuals; and
> WHEREAS, The activity on such a highly competitive basis is known to be potentially dangerous to the welfare of boys participating; and
> WHEREAS, The Society of State Directors of Health and Physical Education desires to strengthen its resolution regarding interscholastic boxing adopted on April 19, 1938;
> BE IT THEREFORE RESOLVED, That the Society of State Directors of Physical and Health Education again disavow all intention to give support to this development and again recommend that school officials in positions to control boxing matches between school teams eliminate this activity from their athletic programs.
> BE IT FURTHER RESOLVED, That this Society again encourage the National Federation of High School Athletic Associations to establish an official policy disapproving boxing as an interscholastic sport.

Girls Allowed to Compete on Boys' Teams

The Civil Rights Acts of 1972 and subsequent court decisions (see Chapter 16) have made it clear that schools must provide comparable athletic opportunities for boys and girls. Some states have amended their regulations to allow girls to compete on boys' teams when a school does not provide comparable opportunities for girls. A few have removed all restrictions and permit girls to play on any boys' teams if they have the talent and physical ability to make the squad. The Missouri regulation is typical of those of most associations:

> A school at its own discretion may allow a student to compete on a team with the opposite sex in baseball, cross country, golf, gymnastics, soccer, softball, swimming, tennis, track, or volleyball, provided the school does not offer interscholastic competition for both sexes in that sport.[26]

Girls are not generally allowed to compete on both boys' and girls' teams, which, if allowed, could be considered discriminatory unless the same privilege is allowed all students.

Various high school associations may have other special regulations unique to their state. It cannot be stressed too strongly that all athletic administrators and coaches must be thoroughly familiar with the standards and regulations of their respective state high school associations.

CONTEST REGULATIONS FOR JUNIOR HIGH SCHOOL

It was common in the early stages of high school associations that their memberships were comprised primarily of senior high schools. Junior high schools as organized units hardly existed. Along with the proliferation of these intermediate schools came junior high interscholastic competition and the need for rules and regulations to control it. Today nearly all state associations include both junior and senior high schools, or grades 7 through 12 and any combination thereof. Because of the ages involved and some differences in the philosophy and objectives of junior and senior high school athletics, modifications are found in contest regulations for junior high schools.

Junior high school athletics will be discussed in Chapter 15. All we shall do here, then, is to list and make brief statements about the most prevalent modified regulations.

1. *There is an upper age limit for contestants, providing a student usually shall become ineligible for junior high school competition upon reaching the age of 16.* The purpose of ths standard is to protect the physical welfare of younger athletes whose maturity levels vary more in junior high school. In most states students who reach the age of 16 are allowed to compete on the senior high school team in their districts.

2. *Competition is usually limited to the first two semesters a student is enrolled in grades 7, 8, and 9.* Students repeating a grade are not eligible in most states.

3. *Shorter sports seasons are established.*

4. *Fewer contests are permitted.* The most common limitations are six games in football and 12 in basketball and other sports. Several associations differentiate the number allowed for seventh-, eighth-, and ninth-grade teams.

5. *The length of quarters is shortened for junior high school games and distances lessened in track and field.* Again, these may be differentiated by grade levels.

6. *Junior high students are generally limited to playing on only one team during each season.* This regulation exists because many junior high schools will have a seventh-, an eighth-, and a ninth-grade team. Often students will play on a team a grade higher than the grade in which they are enrolled; they are then limited to the higher grade team.

7. *State associations encourage schools to schedule junior high games in the afternoon following the dismissal of school.* Some have included such a recommendation in their by-laws.

Other less common junior high school contest regulations have been adopted by various associations. All are for the purpose of making athletic competition more appropriate for the age and maturity levels of the students.

SUMMARY

This summary presents a few brief statements regarding each of the contest regulations discussed in this chapter. They are not necessarily conclusions but rather attempts to show some of the actual common practices.

Contracts for athletic contests. Most state athletic associations supply contract forms and will not be concerned with disputes between schools involving contract violations unless standard contract forms were properly executed. Written contracts, properly signed by authorized school officials, should be in existence for all interscholastic athletic contests.

Eligibility list procedures. Virtually all states have some plan for the exchange of lists of eligible players prior to contests. This varies from a formal letter in one state sent by one school principal to the other listing eligible players for a game, to plans in other states for the preparation of complete scholastic and athletic data on all contestants, which are exchanged prior to each contest. In some states schools send complete data to each school in the conference at the start of the season, with a supplementary list being sent later carrying names of eligible players only. In a few states, only the latter lists are sent. In many states data on all contestants is sent to the state association office, either at the start or the end of the season.

Records of transfer students. Such records usually are one of two types: (1) a combination scholastic and athletic blank, or (2) a strictly athletic record blank with only such scholastic information as is necessary to determine athletic eligibility. It is usual for state athletic associations to furnish transfer blanks, thus providing a common procedure for recording and forwarding athletic and scholastic information regarding students who transfer from one school to another.

Certification of athletic coaches. It is an almost universal regulation that only faculty members who receive their pay from public school funds may be engaged as athletic coaches. Usually, they must be regularly certified teachers with specified teaching loads in addition to coaching duties.

Registration of athletic officials.   Nearly one-half of the states require that athletic officials in designated sports be registered with their state associations for the current year in order to be eligible to officiate in high school games. Usually, there are different classifications of officials, depending upon a number of factors, including ratings from schools, experience, examination grades, attendance at rules meetings, and the like.

Faculty managers at contests.   Regulations providing for faculty managers at contests are desirable. They have been incorporated in the by-laws of a majority of state athletic associations. Responsibility for the athletic program rests with the school administration, although phases of it are delegated to faculty managers. Student management always should be under the supervision of faculty managers.

Protests and forfeitures.   A number of states outline protest procedures definitively. Protests must usually be in writing and be made within a specified time. It should be kept in mind, however, that the state association executive body always has the right to make investigations of alleged violations, even though no formal protest has been filed. In almost all states the use of ineligible players by a school automatically results in forfeiture of all games in which such contestants participated.

Approval of meets and tournaments.   When three or more schools compete in an ahtletic event, it is common practice in most states to require that there be state association approval of it. This procedure is designed to ensure that regulations will be in effect which are comparable to those under which regular state association events are conducted. Thus, competing and entertaining schools, as well as contestants, are protected to an extent greater than otherwise might be the case.

Limitation in number of contests and duration of seasons.   There is a definite trend among state associations to limit the number of contests permitted in most sports and to establish specific practice and playing seasons.

Special contest rules.   The following matters are subjects of special attention found in the by-laws of one or more state high school associations:

1. Conduct of players
2. Conduct of coaches
3. Conduct of team followers
4. No Sunday or Christmas day games
5. Midweek contests
6. Elimination of interschool boxing
7. Girls allowed to compete on boys' teams
8. Modifications for junior high school athletic contests

QUESTIONS AND TOPICS FOR STUDY AND DISCUSSION

1. Of what importance are state association contest regulations to individual schools? How do they differ from eligibility requirements?

2. Why are contracts for athletic contests important?

3. Of what value is the exchange of eligibility lists? Of what interest are they to coaches?

4. What are the purposes of transfer of eligibility forms? How do they prevent eligibility problems for schools?

5. What is the common requirement for high school coaches? Under what circumstances is this requirement sometimes waived? Give arguments for and against requiring a special coaching certificate for all coaches and assistant coaches.

6. Discuss the importance of plans in effect in various states concerning registration and classification of officials. Of what value are they to local schools?

7. Why should principals or their designated representatives be present at all interscholastic games? What should be their responsibilities?

8. What are some of the established procedures for filing protests which are contained in high school association by-laws? When should a protest be filed? What protests generally are not heard by association executive boards?

9. Why do some state associations require approval of all meets and tournaments?

10. What are the reasons for limiting seasons and the number of games for various sports? Assuming you are the athletic director of a particular school of your choice, outline the sports seasons you would recommend for the sports under your supervision.

11. List several special contest and administrative regulations indicated in this chapter and give reasons for them. Why do some states have special regulations not generally found in other states?

12. Why are contest regulations modified for junior high school interscholastic athletic competition? Explain some of the most common modifications.

13. Should girls be allowed to compete on boys' teams? Why?

NOTES

1. Pennsylvania Interscholastic Athletic Association, *1980–81 PIAA Handbook*, p. 6.

2. Indiana High School Athletic Association, Inc., *1980–81 By-Laws and Articles of Incorporation*, p. 23.

3. New Jersey State Interscholastic Athletic Association, *1981–82 Constitution, By-Laws, and Rules and Regulations*, p. 39.

4. Michigan High School Athletic Association, *1979–80 Handbook*, p. 41.

5. Pennsylvania Interscholastic Athletic Association, *1980–81 PIAA Handbook*, p. 14.

6. Michigan High School Athletic Association, *1979–80 Handbook*, p. 41.

7. Iowa High School Athletic Association, *1980–81 Constitution and By-Laws*, p. 49.

8. Ohio High School Athletic Association, *1981–82 Constitution and By-Laws*, p. 30.

9. Tennessee Secondary School Athletic Association, *1981–82 Official Handbook*, p. 16.

10. Wisconsin Interscholastic Athletic Association, *1980–81 WIAA Handbook*, p. 21.
11. Illinois High School Association, *1981–82 Official Handbook*, p. 13.
12. Kentucky High School Athletic Association, *1979–80 Constitution, By-Laws and Tournament Rules*, pp. 24–25.
13. Ibid., pp. 25–26.
14. University Interscholastic League (Texas), *Constitution and Contest Rules for 1981–82*, pp. 147–49.
15. Ohio High School Athletic Association, *1981–82 Constitution and By-Laws*, p. 21.
16. Illinois High School Association, *1981–82 Official Handbook*, pp. 28–29.
17. National Federation of State High School Associations, *1982–83 Handbook* (Kansas City, Mo.: National Federation, 1983), p. 73.
18. Virginia High School League, Inc., *1981–82 Handbook*, p. 47.
19. Alabama High School Athletic Association, *1981–82 Handbook*, p. 73.
20. Florida High School Activities Association, *1981 By-Laws*, pp. 31–32.
21. Alabama High School Athletic Association, *1981–82 Handbook*, p. 72.
22. Missouri State High School Activities Association, *1982–83 Official Handbook*, p. 30.
23. Tennessee Secondary School Athletic Association, *1981–82 Official Handbook*, p. 20.
24. Ohio High School Athletic Association, *1981–82 Constitution and By-Laws*, p. 34.
25. Michigan High School Athletic Association, *1979–80 Handbook*, p. 46.
26. Missouri State High School Activities Association, *1982–83 Official Handbook*, p. 27.

BIBLIOGRAPHY

ADAMS, SAM. "Coaching Certfication Based on Competencies." *Interscholastic Athletic Administration*, 6, no. 4 (Summer 1980), 19–20, 30.

ALABAMA HIGH SCHOOL ATHLETIC ASSOCIATION. *1981–82 Handbook*, pp. 72–73.

FLORIDA HIGH SCHOOL ACTIVITIES ASSOCIATION. *1981 By-Laws*, pp. 31–32.

ILLINOIS HIGH SCHOOL ASSOCIATION. *1980–81 Official Handbook*, pp. 13, 28–29.

INDIANA HIGH SCHOOL ATHLETIC ASSOCIATION, INC. *1980–81 By-Laws and Articles of Incorporation*, p. 23.

IOWA HIGH SCHOOL ATHLETIC ASSOCIATION. *1980–81 Constitution and By-Laws*, p. 49.

KENTUCKY HIGH SCHOOL ATHLETIC ASSOCIATION. *1979–80 Constitution, By-Laws, and Tournament Rules*, pp. 24–26.

MAETOZO, MATTHEW G., ed. "A Survey of Special Certification Requirements for Athletic Coaches of High School Interscholastic Teams." *Journal of Health, Physical Education, and Recreation*, 41, no. 7 (September 1970), 14, 16.

MICHIGAN HIGH SCHOOL ATHLETIC ASSOCIATION, INC. *1979–80 Handbook*, pp. 41, 46.

MISSOURI STATE HIGH SCHOOL ACTIVITIES ASSOCIATION. *1982–83 Official Handbook*, p. 30.

NATIONAL FEDERATION OF STATE HIGH SCHOOL ASSOCIATIONS. *1982–83 Handbook*. Kansas City, Mo.: National Federation, 1983, p. 73.

NEW JERSEY STATE INTERSCHOLASTIC ATHLETIC ASSOCIATION. *1981–82 Constitution and By-Laws*, pp. 21, 30, 34.

PENNSYLVANIA INTERSCHOLASTIC ATHLETIC ASSOCIATION. *1980–81 PIAA Handbook*, pp. 6, 14.

TENNESSEE SECONDARY SCHOOL ATHLETIC ASSOCIATION. *1981–82 Official Handbook*, pp. 16, 20.

UNIVERSITY INTERSCHOLASTIC LEAGUE (TEXAS). *Constitution and Contest Rules for 1981–82*, pp. 147–49.

VIRGINIA HIGH SCHOOL LEAGUE, INC. *1981–82 Handbook*, p. 47.

WISCONSIN INTERSCHOLASTIC ATHLETIC ASSOCIATION. *1980–81 WIAA Handbook*, p. 21.

7

Athletic Contest Management

The management of a school's athletic contests may be the barometer which indicates the administrative efficiency of its entire interscholastic athletic program. Observers are inclined frequently to judge a school by the manner in which these events are administered, and efficient management builds respect for the school. Poor management, even of seemingly minor details, lessens the educational value of athletic events for both players and student spectators. Since public support through gate receipts is needed to help finance the athletic program, it is important that contests be managed so as to encourage attendance. It therefore behooves high school educators to establish and conduct their interscholastic programs so they will command the respect of the public and gain its support. The key person in this process is the athletic administrator. He or she, more than anyone else, will determine the quality of the school's athletic administration, which in turn will be a measure of his/her administrative capabilities.

We shall make no attempt in this chapter to discuss the numerous details involved in administering specific sports, all of which can be found in the various rules books and accompanying manuals published by the National Federation. The discussions which follow will concern those matters that are common to proper management of all high school sports events.

IMPORTANCE OF EFFICIENT MANAGEMENT

Well-managed contests. The well-patronized, successful enterprises in any community usually are those which are well organized and efficiently managed. Every athletic contest should be handled in such a manner. Of course, the interest and welfare of student participants and student spectators must receive first consideration. We must not forget that athletic games are provided to offer educational experiences to supplement those found in the classroom. Following the educational value, however, is the entertainment value to the public. Team followers are interested in the diversion athletic games provide, and good contest management will add to their enjoyment. This should in no way conflict with the school's interscholastic athletic objectives, especially if proper effort has been exerted to make the public aware of the educational goals of its athletic program. Educators must try (1) to make athletic games community events, which will enhance the school's role in the community; and (2) make the athletic contest businesslike, attractive, and a well-organized sports event. The public will recognize it as such, and its educational and good-sportsmanship implications will be primary achievements almost to be taken for granted. In many instances, the reputation of a school may be measured by the manner in which its athletic contests are conducted. Certainly the importance attached to such events offers an opportunity to establish the good name of the school in a community, which should not be overlooked by educators.

Size of school.   The size of the school and the extent of its athletic program make absolutely no difference in the importance of management of contests. Small schools have smaller squads, smaller student bodies, and smaller communities from which to draw adult crowds. The necessity for efficient management, however, is just as great as for the largest city schools. Games can start on time in these schools, crowds can be controlled, and squads can be neatly uniformed and competently coached just as well as in large city schools. Both students and adults in small communities will be as appreciative—if educated to an experience of this kind—as will those who attend larger school contests.

In the attention given to details of management of athletic contests, it will be assumed that schools of different sizes will consider only those items which are applicable to themselves. Naturally, some matters to be discussed will not be of interest or concern to small schools. For example, publicity is not an important matter in connection with small-school athletic contests. An announcement made in the school assembly will reach virtually all the patrons and followers of teams in a village school. This is not true in larger schools. Thus, for them a publicity program is important in order that details of a given contest may be known to those who are interested in it.

Responsibility.   No attempt will be made here to designate every individual responsible for certain details, which will be assigned according to the organization in the school itself. In some schools the superintendent may serve; in others, the principal or athletic director. Often the coach or a student manager will have particular jobs to perform. These persons should be kept in mind when considering the suggestions offered, because plans for administering athletic programs differ to such an extent in schools of various sizes. The specialized function of coaching is not discussed here as an administrative function. That the team will be trained and instructed to the best of the coach's ability is taken for granted.

Phases of contest management.   The other matters to be discussed are those additional to the actual handling of the team at the time of the game or contest. Contest management for home games will be considered under three headings: (1) before-game preparation; (2) game responsibilities; (3) after-game responsibilities. Management details for out-of-town games are discussed separately. The last part of this section will deal with general management items which must receive attention during the course of the year. No attempt has been made to list topics in chronological order. Their importance will vary in different schools, depending upon the individual(s) who are assigned definite responsibilities in the athletic program, but they will serve as a checklist of reminders. It is recognized, of course, that some management details may have been omitted, again because of variations in local situations.

BEFORE-GAME PREPARATION (HOME CONTESTS)

Well-managed athletic contests are not the result of accident. Attending well in advance to all the details pertaining to a home game is evidence of efficient administration and of good planning. It should be possible, in most instances, to have the following items ready well before the rush of last-minute details.

Contracts.   Complete check should be made of dates and days appearing on contracts. When a game is scheduled for Friday, February 10, be sure that February 10 actually is a Friday. Both the date and day should appear on the contract. If contracts are made for two or more years, write in actual days and dates for games each year and not "Return game on corresponding date next year," which is bound to lead to confusion and misunderstanding. Contracts should be typewritten in duplicate and signed in all places indicated. Many state associations require that their standard contracts be used for all games, including league schedules. Discrepancies in a contract should be made known to the other school immediately upon discovery. Have a regular filing place for all athletic contracts, so that they will be available at the time of contests (refer back to Fig. 6–1).

Athletics officials.   The host school is generally responsible for engaging the game officials. This is usually done by contacting available officials directly or securing them through an officials' association. Conference secretaries are sometimes delegated this duty. Regardless of the method, it is important that both schools agree on the officials to be used. Some state associations have regulations requiring such a procedure. Special forms are an aid in getting approval from visiting schools (refer back to Fig. 6–2). Be certain that the officials are registered for the current year. They should be engaged by contract, made out in duplicate, signed, with the school and official each keeping a copy. Schools should keep such contracts filed in a regular place, and those involving officials for a particular game should be accessible at that time. Some schools have found it convenient to place game contracts, eligibility lists, and officials' contracts in a large envelope for each game and to file them in this manner. Arrangements should be made to pay officials immediately following games.

Physical examinations.   Practically all state associations require a physical examination before a contestant can be considered eligible. The record of an athlete's examination should be on file before a contestant can be considered eligible. In fact, for the protection of the coach and school from any liability, it should be on file before he or she is permitted even to participate in practice. Allowing an athlete to engage in practice or competition without it could be a matter of negligence if a court suit were brought in case of a serious injury (refer back to Fig. 5–1).

Parents' permission.   It is a good policy to secure parents' permission for all contestants. Such procedure clarifies athletic injury policies and aids in preventing problems for schools and coaches. Permission cards should be on file before a student is allowed to report for practice. Report the filing of parents' permission cards to your state association if such is required (refer back to Fig. 5–1).

Athlete's application to participate.   Requiring an athlete to make application for permission to participate helps to ensure that this individual understands both the standards of eligibility that he or she must meet and the school policies (refer back to Fig. 5–2).

Eligibility records.   If a list of students eligible to participate in the approaching contest is required from the visiting school, check to see that it has been received. Be certain that the eligibility list of the home school has been sent in accordance with state association regulations. The coach should have a copy of the eligibility list in order that there may be no misunderstanding regarding those who are eligible for a particular game. Eligibility lists of both schools should be at hand for possible reference at the time of a game (refer back to Fig. 6–3).

Methods of securing current eligibility data vary in schools. In some cases a list of all candidates for teams is kept in the school office, to which teachers come on a designated day and check students in their classes for eligibility for athletics. In others, teachers are given a list of athletes in their classes. They mark this list and return it to the office or faculty chairman of eligibility. Still another plan is that of having each athlete, on eligibility-marking day, take to all his or her classes a special eligibility card which the teachers sign, indicating the student's eligibility or ineligibility in each subject. Athletes absent on this day are checked by student managers, who take the cards of the absentees to the teachers concerned.

Claims are made for the value of each scheme. Local conditions, size of school, and precedents are undoubtedly the determining factors. Apparently the most generally efficient plan is that which places in the hands of each teacher a list of students in his or her class who are candidates for an athletic team. The teacher then may mark the list and note ineligible students or those whose work is of such low grade that ineligibility at the next marking period is inevitable unless there is a change in attitude or accomplishment. Students should be warned before they are marked ineligible.

Equipment. Personal playing equipment usually furnished by the school will be discussed in Chapter 10. In this discussion, equipment includes whatever is necessary, in addition to uniforms, for playing the contest. Each school official charged with the responsibility for having all items on hand for a game should have his or her own checklist. Often a student manager may be delegated to take care of these details. They are important factors in efficient management.

Field or court. Unusual locations or temporary circumstances may make special arrangements necessary concerning fields or courts where contests are to be held. Confirm all such arrangements in writing in order that misunderstandings may be obviated. Be sure that the visiting school is fully informed regarding any such changes in plans. If a game or meet is to be held at another school, rather than at the host school, be certain that all details are thoroughly understood by the administration of the school concerned. Athletic directors and coaches, especially, should be certain that the complete schedules of athletic events or special athletic functions are in the hands of the principal or superintendent so there will be no conflicts in assignments to gymnasiums, fields, or other facilities on specific dates.

Publicity. The regular and accepted means of publicizing athletic events of a school should be followed. The extent of the advertising will depend on school policy, seating capacity, and interest in the game on the part of student body and adults. The news-releasing agency should be either the coach, athletic director, or principal, as they may agree among themselves. Paid advertisements in newspapers may be advisable in some instances. Radio "spots" and theater notices are other advertising mediums. Since the athletic program should give first consideration to the students themselves, they should be made as familiar as possible with it. Athletic assemblies offer this opportunity. This does not mean that student interest should be fanned to a white heat prior to each game. One or two athletic assemblies during each season will provide a means by which the student body may be educated to the objectives of the athletic program and school athletic policies. Standards of conduct and sportsmanship should be explained. Sections in the game rules and in state association by-laws applying to sportsmanship should be reviewed. The following program suggestions will also help to provide interesting assemblies:

> Analysis of plays and demonstration football games are the basis of a football assembly. The entire student body should be seated in the bleachers. Cheerleaders should be on hand for the game. A public address system should be used.
>
> Two full teams should be dressed and used for demonstration purposes. An off-tackle play, a reverse, a punt and a simple forward pass could be analyzed. After an explanation, each boy should do his part separately in slow motion. Then the whole eleven may execute the play together.
>
> The student body will soon realize that there are other players on the team besides the ball carrier, the quarterback, and the forward pass receiver. The value of tackles, guards, and blocking backs can be impressed upon them. In the game that follows, common fouls may be explained and then demonstrated by specific individuals.
>
> In such an assembly students are made acquainted with the personnel of their team and the details of executing a few simple plays.

Similar assemblies in track and basketball have been held in high schools, which stress the following points: Assemblies must be thoroughly planned in order to carry out their purpose. They must be simple and they must be explained. They should be short and well executed. Since a great amount of adult interest in high school athletics is stimulated by the interest and enthusiasm of a son or daughter, it is apparent that school athletic assemblies may be good means of publicity as well as good educational media. Some schools have held public clinics in various sports for students and adults, usually before the first game of the season.

Courtesies to the visiting school. The visiting school should be written to a week or ten days prior to a contest and advised concerning the location, time, date, and officials for the game. It is important to be sure that the visiting school has all the necessary data regarding the game. It should be advised concerning admission prices for students and adults, number of complimentary passes it is to receive, and arrangements for its band if it is to be brought to the game. Exact directions as to the dressing place for the visiting team should be sent.

Reserve games. If a reserve game is to precede or follow a varsity team game, complete arrangements should be made for it. Many schools find it more convenient to play outdoor reserve games on dates other than those on which

CENTRAL HIGH SCHOOL

BASKETBALL GAME COURTESY INFORMATION

Central High School vs _____

Date of game _____ Place _____

Time: _____   _____
           (Junior Varsity Game)   (Varsity Game)

Officials: Junior Varsity Game   Varsity Game

          _____   _____

          _____   _____

Color of home team jerseys: Junior Varsity _____

                              Varsity _____

Ball to be used _____

Space will be reserved for your team and pep club buses at _____

_____

Our gymnasium will open at _____ o'clock.

_____ will guide your team to its dressing room.
(Name of student)

_____ will greet your pep club.
(Cheerleader)

Admission: Students $_____ Adults $_____

Please send me the names and numbers of your players for inclusion
in our program and contact me for any further information.

Signed_____
        (Athletic Administrator)

Date _____

FIGURE 7–1   Suggested courtesy information form

varsity or first-team games are held, especially if fields are likely to be in poor condition for main games. Where schools are in the same or nearby cities such reserve-team games usually can be played without interference with school time. Arrangements should be definite for such games, good officials should be secured, and participants should be properly equipped. Precautions against injuries should be just as definite, or even more so, in these games as in any others, because the participants usually are less experienced. If two games are held the same afternoon or evening, they both should be started on time as announced and advertised.

Tickets. If special, season, or complimentary tickets are to be prepared and distributed, do it early. Tickets should be distinctive but not necessarily expensive. Have a definite method of charging them out to any students who serve as salespersons. Insist on businesslike methods in handling this and all financial matters pertaining to tickets. This point is of particular importance because, in some instances, state admissions tax reports must be prepared. If agreement has been made accordingly, make sure that the visiting school has an available supply of tickets for advance sale to its student body. Keep duplicate records of all ticket releases and sales. Have a definite policy in effect regarding complimentary tickets. The athletic council or board of control usually can remove considerable pressure for complimentary tickets by adopting a list of persons entitled to them and then adhering strictly to this list. In most cases those who make themselves nuisances in seeking complimentary tickets are not entitled to them, and athletic council action can provide a legitimate reason for not granting them. Adequate provision should be made for the selling and taking of tickets at the contest. Adults should usually serve in these capacities.

Contest programs. In general, an athletic contest is raised to a higher level if a simple, informative program can be placed in the hands of spectators. A program nine-tenths of which is advertising does not accomplish this purpose. It is far more important to include statements which explain the school's philosophy and objectives of interscholastics and sportsmanship standards. Names and numbers of players and the names of the coaches provide information spectators desire. A few major game rules interpretations can be included. If a small amount of legitimate advertising is necessary, there should be no objection to it. Sometimes ill will is engendered in advertisers if they are continually asked to contribute to school athletic progams more than the advertising is worth. The type of contest and the interest taken in it, as well as the size of the community, are determining factors in the furnishing of programs. In most instances they should be sold. Reliable, trustworthy students can be assigned to distribute them.

Concessions. Concessions can be a source of revenue for a school's athletic program. If city or board of health permits for such concessions are necessary, they should be arranged for in sufficient time prior to the season or contest. Uniformed vendors add to the neatness and appearance of the project. If the concession rights are sold to a club or commercial firm, the high school should know what is to be offered for sale and the methods to be employed. Many schools find that local high school clubs or student organizations are glad to take charge of the concessions. Usually such organizations are worthy ones, and often they perform services for the athletic department that more than offset what might be realized from concession sales if they were handled by the school itself. Regardless of the method of handling the concessions, the athletic administrator should insist on sanitation, neatness, and the employment of businesslike methods.

Ushers.   Ushers are valuable adjuncts at an athletic contest. They not only assist the paying public to find their places in the stadium, gymnasium, or bleachers, but also actually help to enforce laws and rules. Definite arrangements for ushers should be made for all contests where a stadium or bleachers are used. They need not necessarily be uniformed, but they should have some distinctive apparel, badge, or button as identification. Students may be delegated and trained in ushering, and they can do much to maintain a high level of conduct at athletic contests. Some schools use varsity lettermen in sweaters as ushers. Others use Boy Scouts, girl reserves, or boys and girls from other uniformed organizations for ushering. Some recognition should be given to ushers. This may be made in the form of school letter awards, invitation to the athletic banquet for the sport, formation of an ushers' club, or the like.

Police protection and parking.   As public servants, city and state police should be used at athletic contests for handling crowds, directing traffic, and parking. Most local police departments are willing to detail special officers for duty at a high school game. Some schools feel that the presence of an officer at their contests is an indictment against them. This is not true. Law enforcement officers are present at all large gatherings, and their presence may be defended because of the possibility of an emergency which might arise. In too many instances school officials have not taken advantage of this public service, which is usually theirs for the asking. The presence of a uniformed officer also adds dignity to a contest and provides a method for enforcing local regulations regarding conduct of spectators and sportsmanship at contests. When an individual buys a ticket for a high school athletic contest, it should be with the understanding that he or she may, under certain circumstances, be asked to leave the stadium, field, or gymnasium. The management reserves the right to refund the purchase price of the ticket and, with the aid of an officer of the law if necessary, to eject an unruly spectator whose conduct is not in accordance with established standards. An occasional justified ejection has a wholesome effect on the general conduct of the crowd. For this reason, if for no other, the presence of uniformed officers at high school athletic contests is justified. It is advisable that law enforcement officials designate one officer to be in charge of other officers and to whom the athletic director should report any crowd control problems needing attention.

Reserved areas. If the stadium or bleachers are to have reserved sections, these should be plainly marked and roped off or guarded. When a patron buys a reserved seat, he or she is entitled to it and should also be free from abuse of molesting students. Adults sometimes hesitate to attend high school games because of the rowdyism of younger students which occasionally occurs. Reserved areas for bands, parking, or players' spaces should be provided and plainly designated prior to the game.

Cheerleaders. Well-uniformed and courteous cheerleaders can do a great deal to keep the crowd in the right frame of mind. Considerable attention ought to be given to the selection of cheerleaders, who can be sportsmanship leaders as well. Their big job should be that of securing recognition of outstanding plays and examples of good sportsmanship on the part of both teams, and of aiding the school and game officials as the contest progresses. They may also help much in maintaining proper order, and in assisting ushers and officers. A school letter award should be granted to cheerleaders who do the right kind of job.

Scoreboards. Scoreboards are almost essential pieces of equipment in modern high school athletic contests. Some excellent electric types are on the market, but these are not a necessity. Usually it is sufficient to have a device that shows the score of each team and the quarter, inning, or amount of time remaining to be played in the period. Definite arrangements should be made to have one or two students manage the scoreboard regularly.

Condition of stadium, bleachers, or gymnasium. Upkeep of facilities should be a janitorial rather than an administrative duty. However, some members of the athletic staff may have to see that these facilities are in proper order for a contest. The stadium and bleachers should be clean. Out-of-date notices and paper and other debris should be removed. Rest rooms should be fully equipped, sanitary, and readily available. Temperature controls for indoor games should be inspected and regulated so that they are working properly at the time of the contest. Be sure that temporary bleachers have been properly inspected by authorized officials to ensure their safety.

Bands and half-time arrangements. If bands are to be present at a game, make certain that reserved seats are provided for them in the bleachers or stadium or on the field. Advise each band of the amount of time it will have for maneuvers between halves. If a flag-raising ceremony is to precede the game, make arrangements for all details and advise band directors accordingly. At football games especially, the local school band often can be of service in protecting the playing field from encroachment by spectators, which sometimes occurs near the end of the game if the field is not well roped off. The members should be instructed concerning this service and made to realize that spectators will respect their uniforms. Band directors should be cautioned that they must adhere to time limits to avoid any delay of game. Students must not be permitted to use musical instruments and noisemakers during contests.

Decorations.   If the field or gymnasium is to be decorated for the contest, include the color schemes of both schools. Be sure that the decorations do not interfere with the playing facilities. Crossbars of goal posts or basketball backboards never should be decorated or marked in any manner. Offensive posters or banners should be prohibited. It is generally wise to exclude all but official school banners. Other types often serve as a source of trouble and contribute nothing to the most worthwhile objectives of interscholastic athletics.

Public address system.   Some schools own their public address or loudspeaker systems. Often they may be used to advantage at athletic contests, outdoor ones especially. A regular policy relative to their use should be established. If the announcers are high school students, they should be trained in their job before the contests. Public address announcements regarding athletic events generally are most effective when made sparingly. Pertinent information regarding completed plays, substitutions, and explanations of penalties usually are sufficient. Do not attempt to give a running account of a contest for those who are seeing it. Criticisms of officiating should definitely be prohibited.

Physician at contests.   Arrangements should be made well in advance of a contest to have a physician present. In football, especially, it is recommended that a physician be present, or on call, for all practice sessions as well as at games. In many cities and towns there are physicians who are interested in athletics and like to attend the games. Sometimes it may be necessary to pay for the services of a physician in order to have one present. In either case it is a desirable policy to have one present to protect both the contestants and the school. Often, the physicians in a community are willing to arrange their schedules so that one of them is free to attend one or more home games, and thus little hardship is imposed on any one of them. Complimentary tickets, of course, should be available to cooperating physicians as a minimal act of courtesy. When it is impossible to have a doctor present at all contests, special arrangements should be made to provide for proper medical supervision (see pages 295–296).

Scorers, timers, judges.   Adequate provision should be made to have trained scorers, timers, and judges at any contests that require their services. Care should be taken that they are competent. An error made can lead to a protest of a game. Some schools have a program to provide them with proper training. It is wise to furnish them a bulletin of instructions or rules book outlining their responsibilities. Members of the faculty are usually the most dependable for these assignments. Use the same persons regularly if possible. Timers and judges for track and swimming meets are sometimes difficult to secure. It is best to arrange for a few more than is needed to ensure an ample staff.

Organizing the school staff.   An efficiently managed athletic contest requires the help and cooperation of both faculty and students. The final responsibility is that of the athletic administrator, but he/she must secure the assistance of other faculty members for duties not appropriate for high school students. Many schools pay teachers for such extra duties, which, if it can be afforded, is a good policy that contributes toward a feeling of loyalty and responsibility. Among the tasks that need to be assigned are ticket sellers, ticket takers, scorers, timers, and supervisors of students.

   Students can assume many minor responsibilities such as serving as visiting team and cheerleader hosts, dressing room attendants, equipment managers, and so on. Involving as many students as possible promotes their interest and provides educational values for them.

   It is the job of the athletic director to organize the support system essential for good contest management. It is recommended that brief outlines of instruction be provided, listing the responsibilities each person is to assume. A sufficient number of such outlines for a sports season can be prepared before the first game is played.

   Athletic administrators of large high schools frequently have contests in different sports in progress simultaneously. Since the administrator cannot be in more than one place at a given time, some of these large schools have assistant athletic directors for such situations, while others simply designate some other person, generally the coach, to be in charge. Clinton High School of Clinton, Iowa employs *A Game Manager Plan* under the supervision of the athletic director.[1] Those selected as game managers are paid nominal fees and are provided job descriptions outlining their responsibilities. A report is filed with the athletic director following each contest. The plan fosters uniform management of all athletic contests.

GAME RESPONSIBILITIES (HOME CONTESTS)

The items listed and discussed in this section will be those to which attention must be given at the time of the contest. Preparation for some of them will have been made previously, but when the day of the game comes around, time is limited and every detail must have received its proper attention. In some instances the checklist items under Game Responsibilities will be re-statements of those appearing under Before-Game Preparations. This simply means that such matters necessitate consideration at both times.

Supplies and equipment.   With regard to game supplies and equipment, exclusive of uniforms for players, the following is a suggested list of supplies and playing equipment which should be available at game time for the common sports:

Baseball

Balls	Catcher's outfit	Official rules book
Bases	Drinking water	Resin
Batters' helmets	First-aid kit	Score book
Bats	Lime	Towels

Basketball

Balls	First-aid kit	Score book
Bonus throw signals	Gun	Towels
Cartridges	Horn	Watches
Drinking water	Official rules book	Whistles
Electric scoreboard controls		

Cross Country

Cartridges	Gun	Watches
Drinking water	Official rules book	Whistles
First-aid kit	Route markers	Yarn
	Towels	

Football

Balls	Head linesman's chain	Resin
Cartridges	Horns	Scoreboard equipment
Drinking water	Jackets for chain carriers	Stretcher
First-aid kit	Mouth and tooth protectors	Towels
Goal-line flags	Official rules book	Watches
Gun	Participation record book	Whistles
Head linesman's box		Yard markers

Golf

Balls	Official rules book
First-aid kit	Score cards
Local course rules	

Swimming

Cartridges	Gun	Score sheets
Diving judges' cards	Heat sheets	Towels
False start line	Lane markers	Watches
First-aid kit	Official rules book	Whistles
	Rope finish line	

Tennis

Balls	Official rules book
First-aid kit	Towels
Nets	

Track

Batons	Javelin board	Starting blocks
Cartridges	Judges' stands	Tape (measuring)
Crossbars	Jumping standards	Towels
Drinking water	Line marking material	Vaulting poles
Discus	(not lime)	Vaulting standards
First-aid kit	Official rules book	Watches
Gun	Score sheets	Whistles
Hurdles	Shot (12 lb.)	Yarn
Javelins	Spade or shovel and rake	

Volleyball

Antenna	Line tape	Official rules book
First-aid kit	Net	Standards
		Scorebook

Wrestling

Clock or watch	Official rules book
First-aid kit	Points indicator
Gong or whistle	Towels

Tickets. Tickets should be at booths with sellers and takers stationed as previously assigned.

Ushers. Ushers should be at stations previously assigned.

Contest programs. Supplies of programs should be in the hands of distributors who have previously been instructed as to their stations. Distribution of programs should never be wasteful. It is better to have unused programs turned in after a game than to have the stands littered with them during a contest.

Officials' quarters. Officials should have private dressing rooms apart from either team. A student manager should be assigned to direct officials and be at their service. Officials should be requested to arrive at their dressing rooms and be dressed to report to the playing field or floor at least 30 minutes before game time.

Visiting-team quarters and courtesies. At least one student manager should be assigned to the visiting team. He or she should show the visiting school officials their team dressing quarters and the method of reaching field or gymnasium, inquire if they have all the equipment they need, furnish them a supply of drinking water (individual cups or bottle if a fountain is not available on field or in gymnasium), and remain on constant call for any services the visiting coach or athletic director might desire.

Flag raising. Be sure that an American flag is on hand and that students are instructed as to their functions in the flag-raising ceremony. Bands also should understand their part in the program.

Intermission program. If a program is planned between halves of the game, be certain that all arrangements are completed and that student managers know their duties.

Players' benches. Reserved areas for substitute players and coaches of visiting and home teams should be roped off or protected by student guards. No one else should be allowed on these benches.

Physician. Check to see that the physician expected for this contest is present.

Bands. Reserved seats or benches should be provided for visiting-school and home-school bands. Check to see that they are available. Student managers may be assigned to this detail. Be sure that band leaders know the time allotted them between halves, and also what is expected of them after the game.

Contracts. The principal, athletic director, or coach should have game and officials' contracts in his/her possession at game time for possible reference.

Contract guarantees and payments. Have school athletic association checks available for the visiting school (if contract calls for a guarantee) and also for officials. These should be given to the persons concerned during the intermission period or immediately after the game.

Eligibility lists. Have the eligibility lists for both competing schools accessible at the time of the contest.

Scoreboard arrangements. Student managers can be assigned to scoreboards. They should be students who have had experience in this work.

Guards for dressing rooms. It is advisable to have a guard on duty in the visiting and home team dressing rooms during the progress of the game. Even though valuables should be checked, clothing and other articles sometimes disappear if the locker rooms are left unguarded. An alternative is to assign the visiting team to a room that may be locked and then give the key to the coach or faculty or student manager.

Extra clothing for substitutes. Adequate clothing is especially important in football. Parents legitimately object if their sons are insufficiently protected while sitting on the bench. Have an adequate number of warm coats or blankets for all substitutes, or else have fewer substitutes. Treat them all alike.

Concessions. Check to see that concessions are being handled properly.

Cheerleaders. Cheerleaders should be on their assignments at least a half hour before game time.

Police. Police officers assigned to duty at the game should be available before or soon after gates or doors are opened. An officer stationed near the main gate or stadium entrance has a good psychological effect.

Supervisors. Faculty supervisors should report to the athletic director at a specified time and be at their stations well before the game starts.

Public address system. Check the public address system prior to the start of the game to see that it is working properly.

Rest rooms. Make certain that rest rooms are properly equipped and are available when the gymnasium door or field gates are opened.

Scorekeepers and timers. These should be adults who have had ample training for their responsibilities. An error by either can cause serious problems and even lead to the protest of a game. They should report at least 30 minutes before contest time.

Guarding extra equipment. Student guards should be assigned to see that extra equipment, such as balls, bats, helmets, jackets, sweaters, blankets, and pads, is not lost during games.

Checklist. A checklist containing the supplies, equipment, and all the details related to game responsibilities of the athletic administrator for the sport concerned should be prepared. This decreases the possibility of overlooking any important particulars and tends toward good contest administration.

AFTER-GAME RESPONSIBILITIES (HOME CONTESTS)

After a game is over, there are still several things to be done. Usually it will be the faculty manager, athletic director, or coach whose responsibility it is to see that they are finished. These items will be indicated in the form of a suggested checklist.

Payment of officials.   Officials should be paid between halves or immediately after the game. An official should be free to leave the school after the contest. Do not make it necessary for him or her to hunt up someone in order to get paid. The fee should be ready for the official unless it is to be mailed.

Payment of visiting school.   Again, if this detail was not attended to during or before the half, it should be done immediately after the conclusion of the game. Be sure that the payment is in accordance with contract guarantee provisions.

Storage of equipment.   Student managers should be assigned the responsibility of collecting and storing all field, court, or game equipment after each contest.

Contest receipts.   At least within a day or two after a game the athletic director, faculty manager, or coach should check receipts for the contest. Such a report should be received from the individual in charge of ticket sales at the game.

General financial statement.   It is good business practice to have a complete financial statement, showing receipts and expenditures, ready within a week after each game. The report should be placed in the hands of the high school principal or superintendent of schools.

Concessions report.   If the concessions are handled by the high school athletic association, there should be a complete report of receipts, expenditures, and inventory after each game. If concessions are in the charge of local school clubs or organizations, a financial report still should be made to the athletic director or high school principal. School officials have the right to know the financial status of this agency in order that they may be in a position to answer inquiries concerning it.

Record of officials.   Many state athletic associations ask that schools rate officials either after games or at the end of the season. In the latter case it is desirable to keep a record of all officials until the state blank is received. A simple method is to list the name of the official, the game in which he or she worked, the date of the game, a rating based on the state rating plan, and a few remarks about the work. This record will also be of value when officials are being considered for subsequent years. Such records should be kept for out-of-town as well as for home games.

Participation records.   Shortly after each game a record of all participants should be made, usually by the coach. This may be used for award purposes, if that policy is followed in the school, and also for final season reports to the state athletic association in states where such reports are required. Oklahoma supplies an Individual Participation Record Form typical of those used in states desiring such information. A copy of this information also is retained as a permanent record of the school (see Fig. 7–2).

Filing of contest data.   Usually it is desirable to have all the information concerning a particular contest available in one place. Such a filing procedure is possible if data regarding a game are compiled shortly after its conclusion, while it still is fresh in mind. One plan for keeping complete contest records is to use a 10-by-13-inch envelope, properly labeled for the contest concerned, into which are filed all related materials for each game, including game and officials' contracts, correspondence, school and newspaper clippings, and so forth. This method provides a complete accumulative record related to the contest.

A simpler plan involves the use of a single form to record a summary of game results, officials, and receipts for home games (see Fig. 7–3). These forms are easy to file and they can become part of a school's total interscholastic record.

Obviously, either system enables data concerning any contest to be found readily. It requires only a minimum of effort, but the information must be filled in soon after the game has been played. Some schools keep record books of all games, with satisfactory results. Whatever system is used, the important thing concerning it is regularity and keeping it up to date. Records become valuable with age and they should be kept faithfully.

PREPARATION FOR OUT-OF-TOWN GAMES

Definite preparation must be made by visiting-school officials for athletic contests to be played away from home. Coaching of the team is not included in this discussion. Regardless of the size of the school, there are numerous matters regarding the trip, management of the team, and financial considerations to which attention must be given. In the smaller schools the superintendent, principal, or coach will attend to them. In larger schools the athletic director or faculty manager usually will take care of these administrative matters. The items presented here may be considered as a checklist of duties from which schools may select, or to which they may add, those pertaining to their local situations.

Oklahoma Secondary School Activities Association

INDIVIDUAL PARTICIPATION RECORD

(To be kept as a permanent record of your school)

DIRECTIONS—

After each game put name of school and date of game on vertical line. Following each student's name and in the column of the school against which he has participated, indicate with ink the amount of time he participated.

Season's Schedule	in	School	Date Played																	
NAME OF STUDENT																				

I certify that the above is a complete record of all students who have participated in any part of any game during the

season ending _____ 19___ .

School _____

By _____

Principal or Superintendent

FIGURE 7–2 Individual participation record (Oklahoma)

CENTRAL HIGH SCHOOL
ATHLETIC CONTEST SUMMARY

Sport _____ Date _____ Played at _____

Score:

Central High school _____ vs _____High School ___

Officials:_____   _____

_____   _____

Scorekeeper _____ Timer _____

Home Game Gross Financial Summary:

Attendance _____ Total Gate Receipts $_____

Concession Receipts $_____

Remarks:

FIGURE 7-3 Suggested contest summary form

Transportation. Transportation of an athletic team is the most important item in connection with games away from home. Often, especially among small schools, teams cannot be transported in the most acceptable manner because of lack of funds. If at all possible, school athletic teams should be carried only by bonded, public common carriers. School buses also are highly desirable, but some states have questioned the right to use such vehicles for out-of-school activities as they have defined them. Private cars driven by adults should not be used unless absolutely necessary. Schools and private car owners should be sure they understand the public utility and public liability laws of their states where such an arrangement is in effect. Special precaution should be taken to see that there is proper insurance coverage for all vehicles.

Under no circumstances should student drivers of private cars be allowed to transport athletic teams. Where such a policy is followed, school authorities may be charged with negligence in case of accident, with subsequent court action a possibility. Team members should be required to go to the entertaining school together and return the same way. The one exception to this rule is where parents personally request permission of the school official in charge of the team to take their son or daughter home with them. Have a definite time for starting the trip. Plan a definite range in time for arrival home, and notify parents accordingly. Usually only team members, student managers, coaches, and school officials should make up the party if a bus is chartered for the trip. The same applies if a school bus is used. Discipline problems are lessened to a considerable degree if no student other than team members, student managers, and possibly cheerleaders are allowed.

Parents' permits. Some schools do not think it is desirable or necessary to require permission of parents of students for each out-of-town trip that the school athletic team takes. They feel that the original permission for the student to participate covers scheduled trips as well as actual play. This opinion is reasonable. Other schools have forms that they require the student to take home, have signed by one of the parents, and return to the coach, faculty manager, or principal before he or she may go on the trip with the team. These forms usually state the location, date, and time of the contest. They also indicate the type of transportation to be used, hour of departure, probable hour of return, and a source where information may be obtained in case the return trip is delayed. In signing such a form the parent usually indicates that the school is released from any liability in case of accident. Just how much this apparent release of liabilty amounts to is questionable. The chief justification for a procedure of this kind is that it keeps parents informed of the school's efforts to cooperate with them in the care and safety of their sons or daughters.

Figure 7–4 is an example from which a school can devise a form of its own for all out-of-town athletic contests for a sports season. It can also be a pattern for developing one to be used for each trip if the school prefers that

CENTRAL HIGH SCHOOL

PARENTAL PERMISSION FOR OUT-OF-TOWN ATHLETIC TRIPS

Your son/daughter has been selected as a member of the Central High

School _____ squad and will make, with your consent, out-
            (sport)
of-town trips with the team. Players will travel by school bus.

Every precaution will be taken for his/her safety. He/she will be

required to leave and return on the school bus, except upon your

personal request, he/she will be allowed to travel with you in your

personal automobile. He/she will be informed of each time of

departure and return and will be instructed to so inform you. He/

she is asked to dress neatly and to conduct himself/herself properly

to help establish a favorable impression for our school.

We hope you will give your consent by signing and returning the

form below immediately. If you have any questions or desire any

further information, please call me at (telephone number) .

Signed_____
                     Athletic Director

- -

To: (name of athletic director)

We hereby grant our consent for _____
                                 (name of son or daughter)
to make out-of-town athletic trips under the conditions explained in

your memorandum, and we will not hold Central High School or its

representatives liable in case of accident.

Signed_____
                     Parent

FIGURE 7-4 Parental consent form for out-of-town athletic trips

procedure. If a school adopts either procedure, a student should not be permitted to make a trip until the bottom form is signed by a parent and returned to the athletic director. All returned forms should be filed and kept until the end of the particular sports season. If a school transports its pep club by school bus, the same type of form could be developed for pep club members.

Finances for trip. The member of the faculty in charge of the trip should be the custodian of all funds. Sufficient money should be withdrawn from the school treasury to take care of meals, lodging (if necessary), and incidentals. A strict accounting of all expenditures should be made to the principal, superintendent, or athletic director immediately after the return. Bus charges should be paid by the school by check. Contract guarantee checks should not be cashed by sponsors on trips unless absolutely necessary. It is much better to have them pass through the regular financial channels of the school or athletic association treasury.

Equipment. Each player should be charged with responsibility for his or her personal playing equipment. Duffle bags, with names or numbers on them, are satisfactory means for carrying it. Game equipment, bats, balls, helmets, first-aid supplies, extra shores, cleats, jerseys, sweaters, coats, and the like should be the responsibility of one or two student managers. They should see that they are properly assembled, placed in trunks or bags, and loaded at the start of the trip, and they should assume responsibility for their safekeeping during the games, and check to be sure that they are returned. If additional equipment is issued to a player on a trip, it should be charged to that player by the person issuing it.

Game details. Complete information should be available before the start of the trip regarding game details. Know the time of the game, the place where it will be played, the location of dressing rooms, who is to officiate, the price of admission, and the regulations concerning complimentary tickets for the visiting team. Band, manager, and cheerleader arrangements should be understood. Having this information ahead of time will lessen the confusion upon arrival.

Eligibility records. Be sure that all players making the trip are eligible for the contest to be played. Make certain that their names appear on the eligibility list. Take this list, and the one received from the competing school, on the trip for possible reference.

Game contract. The game contract should be accessible for reference in case any differences of opinion arise. It should be in the possession of the individual in charge of the trip, together with special correspondence concerning the game and both eligibility lists.

Trip personnel.   Have a definite time when the coach will post a list of team members and student managers who will make the trip. State the time the team will leave and then leave at that time. If players know this hour is the deadline they will be on time. Require athletes to dress neatly and impress upon them that they are *ambassadors* for their school. Standards of conduct for trips should be well established.

Supervision.   Providing adequate supervision on buses, in private cars officially carrying students, and at away-from-home games is very important. Several state associations hold the school responsible for the conduct of followers at all contests. Faculty supervisors should be carefully instructed as to their authority and responsibilities.

Participation record books.   If it is the policy of the school to keep an accurate record of all participants, the record book should be carried on the trip. Responsibility for compiling data in it may be delegated to a student manager.

GENERAL MANAGEMENT DUTIES AND POLICIES

In the preceding sections of this chapter, administrative or management matters have been discussed involving before-game, game, and after-game duties. Likewise, items necessitating attention concerning out-of-town games have been considered. Obviously, these all are administrative or managerial functions. In addition, however, there are matters which are not specifically allied with any one event but which concern the whole program. These are what might be classified as school athletic policy administrative functions. Most of them will be or have been submitted to the athletic council or board of control for its approval. Insofar as it is possible to distinguish them from those matters previously considered, they will be presented here. It is obvious that most of the items discussed under the headings previously mentioned also will have been approved by the athletic board.

Permanent athletic eligibility, participation, and scholastic records.   The amount of clerical work necessary in compiling eligibility-list data may be lessened considerably by centralized records. Some local schools and state athletic associations have devised forms to accomplish this end. In some instances copies of the regular eligibility lists are retained and filed by schools for use the following year in compiling athletic data and statistics. This is an excellent procedure if no other plan is in effect. Iowa is one of the state athletic associations which require that a "permanent book of record" be kept on file in each school.[2] The information requested or contained in it includes eligibility data for all athletes during the year; rules and regulations of the Iowa High School Athletic Association; data concerning athletes representing the school during the year; personnel of various teams; results of games and contests held in each sport; school track records; schedules for the ensuing year; high school athletics cash book; and notes on each athletic season during the current year. This record book becomes a permanent school record and must be completed upon penalty of loss of membership by the school. In Oregon, a Report to Secretary is made by designated dates, with a copy being retained by each school. In this way a permanent record of athletics and considerable scholastic data are centered in one place, thus resulting in easier access to sources of information for the preparation of subsequent eligibility lists.

Some associations require each school to file with the state office a copy of the eligibility lists exchanged with other schools for each sport. These copies and the ones retained by the athletic administrator become permanent records of participation.

Florida requires each member school to file an annual eligibility list with the Executive Secretary containing the eligibility status of each athlete.[3] Forms are provided for this purpose and must be submitted at least five days prior to any contest in which the students listed participate. A few other high school associations require similar reports in lieu of member schools' exchanging eligibility lists, unless one of the competing schools requests it. A copy of this report provides a convenient way for the athletic director to keep a permanent record of the eligibility status of athletes.

Regardless of the scheme followed in recording permanent athletic records of students, be consistent and faithful. New administrators and coaches coming into schools should find complete records available. Also, there are many cases when information is desired concerning the athletic participation of former high school students several years after they have graduated. The school athletic department is the place from which it should be obtainable.

Athletic finances and budgets. These items will be discussed in Chapter 11. They are mentioned here, however, because they should properly be considered general administrative duties. It is impossible to overemphasize the importance of sound financial policies and accurate bookkeeping in connection with a high school progam of interscholastic athletics. That is one reason why an entire chapter will be devoted to this subject.

General reports. In some instances the general report for the athletic year may be the permanent record. In others part of it may appear in the school paper or school annual. It is highly desirable, however, that a brief but complete athletic report be placed in the hands of the superintendent or principal at the close of the school year. It is good information for either or both of them to have and is in line with policies in many schools that teachers shall report their year's work at the end of the final semester. The report should include at least: (1) financial statement; (2) results of games and meets; (3) number of participants; (4) outstanding features of the year's activities; and (5) proposed schedules for the ensuing year.

Contracting officials.   Athletic officials for home games for the following year should be engaged as soon as possible. There are always many officials, but sometimes there are not enough good ones. Ninety-nine percent of them are honest and eager to do a good job because that is their best method of receiving other assignments. It is a fact, however, that certain officials are better known and handle games in a more satisfactory manner than others; such persons generally are acceptable to all schools. These are the individuals whose services have to be contracted for early. Home schools should submit lists of officials to visiting schools. Names of officials mutually agreeable should be submitted to the athletic council for approval. Officials then should be approached concerning their availability, and contracts should be sent them. In some cases it may be desirable to ask officials to hold a date or dates tentatively for later confirmation. This procedure will enable the securing of formal approval from the visiting school.

Keep a file of all correspondence regarding approval of officials. As far as possible, officials should be secured from six months to a year in advance of the games in which they are to work. It should be understood that contracts are binding only in case an official is properly registered with the state association, if state regulations require such a procedure. Do not use the same official in too many games. This is not a good policy either for players or spectators. Some athletic coaches practice "trades" in officiating, in which a coach from one school works as an official in a game for another school with the understanding that the coach of the latter school will work a contest for the coach of the former institution. This policy leads to difficulties.

A word to the athletic official may not be amiss in this discussion. Having an important part in the successful conduct of an athletic contest, the official should be businesslike in his or her correspondence, be on time, know the rules, and, above all, be honest and fearless.

Officials with the best reputations do not solicit games. School officials know which ones they want to officiate their games. If an official's work and reputation are what they should be, that person will receive a proper share of assignments and should not have to make himself or herself a nuisance or cause embarrassment to athletic directors or coaches by asking them for games. All that representatives or coaches want of the official is to perform the duty of officiating a game fairly.

The following list provides excellent standards for officials to follow:

OFFICIAL'S CODE

1. To know fully the rules and accepted officiating procedures for each sport in which I will serve as arbiter.
2. To build my game schedule through my accepted worth, potential possibilities, and inherent character rather than through transitory acquaintance or trading of favors or attempted pressures.
3. To honor my contract, even though this may occasionally result in financial loss or loss of opportunity to work for a larger school or one involving less travel.
4. To keep myself physically and mentally fit.
5. To be systematic, prompt, and businesslike in all my dealings with those I serve.
6. To wear the accepted official's attire and to maintain a neat and creditable appearance.
7. To act in such a way as to be a worthy example to those under my supervision.
8. To remember that my responsibility also extends to my fellow officials and that I must work as one member of a team.
9. To make my decisions promptly but without snap judgment, firmly but without arrogance, fairly but without officiousness; and to base them on the rules, regardless of the type of school, the closeness of the score, or the opinions of partisan spectators.
10. To keep in mind that my first charge is the safety and general welfare of those under my supervision.[4]

Dressing rooms for visiting teams and officials. The dressing or locker room facilities for visiting teams should be adequate, clean, and available upon the team's arrival. A separate room away from both teams should be available for officials. A student manager should be assigned to meet the officials upon their arrival and be ready to assist them in any way.

At least one student manager should be assigned to the visiting team to show its school officials their dressing quarters and the way to reach the field or gymnasium. He or she should inquire if they have all the equipment they need, furnish a supply of drinking water with individual cups or bottles if a fountain is not available, and remain on constant call for services to the visiting coach or athletic director. It is advisable to have guards on duty in visiting and home school dressing rooms during the progress of the game if they cannot be securely locked.

Schedules and practice. As indicated previously, schedules should receive the approval of the local school athletic council or board of control. Generally, they should not be the final responsibility of any one individual. Of course someone will have the task of making arrangements for schedules, but this always should be done subject to the final approval of the council. Schedules usually should be made at least a year in advance. In some sports in which yearly home-and-home games are played, two years will be involved. In general, games should be arranged as nearly as possible so that home contests alternate each week with those away from home. Likewise, they should be arranged so that they do not interfere with school time. The North Central Association of Secondary Schools and Colleges recommends that no high school athletic contest be scheduled for an evening preceding a school day. Leagues, conferences, or local athletic associations can aid schools in establishing regular schedules and deciding on days of the week on which games will or will not be played.

Both boys' and girls' programs must be taken into consideration when planning games and practices, particularly if facilities have to be shared. The scheduling of both practice sessions and games should provide for fairness and equity between the sexes. Because of concerns regarding civil rights and discrimination, any special favoritism toward either sex must be avoided. Some schools have found that scheduling practices for boys and girls simultaneously for such sports as golf, tennis, track, and swimming is practical and helps to prevent conflicts.

When schedules have been approved, they should be mimeographed or printed for student and adult distribution. This is an effective means to publicize a school's athletic program. By this method it also is possible for administrators to protect themselves from pressure for post-season games, especially in those states in which games other than those regularly scheduled are prohibited.

There are differences of opinion as to the desirable length of seasons. There is a tendency on the part of some state athletic associations to aid schools in establishing maximum limits in the number of games to be played in some activities. Local schools themselves, or regional leagues, frequently set up their own limits.

There is no question that many school administrators have often not heeded their better judgment in setting up athletic schedules. This same criticism might be levelled against coaches as far as the frequency and length of practice periods is concerned.

The number and length of practice periods will vary with the discretion of coaches, the experience of the team, and the availability of facilities. Undoubtedly the claim that high school players tend to become "burned out" is a greater indictment against practice policies than against the number of games played. Approximately one and one-half hours for basketball and two hours for football are generally sufficient. If players begin to lose their enthusiasm and are not making concerted efforts to improve their skills, it is usually best to terminate the practice session at that point. The "quality" of practice determines improvement more than the length of practice. It is believed by many that more coaches hold practices that are too long than not long enough. Under no circumstances should they cause practices to become wearisome for their athletes. Unless practice sessions are enjoyable, some of the "fun" will be taken out and the recreational value reduced. A coach properly trained in the science of physical education should understand the elements of fatigue in adolescence and the degree of strenuousness occasioned by participation in various sports. Practice periods should be governed accordingly. In general, it will be a safe rule to practice a shorter period than had been planned. The following suggestions as to number of regular season games are based on state association recommendations or regulations. They may be of aid to schools in setting up schedules in the more commonly sponsored activities.

BASEBALL. One or two games per week with at least two or three days between games. (No high school player should pitch more than one game per week.) Recommendation of twelve to fifteen games.

BASKETBALL. Generally one game per week with possibly one or two weeks during which two games are played. Recommendation of fifteen to eighteen games during regular season.

CROSS COUNTRY. One meet per week. Recommendation of five to seven meets.

FOOTBALL. One game per week. (At least three weeks of practice prior to first game.) Plan an open date near midseason if possible. Recommendation of seven- or eight-game maximum.

GOLF. Physical nature of the sport not important in determining number of scheduled meets.

SWIMMING. One meet per week. Recommendation of eight to twelve meets.

TENNIS. One meet per week. (Limit competition of individuals either to singles or doubles, not both.) Recommendation of eight to twelve meets.

TRACK. One meet per week. (Limit number of events for individuals.) Recommendation of eight to ten meets.

WRESTLING. Not more than one meet per week. Recommendation of eight to twelve meets.

The matter of sectional or state tournament and meet competition naturally is closely associated with schedule making. A number of state association regulations regarding maximum number of games to be played by schools have been established, with tournament or meet competition in mind. Local schools should adopt their own policies relative to such participation. In all states participation in tournaments is voluntary. If the school officials of the state feel that the state association-sponsored tournaments and meets fill a need, undoubtedly they will be set up and controlled with that end in view.

Athletic alumni and varsity clubs. School administrators hold different opinions regarding the advisability of encouraging the activities of varsity, lettermen, or alumni athletic clubs. Some feel that such organizations may attempt to dictate the athletic policy of the school and hence should not be recognized. Others see in them the opportunity for another contact in the proper administration of the athletic program. The latter view seems to be the more prevalent. The varsity and lettermen of a school should have had enough experience in athletics to understand some of the problems connected with them. This observation may not be valid for alumni athletic clubs. It seems best to work closely with all these organizations, however. They should be provided an understanding of the school's philosophy and objectives for the athletic program and should be guided in formulating objectives of their own that are compatible. Keep them informed of school athletic policies, send them copies of schedules, aid in the arrangement of details for their meetings, and advise them concerning special athletic functions and banquets. By following such a procedure it generally will be possible to use such organizations for the purposes desired by the school rather than vice versa.

Athletic equipment. The purchase and care of athletic equipment represents the largest item of expense, except salaries, in the administration of the athletic program. It is mentioned here under general administrative duties and policies because of its major importance. Discussion of this subject appears in Chapter 10.

Local league or conference obligations. Most schools find it advantageous to join leagues, athletic associations, or athletic conferences. As long as membership is maintained in such an organization, all obligations should be fulfilled. These include attending meetings of the league, maintaining full league schedules, remitting dues promptly, and remaining loyal to the group of schools in the association. If these repsonsibilities and courtesies cannot be maintained, ask for release from the organization.

Athletic banquets. Every school should have a definite policy regarding athletic banquets. They should be regarded as regular affairs if a school is going to have them at all. Teams that lose all their games have as much, or more, reason to be banqueted as those whose records constitute what is considered a "highly successful season." The athletic banquet should be a school, or school and community, affair rather than something to which the athletes are entitled. The school owes the athletes nothing, a fact they should be made to realize early in their athletic careers. Instead of limiting an annual or seasonal banquet to members of an athletic team alone as the honored guests, it seems more justifiable to recognize all the activities of the school during the period. Include music, forensics, dramatics, and scholarship as well as athletics. Such an array of talent really gives a community an opportunity to see the broad scope of the school's program.

Athletic blanks and forms.   Each local school uses blanks and forms in the administration of its athletic program. It prepares these forms itself or receives them from the state athletic association. The supply of both these types should be checked frequently. Schools can get excellent ideas for record keeping by exchanging samples of blanks and forms. If forms, reports, or accounts of meetings are to be printed, be sure that the copy is correct before it is sent to the printer. It is much easier and cheaper to make corrections before the type is set than after.

Selection of student managers.   Some of the responsibilities of student managers have already been discussed in this chapter. They might be elected or appointed but they should not be members of athletic squads. High school students interested in athletics are usually eager to be of help. Make their selection a definite and businesslike procedure. Let it be known that the jobs are open to those interested who meet the qualifications. Usually an apprenticeship period should precede full management appointment. Student managers should be eligible for school letter awards. Definite requirements for senior, junior, and assistant manager awards should be established and understood, if that many are necessary. Generally, student athletic managers should not be paid by the school for their services. It is a good policy to provide a distinctive shirt, coat, or jersey to be worn by student managers when on duty.

Awards recommendations.   Each school should have a definite policy relative to athletic awards. *This is an administrative matter of the first rank.* Recommendations regarding awards, standards, and policies followed in schools are discussed in detail in Chapter 9.

Crowd control measures.   Effective crowd control procedures are a must in planning for athletic contests. The trend toward disrespect for law and order in our society and, simultaneously, an increased interest in athletic competition make it both advisable and necessary. Some schools have discontinued night football games and many have had to use larger numbers of law enforcement officers to supervise at athletic events. Teaching sportsmanship is no longer sufficient. Procedures for enforcing sportsmanship in the form of crowd control plans are being sought. Such steps are important if interscholastics are to maintain their educational value. Proper planning for teaching and enforcing sportsmanship at games will enhance the educational values inherent in athletics, while tolerating misconduct will jeopardize these values and in extreme cases may lead to the discontinuance of the interscholastic program.

A good crowd control program must be a positive one which includes three phases: (1) education, (2) involvement, and (3) enforcement.

The educational phase must reach adults as well as students. The public should also be educated to the objectives and policies of the athletic program, as well as the standards of sportsmanship found in the game rules and those contained in state association by-laws. In most states a serious breach of sportsmanship by a player, coach, student, or fan can jeopardize the school's membership in the state association and result in a loss of the privilege of competing in interscholastic contests with other schools. Assemblies, parent-teacher meetings, booster club meetings, statements in game programs, bulletins, posters, and news releases can be used to reach adults and students.

An effective plan must be a comprehensive one which involves a number of individuals and groups. Some of those to be inlcuded are the high school principal, athletic director, coaches, other faculty members, pep club sponsor and cheerleaders, lettermen's club, boosters club, parents, and law enforcement officials. Planning the part each is to take and the responsibilities to be assumed is a significant phase of crowd control. The specific responsibilities for each group should be appropriate and well understood. Provisions must be made for channels of communication at game sites. One person—preferably, the high school principal or athletic director—should provide the leadership for coordinating the cooperative efforts of those involved.

Enforcement procedures must be definite and well understood. Faculty members, selected school patrons, and some student representatives should act as observers to report any potential problem to the athletic director, principal, or person designated. Some of the larger schools use walkie talkies to communicate with this individual, who in turn signals the police officer in charge if necessary. This procedure has proved very helpful. The person in charge must have the authority to decide what action should be taken. He or she must resolve whether it is a matter that should be handled by the police or by some other means. Schools should not expect law enforcement officials to relieve them of the responsibility for supervision. Police officers are there basically to supplement the efforts of the school staff and to take corrective steps in case of an emergency. If there are several police on duty, it is generally best to have the principal or his chief representative communicate with only one officer, who has been designated in charge. This officer should be responsible for instructing other officers as to their stations and their responsibilities. When enforcement procedures are well planned and administered, they are educational as well as corrective.

One cannot discuss crowd control plans without emphasizing the strategic position of the coach in influencing students and spectators. His or her position can be a most positive force, or it can work negatively. The coach who shows respect toward the game officials and opponents and makes certain that the players do likewise will contribute more than any other single person to maintaining good sportsmanship and crowd control. Some schools wisely set standards of sportsmanship which they require their coaches to meet. Such action is evidence of the importance attached to the coach's position and should be welcomed.

Familiarity with state athletic association regulations. It is the responsibility of the local school to know and to understand the minimum eligibility and contest regulations established cooperatively through its state association. These standards become the standards of the school by virtue of its membership and are the same for all member schools. Each has the responsibility for upholding them. Most state associations publish various bulletins, journals, posters, and so on to help in educating students and the public to the regulations applied in interscholastics. Posters should be displayed on bulletin boards and publications should be available in school libraries. These procedures will increase student and faculty interest in and respect for the school and state association activities, and also help them to see that local school athletics are a part of a statewide educational athletic program.

MEET AND TOURNAMENT MANAGEMENT

In addition to regular season contests, schools participate in meets and tournaments which require efficient management. We shall make no attempt here to discuss the many meets and tournaments held in the various high school sports. The rules books for some of them, including track and field and wrestling, contain sections on the organization and administration of meets in these sports. In this section we shall discuss only those general management matters which are more or less common to all tournaments and meets. It is usually the athletic administrator who must assume the duty of managing them, or delegate the task to a staff member. In either case, he/she must be thoroughly familiar with the responsibilities entailed.

Types of Meets and Tournaments

We can consider the meets and tournaments in which schools engage under three headings: (1) invitational, (2) conference, and (3) district and state high school association meets and tournaments.

Invitational meets and tournaments. These are athletic events sponsored by individual schools which invite other schools to participate.

Conference meets and tournaments. It is common for conferences to sponsor meets in which member schools compete for a so-called conference championship. A school is selected by conference action to host the event, and many of the regulations and some management details are also determined by the conference. Frequently, a committee is selected by the conference to assist in management, but the host school must also provide a manager. It is a general practice to rotate, as far as possible, the responsibility for hosting these events among those schools having adequate facilities.

District and state events.   These athletic events are sponsored by the state high school association, which, at least in part, is responsible for organizing them. A member school is chosen to host such a tournament and a manual of instructions is provided for managing it. It is more common for high schools to host district meets and tournaments than state contests. Many of the latter are held at colleges and universities which have larger facilities essential for conducting them.

Considerations in the Decision To Host

High school administrators will naturally want to assume their fair share in hosting conference sponsored and/or state high school association sponsored events, but certain considerations must be taken into account, both in accepting an invitation and also in deciding to sponsor an invitational meet. Among the most important are the following:

1. *Facilities.* It must be decided whether the gymnasium or playing field is adequate for the competition, whether dressing room facilities are ample, whether enough parking is available, and so on. An individual school may have sufficient facilities for one type of sports tournament but not for others.

2. *Support of administration and faculty.* It must be made certain that the school administration and the faculty desire and will cooperate in hosting the event. The support of both, of course, is needed for it to be successful.

3. *Manager.* The host school virtually always provides a manager for the tournament, which in most cases is the athletic director. This person must decide whether he/she can devote the necessary time required and whether he/she is sufficiently knowledgeable about the administration of the particular event. If not, is there a member of the staff who can and is willing to assume this responsibility?

4. *Finances.* Most meets and tournaments depend on gate receipts for financing. Is the community sufficiently interested to support the event through attendance? Schools, in general, should not host events which are not self-financing, except in the case of conference meets and tournaments in non-income sports for which the conference or participating schools will pay their share of the expenses.

5. *Conflict with academic program.* Athletic contests should supplement the high school academic program and not be a substitute for classwork. Some conflict is unavoidable, particularly in the case of district and state meets, but most contests can be scheduled at times which will not interfere with the academic responsibilities of students. If class time is to be lost, there should be careful planning to involve as many students as possible in hosting an event and to make certain there will be educational experiences extended to students through their involvement.

6. *Other considerations.* For district or state tournaments, it is often necessary to secure ample housing and eating facilities for visiting teams.

Pre-Tournament Organization

Just as there are pre-game responsibilities for regularly scheduled contests, so there are advance details which must be worked out well in advance of the date(s) of a meet or tournament. After the tournament manager and any necessary assistant managers have been selected, the following are some of the important organizational matters to be considered:

1. *Invitations.* If the meet is not a conference event or one sponsored by the state association, participating schools must be selected. It is always best to choose those within reasonable distance and which have teams well enough matched to make the competition interesting. Contracts containing a guarantee should be signed by schools accepting invitations.

2. *Tournament committee.* Conferences often appoint a committee to help organize and manage a conference event. Committees for district and state contests may be appointed by the state association. If such committees have not been appointed, it is advisable for a local committee to be selected, especially for invitational meets. These persons can be chosen by the athletic administrator or high school principal, and it may be appropriate to select one or more committee members from the faculties of participating schools.

3. *Information table.* A table or booth where visiting teams are to report to secure information aids in management. Students under the supervision of a faculty member can assume this responsibility.

4. *Tournament officials and workers.* Game officials, announcer, scorer(s), timer(s), and a statistician(s) must be secured. These must be competent and experienced individuals for their tasks.

5. *Dressing room and equipment managers.* These are appropriate responsibilities for students.

6. *Ushers.* If needed, both faculty members and students can be assigned to ushering duties to direct visiting pep clubs and visiting team followers to the sections where their groups will be seated.

7. *Team hosts.* Properly instructed team hosts can make teams feel welcome. Two students can be assigned each team as co-hosts to direct players and coaches to their dressing rooms and extend other courtesies to them. Providing a courtesy room for visiting coaches and school officials is a good gesture, and students can serve as hosts in this area with the help of a faculty member.

8. *Crowd control.* Tournaments frequently require more crowd control

measures than do regularly scheduled contests. Arrangements must be made for adequate police protection both around the playing area and about the premises. One law enforcement official should be designated to be in communication with the tournament manager for mutual reporting of any potential problem. Others should report through these persons to prevent any misunderstanding or confusion.

9. *Concessions.* Patronage at concession stands tends to be greater at meets and tournaments, and proper planning must be made to handle it.

10. *Medical supervision.* A physician should be present at all meets and tournaments, or other adequate arrangements must be made for proper medical supervision.

11. *Insurance.* If the host school's insurance does not protect the school and its representatives from liability arising from meets and tournaments, it is advisable to secure liability coverage for the particular event, which can usually be purchased for a reasonable premium.

12. *Publicity.* Plans should be made for publicizing the event through local and area press, radio, and television media representatives well in advance of the meet or tournament. They should be provided advance information and data and have spaces reserved for them during the event.

13. *Tickets.* If the school does not have an adequate supply, these must be ordered in ample time.

14. *Programs.* A neat, well-arranged meet or tournament program adds to the pleasure of fans. Information to be included in the program, such as names and numbers of players, must be obtained from participating schools in time for composition and printing of the brochures.

15. *Maintenance.* Arrangements must be made to have maintenance personnel available throughout the event.

16. *Awards ceremony.* A well-planned awards ceremony provides a fitting climax for a high school meet or tournament. Some schools have found that cheerleaders or other student representatives who have received special instruction in presenting awards can do an excellent job; presentation by students is also a way of showing that the event has been primarily for the benefit of students.

If each person who assists even minimally in the management of the tournament receives a brief bulletin of instructions, it is more likely they will assume their responsibilities in a way that will enhance the overall administration of the event.

Administration

The administration of a meet or tournament, of course, begins with the organizational planning, but it further involves procedures to put those plans into effect. Several of the administrative procedures are implied in the discussions above, but there are a few others which should be emphasized.

State association approval. A number of high school associations require that the state office sanction all conference and invitational meets of more than three schools. In this case, the manager must either secure approval or make certain state association sanction has been given.

Instructions to participating schools. The administration of any tournament is greatly enhanced by providing participating schools with adequate information regarding management plans. This can be accomplished by preparing a bulletin of instructions which contains:

1. List of participating schools
2. Time and place of coaches' meeting for pairings or drawings
3. Location of parking areas
4. Time schedule
5. Location of dressing rooms
6. Where to report (information table)
7. Color of uniforms to be worn (top bracket—light; bottom bracket—dark)
8. Warm-up times and places
9. Financial arrangements
10. Admission prices and ticket information
11. Housing arrangement (if necessary)
12. Location of courtesy room (if any)
13. Between-game entertainment (if any)
14. Name of manager and persons in charge of specific details
15. Equipment and supplies which will be made available
16. Medical supervision to be provided
17. Other (information important for certain sports)

Supervision. Adequate supervision, in addition to police protection, of all phases of a meet or tournament contributes to smooth administration. These duties can be assigned to the athletic staff or other members of the faculty who will help to see that all individuals assigned responsibilities are properly assuming them.

Follow-up responsibilities. Following the conclusion of a meet or tournament there are additional responsibilities which require attention. A record of the competition should be compiled and a financial statement prepared. Copies of these should be sent to each participating school together with any amount due it. Payment should be made as soon as possible to tournament officials and others who receive remuneration. A final check should be made to see that all helpers have returned supplies and equipment to their proper places.

Properly planned and administered athletic meets and tournaments provide worthwhile learning experiences for students as well as wholesome entertainment for athletic patrons.

SUMMARY

Efficient contest management is one of the most important responsibilities of athletic administrators.

Contest management comprises three phases: (1) before-game preparation, (2) game responsibilities, and (3) after-game duties.

Preparation for out-of-town contests involves arranging for insured transportation, requiring parental permission be obtained by students, and providing for adequate supervision.

Also inherent in contest management are general responsibilities for which policies should be established and carefully followed.

Athletic administrators must be prepared to administer meets and tournaments. The three general types include: (1) invitational, (2) conference, and (3) state association-sponsored meets and tournaments.

QUESTIONS AND TOPICS FOR STUDY AND DISCUSSION

1. Why is efficient management of athletic contests important? State several reasons.

2. List and discuss briefly the matters to be considered in the before-game preparation for home contests.

3. Assuming you are the athletic administrator of a high school of your choice, prepare a chart for organizing the faculty staff and students to assist in the management of an athletic contest under two headings such as:

Assignment	Teacher or Student(s)
Announcer	(Teacher)
Host for officials	(Student(s))
Etc.	

4. Prepare a checklist to aid the athletic director in attending to responsibilities for home contests.

5. There are several responsibilities following home contests. State as many as you can and enumerate the duties.

6. Discuss the important responsibilities which must receive attention for out-of-town games.

7. There are many general management duties and policies concerning the interscholastic program. List and discuss their importance.

8. Are you in agreement with the recommendations made in this chapter regarding the number of games and practice schedules for the various sports? Why?

9. Outline a practice schedule for boys' and girls' teams you as athletic director would recommend for three selected sports seasons during which it would be necessary to share facilities.

10. Outline the duties you think are appropriate for student managers.

11. Present a plan for organizing and administering crowd control measures.

12. Give reasons why it is important for any athletic director planning a series of meets to be thoroughly familiar with the regulations of his/her state high school association.

13. Select a sport and prepare an outline or chart listing matters which must receive attention in organizing for a meet or tournament in that sport.

14. Prepare a bulletin of information you would provide schools participating in the meet or tournament you have planned in question 13.

NOTES

1. Bill Holmstrom, "The Game Manager Plan: A Game Saver for the Athletic Director," *Interscholastic Athletic Administration,* 7, no. 4 (Summer 1981), pp. 24–25.
2. Iowa High School Athletic Association, *1980–81 By-Laws,* pp. 13–14.
3. Florida High School Activities Association, *1981 By-Laws,* p. 17.
4. National Federation of State High School Associations, *So Now You're An Official* (Kansas City, Mo.: National Federation), p. 19.

BIBLIOGRAPHY

AMERICAN ASSOCIATION FOR HEALTH, PHYSICAL EDUCATION, AND RECREATION. *Crowd Control for High School Athletics.* Washington, D. C.: The Association, 1970.

FLORIDA HIGH SCHOOL ACTIVITIES ASSOCIATION. *1981 By-Laws.*

HILL, DICK. "Job Description for Athletic Administrators." *Interscholastic Athletic Administration,* 6, no. 3 (Spring 1980), 25–26.

HOLMSTROM, BILL. "The Game Manager Plan: A Game Saver for Today's Athletic Director." *Interscholastic Athletic Administration,* 7, no. 4 (Summer 1981), 24–25.

IOWA HIGH SCHOOL ATHLETIC ASSOCIATION. *1980–81 By-Laws.*

NATIONAL FEDERATION OF STATE HIGH SCHOOL ASSOCIATIONS. *So Now You're An Official.* Kansas City, Mo.: National Federation.

NEWCOMER, ART. "Boosters Clubs Support Your School." *Interscholastic Athletic Administration,* 5, no. 4 (Summer 1979), 14.

RESICK, MATTHEW C., and CARL E. ERICKSON. *Intercollegiate and Interscholastic Athletics for Men and Women,* Chapters 8 and 9. Reading, Mass.: Addison-Wesley, 1975.

8

Administration of the Local Interscholastic Athletic Program

High school associations in all states establish minimum standards and regulations which influence and give direction to high school athletics, but these organizations do not administer these activities, except for the district and state competition they sponsor. The importance and value of each school's program is determined by how well that school plans and administers it. Careful planning is an essential ingredient in successful administration of any program, and in high school athletics it involves the efforts and cooperation of many individuals, beginning with the board of education and extending to high school students. An initial step is to establish an organizational plan which defines the authority and responsibilities of the persons, or positions, included. Local policies and procedures must be developed and serve as guidelines to those to whom responsibilities are delegated. The administrative organization will differ in relation to the size of schools, but in all schools it will have a common purpose: to provide worthwhile educational experiences through athletic activities.

DIVISION OF RESPONSIBILITY IN LOCAL HIGH SCHOOL ATHLETIC ADMINISTRATION

Responsibility for the athletic program will vary with the size of the school and may range all the way from a one-man operation to plans involving several persons delegated authority and responsibility.

The Board of Education

State legislatures delegate the legal authority for administering educational programs to boards of education. Included is the authority to govern interscholastic athletic programs and to establish the requisite policies and regulations. Professional school administrators are employed by boards of education and delegated the responsibility for developing and recommending standards and policies for the districts and their schools to be considered for board adoption. Authority for implementing such policies may then be delegated to other professionals on the administrative staff or to members of the faculty.

It is important to emphasize at this point the importance of having all policies, including athletic policies, officially approved by the board of education, which gives them some semblance of legal status and makes it more difficult for anyone to challenge them in a court of law.

The Superintendent of Schools

The superintendent of schools is the professional employed to represent the board of education and to implement its policies. He/she is also expected to recommend policy for the board's consideration and has the final responsibility to the board for the athletic program just as for any other phase of the educational program. The complexities of the superintendent's job make it necessary in virtually all school districts for this administrator to delegate many responsibilities to other professionals serving under him/her, but all of us must remember that the final responsibility to the board of education is that of the superintendent.

It is only logical that members of the board of education should understand the school's philosophy of interscholastic athletics and the educational objectives it is trying to achieve through the interschool program. It is a primary responsibility of the superintendent to provide this understanding. He or she should also inform the board about the state high school association to which the high school belongs and explain its most important functions. Unless this is done, a school board member may misinterpret the situation as one in which the state association is a separate entity which imposes regulations and restrictions upon the school from the outside. It is important that the school board understands that the state high school association is an organization through which the high schools of the state work cooperatively in establishing statewide standards and regulations which become the minimum standards and regulations of each member school. Such knowledge will help the board of education better to evaluate athletic policies.

The superintendent should have a definite understanding with principals, athletic directors, and coaches that the athletic policies adopted shall be supported. They should be reviewed and reevaluated periodically and, if found unsatisfactory, should be changed rather than violated. The superintendent should also see to it that the policies are interpreted to the public. Arrangements should be made for the athletic director and coaches to speak to community organizations to which they will present the philosophy and objectives of the interscholastic program and the policies established to guide it. The administrator must decide on the type of organization school representatives will form for working out the school's athletic policies. Some of these types are discussed later in this chapter.

Finally, the superintendent should have an understanding with the board of education that it will firmly support any local policies and standards it adopts as well as those of its state high school association. Some state associations require official board of education approval of their minimum statewide standards as a prerequisite for membership in the association. Unless the board of education staunchly supports district policies, they are of little value.

The High School Principal

Superintendents generally delegate responsibility for the interscholastic program to the high school principal(s). They are the persons accountable for the secondary education program in their respective schools.

The relation of the high school principal to the athletic program is more specific than that of the superintendent in most instances. Athletics in physical education is a part of the curriculum. Interscholastics is a supplement to the curriculum through which additional learning experiences are offered. Both are under the supervision of the principal. The evaluation of a school by its patrons is influenced by what they observe at interschool games. Smooth administration of contests, well-disciplined students, and good sportsmanship leave a favorable impression for the school. Therefore, principals must provide active leadership for the interscholastic program and assume final responsibility for the numerous details, although they may delegate many of them to others on the staff. Principals must understand the athletic philosophy, objectives, and policies of the entire school system. If a school is one of several in the system, the athletic program in that institution should be conducted in accordance with the general scheme advocated or in effect in the system as a whole. Early in the school year, all concerned with the program should understand their individual responsibilities. The principal should make sure they do and then give unqualified support to each individual.

The primary responsibility of the principal is to make certain that interscholastic contests produce worthwhile learning outcomes. If they do not, they cannot be justified as a part of the educational progam. He or she must see to it that coaches and others on the faculty understand this and that they strive to make interscholastics educationally significant.

Among the details for which the principal is responsible is that of eligibility of contestants. Such certification always should be based on complete information concerning students' athletic and scholastic histories. Student bodies should be instructed in their responsibilities for contributing to the value of the athletic program. The principal may do much to bring about better relations between schools by attempting to foresee and forestall any possible differences or misunderstandings. Attempts should be made to settle them before they develop, and for most of them every possible effort should be made to avoid publicity. As evidence of interest in the athletic program, the principal should attend as many of the contests as possible. Commendations of outstanding examples of good sportsmanship or fine citizenship should be given to visiting schools. There should be a definite understanding with all school athletic officials regarding their responsibilities concerning game officials, finances, schedules, care of playing facilities, control of spectators, care of contestants, and so on. Usually it is the principal's duty to apportion existing facilities of the school's physical plant between intramural and interscholastic athletics, as well as between boys' and girls' activities. The principal should see that athletics are an integral part of the school's physical education program.

The extent to which responsibility is personally exercised by the principal will depend upon the size of the school. He or she may assume nearly all of it in the smaller high school, and in some of the smallest even the superintendent may do so. In larger schools the numerous duties of the principal leave too little time for proper athletic administration, and in those schools the responsibilities are more and more being delegated to other professionals.

The Athletic Administrator

The terms *athletic administrator* and *athletic director* have been used interchangeably in our discussions. Either designates an individual primarily responsible for the administration of the athletic program of a school. In smaller schools the position *director of athletics* may not exist by title but the duties entailed are assumed by the principal or delegated to an assistant principal.

The position of athletic director is becoming one of increasing importance in the interscholastic athletic program. Frequently, this person is also the director of physical education. The trend toward larger administrative units has added many responsibilities for both the superintendent and the principal. Attending to the many details of secondary administration limits the amount of time that the principal can give to supervising the athletic program. The interest of the public in interscholastics and the problems that arise when there is no adequate supervision have made it necessary to delegate much responsibility to an athletic director. Also, the fact that many younger principals have not come up through the ranks of athletics and coaching is another factor in their relying more and more upon professional athletic directors for assistance. Specialized preparation for the principalship today and the demand for principals with advanced degrees is causing prospective principals to bypass these experiences.

As the position of athletic director becomes more firmly established, candidates for the position are becoming much better trained individuals. They are generally former coaches, or coaches with reduced teaching loads, who have had additional preparation beyond the undergraduate level. Many have their master's degrees. The position is also a changing one. Formerly, its task was primarily to relieve the principal of the responsibility of such administrative details as scheduling games, hiring officials, checking equipment, arranging for faculty help at contests, seeing that the facilities were in order, and so on. With varied background and increased formal educational preparation today, the athletic director is becoming the person who is increasingly giving direction to the athletic program and is expected to recommend policies to the principal to be submitted to the superintendent. This added responsibility is a proper one and makes full understanding of the philosophy and objectives of interscholastic athletics mandatory. It must be realized that the policies recommended shall have the approval of the principal and superintendent, who are the final authorities. (See pages 5–6 for responsibilities of the athletic administrator.)

The Activities Director

The extracurricular programs in many of today's larger high schools have become so broad that the principal does not have sufficient time to supervise adequately and to coordinate all of the many intraschool and interschool student activities. Just as department heads have been appointed to supervise subject matter areas, a relatively new position of director of activities has been created in some schools, with responsibility to the principal for directing the entire extracurricular program. In some instances the title may be "assistant principal" with this responsibility. If the school also has a director of athletics, this work will be under the supervision of the director of activities, as will be those of the music director, speech director, club sponsors, and others.

This position demands qualifications similar to that of the principal, such as a broad understanding of school activities, supervisory capability, and administrative leadership ability. Schools with good directors of activities have improved their programs, and we can expect that the status of this position will become more significant in the future in determining school policies.

The Coach

By virtue of his/her position, the high school coach will always share in the responsibilities of athletic administration, which will vary with the size of the school and also with the sport he or she coaches. In some of the smaller high schools, except for certifying the eligibility of players, the coach may be delegated many administrative responsibilities. Often in such sports as golf, tennis, and others in which larger schools compete, he/she will be the only school representative present at out-of-town contests and will be in full charge of supervising players and any other students present.

The coach will want to share in establishing athletic policies and should be permitted to do so. This person must understand, however, that his or her authority generally consists of making recommendations for consideration by the athletic director and principal. It is important that the difference between interscholastic athletics and other types of athletics be realized. The policies presented for consideration must stem from an understanding of the philosophy and objectives on which the school's athletic program is based. The coach shall be cognizant of the fact that teaching youth through athletics is more important than providing entertainment for the public. If the policies suggested reflect this, the coach will become an influential member of the team.

The coach is usually given considerable latitude in establishing policies on training rules for athletes. He or she may find it both helpful and advisable to involve athletes in the formulation of training standards. Regardless of how they are developed, it is strongly recommended that training policies be submitted to the athletic director and principal for their approval, for the coach may need their support when serious violations occur. Their approval of the training standards will help to ensure this support. Some coaches have experienced embarrassment by setting training rules without the knowledge of the school administrators.

It is imperative that the coach adhere to the school policies established until such times as they are changed.

The Director of Physical Education

Often the athletic director is also the physical education director, which is a logical combination. Because of the relationship between the two programs, the director of physical education, when not also the director of athletics, should always be consulted on athletic policies and should assist in the administration of the athletic program. When the two positions exist separately in a school, mutual cooperative attitudes must prevail to allow each program to complement the other.

Faculty Representatives

Members of the faculty participate in the administration of athletic events in various ways ranging from selling and taking tickets to other duties assigned them. One or more members generally serve as the pep club sponsor(s), and the supervision of that organization is important in contest management, especially in contributing toward better sportsmanship and crowd control.

It is well that at least one faculty member other than athletic personnel be involved in considering policy for the school athletic program. Although such a representative may not have had wide experience in athletic matters, there are some distinct advantages in having the general faculty represented. The faculty will be in a position to give its view in regard to the relationship of interscholastics to other phases of the school program. Better faculty support for the athletic program can be expected if it is represented in policy making.

Students

High school students can assist in athletic administration in several capacities. Serving as student managers, hosts, and ushers have already been mentioned, but there are other responsibilities they may assume such as selling programs, working in concession stands, keeping statistics, and assisting faculty members in their assignments.

Today's students want to be involved, and it is advisable to involve them as much as their level of capability and maturity permits. They should understand that they cannot determine policy for the school but that their views will be considered. As stated above, athletes may participate by recommending training standards subject to the approval of the coach and with the realization that the coach reserves the right to reject them or to set additional standards which are deemed necessary and in the best interests of the majority of athletics. Athletes will often set more rigid training rules for themselves than those imposed by the coach.

The pep club has become an integral part of the interscholastic athletic program and involves large numbers of students. A cheerleader representative can well be included in the policy-making group.

The benefits of having students involved in policy-making discussions derive not so much from what they will contribute in the way of policy as from the results in having them in a position to understand better the reasons for the policies.

The administration of the high school interscholastic program is a cooperative endeavor which involves the cooperation and assistance of many persons. Proper organization and clear policies tend to make their efforts more effective.

ADMINISTRATIVE ORGANIZATION

In some small high schools there may be little semblance of any type of organization to administer the interscholastic athletic program. Quite often it is directed by one person, the principal or the superintendent, who also determines policies and procedures. Administrators of other small schools have seen fit to establish an athletic committee, commonly referred to in larger schools as an athletic council, to advise them by making recommendations on matters of policy and liaison with other groups. However, organizations of this type are more common in medium-size and large high schools, and in school districts having multiple high school units there may be a district-wide committee or council.

Organizational Plan for Small High Schools

Regardless of the size of the school, it seems desirable to bring faculty members and students into close contact with the athletic program. Good administrators do this through curricular activities and other school functions. Obviously, the superintendent or principal who is acting as the athletic administrator will have to take the initiative in forming an athletic council. The problems of the small school athletic program are generally fewer and not of such magnitude as to require regular meetings. The value of establishing an organization of this type lies in the fact that it is ready to function if called upon to do so. It can assist in policy making if desired, and such other matters as schedules, equipment, awards, and finances may be considered. These are sometimes unique problems for the small school which also may be studied.[1] Considerable time may pass before anything unusual requires the attention of this organization, but if an emergency should arise, the machinery for handling it is in existence and should facilitate somewhat smoother functioning.

It is recommended that the athletic council of a small high school be comprised of the following:

1. The superintendent of schools (chairperson)
2. The high school principal
3. A coach
4. One or two other members of the faculty
5. A member of the board of education
6. An elected or appointed representative of the student body

There is a difference of opinion among superintendents regarding whether a member of the board of education should be on the athletic council. Some feel that the board delegates its administrative functions to the superintendent and principal and should not be represented on the council, which might thereby be unduly influenced to conform to expressed board opinions. Others consider membership on school committees a good way of keeping board members better informed of potential problems in school administration. This of course is a matter which must be decided by the administrators of each individual school.

It is important that members of any athletic council understand that they are serving in an advisory capacity and that their responsibility and authority is limited to making recommendations to be considered by the superintendent and principal. It must be left to these individuals to decide whether official board of education approval of any recommendation is warranted.

Plan for Medium-Size Schools

What is meant by a medium-size school? It may have somewhat different meanings in different states depending upon the range of high school enrollments in those states. For the purpose of this discussion, we shall consider it a school with an enrollment between 150 and 500 students with a faculty of some 10 to 20 members.

An organizational plan for the control of athletics in the medium-size high school presents unlimited educational possibilities. Chief among them is the opportunity to keep the athletic program in its proper place in the curriculum. Sometimes, in the "nearly big" towns, there is an overemphasis on the importance of athletic teams, especially winning ones. In the same way that it is valuable in the smaller schools, so an athletic council may function well in schools of this size. Recommendations for the personnel of such a body in the medium-size high school are as follows:

1. The superintendent of schools
2. The high school principal (who should act as chairperson)
3. The athletic director (if there is one)
4. The coach or coaches
5. One or two additional members of the faculty
6. A member of the board of education
7. The pep club sponsor
8. Two high school athletes (boy and girl)
9. A representative of the pep club

It will be seen that the suggested form of organization for schools in this group is, naturally, more elaborate than that for smaller schools. It should not be assumed, however, that proper administration of the program is more important in one instance than in another. Rather, this more complex arrangement simply reflects the fact that the larger school system generally lends itself to more efficient organization for the administration of all educational matters, including athletics. It will be noted that the principal has been designated chairperson of the athletic council in place of the superintendent. The principal is in charge of the administration of other high school subjects; hence it is logical that he or she should have immediate responsibility for athletics. In schools of this size the relations and contacts between superintendent and principal are very close, and ideally they work as a unit. In most cases, however, superintendents are glad to delegate immediate responsibility for the athletic program to their high school principals. The athletic coaches should be members of the council because of their obviously vital connections with the program. In considering matters of policy or procedure, it is recommended that only the head coach should vote. One high school faculty member, and possibly two, should serve on the council in addition to the principal and coaches. It is desirable to rotate this faculty membership frequently in order that more faculty members may understand the school's athletic program and its objectives.

Meetings of the athletic council in schools of this size are generally more formal than those in smaller schools. Usually, there are more matters of policy to be discussed as well as decisions to be made. Accounts of the meetings should be kept, and it may be advisable to publish them in the local newspaper or school paper, if one is issued. If publication is not feasible, it is suggested that reports of council meetings be made to the student body at assembly periods. The purpose of these suggestions is to keep students and the public informed of the athletic policies and program of the school. It is common knowledge, of course, that school athletics, dramatics, forensics, musical activities, and the like attract the attention of both students and school patrons to an extent greater than do most other school functions. Keep everyone informed regarding the things for which the school stands in all these activities. Precedents can be established and publicized more easily through regular procedures than when unusual circumstances arise.

Plan for the Large High School

The large high school has much the same setup as the medium-size high school discussed in the preceding section, except that it has a well-established physical and health education program and usually sponsors a much greater range of athletic activities. Much of the detail work in administering the athletic program is delegated to the athletic director or faculty manager, the title of this official being dependent upon school terminology. Several coaches and assistant coaches make up the athletic coaching staff. School policies vary as to whether these individuals are members of the physical education department.

As in the suggested plans for athletic organization in the small and medium-size high school, it also is recommended that an athletic council be established. Its personnel should include:

1. The superintendent of schools (Undoubtedly his or her connection with the administration of the athletic program in the high school will be entirely advisory.)
2. The high school principal (who should act as chairperson)
3. The athletic director or faculty manager of athletics
4. The head coach of each boys' and girls' sport sponsored by the school (Assistant coaches should meet with the council, if possible, but only in an

advisory capacity and in order to be familiar with all action relative to the school athletic policy.)

5. One or two members of the high school faculty, to be appointed by the principal (The head of the physical and health education department should be included if this person is not the athletic director or a head or assistant coach.)

6. One member of the local board of education (This courtesy should be extended to the board with the request that it appoint a member.)

7. The supervisor of physical and health education for the local school system

8. The pep club sponsor

9. A cheerleader (elected or appointed)

10. Two high school athletes (boy and girl, elected or appointed)

This may seem like quite an extensive membership list for an administrative board to handle a high school athletic program. The scope of the council's activities, however, usually justifies the inclusion of all these individuals.

Meetings of the athletic council should be conducted in a businesslike manner. An agenda should be prepared for each session. Complete records of all meetings should be kept. It is obvious that matters which will come before the council for consideration in the large high school will be similar to those of the medium-size school. Many of these also will be the same basic ones that are important to the smallest high school sponsoring interscholastic athletics. The chief differences will be in their number and extent.

Plans for Larger Cities and Districts With Multiple High School Units

Although each school within a large city system, or within a reorganized district with two or more high schools, should have its own athletic council, it is important to have a broader plan which takes into consideration all the high schools in the system. In these situations there is a need for uniform policies and standards, which require more supervision and centralized control. Generally, the membership of the central council will be comprised of the athletic director for the district, an administrative representative from the superintendent's office, and the principal of each high school or an assistant principal designated by him/her. Cedar Rapids Community Schools (Iowa) has such a council.[2]

St. Louis, Missouri, has a well-organized plan for the administration of interschool athletics through the St. Louis Public High School League. A league manager is appointed to supervise the citywide program. A board of directors is selected from representatives of each school to determine league policies subject to review of the high school principals. An athletic director in each high school is responsible for the admninistration of interschool activities within the school in accord with the policies established by the board of directors and contained in the *League Handbook*. Excerpts from this handbook are printed herein to illustrate a plan of administrative organization for a large city school district and to offer ideas whch may be used in smaller school systems.

The foreword written by Dr. William Kottmeyer, former Superintendent of Instruction, provides the philosophy which guides the program:

ST. LOUIS PUBLIC SCHOOLS—SECONDARY ADMINISTRATION REGULATIONS FOR AFTER-SCHOOL ACTIVITIES

Foreword

You are familiar with the divergent attitudes taken toward high school athletic programs. One attitude is that the school's business is to offer academic learning and vocational skills and that elaborate athletic programs detract from these major purposes. Other critical observations are that the usual athletic programs lavish inordinate attention upon relatively few students, that the values of athletic prowess are distorted, that youngsters get the notion that one must win at all costs, that silly rivalries are encouraged, and that the costs of such progams are excessive.

Conversely, it is held that athletic programs promote health and endurance among the considerable number who do participate, that they furnish college opportunities to poor boys and girls, that they build character and fortitude in competition, that they teach sportsmanship, that they provide unifying interests and establish school loyalties for the student followers who do not actively participate, and that they provide for all students healthful and recreational opportunities.

In these large cities of the country, we are upon changing and critical times and, granting some of the virtues and vices of athletic programs, we can profitably reassess some of our favorite attitudes. Among our many school vexations, we are plagued with the problems of dealing with increasing numbers of boys who see little relationship between our academic program and making a living. Only vaguely aware of the transformation American industry is undergoing which almost daily diminishes the need for unskilled labor, they become our dropouts, our itinerant suspensions, our local discipline problems. When they remain in school, they enervate and sap the instructional program and they influence the attitude of the other students. Often their only stake in school is participation in the athletic program, and their only source of intelligible communication is with the coaches who represent masculine values which they understand and respect. Many boys come from broken homes in which there is no guiding or controlling male influence. A substantial athletic program, systematically organized, judicially manned, and aggressively regulated gives promise of becoming a more integral and important part of the total educational program of the large city school systems of the United States than it has in the past.

If our athletic programs are to perform such a function and to become a substantial educational force in our schools, certain duties and responsibilities will have to be assumed by the coaches, the athletic directors, the principals, and the central administrative units.

The coaches are expected to teach athletic skills efficiently and faithfully without being regulated by time tickets. The object of playing games is to win games and we can do without excessive piety about "how we play the game"; nevertheless, any coach destroys his educational usefulness who prizes winning so much that he tolerates abusive or profane language by his players, who permits or encourages dirty playing or fighting, who allows his players to quarrel about judgment decisions of game officials or to threaten them. If coaches are to be effective teachers, they will have to serve as unofficial advisors and counselors for the boys whom they direct in athletics and they should assume responsibility for their attendance, conduct, and academic performance. Above all, the coaches should lead these boys to understand the primary importance of their educational program.

The position of Athletic Director will have to become one of much greater responsibility than it has been in the past. We have tried to stress the role of the principal in improving instruction and if he/she is to do so, the many details of athletic supervision will have to be delegated to a responsible school official. The specific duties and responsibility of this official, the Athletic Director, are spelled out elsewhere. Principals will continue to be responsible for the total school program. Athletic directors are to be appointed annually by the principal, with the approval of the district director and the Director of Physical Education and Athletics. The athletic director will be immediately responsible to the principal for the conduct of the interschool and intramural athletic progam.

The principal's relationships to the athletic program are more or less obvious. He/she must, of course, make judicious appointments to the athletic staff and must, through the athletic director, hold the staff responsible for the efficient conduct of the program. More difficult is the principal's role in establishing in the school, and particularly among the academic faculty, an understanding and appreciation of the educational function of the athletic program within the total program of the modern large city high school. Equally challenging is the need to get the athletic staff to recognize the primacy of the total learning program and to capitalize upon their potential talents for motivating and guiding youngsters who are not amenable to the traditional disciplines and controls. The interschool contests, involving small numbers of students in tense competitive situations and great numbers of students as factional spectator groups, become realistic and standardized tests of the effectiveness of the total high school staff through the principal's leadership in developing attitudes and conduct patterns which are important objectives of our instructional programs.

Citywide administrative controls over the Physical Education and Athletic program are now vested in the Division of Physical Education and Athletics. The supervisory functions of the Division are presumably well understood. The Division is responsible with the principal and athletic director for efficiency of instruction in the Physical Education classes, for the production of and adherence to the curriculum, for the appointment, in collaboration with the Personnel Division, and, with the principal, for the evaluation of the teachers and for their in-service activities. It is responsible to the Assistant Superintendent of High

School for the compiling and control of the athletic budgets, for the customary management functions of the High School Athletic League, for the supervision of the interschool athletic contests, and, with the principal and through the athletic director, for supervision and control of the intramural programs.

The Division is to function as a useful and cooperative agency to relieve the high school principal of the many technical management and supervisory chores which are necessary in a local program for which the principal is ultimately responsible. It is expected that the Director, with the District Director, will approve all Physical Education and athletic appointments in the local schools, will advise and assist the principal in his/her staff evaluations, and will coordinate the various local programs through the athletic directors.

CONSTITUTION OF THE ST. LOUIS PUBLIC HIGH SCHOOL LEAGUE

Article I. Name

The name of this organization shall be "The St. Louis Public High School League."

Article II. Jurisdiction

The St. Louis Public High School League shall control all interscholastic athletic activities of the member schools scheduled by the League, subject to the Constitution of the Missouri State High School Activities Association. The action of the Board of Directors shall be final unless one of the Principals requests the Assistant to the Superintendent to call a meeting of the Principals to review the action of the Board of Directors.

Article III. Membership

The League shall consist of all the Public High Schools in the City of St. Louis.

Article IV. Representation

Each school shall be entitled to one faculty representative to be selected by the Principal. These representatives shall constitute the Board of Directors.

Article V. Officers

Section 1. The executive power of the League shall be vested in the Manager.

Section 2. The manager shall preside at all the meetings of the Board of Directors. He shall also act as secretary at all meetings, shall act as treasurer of the League Funds, and shall be responsible for carrying out the measures passed by the Board of Directors. The League Manager shall be appointed by the Board of Education.

Article VI.   Board of Directors

The Board of Directors shall have charge of the arrangement and administration of all games, contests, tournaments, and meets scheduled by the League.

Article VII.   Meetings

Section 1.   Meetings shall be held at the call of the League Manager, or on written request of any school. Due notice of all meetings shall be given in writing by the Manager to each school.

Section 2.   A quorum shall consist of a majority of the representatives of the schools.

Article VIII.   Eligibility—Participation and Eligibility Lists

A.   In order to represent his school in any contest, tournament, meet or as a cheerleader, a student must meet all the requirements of the Missouri State High School Activities Association and, in addition, any other requirements or limitations as may be imposed in Section 1.

B.   A student shall be permitted to compete in interscholastic high school athletics for no more than four (4) consecutive years after having entered the ninth grade of any secondary school. This requirement shall be waived in the case of students entering the Armed Forces of our Country, as provided in Article V, paragraph K, of the Constitution of the Missouri State High School Activities Association. This amendment shall become effective and in force with the beginning of the 1946–1947 school year.

C.   A student enrolling in a member secondary school other than that of his home school district may not represent that school in athletic competition for a period of forty weeks and not before the fifth semester.

D.   A student residing in two overlapping districts (technical and cosmopolitan) may choose his "home" school when he enrolls the first time in a St. Louis public high school. This is interpreted to mean that a student shall make a choice of a general or technical high school at his initial enrollment in a member school. Thereafter, if he moves from the school of his first enrollment to another school, e.g., from technical to general or from general to technical, he must attend his new school for a period of 40 weeks before becoming eligible for athletic competition.

E.   The condition of "C" shall apply to a student transferring to another member school without a change in his legal residence.

F.   A student who changes his school district by changing his legal residence may remain at the school he is then attending without affecting his eligibility for League competition, provided he is eligible at that time. He may also change to the school of his new home district and become eligible for League competition immediately.

G. A student is not eligible when under suspension from classes by his administrator and a student who withdraws from school because of disciplinary measures shall not be eligible in any sport for one full calendar year from the date of withdrawal. When applied to the Lincoln High School and Tutorial School, it is interpreted to mean a boy or girl becomes eligible upon reassignment to a school a year from the date he was suspended provided the other requirements of eligibility are met.

H. Terminal Education students are not eligible. There is no possibility for them to be eligible.

I. An interpretation of the Athletic Eligibility for schools with annual promotion is as follows: An athlete must be passing in three solid subjects (full credit) at the end of the first semester in order to be eligible for competition during the Spring Term. To become eligible for the Fall Term, the athlete must have passed three solid subjects during the preceding Spring Term. A solid subject is one that has the equivalency of a half unit value for one semester; it can be either half of the full year unit course or a one semester course with one-half unit credit.

J. The Manager is to use the postmark date as the date of receipt of the eligibility lists.

K. Each school will send eleven (11) copies of each eligibility list to the League Manager. He will, in turn, prepare eleven packs of each, keeping one in the League files, and sending one pack to each member school.

L. Eligibility lists changes will be due on Wednesday of the first week of the second semester (this exception to the 5-day rule for this period only). If a team participates before this date, eligibility lists for that event must be in the League Office by the date of participation.

M. When a player or team appears for any contest or meet scheduled by the League without being accompanied by a coach or other faculty representative of the school they shall not be allowed to compete.

N. A student entering a member school other than that of his home district, by reason of permissive transfer regulations, will be ineligible for forty weeks and not before his fifth semester.

Article IX. Protests

A. All protests shall be presented in writing by the Principal of the protesting school to the League Manager, who will send a copy of the protest to all member schools.

B. Protests arising from the interpretation of the Missouri State High School Activities Association Constitution shall be referred to and settled by the Board of Directors of the Missouri State High School Activities Association, whose decision shall be final.

C. Protests not involving an interpretation of the Missouri State High School

Activities Association Constitution shall be decided by the Board of Directors of the St. Louis Public High School League, whose decision shall be final.

D.   If a team shall play an ineligible contestant, such team shall forfeit all games, contests, or events in which said ineligible contestant shall have participated.

E.   It is the duty of the Principal of the member school to notify the League Manager immediately if a contestant previously certified as eligible becomes ineligible or is found to be ineligible. The League Manager will then notify all other member schools of this change in eligibility. The use of a contestant known to be ineligible is unthinkable, and a school violating the spirit of this clause is subject to severe disciplinary action by the Board of Directors of the St. Louis Public High School League.

Article X.   Officials

Officials shall be chosen as follows:

A.   The League Manager will prepare a list of the officials available.

B.   All Head Coaches for a particular sport will meet and add to the list of names any officials that they desire to be considered.

C.   The final list of officials compiled by the Manager and Coaches becomes the approved list.

D.   From this list each coach selects the officials that he approves for his games. The Manager assigns officials for all League Games from his list. All assignments made by the Manager are final.

E.   The approved list of officials shall be made new for each season.

Article XI.   Finances

Section 1.   The Public High School League shall be financed by the money derived from the sale of tickets at the gate in the various sports and money appropriated by the Board of Education.

Section 2.   All receipts from the sale of tickets at the member schools for the scheduled League games of a regular season shall belong to the school at which the tickets are sold.

Article XII.   Amendments

The Constitution and By-Laws may be amended by an affirmative vote of a majority of the schools constituting the League, provided the proposed amendment has been submitted in writing to the representative of each school at least two (2) weeks before the meeting in which the amendment is presented for adoption.

Article XIII. Unsportsmanlike Conduct

Section 1. Unsportsmanlike conduct by a participant or participants shall be construed to mean using vulgar or profane language, striking or attempting to strike an official, coach, or spectator during League competition in which any St. Louis Public High School team is involved.

Section 2. If any of these acts is committed, it becomes mandatory for the League Manager to obtain the information as soon as possible and immediately report the matter to the League Board of Directors. Pending final action by the League Board of Directors, the participant or participants involved shall be suspended from all League Competition.

Section 3. The Board of Directors of the St. Louis High School League shall weigh the facts and take such action as it deems advisable. Its decision shall be final upon approval by a majority of its members.

BY-LAWS

I. Entering and Withdrawing from Sports

Section 1. There shall be annual contests for the championship of this League in any sport in which a majority of the member schools express a desire to compete by applying in writing to the Board of Directors, requesting that regulations be adopted and a schedule be set up.

Section 2. A member school may withdraw from active participation in any sport provided the decision to withdraw has been filed in writing with the Manager before a schedule in that sport has been drawn. The school that has withdrawn from a sport shall enjoy all the privileges and assume equal responsibilities of the League, except that the school shall not share in any surplus remaining in the treasury, or be assessed for any indebtedness at the close of the playing session.

II. Awarding Championship

The Board of Directors shall meet within four (4) days after the last contest of each sport for the purpose of declaring a championship in that sport. Failure of the Board of Directors to comply with this rule shall be interpreted as automatically awarding the championship in the manner provided for in the By-Laws of this Constitution.

III. Awarding of Trophies

Section 1. A suitable trophy shall be awarded to the school winning the championship in each sport. The cost of the trophy to the League shall not exceed thirty dollars ($30.00) per trophy. All championship trophies are to be awarded by the League Manager as follows:

Championship: League Manager—Team Captain—Principal of the School
All Sports: League Manager—Athletic Director—Principal of the School
Sportsmanship: League Manager—Student President—Principal of the
   School

Section 2.   The League shall not accept Athletic Trophies other than those sanctioned by the Board of Education.

IV. Suspension of Rules

Any provision of these By-Laws may be suspended, for a specifically stated time and purpose, by an affirmative vote of three-fourths (¾) of the members of the Board of Directors.

V. Administering Aid to an Injured Athlete

No person shall give aid to injured athletes at any game, contest or meet under the direction and supervision of the League, except coaches, other school personnel, and authorized physicians.[3]

ATHLETIC LEAGUES AND CONFERENCES AS ADMINISTRATIVE AGENCIES

School conferences and leagues, as discussed in Chapter 2, were first established to control abuses that individual schools were powerless to change. Their initial function was to formulate rules to eliminate outside players from high school teams by providing that all participants had to be bona fide students and by adopting standards for eligibility purposes. It quickly became evident that conferences also offered definite administrative advantages in such matters as expediting the scheduling of games, sponsoring league championships, maintenance of records, assignment of officials, resolving disputes between schools, and so on. Later they began to give attention to improving sportsmanship, creating better relations among schools, and promoting the educational and recreational values of conference activities. Their functions now include at least three phases: (1) control, (2) administration, and (3) promotion of the educational and recreational values of interschool contests.

The fact that nearly all schools are now members of conferences or leagues is proof of their success. It is general practice to operate under a constitution and by-laws consistent with the state associations to which all members adhere, which results in greater uniformity in the administration of interscholastic games among the schools. Local school policies are, therefore, greatly influenced by conference regulations.

Optimum Size

Usually the league or conference includes a comparatively small geographical section of the state, with its membership composed of schools of comparable size and sponsoring similar or identical activities. Preferably, leagues should be small in size (five to eight or ten schools), because an unwieldy organization is ineffective. All member schools should meet each other in all sports sponsored by the league during the season. If they cannot, it is safe to say that the organization is too large.

Services of Athletic Conferences

The value of the services rendered to member schools by athletic conferences and leagues depends on their local administration. Athletic conferences may serve to:

1. Enable member school officials to become better acquainted with each other through their league meetings
2. Provide opportunities for schools of comparable size to compete with each other
3. Allow the determination of league championship through comparatively local competition and without excessive team travel
4. Provide methods for keeping league records of individual achievements and school standings
5. Assign contest officials by league officers and establish uniform fees
6. Develop definite ways for the improvement of sportsmanship at athletic contests through programs, exchange assemblies, school visits, and the like
7. Ensure full schedules of all member schools in league-sponsored sports
8. Conduct league meets and tournaments in appropriate sports
9. Act in an advisory capacity with state athletic association officials on matters of general athletic importance
10. Establish local league regulations for the conduct of games, including student and spectator control, admission prices, complimentary tickets, program arrangements, and so on
11. Resolve any disputes between or among its member schools

MATTERS APPROPRIATE FOR ATHLETIC COUNCIL CONSIDERATION

It should be remembered at this point that the athletic council is an advisory body and does not assume the authority of the superintendent of schools or the principal, nor of the athletic administrator to whom authority has been delegated. Neither should it be expected to have the final say in decisions properly belonging to any of these persons. Decisions such as the percent of the total school budget to be allocated for the athletic program had best be left to the superintendent and board of education. They will want to discuss with the high school principal and athletic director the needs and estimated cost of the athletic program, but the decision must be theirs. Members of the council would have insufficient knowledge to determine allocations within the total school budget. The athletic council can best consider those matters on which the administrators believe they can benefit from its advice. Routine athletic administrative responsibilities can be discussed, but time should not be wasted in considering those the athletic director will handle.

The following areas are some on which recommendations can be found helpful:

1. *Philosophy and objectives.* Council members can be asked to assist in formulating a statement of philosophy and objectives for the school, which will give the interscholastic athletic program a sense of direction. One of the principal values of securing its assistance is to better educate the members as to why the school offers the program. Any statement prepared and approved by the superintendent and principal should be presented to the board of education for official adoption.

2. *Policies.* Policies are essential to good athletic administration, and recommendations from the council should be for the purpose of establishing guidelines for administering the program. Again, policies developed should preferably receive the approval of the board of education.

3. *Review of schedules.* Review of tentative schedules before they are officially approved and announced can help to avoid conflicts and resulting problems.

4. *Finances.* Recommendations can be helpful regarding fees to be paid officials, admission prices, use of profits from concessions, special fund raising projects, cost of awards, and so on.

5. *Sharing of facilities.* This is an area of conflict in many schools, particularly those with inadequate facilities for both boys' and girls' athletics. The council can recommend times for practice for boys' and girls' teams, athletic contests, and intramurals, which may make it easier for the athletic director to arrange schedules.

6. *Sportsmanship and crowd control.* Involving the council in suggesting measures for crowd control and procedures for improving sportsmanship fosters faculty and student cooperation in these matters and assists in identifying potential trouble spots.

7. *Review of state high school association standards and regulations.* This task will help provide a better understanding of the regulations to which the school must adhere and of the eligibility standards students must meet to

participate. Ways of educating students and parents to these standards are also worthy of discussion.

8. *Additional local school standards.* Some individual schools frequently adopt local standards higher than those of the state association. Some set more specific standards for citizenship and conduct. The council's opinion on whether such standards are needed or advisable can be useful, as well as what additional standards should be considered.

9. *Publicity.* Council members may contribute ideas on ways athletic contests and the purposes of the athletic program can be better publicized.

10. *Awards.* This includes such matters as the types of awards the school should give, qualifications for awards, and award ceremonies.

11. *Guidelines for cheerleaders.* Policies to guide the cheerleaders, such as when and when not to cheer, will aid the pep club sponsor in improving the educational values of that organization.

12. *Special events.* Athletic banquets, invitational tournament sponsorship, parents' night, and other special events are appropriate topics on which the council might be asked to give advice.

The above represent some of the areas in which an athletic council can contribute, but it must be understood that the principal and/or superintendent shall have *veto power* over any action of the council. Depending upon the overall administrative organization of the school and the size of the school district, one of these individuals is accorded final responsibility for administering the high school program and is, therefore, accountable for resultant acts and events. This presents no problem by virtue of the fact that the great majority of the council's recommendations will be approved. When any are disapproved, valid reasons for the veto should always be made known. There may be provisions for appealing vetoes to a higher authority, but appeal should not be exercised without the consent of the person who has denied the recommendation. It is administratively unwise for any school committee to "go around" the principal or superintendent to a higher authority. We must not forget that the function of an athletic council—even its very existence—is determined by the school administrators and board of education.

ESTABLISHING AND DEFINING HIGH SCHOOL ATHLETIC POLICY

If well-defined athletic policies are in existence in a school, they can be upheld as guidelines for the interschool and intramural programs. Establishing general policies ahead of time may prevent or alleviate many difficult situations.

Responsibility for Developing Athletic Policies

The final responsibility for developing school athletic policies rests with the board of education; however, in practice it is delegated to the superintendent of schools, who in many school systems will further delegate it to the high school principal. In large high schools it is becoming increasingly typical to give the athletic administrator this responsibility under supervision of the principal.

The procedures and individuals involved in the process will vary from school to school and from administrator to administrator. Several will seek the advice of an athletic council, while others will do it in consultation with the coaches and other faculty members concerned, and some will develop policies in a unilateral fashion, which is the least desirable procedure. Regardless of the procedure employed, it is advisable to have all significant policies officially approved by the board of education.

The athletic policies must be appropriate. To be appropriate they must be consistent with the philosophy and objectives of the school's interscholastic program. The school must decide why it has an athletic program and what it is trying to achieve through it. Policies are for the purpose of helping to achieve the desired objectives. When they aid in attaining this purpose, they are appropriate. Before establishing policies, the philosophy and objectives must be clarified. This was the function of Chapter 2, which you may want to review in order to better understand the policies discussed later in this chapter.

Relation of Athletic Policies and Outside Groups

Any school, regardless of its size, can and should define its athletic policy and inform its patrons accordingly. This statement simply means that the administration should decide on the program to be followed throughout the year and adhere to it. Circumstances and local situations often affect school administrators—sometimes either seriously inhibiting or overstimulating them—in determining the number and extent of their schools' athletic activities. There are the "downtown" interests that frequently are more concerned with the athletic record and superiority of the local high school team than with the educational values of athletics and the welfare of the participants. Also, there are those individuals who have no idea of the problems involved in some of the suggestions made by students themselves or by apparently well-wishing school patrons. The activities of such people present a real problem to the school administrator. They make it all the more important that the school's athletic policy be understood, and this will not happen unless it is discussed and brought out into the open. However, one should not be too intent upon an immediate change in the entrenched attitudes of a community.

No outside group should be allowed to determine athletic policy for the school, such as invariably happens when a vested interest is allowed to influence the athletic director or the school administration. There is nothing wrong and no difficulty is likely to develop from an outside agency donating money to the athletic fund, or any other fund of the school, provided there are no strings attached. On the other hand, if an outside group wishes to donate money only for a specified purpose, such as purchasing a new football scoreboard with advertising on it, acceptance will set a precedent which may eventually lead to serious problems when others request a similar privilege, and it may well be the money could be better used elsewhere in the athletic program where there is a greater need. A school may accept donations for any program without encountering problems if it is clearly understood in advance that the board of education and the school administrators will determine the use of the funds.

Athletic Policy Considerations

Several areas of policy considerations were discussed on pages 213–215. There are additional policy issues to which school administrators might well give consideration, depending on the school's locality:

1. The relation and division of available facilities and personnel between intramural and interscholastic athletics
2. The number of sports activities in which the school can offer (a) proper teaching and coaching; (b) adequate equipment; and (c) satisfactory playing facilities
3. Educationally justifiable athletic schedules—length of them and frequency of games
4. Methods of financing the athletic program
5. Determining ways of providing comparable interscholastic opportunities for boys and girls
6. The place of junior high school athletics in the general athletic program (see Chapter 15)
7. The student and faculty relation in the organization for control of athletics
8. Understanding of the relation of the local school to its league and state athletic association
9. The policy of the school in the care of, and payment for, athletic injuries
10. Delegation of authority to coaches or faculty managers in matters pertaining to contracts, eligibility, equipment, schedules, officials, and the like
11. Transportation of athletic teams
12. Guidelines for booster club cooperation and support

IMPLEMENTING LOCAL ATHLETIC POLICIES

Adopting athletic policies must not be considered an end in itself. To be effective, these policies require a definite plan of implementation. It is the responsibility of the athletic administrator to plan practical procedures for accomplishing this objective, and the superintendent should insist that these plans be made available. A comprehensive approach is recommended in which the duties of the high school administrator, the athletic director, coaches, the pep club sponsor, athletes, and cheerleaders are outlined. Attention must be given to providing full information in regard to athletic policies and procedures for enforcing them.

Basic to an understanding of interscholastic policies is a clear knowledge of the school's philosophy and objectives for the athletic program. The policies will be more readily accepted by the public if it understands the school's purposes in promoting an athletic program. This underlying philosophy should be reviewed as an introduction to any discussion of the policies that guide the program.

The Superintendent

The primary responsibility of the superintendent is to make certain that the board of education has full knowledge of the athletic policies and approves of them. These policies can be explained when they are presented to the board for consideration of approval. In many school communities the superintendent is invited to speak on the athletic program before the chamber of commerce, service clubs, and other community groups. The superintendent should use these opportunities to discuss the interscholastic athletic policies. Because of the pressure on this person's time, a member of the athletic council or staff may be suggested to substitute at a speaking invitation.

The Principal

The entire faculty should have a knowledge of the athletic policies applied by the school. It is logical to expect the principal, as supervisor of the faculty, to be responsible for the faculty's understanding. Using part of a scheduled faculty meeting for this purpose will help to emphasize that the athletic program is an integral part of the total educational program of the school.

It is generally considered that the principal has the final responsibility for the school's interscholastic program and is held accountable for such by the superintendent and the board of education.[4] Hence, supervision must be given to the athletic director, coaches, and pep club sponsor to ensure that they properly carry out the implementation of athletic policies. In the larger schools the school administrator may find it necessary to delegate supervisory authority to the athletic director under the general supervision of that person's office. In such cases it is important that they work closely together.

The Athletic Director

This individual is the chief lieutenant of the principal. Some schools do not have an athletic director by name but delegate the responsibilities of this position to an assistant principal. We shall not be concerned with the title but shall devote our attention to the duties of the position when the principal does not directly supervise the athletic program.

The position of athletic director shall be regarded as an administrative one. The athletic director must be certain that all coaches fully understand the school's philosophy, objectives, and policies.[5] Coaches should have an opportunity to suggest policy changes, but until such changes are made, they must abide by those policies in effect. Each coach should be required to discuss the athletic objectives, policies, and standards of eligibility with members of his or her sport squad. The purposes and reasons for these rules should be emphasized. Athletes who understand why the school offers them interscholastic opportunities and realize what the school is trying to help them achieve make better ambassadors for the school. Likewise, coaches who give ample attention to the most worthwhile objectives of athletics are more highly respected by players and long remembered as "teachers." Coaches must fully enforce policies applying to athletes and take prompt action when violations occur. It is the duty of the athletic director to give the necessary supervision to see that coaches carry out these responsibilities and those discussed in the next section.

The High School Coach

The high school coach occupies a most strategic position in the interscholastic program. He or she is in direct contact with players and has more influence upon them than any other single individual. The coach also is most influential in developing proper attitudes in student and adult fans.

Because coaches are accountable to the athletic director and/or high school principal, it is important that these persons be afforded the opportunity of recommending coaches to be employed. Care must be exercised in selecting a coaching staff.[6] A prospective coach has a right to know the school's philosophy and objectives of athletics and the policies applied in implementing them. School officials must be certain he/she will accept and support them. A mutual understanding should be derived from the interview in the hiring process.

Shortages of coaches in some cases have forced schools to employ nonfaculty coaches if they want to continue particular sports in their programs.[7] This should be only a last resort, and, advisably, such persons should be fully certified teachers who are not currently teaching. It is even more important that these coaches understand school policies and adhere to them.

If athletics are to be educational, *teaching students through athletic activities* must be as much a concern as winning games. The following is taken from a manual published by the Missouri State High School Activities Association to aid coaches in assuming this responsibility.

THE COACH'S RESPONSIBILITIES

The athletic coach, in his/her strategic position, is the most influential person upon the educational outcomes and the sportsmanship and conduct of players and spectators. Hence, he/she shall be expected to assume the following responsibilities:

1. To set a proper example. He/she shall maintain a professional attitude toward fellow coaches and toward athletic game officials. His/her complaints should be filed through the proper channels, and he/she should avoid showing any disrespect on the athletic field or playing floor either during or following games.
2. He/she must instruct his/her players regarding the philosophy, objectives, policies, and standards of conduct set by his/her school.
3. He/she must repeatedly explain the potential values that interscholastic athletics offer for personality and character development of players. These will not come automatically without his/her guidance.
4. He/she shall distinguish between emphasis on competition and overemphasis on winning. Learning to do one's best is a worthwhile educational goal, but an obsession on winning which causes loss of sight of the educational and recreational values of competition is detrimental to the interscholastic program.
5. He/she shall view and cause others to view games in their proper perspective. Although he/she must stimulate a desire to win, he/she must teach players the enjoyment and values of competing regardless of whether the game is won or lost.
6. Standards of sportsmanship and training standards must be developed. It is strongly recommended that these be approved by the school administration and board of education. Sportsmanship standards contained in game rules and the provisions of MSHSAA By-Law Section 11 should be carefully explained to players. *(See MSHSAA By-Law Section 11 in MSHSAA Handbook.)* The reasons for these standards must be well understood.
7. He/she shall enforce the standards of sportsmanship and conduct. Substitution should be made for any player who shows any signs of a display of temper, disgust, etc. A player who is assessed a penalty by a game official for unsportsmanlike conduct should be removed from that game and the player should not be permitted to play in the next succeeding game if the violation is flagrant. Players should understand that intentionally striking a player, etc., will result in their not being permitted to play in the following game. The player must understand that his/her action casts a reflection on the coach, the entire team, and the school community.
8. The standards of eligibility that a student must meet for the privilege of representing his/her school in interscholastic athletics shall be thoroughly reviewed at the beginning of each sport season. A proper understanding of the nonschool competition and award standards is of particular importance. *(See MSHSAA Handbook, Article VIII, Section 5.)*

WHAT H. S. ATHLETES SHOULD BE TAUGHT IN ADDITION TO SKILLS

1. The history of school athletics, including:

    a. That athletic activities in the beginning were initiated by students themselves for one predominant purpose, recreation.

b. That school officials eventually recognized that they could have significant educational values.

c. That the schools individually and cooperatively adopted standards to guide interscholastic athletics so that they would provide:

(1) Educational and recreational values to participants and student spectators.

(2) Fairness and equity among players.

2. The school's philosophy of interscholastic athletics. This can best be done by helping students to understand the answer to the question, "Why does this school have an interscholastic athletic program?"

3. A student should understand that the interscholastic program provides a laboratory in which he has the opportunity to learn:

a. Skills (taught through practice in the sport concerned)

b. Knowledge

(1) Rules of the game (game standards).

(2) Importance of abiding by the rules (upholding the standards contained in the rules).

(3) That consequences follow violations.

(4) Eligibility standards. A student should be taught that the concept of eligibility is fundamental in our representative form of democracy. No student has an inherent right to represent a school in interscholastic athletics. This is a privilege to be attained by meeting the standards set for that privilege. This is the basic theory that caused our forefathers to set careful standards for persons wishing to represent others by being chosen to public office. *(A brochure, "How to Protect your High School Eligibility," is available from the MSHSAA for this purpose.)*

c. Emotional patterns and their importance *(This area includes attitudes, ideals, sense of fair play, respect, courtesy, etc., which involves a "feeling" on the part of the participant.)*

(1) Ideals of fair play.

(2) Respect for authority.

(3) Self-control.

(4) Sportsmanship.

(5) Ideals of honesty demonstrated by playing in strict accord with the rules.

(6) Respect for opposing players.

(7) A desire to excel.

(8) An appreciation of the educational and recreational values of competition.

d. To provide educational recreation. *(Students should understand that educational recreation differs from other types of recreation in that in addition to leisure time activities, it has an educational purpose.)*

4. The interschool contests provide opportunities to demonstrate and to evaluate the best that the students have learned in the following areas:

   a. Skills.

   b. Knowledge.

   c. Emotional patterns.

5. Officials shall be respected and shown proper courtesies. Students shall be caused to understand that the athletic game officials provide for fairness among players by enforcing the game rules. Although an official may occasionally make a mistake in a judgment decision, it is the mistakes made collectively by players that really determine the outcome of games.

6. Players shall be taught the values of competition. Teaching students to try to do their best, even better than any other, is educationally sound and a worthy objective in any endeavor. They must, however, fully understand the difference between emphasizing competition and overemphasizing winning. When winning is emphasized to the extent that it causes a loss of sight of the educational and recreational values of competition, it is being overemphasized and interscholastic games then can be detrimental to the educational and recreational purposes of school athletics.

These are the important educational outcomes inherent in the objectives of interscholastics. A good reference for more detailed information regarding the philosophy and objectives of school athletics will be found in the bulletin, "A Clarification of the Philosophy and Objectives of Interscholastic Athletics," which is available to you free-of-charge from the MSHSAA Office upon request.

PROCEDURES COACHES MAY EMPLOY TO TEACH THESE OUTCOMES

1. Frequent short lectures of approximately five minutes near the beginning of the practice period planned in such way from day to day, and week to week, to include items in the above outline.

2. Provide students with written bulletins. Many coaches now send home with students informative bulletins for instructional purposes. This has an advantage in that the parents frequently become better informed. This bulletin should contain a statement of the school's philosophy and most worthwhile objectives of interscholastic athletics and the most significant values to be received through them.

3. Frequent generalizations in the form of relaying to players and students complimentary remarks about team plays, acts of sportsmanship, good behavior, etc., received by the coach from officials and others, and emphasizing the significance of them will do much to enhance the most important values inherent in interscholastic athletics. Clippings and letters of this type make excellent material for the coach's bulletin board. A famous juvenile judge once said, "Goodness needs a press agent!" Too often we become too busy to note the good phases of our program. Neglecting this can be confusing and misleading to youth in their groping for a sense of values.

4. School assemblies. Coaches and their players can present good assembly

programs on the educational and recreational values of interscholastic athletics.

Whether the interscholastic sport which you coach will have significant educational and recreational values for the students in your school will, in the final analysis, depend upon the attention that you as a teacher devote to them.[8]

It is general practice for the coach to be invited near the beginning of the sport season to speak to the booster club and various service clubs on the team's chances for the season. This is an appropriate time for him or her to review the interscholastic philosophy, objectives, and policies. It is highly important that fans have a clear understanding of them in order to avoid problems for both coach and school.

In addition to the policies of the athletic council, the coach will generally have training rules for his or her athletes which also involve policy. As stated before, it is suggested that athletes be encouraged to recommend training standards to the coach, and that those finally adopted be presented to the athletic council for approval, or to the administration if the school does not have an athletic council. After being established, they should be put in writing along with the official school athletic policies and provided to the players and their parents. Experienced coaches have long recognized the significance of and help afforded by keeping parents fully informed. Some prepare manuals for athletes and their parents which contain a statement of the interscholastic philosophy and objectives, school policies, standards of eligibility, training rules, and any other pertinent information which they desire them to have. This practice is a great help in implementing school athletic policies.

The Pep Club Sponsor

The pep club generally includes far more students than does the team on the field or floor. There will be school policies to guide this organization. It is the responsibility of the pep club sponsor to see that all members thoroughly understand them. As the principal representatives of the club, cheerleaders should be expected to aid the sponsor in communicating with other members these policies as well as the philosophy and objectives of the interscholastic program.

Media To Be Used

The practice of having school representatives speak to community groups has been discussed earlier in this chapter. There are other media that the school might well use, as the following suggestions indicate.

1. Written statements of the school's philosophy, objectives, and policies for the athletic program are strongly recommended. These can be in the form of a prepared bulletin or can be contained in athletic manuals. Wide distri-

bution of them is advisable. Some schools have involved art classes in the making of posters displaying school policies and standards. Involving students other than athletes and cheerleaders helps broaden the understanding among the student body.

2. If a school newspaper is published, athletic policies should be presented through it.

3. Cooperation of local news media should be solicited. Prepared statements for the press, radio, and television are recommended. Some schools require radio stations broadcasting games to give statements prepared by the principal or athletic director in return for the privilege of broadcasting and consider this practice more advantageous than charging for broadcast rights.

4. Athletic philosophy, objectives, and policies should be included in game programs. It is quite common for game programs to contain advertising of local businesses. It is far more important that they be used to advertise the school program and its objectives. The former generally has no relationship to education; the latter helps to publicize an important phase of the educational program.

Enforcement of School Policies

Proper enforcement of school policies requires that responsibilities be shared and fully assumed by all who have a part in the administration of the program. The athletic council or school administration must provide leadership in formulating procedures for enforcement. The responsibilities of the principal, athletic director, coaches, pep club sponsor, cheerleaders, team captains, and players should be clearly outlined.

Steps should be formalized for handling reported violations. Because the courts today give attention to whether due process has been provided in practically all instances wherein rules and regulations are involved, it is strongly recommended that each school have an established and published due process procedure (see Chapter 16). It is important that a hearing be afforded before penalties are assessed. Asking the offender to appear before the athletic director or principal to show cause why action should not be taken is a wise initial step. This in itself is in accord with the principle of due process and places the individual(s) on the defensive rather than the school. The right of appeal of a ruling of the athletic director or principal to an appeals committee, or to the board of education, is important, particularly in serious cases. In most instances the violator will not request a hearing or appeal, but it is important to inform the person involved of the course that may be followed. This will help to avoid court cases and will be a significant factor should there be one.

Action taken should be reasonable but firm and appropriate with the offense. When policies are adopted, they should be consistently upheld. One or two instances when they are not enforced greatly reduces their effectiveness.

The Booster Club

The booster club is mentioned here because if its members understand athletic policies, they will avoid engaging in any activities or projects objectionable to the school. It is wise for the athletic director or someone designated by him/her to attend all booster club meetings to make certain its members understand school policies and adhere to them. With proper guidance, the booster club can be an asset to the athletic program and assist in implementing school policies.[9]

EVALUATION OF THE HIGH SCHOOL ATHLETIC PROGRAM

Concern about competencies and accountability in all phases of education has stimulated a trend toward evaluation of coaches and the athletic program. When these conditions prevail, assessment of interscholastic programs can well be considered essential and important to survival. More important is evaluation as a significant basis for the improvement of high school athletics.

A school planning assessment should first establish purposes for the evaluation. To be valid it must determine whether a philosophy is being implemented and whether objectives have been formulated which are being achieved. Both must be in written form and based on the interests and needs of students to be meaningful. The public is inclined to evaluate the athletic program and the coaches by observing contests, but its judgment is generally based on whether games are won or lost, which may be an invalid measure.

What Is To Be Evaluated

There are at least four primary elements to be considered in the assessment of a school's athletic program:

1. An appraisal in terms of philosophy and objectives
2. Whether significant learning outcomes (knowledge, emotional patterns, and skills) are resulting from the program
3. Involvement of students (players and nonathletes) actively participating
4. An evaluation of the athletic staff (athletic administrator and coaches)

Figures 8–1 and 8–2 will reveal phases involved in the evaluative process.

Methods and Techniques of Evaluation

Evaluation of an athletic program employs subjective judgments based on observations, but certain methods and techniques can add some degree of objectivity, which can also be used for self-evaluative purposes.

After determining specifically what it desires to evaluate, the school

CENTRAL HIGH SCHOOL

EVALUATION OF INTERSCHOLASTIC ATHLETIC PROGRAM

(Rate each phase as follows: 1 - Very Good, 2 - Above Average,
3 - Average, 4 - Needs Improvement, and 5 - Poor.)

<u>Phase</u>   <u>Rating</u>

1. A written statement of philosophy and objectives   ____
   is understood by athletes and parents and gives
   direction to the athletic program

2. Written policies are in effect to implement the   ____
   philosophy and objectives

3. A sufficient variety of sports is offered to   ____
   meet the interests and needs of the majority of
   students

4. Comparable opportunities are provided boys and   ____
   girls

5. Good sportsmanship and conduct are evident at   ____
   athletic contests

6. Contests are well managed   ____

7. Schedules are arranged to keep conflict with   ____
   academic program at a minimum

8. Adequate provisions exist for health and safety   ____
   of athletes and for medical supervision

9. Good relationships exist between coaching staff   ____
   and other members of the faculty

10. Facilities are adequate   ____

11. Fields and gymnasiums are well maintained   ____

12. Community supports program and its objectives   ____

Total rating points: ____

Divided by 12 = final rating: ____

FIGURE 8-1   Form for evaluating athletic program

CENTRAL HIGH SCHOOL

EVALUATION OF COACH

(Rate each phase as follows: 1 - Very Good, 2 - Above Average, 3 - Average, 4 - Needs Improvement, and 5 - Poor.)

<u>Phase</u>	<u>Rating</u>
1. Possesses philosophy of athletics compatible with philosophy of secondary education	____
2. Personal qualities	____
3. Professional preparation	____
4. Plans coaching to develop knowledge and emotional learning in addition to athletic skills	____
5. Has positive influence upon high school students	____
6. Uses effective coaching methods and techniques	____
7. Sportsmanship displayed at athletic contests has positive influence upon players and fans	____
8. Ability to manage and discipline players	____
9. Provides written statement of reasonable training rules to athletes and parents	____
10. Gives proper attention to sanitation and health and safety of athletes	____
11. Maintains professional relationships with game officials and opposing coaches	____
12. Relationship with other members of faculty	____
13. Relationship with parents	____
14. Cooperation with school administration	____
15. Participation in community activities	____
Total rating points:	____
Divided by 15 = final rating:	____

Coach evaluated _____ Sport _____

FIGURE 8-2 Form for evaluating coaches

must then develop appropriate methods and techniques for the assessment. It is best for each school to design its own evaluation forms to ensure compatibility with its philosophy and objectives. Figure 8–1 represents one suggested type. Additional phases can be added, or those listed can be further refined for better adaptation to the school's program.

A similar form for evaluating coaches can be formulated as shown in Figure 8–2.

An evaluation committee can be selected to use the forms devised, and a final rating from their judgments can be computed by dividing the sum of the members' total collective rating points by the number comprising the committee. After an evaluation has been completed, use should be made of it in accord with the purposes established for it. The results should be discussed with any person(s) concerned as a basis for personal and professional improvement. The athletic director, principal, and superintendent will want to study the reports carefully, and they should be reviewed with the board of education. Particular notice should be taken of whether worthwhile educational outcomes are being developed and how the athletic program can better contribute to the educational aims of the school. The evaluative process can be an important diagnostic and remedial tool for improving the school's athletic program. Strengths should be publicized as well as steps taken to remedy weaknesses. This kind of evaluative process is important to the survival of high school athletics in an era of educational accountability.

SUMMARY

Good interscholastic athletic administration requires a sharing of responsibilities. The board of education has the final authority, and the superintendent is responsible to it for the athletic program of the school, but he/she will delegate responsibilities to others on the school staff. The responsibilities of principals, athletic directors, and coaches will vary according to the size of a particular school.

Organizational plans for interscholastic athletic administration will range from a one-man operation to a representative athletic council.

Well-defined school policies should be established for the athletic program. They should be developed cooperatively and be officially approved by the board of education.

A school must develop plans to implement its policies. The athletic director is held accountable for enforcing them, and the coach is in a strategic position to assist in their implementation.

The evaluation process is becoming increasingly important. It should be used to determine the strengths and weaknesses of an athletic program and as a basis for planning improvements.

QUESTIONS AND TOPICS FOR STUDY AND DISCUSSION

1. Draw a diagram which shows the division and lines of responsibility for the athletic program in a school in which you are, or would like to be, the coach.

2. List responsibilities students can assume in the athletic program.

3. Assuming you were the athletic administrator initiating an athletic council, list the persons you would include on the council:
   a. in a high school with an enrollment of 150
   b. in a high school with an enrollment of 450
   c. in a high school with an enrollment of 1,500

4. List and discuss the different policy areas included in the excerpt from the Constitution of the St. Louis Public High School League.

5. Discuss matters you consider appropriate for athletic council consideration.

6. Why must an athletic council be considered an advisory body? Explain.

7. What are some of the benefits and services school conferences have for individual member schools?

8. Explain why a specific plan to implement school athletic policies is important?

9. Why is approval of athletic policies by the board of education of importance?

10. Discuss practical methods of enforcing athletic policies. Explain the responsibilities of various individuals in enforcement.

11. Why should evaluation be considered an important aspect in the administration of a local high school athletic program?

NOTES

1. Jim Dutcher, "Understanding the Unique Problems of the Small High School Program," *Interscholastic Athletic Administration*, 8, no. 4 (Summer 1982), 14–15 and 29.

2. Tom Ecker, "Organizing an Athletic Council," *Interscholastic Athletic Administration*, 5, no. 4 (Summer 1979), 15.

3. St. Louis Public High School League, St. Louis Public Schools, St. Louis, Mo., *Constitution and By-Laws, League Handbook, 1981–82*, pp. 57–62.

4. Santee Ruffin, *The Principal's Role in Interscholastic Sports* (Reston, Va.: National Association of Secondary School Principals, 1982).

5. Albert L. Burr, "What Every Athletic Director Should Tell Coaches," *Interscholastic Athletic Administration*, 5, no. 4 (Summer 1979), 17–30.

6. Paul E. Hartman, "Selecting the Right Person To Be Coach," *NASSP Bulletin*, 62, no. 418 (May 1978), 23–27.

7. Warren C. Bowlus, "Should Athletic Administrators Hire Non-Teaching Coaches?" *Interscholastic Athletic Administration*, 6, no. 1 (Fall 1979), 11.

8. Missouri State High School Activities Association, *Coaches Manual For Teaching Youth through Interscholastic Athletics*, pp. 7–10.

9. Larry Canfield, "Forming An Effective Booster Club," *Interscholastic Athletic Administration*, 7, no. 1 (Fall 1980), 18–20.

BIBLIOGRAPHY

ADAMS, SAMUEL H., and KENNETH A. PENMAN. "Assessment of an Athletic Program." *Interscholastic Athletic Administration*, 6, no. 1 (Fall 1979), 7–8.

ARNOLD, DON E. "Staffing The Interscholastic Program." *NASSP Bulletin*, 62, no. 419 (September 1978), 75–87. Reston, Va.: National Association of Secondary School Principals.

BOWLUS, WARREN C. "Should Athletic Administrators Hire Non-Teaching Coaches?" *Interscholastic Athletic Administration*, 6, no. 1 (Fall 1979), 11.

BURR, ALBERT L. "What Every Athletic Director Should Tell Coaches." *Interscholastic Athletic Administration*, 5, no. 4 (Summer 1979), 27–30.

CANFIELD, LARRY. "Forming An Effective Booster Club." *Interscholastic Athletic Administration*, 7, no. 1 (Fall 1980), 18–20.

DOUGHERTY, JOHN W. "Supervision and Evaluation of Teaching in Extracurricular Activities." *NASSP Bulletin*, 62, no. 416 (March 1978), 31–34. Reston, Va.: National Association of Secondary School Principals.

DUTCHER, JIM. "Understanding the Unique Problems of the Small High School Program." *Interscholastic Athletic Administration*, 7, no. 4 (Summer 1982), 14–15 and 29.

ECKER, TOM. "Organizing An Athletic Council." *Interscholastic Athletic Administration*, 7, no. 4 (Summer 1982), 15.

HAMMER, WARREN. "Upgrading Your Athletic Department." *Interscholastic Athletic Administration*, 8, no. 2 (Winter 1981), 22–24.

HARTMAN, PAUL E. "Selecting the Right Person To Be Coach." *NASSP Bulletin*, 62, no. 418 (May 1978), 23–27. Reston, Va.: National Association of Secondary School Principals.

HOLSBERRY, JOHN, JR. "Sportsmanship: Athletic Directors Influence Establishment of Code." *Interscholastic Athletic Administration*, 8, no. 4 (Summer 1982), 10–13 and 29.

MISSOURI STATE HIGH SCHOOL ACTIVITIES ASSOCIATION, *Coaches Manual for Teaching Youth Through Interscholastics*, pp. 7–10.

POTTER, GLEN, and THOMAS WANDZILAK. "Athletic Evaluation: Assessment For Survival." *Interscholastic Athletic Administration*, 8, no. 4 (Summer 1982), 6–9.

RESICK, MATTHEW C., and CARL E. ERICKSON. *Intercollegiate and Interscholastic Athletics for Men and Women*, pp. 24–31 and 44–51. Reading, Mass.: Addison-Wesley, 1975.

RUFFIN, SANTEE. *The Principal's Role in Interscholastic Sports*. Reston, Va.: National Association of Secondary School Principals, 1982.

9

Athletic Awards

GENERAL AWARDS POLICIES

Since time immemorial, it has been customary for victors to receive rewards as evidence of their successes. In some instances the reward was wealth, position, or the granting of power. These traditions have carried over into athletics. Because of the different types of athletics and the various awards policies, it is sometimes difficult for lay persons to understand why there are limitations on awards for interscholastic athletics.

Professional athletics, of course, offers rewards in the form of salaries and bonuses for services in what is in actuality a business enterprise. Some amateur athletic organizations permit the giving of merchandise within set limits without jeopardizing an athlete's eligibility. In the early period of interschool athletics, the idea used to prevail that awards should be given high school athletes for the services they rendered the school. After athletics were recognized as a part of the total education program, the fallacy of this point of view was realized. It was noted that the participants were receiving special educational and recreational benefits not afforded all students. Therefore, interscholastic awards generally are now limited to symbolic awards of a similar nature to those provided students for their achievements in other interscholastic activities. Typical awards given by schools are medals, ribbons, plaques, trophies, athletic insignia, and certificates of recognition. A few schools follow the policy of giving "school" letters instead of an athletic letter only. Students may earn the school letter by participating in various activities of which athletics is one. Points necessary to earn the letter may be accumulated in different activities, and these are generally designated on the letter by insignia. The policy seems to be a good one and relieves the school of any complaint of favoritism or discrimination related to awards.

Practices found in collegiate athletics were imitated in early high school athletics. The giving of athletic letters and lettermen's sweaters or jackets was one of them. It became customary in many states for the high schools to give their athletes a varsity sweater with the school letter in recognition of their athletic achievement. This often led to one school attempting to outdo another, or at least to keep up with it, which eventually proved to be an item of considerable expense. Leading school administrators began to question the giving of any type of material award to athletes for participating in a program which was to be primarily for the educational benefits of the participants. It was also realized that high school athletes were motivated more by the opportunity to play than by the award received. Thus attention has come to center more on the values received by playing than on any type of reward. Most administrators are of the opinion that it is proper to give recognition in some form for athletic excellence.

Out of these circumstances the philosophy emerged that high school athletic awards should be symbolic. Cooperatively through their state association the schools began to establish award standards limiting them to ribbons, medals, trophies, and the like, until today most state associations have such regulations. Those states which do not completely ban awards have certain limits for any type of material award given. The fact that the interscholastic program has continued to grow and attracts more students than any other athletic program is sufficient proof of the soundness of the philosophy of school awards and the standards created to implement that philosophy.

The problem of awards from outside sources confronts school administrators frequently, especially when a high school team has had an outstanding season as measured by the number of games won or championships annexed. Teams often are feted on numerous occasions. Unless the situation is watched, some well-intentioned, community-minded individuals or groups will want to present team members with awards having intrinsic values greater than school or state association regulations allow. They seem to think that the athletes must be given something for what they have done. Recognition of honor brought to their school or to themselves may be all right if kept within reason. Rewards for having done that which was a benefit and pleasure for them to do are not only unnecessary but unjustifiable.

State athletic association regulations relative to awards are helpful limitations to which local school administrators may refer when community groups consider giving gifts to team members.[1] It behooves athletic administrators to have their local athletic and other activity award policies well understood by student bodies and public alike. Publicizing them in advance will be an effective means by which the athletic program of a school may be kept in its proper place in relation to the other educational phases of the curriculum. It will help keep athletics on an even keel no matter whether a school team wins or loses all its games or finishes first or last in its city, league, section, or state standings.

SCHOOL AND SPORT AWARDS POLICIES

The policy of granting school awards for interscholoastic athletic or activity participation should not be a haphazard one. Definite policies and participation requirements should be established, tempered in most cases by recommendations of school authorities concerned. The same awards should be offered to both boys and girls. These policies will enhance the significance of the award and make it actually one of school recognition.

As indicated previously, state associations in virtually all states have set limits as to costs of awards. Usually the number of awards an athlete may receive of value exceeding a few dollars is fixed. However, the determination of standards for award qualifications has been left to individual schools. Policies vary from state to state in accord with high school association regulations, and they also vary from school to school. Following are some of the various practices employed by schools in their awards programs:

1. Some schools give a school letter which often is based on a point system, and which may be earned for participation in various student activities of which athletics is one.
2. The same size letter is given in all varsity sports. (There is no general distinction between major and minor sports as once existed.)
3. Smaller letters are usually presented for junior varsity and junior high school sports.[2]
4. Several schools make their awards at the end of a semester or school year and also take into consideration an athlete's citizenship and scholastic status.
5. Costs have caused a number of schools to award only one letter to an athlete for participation in a particular sport, after which chevrons are presented to attach to the letter to indicate the number of years he/she has lettered.
6. Most awards are limited to a cost of ten dollars or less.
7. Qualification for athletic letters is usually based on participation in an established number of quarters or games.
8. Special awards in the form of metallic basketballs, for example, are often presented members of teams winning conference or state association championships.
9. Some high schools present awards in intramural athletics.
10. Certificates are often awarded non-letter athletes for their participation as a member of an athletic squad.

With a few exceptions the above practices may be taken as fairly indicative of the general policies now in effect in schools throughout the states. One exception is the plan in some states that allows a school to award a sweater or a blanket to a boy or girl once during his or her high school athletic career. Other states definitely rule against such a practice. In general, the most desirable policy to follow seems to be that of making awards of little or no intrinsic value. Some schools find that certificates serve this purpose. Certainly, giving a school letter to an athlete is a manifestation of trust in him. He should consider the receipt of it in this light and wear it with honor because his school has given him that privilege. In reality, the awarding of the school letter to a student is giving him the second highest recognition of which the school is capable, the highest, of course, being the diploma. More than mere athletic ability should be the basis for awarding a school letter.

Method of Granting Awards

In our previous discussion of awards it was suggested that awards (letters) be granted by the athletic council or board of control in a local school. The following procedure is recommended:

1. At an early season practice session the coach should advise all team candidates of the award policy of the school.
2. Records of the amount of competition of each individual should be kept if that is a criterion on which awards are granted.
3. A recommended list of those to receive the school award should be prepared by the coach and submitted to the athletic director and principal.
4. The athletic director and the coach should confer with the principal in order to check on school citizenship, attitude, character, and scholastic standing of those recommended.
5. Combined recommendations should be submitted to the athletic council or board of control for final approval.
6. Letter awards should be made at a school assembly as near the end of the semester as possible.

Basis for Granting Awards

There are different plans in effect which form the basis for granting athletic awards in various schools. In some instances they are given solely on the recommendation of the coach. In others this recommendation is combined with those of other school officials. Certain schools pay much attention to the amount of participation as the basis for awards. They set up definite requirements that a student must have played in so many quarters or innings or have won a required number of points. Another plan is that of awarding only a limited number of letters per year and determining the recipients on the basis of a point system which includes all the sports sponsored by the school. Most schools require that, to receive awards, students must be good school citizens, receive passing grades in their work, have been regular in attendance at practice sessions, and have observed training rules as formulated by the coach.

Example of Awards System

The following are the regulations for awards given by the member schools of the St. Louis Public High School League:

REGULATIONS FOR ATHLETIC AWARDS

Member schools may award letters to students in their school who have participated on the athletic team when they meet the following requirements:

Basic Requirements

1. All eligibility requirements of the Missouri State High School Activities Association and of the St. Louis Public High School League must be met for an athlete to be considered eligible for consideration for an athletic letter.
2. The athlete, to be considered for an athletic letter, must have displayed good sportsmanship in competition and have been regular in attendance at practice and at games.
3. The coach shall recommend the athletes to be considered for athletic letters at the end of each sports season.
4. This list of recommendations by the coach shall be submitted to the principals and each athlete so recommended must be approved by the principal.
5. A letter and a certificate shall be awarded to each athlete the first time he/she qualifies in each separate sport. Thereafter, he/she shall be awarded a certificate only in lieu of a duplicate letter for the sport.

Specific Requirements

1. *Football:* Participation in at least one-third of the quarters played by the team in the total schedule.
2. *Basketball:* Participation in at least one-third of the quarters played by the team in the total schedule or participation in State Tournament.
3. *Baseball:* Participation in at least one-fourth of the innings or one-third of the games played by the team in the total schedule or participation in State Final. Exception: Pitchers may be recommended for letters without an established requirement of participation. No more than two base coaches may be recommended for letters without an established requirement of participation.
4. *Track:* Score an average of two (2) points for the dual meets in the total schedule of the team or qualify in the District or League Meet.
5. *Swimming:* Score an average of two (2) points for the dual meets in the total schedule of the team or qualify in the State Meet.
6. *Tennis:* Participation in at least one-half of the matches played by the team in the total schedule.
7. *Cross Country:* Participation in at least one-half of the meets run by the team in the total schedule and finishing among the first seven (7) men of his school in one-half the meets.
8. *Soccer:* Participation in at least one-half of the halves played by the team in the total schedule.

9. *Wrestling*

   (a) A boy will score points in each match according to the rules—2 for draw, 3 for decision, 5 for pin.
   (b) If no points are scored, one point per match will be awarded for participation.
   (c) A letter will be awarded: For averaging one point per match in the total schedule of the team, or scoring two or more points in District Meet.

10. *Field Hockey:* Participation in at least one-half of the matches played by the team in the total schedule.

11. *Gymnastics:* Participation in at least one-half of the meets in the total schedule of the team.

12. *Volleyball:* Participation in at least one-half of the matches played by the team in the total schedule.

13. *Cheerleaders:* Participation in at least one-half of the events participated in by the squad in the total schedule.

14. *Service Letter:* May be awarded to a student who has been faithful in practice and participation for at least two years and has completed the sport season during his senior year without having reached the required standard, either because of injury or lack of skill.

15. *Manager's Letter:* May be awarded for a minimum of one season of service as Team Manager and such letters shall be limited to not more than two per sport year.

Style of Letter

1. *Athletic Letter:* The approved athletic letter award for member schools of the St. Louis Public High School League shall be full block letter, six (6) inches in height. Identifying insignia may be superimposed on the letter.

2. *All Other Letters:* All school organizations, other than interscholastic athletics, are authorized to award letters or emblems which are descriptive or indicative of the activity. The letters awarded shall be four (4) inches in height.

   Specific regulations for earning these other letters shall be established by individual schools similar to those set up for the athletic letter.[3]

The giving of a manager's letter is being done by an increasing number of schools. These students perform a service for both the athletes and the school. Recognition of these services certainly is appropriate.

Athletic Banquets

A word about athletic banquets is appropriate in discussing awards for high school athletic competition. They are a form of recognition and are sometimes considered a form of reward. Most state associations do not permit nonschool organizations to give high school athletes any type of award except certificates of recognition for their participation in interscholastics. This regulation is a good one because most of these groups want to make the presentations as much, or more, for the purpose of gaining recognition for themselves; thus, their making awards to athletes who have received attention all during the season of play is not necessary and is often unjustifiable, as was stated earlier.

The practice of holding an athletic banquet within the local community, however, is traditional in some school systems. If properly planned and administered, such banquets may add to the values of the athletic program and can provide a worthwhile culmination for the high school sports season. Speakers selected should be those who understand the philosophy and objectives of interscholastic athletics and who can help to educate better the athletes and school patrons to the most worthwhile objectives and values of high school athletic competition. Planning the program and choosing the speakers should remain within the control of the school officials.

PROBLEMS SCHOOLS FACE
IN REGARD TO AWARDS AND AMATEURISM

Although schools through their state associations have done much to cause high school athletics to remain amateur and have exercised considerable control over the matter of awards, some problems still persist.

Organized summer athletic program sponsors frequently desire to have outstanding high school athletes compete in nonschool summer sports. Athletic administrators generally approve of having students participate in summer athletic programs provided they meet standards similar to those inherent in the interscholastic program. Until recently there have been few summer athletic programs specifically planned for high school youth. The best high school tennis players, golfers, baseball players, wrestlers, and swimmers are often sought by sponsors of adult teams or meets during summer months. Many of them offer cash or merchandise awards of some type which violate the award standard established by the schools through their state association. When a student becomes ineligible because of receiving an award in violation of state high school regulations, it often causes a cry of protest and criticism of the high school standards. The state associations and their member schools might do well to better inform sponsors of nonschool athletic contests about the interscholastic award standards and the reasons they are important for both the high school athletes and the interscholastic program.

The possibility of an award after high school eligibility is completed in the form of a college athletic scholarship estimated as being worth up to as much as $8,000 and more over a four-year period is causing many athletes and their parents to look upon high school athletics as a means to an end. Having the fun of playing and enjoying high school games as recreation is being replaced as a primary objective by the objective of winning the athletic scholarship. Recruiting activities of college coaches frequently interfere with the academic work of the high school athlete. These conditions are making it more difficult for the secondary school to implement the philosophy and objectives of interscholastics they have developed in the best interests of the great majority of high school youth.

Award standards must be maintained. Some proclaim that high school athletics are the only remaining *pure* amateur program. If this is so, credit can be given to those educational leaders who had the foresight to establish the award standards to which the secondary schools adhere. In the interest of providing a wholesome athletic program with educational values for youth, these standards must be maintained!

SUMMARY

The giving of awards for participation in high school athletics is traditional.

All state associations have established limits for awards which may be given by member schools. The qualifications for awards are left to individual schools.

The athletic or school letter is the most common award.

Awards should be the same for boys and girls and for the various sports.

Banquets in recognition of athletic participation are often held in connection with award ceremonies.

Nonschool athletic organizations frequently give awards which exceed in value those schools are permitted to provide, which presents some problems.

QUESTIONS AND TOPICS FOR STUDY AND DISCUSSION

1. Discuss prevailing differences of opinion regarding awards for participation in athletic activities. Which do you support? Why?
2. Give reasons for the philosophy that awards for participation in high school athletics should be symbolic only.
3. Discuss the various policies applied by schools in their award programs.
4. Should citizenship and scholastic standing be included in the qualifications for athletic awards? Why?
5. What effects have increasing costs had on high school athletic awards?
6. Discuss the merits of establishing uniform regulations for athletic awards as the St. Louis Public High School League has done for its member schools.
7. Prepare a plan you would propose for making awards to high school athletes in a sport of your choice.
8. Do you agree with the author's opinion that the monetary value of college

athletic scholarships is supplanting the learning and recreational values of interscholastics in the minds of many athletes and their parents? Why or why not?

NOTES

1. See pages 109–110.
2. Joe Tomlinson, "Solving an Awards Dilemma." *Interscholastic Athletic Administration*, 6, no. 4 (Summer 1980), 24.
3. St. Louis Public High School League, St. Louis Public Schools, St. Louis, Mo., *League Handbook, 1981–82*, pp. 79–80.

BIBLIOGRAPHY

NATIONAL FEDERATION OF STATE HIGH SCHOOL ASSOCIATION. *1982–83 Handbook*. Kansas City, Mo.: National Federation, 1982.

ST. LOUIS PUBLIC HIGH SCHOOL LEAGUE, St. Louis Public Schools, St. Louis, Mo. *League Handbook, 1981–82*.

TOMLINSON, JOE. "Solving an Awards Dilemma." *Interscholastic Athletic Administration,* 6, no. 4 (Summer 1980), 24.

10

Athletic Equipment

The purchase and care of equipment for high school athletics represents one of the major problems confronting those in charge of the program. In most schools funds are limited, squads are as large as facilities and equipment will permit, and safety precautions require the purchase of the best quality of merchandise for the money available. Many boards of education purchase general playing equipment (balls, bats, nets, and the like) but are prohibited by law from furnishing personal equipment. In some cases this material must be purchased from other than tax money. Thus, insufficient funds sometimes make it impossible to buy needed equipment. Serious questions can be raised as to the justification for sponsoring football, for instance, by a school unless it properly and adequately equips the students who play on its teams.

THE PURCHASE OF EQUIPMENT

General Policy

Good, substantial, and safety-approved equipment in all sports is a minimum essential. The school must spend its dollar well in order to get the most it can for its money. There should be a regular time and procedure for these important transactions. Items never should be bought just because they are inexpensive, nor should they be bought from unknown firms. Experience will show that recognized and legitimate sporting-goods dealers are the safest ones from which to purchase materials. They need not necessarily be local merchants; but if athletic supplies can be bought as cheaply from them as from anyone, they should be given the business. Equipment should be bought only after needs are known. Regular inventories should be maintained. Purchase orders should be on regular school forms for that purpose and authorized by the athletic council or board of control. Usually the athletic director, faculty manager, or coach will be given authority by the council to issue such purchase orders.

Some of the suggestions in the preceding paragraph may seem superfluous as far as small schools are concerned. Actually they are not entirely so. Instead of having the responsibilities described there assumed by the individuals mentioned, they will be retained in the small schools by the superintendent or principal. There is every reason for the small school to be businesslike in its athletic purchases. Usually there is less funding, proportionately, and equipment has to be used longer. More frequent changes in administration in small schools is an even more important reason why athletic purchases and the handling of funds in connection with them should be entirely clear and justified. Generally it is safe to advise that equipment be purchased with school board money in the same careful way that one's personal funds would be used.

Precautions should be taken to make sure that certain equipment, such as football helmets, meet reasonable safety standards. This will be discussed in Chapter 12.

Equipment Inventory

At the close of each season an inventory of all equipment on hand should be made. A form of inventory blank is shown in Fig. 10–1. By comparing this with the inventory made at the close of the same sport season a year ago and adding any material bought since then, it should be possible to account for all equipment. Of course, due allowance has to be made for worn-out items. Such an inventory will show four things:

1. How much equipment is on hand for the next season of this sport
2. What equipment has to be repaired or replaced
3. How much new personal or game equipment will have to be purchased prior to the start of the next season in this sport
4. Whether managers or equipment persons are efficient, and whether or not athletic equipment is being lost or stolen

In large schools especially, it is desirable to have the coach of each sport responsible for turning in the inventory to the faculty manager, athletic director, or principal. In this way the coach can have firsthand information regarding the equipment for the sport he or she coaches, and as a result should be in a better position to present the requisition for equipment when the next annual budget is being prepared.

The athletic administrator usually has the initial responsibility of reviewing requests from coaches for equipment, and equipment inventories submitted for the various sports are important aids in determining what equipment shall be purchased. He/she can usually anticipate that the total requests

INVENTORY OF EQUIPMENT

_____ HIGH SCHOOL

Close of _____ Season   Year: 19____

(Sport)

Articles Used For This Sport	Previous Inventory Count	Number Purchased During Year	Total Number To Be Accounted For	Present Inventory (First Class Shape)	Present Inventory (Need Repairs)	Number Articles Not Accounted For	Estimated Number New Articles Needed Next Season

Date of inventory, _____ 19____   Coach _____

Athletic Director _____

Student Manager _____

FIGURE 10–1   Suggested after-season inventory form

will exceed in cost the amount allocated in the board of education budget and from other funds available. Hence, priorities must be established. Highest on the priority list must be safety equipment needed, such as football helmets and pads, to ensure there will be no grounds for negligence charges based on failure to provide proper protective equipment for players. Other decisions should be made after consulting individual coaches regarding their greatest needs.

Request for Purchase

The amount and expense of equipment required for interscholastic athletics has caused many schools to develop requisitioning procedures for athletic equipment and supplies. Keeping within budgets makes it necessary that requisitions be examined and approved by the athletic director, principal, or other person delegated this responsibility. Each coach is generally asked to submit his or her needs on a requisition form. Figure 10–2 is the type of form used by the Springfield, Missouri, high schools.

Requisition forms must be completed carefully to ensure the quality of the article(s) desired. Specifications must include the catalog number, serial number (if any), recommended supplier, quantity of various sizes needed, and acceptable substitutions.

FOOTBALL EQUIPMENT

REQUEST FOR PURCHASE

_____   _____
School   Date

NOTE: Please note those items for which a substitute is not acceptable by indicating NO.

ITEM	SPECIFICATIONS W/SUPPLIER AND CAT. NUMBERS	UNIT PRICE	QUANTITY WITH SIZES AND NUMBERS AS REQUIRED	TOTAL COST	SUBSTI- TUTION

Signed

FIGURE 10–2   Request for purchase (Springfield, Missouri)

Procedures for Purchasing

There are three general procedures for purchasing athletic equipment:

1. Purchasing directly from a salesperson or supplier
2. Purchasing by competitive bidding
3. Centralized purchasing

Each of the three procedures has some advantages depending on the total situation. When the cost of equipment involved is of a limited amount, direct purchasing is the simplest and generally the most convenient. By ordering from a reputable salesperson or supplier, it is generally possible to have defective equipment replaced and improper sizes exchanged, and advantage can sometimes be taken of special price offers.

Competitive bidding will save money and automatically require standardized purchasing procedures. It avoids unnecessary interruption of the duties of athletic directors and coaches by calls and visits from salespersons. In the long run, handling all purchases simultaneously saves time, although purchases may be made from more than one bidder. It is strongly advisable to provide each bidder with a copy of the school's competitive bidding policies and to include in them a statement which reserves authority to reject any and all bids and to accept bids on individual items. Submittal of samples should be required.

Districts with multiple school units, and some leagues and conferences, have practiced centralized purchasing by combining their orders and stocking equipment and supplies in quantity. Agreement must be made on the standardization of equipment, except for colors and insignia, with all schools receiving the same quality and brand. Increasing the quantity ordered in this manner and employing competitive bidding often results in substantial savings to individual schools. Care must be exercised in choosing this procedure to make certain administrative costs do not exceed savings, and that ample storage facilities are available.

The *unit purchasing plan* embodies some elements of centralized purchasing. Many schools have "handed down" player equipment from the varsity squad to the junior varsity or junior high school squad, which on occasion has been the cause of controversy. Junior high school coaches and administrators often proclaim it is just as important to purchase new equipment for their teams as for the senior high school varsity teams and that improper fitting, particularly in football, can result in injuries. However, financial conditions have caused many schools to continue the practice. A well-planned unit purchasing procedure provides for the reuse of equipment at each level for a specified period, handing down to the next level, purchasing necessary replacements at each level, and ordering new uniforms for each level at set periodic times. The thrust of the plan is that all equipment needed is ordered as a unit by an athletic administrator or purchasing agent. Franklin School District in southwest Ohio uses one type of unit purchasing.[1]

Purchase Orders

After requisitions have been approved, needs have been ascertained, samples have been inspected, or bids have been received, comes the formality of placing the order. It is best to have one individual in the school responsible for placing orders. He or she should sign the purchase order form, which should be made out in triplicate. After purchase orders have been completed, they should be distributed as follows:

> *Original*—Sent to the firm with which the order is placed.
> *First duplicate*—Retained by the individual signing the purchase order.
> *Second duplicate*—Filed in the high school principal's office.

This procedure provides a double check on all school purchases and is especially valuable if the school is large and there are numerous agencies placing purchase orders payable out of general school activity funds. A typical purchase order form is shown in Figure 10–3. Special attention should be given to the fact that the orders are numbered serially, so that it is possible to account for all of them. They also are made out in triplicate and punched so they may be filed in a two-post binder for ready reference.

ISSUING EQUIPMENT

An efficient method for issuing and keeping records of equipment is an essential factor in athletic management, in order that equipment may be preserved and the expenses for such items kept to a minimum. It also is imperative that business methods be employed in this phase of management because of the effect they have on students participating in athletic competition. Respect for, and care of, property should be one of the lessons to be derived from athletics. If students are made to realize that the material furnished them by the school is merely loaned, that the management keeps an accurate check, and that they are held accountable for it, they will learn a valuable lesson. By this method, proper habits may be taught high school students, and every effort should be made to avoid situations in which carelessness, destructiveness, dishonesty, or thievery may develop. Have definite places for all equipment, with someone charged with the resonsibility for it. If equipment is issued to a student with the understanding that it is to be retuned by him/her at the close of the season, insist that it may be returned or that restitution be made. It is a worse than idle gesture to go through the motions of charging athletic material to students and then to disregard the losses when only part

```
┌─────────────────────────────────────────────────────────────┐
│  PURCHASE ORDER                           No. _____          │
│                                                              │
│              _____   HIGH SCHOOL                  │
│                                                              │
│              _____,  _____                    │
│                                                              │
│                               TO  _____           │
│                                                              │
│                                   _____           │
│                                                              │
│  Date  _____ 19___            _____           │
│                                                              │
├─────────────────────────────────────────────────────────────┤
│  Please fill the following order:                            │
│                                                              │
├─────────────────────────────────────────────────────────────┤
│  Deliver to _____        Invoice to _____          │
│                                                              │
│              _____                   _____          │
│                                                              │
│  Ship via _____                      _____          │
│                                                              │
│                    Signed _____                 │
│                                   (Title)                    │
└─────────────────────────────────────────────────────────────┘
```

FIGURE 10–3   Purchase order form

of it is returned. Due allowance in all instances, of course, must be made for natural depreciation of equipment because of normal usage. It will be surprisingly gratifying to observe how careful high school students can be of equipment issued to them if they are made to understand that they are responsible for it. In this connection, however, every effort should be made by the athletic management to aid them in making it easy to take proper care of their equipment.

Marking Equipment

Various schools have different systems of marking their game and personal athletic equipment. Marking pencils or pens using permanent ink or waterproof stencil paints are most effective on cotton goods and practice equipment. Care should be taken to be sure that the markings will show and remain on new plastics and other types of materials. Usually, the name of the school, a number, and the size should appear on each garment. Quite often the number is the only identification mark for the equipment issued to an athlete.

Inexpensive number or school identification labels may be sewed on the inside of woolen or silk jersey seams if no other numbers or marks appear on them. Game jerseys, of course, will be numbered for football and basketball in accordance with rules provisions, but some other identification usually is necessary for baseball, swimming, and track uniforms. Leather goods should be numbered and sized with India ink on white cloth or should have numbers or marks burned in them. Personal marking also discourages use of another player's equipment, which for health reasons should not be permitted.

Equipment Cards

Every piece of equipment issued to a student should be charged to him or her on a permanent athletic equipment card, which he or she should sign. Signatures are especially important if students take the material to their own lockers and keep it there. Requiring the student to sign the card may be considered an unnecessary formality, but the performance of it at least has the psychological effect of a contractual agreement entered into between the student and the school for the athletic equipment. Separate cards can be prepared for each sport, or a general card can be used for all sports (see Fig. 10–4).

Daily Care of Equipment

Athletic equipment deteriorates more rapidly because of ill treatment than it does from excessive use or wear. The method of taking care of it between practice sessions and between games is the greatest factor in determining its durability and appearance. Wet and perspiration-soaked cotton and woolen equipment must be thoroughly dried between practice sessions or games. Also, it must be laundered or dry-cleaned frequently. Shoes should be brushed with a stiff brush and oiled. Pads should be dried thoroughly, washed with saddle soap, and painted with shellac. Helmets should be aired and dried thoroughly between practice sessions or games.

Obviously, these duties cannot be performed by team members themselves. Neither does such a plan work well if athletes keep their equipment in lockers. Although some locker rooms have elaborate locker ventilation systems, seldom are they efficient enough to do a drying job such as is required for athletic equipment. The recommended plan is to have a separate equipment room in which a special space is provided for the material issued to each team member. No one is to be allowed in this room except the coach, athletic director, or student manager in charge of equipment. The room should have cross-ventilation (or be a drying room) if possible. A hook or two should be provided for each athlete. All the material issued to an athlete should be turned in after each practice. The student manager can check it daily by consulting the student's equipment card, which should be above the number

CENTRAL HIGH SCHOOL

RECORD OF EQUIPMENT ISSUED

Name_____ Sport_____

Locker No._____ Date Issued_____

Article	Issued	Re-turned	Article	Issued	Re-turned
Practice Trunks					
Practice Jersey					
Shoes					
Jockey Strap					
Sweat Pants					
Game Uniform					
Game Stockings					
Knee Pads					

Coach_____ Student_____

FIGURE 10–4 Equipment card

of his or her hook. At the next practice session or game the athlete gives the number at the equipment room window to receive his or her material. On days of games the game uniforms are substituted for those used in practice.

A master record card used at many high schools contains a complete checklist of all material issued to each team member. It also lists the space on the equipment racks in the drying room that has been assigned to each student. Its general makeup is shown in Figure 10–5.

The advantages of such a system follow:

1. Uniforms that are dry before the next practice result in cleaner equipment. Garments wear longer.
2. Clean clothes are available more often, thus preventing infections.
3. When an athlete is dropped from the squad, his or her equipment is in. Thus, there is no opportunity for loss.
4. When a uniform is not used by a player, it remains on its hanger. When the player returns to practice, the uniform is on the hanger, whether is is one day or one month later.
5. A player learns to be careful with his or her uniform or pay a severe penalty.
6. It does away with the temptation to steal or to use some other person's property.
7. It relieves the coach of practically all worries caused by loss or mix-up of equipment.

RECORD CARD													
Space Number	Name	Shoes	Helmet	Shoulder Pads	Pants	Knee Pads	Jersey	Supporter	Socks	Stockings	Under Jersey	Miscellaneous
1												
2												
3												
4												
5												
42												
43												
44												

FIGURE 10–5   Master equipment record card

GENERAL CARE OF ATHLETIC EQUIPMENT

The value of an efficient system for the purchase and issuing of equipment is lost if proper care is not given to the equipment during and after the sport season. This observation applies to repair of equipment during the season as well as storage of it after the season is concluded. The old adage that a stitch in time saves nine may be literally true with athletic equipment, since repairs sometimes will save a school several times the cost of purchasing new equipment. In some of the larger schools a faculty manager is placed in charge of the purchase, care, and repair of all athletic equipment. Judgment, of course, must be exercised as to what to repair and what method is to be used.

Repairing and Cleaning Athletic Equipment

Check equipment periodically. This should be done frequently to discover tears, breaks in leather, or broken parts. Some schools will have their own cobbler's outfits for minor repairs to shoes and leather goods. Others will have arrangements with local cobblers or leather-goods repairmen. Shoes especially should be checked frequently, because those in poor condition may cause foot injury or infection. Helmets also receive a great amount of abuse. When rips appear in linings or chin straps, have them sewed up at once. This also applies to jerseys and pants. Keep them dry, clean, and in repair.

White goods and towels should be laundered frequently. Football pants also can be washed. All laundry service should include mending. By this method clean material in the equipment room will be ready for use. A number of schools have found that a laundry on the premises results in considerable savings, particularly for a large athletic program.[2]

Most woolen goods should be dry-cleaned to prevent shrinkage. It is not advisable to use bleaching materials on white equipment. Generally they do not aid in cleaning the equipment and may be injurious to it. In view of the large number of new materials, both protective and clothing, now on the market it is important that manufacturers' directions for cleaning be followed. This applies to textiles, leather, fibers, plastics, rubber, and metals. Supplying clean, well-fitting athletic equipment to team members is one of the surest means of preventing infection epidemics. Insist on all students using only their own equipment, keep it clean for them, and repair or replace it if it becomes damaged. Some schools have had considerable success in having their repair work on athletic garments done by home economics (sewing) classes. In such instances the equipment has been thoroughly cleaned before being sent for repairs. In some cases the class members have been paid a small fee for their services, and in others a sewing club has taken over the work as a project for raising funds. Variations of these plans may be worked out for minor repairs, a practice that reduces the cost of the athletic program.

Reconditioning athletic equipment for various sports is another source of savings that at the same time provides safe equipment, including protective equipment for football. There are firms which specialize in reconditioning, and the National Athletic Equipment Reconditioners Association (NAERA) established in 1975 has set standards for its members which help to ensure satisfactory performance.[3] Athletic administrators will be wise to check what equipment can be reconditioned before ordering replacements.

Storage of Athletic Equipment

When a sport season has been concluded, have the equipment cleaned. Sort out those items which need repairs and which are worth repairing, and send them to repair firms whose workmanship and services are known. All other equipment should be properly conditioned for the off seasons and stored. Airtight bins or trunks for the woolen goods and special cases or racks for the leather equipment should be provided. Cotton material may be wrapped and stacked on shelves or in bins. Following are suggestions for conditioning and storage of athletic equipment:

Leather shoes—Clean thoroughly. Brush with neatsfoot oil. Replace laces and cleats. Renumber. Rub track shoes with vaseline. Store in dry place (bins or shelves).

Helmets—Buff or sandpaper and repaint. Follow with a coat of shellac. Place on a wooden form on a rack, or stuff inside of helmet with paper and tie ear flaps together with string. Do not fasten elastic strap, because it will stretch. Clean felt or sponge rubber inside of helmet with soap and water. Tag for size. Renumber. Store in dry place.

Hip, shoulder, and knee pads—Wash leather hip, shoulder, and knee pads with saddle soap. Check with manufacturer for care of plastic or synthetic pads. Shellac leather portion of pads. Tag for size. Store in dry place.

Inflated balls—Clean with standard ball cleaners on the market. Deflate to three to five pounds pressure. Store in dry place.

Canvas shoes—Thoroughly dry and brush. Tag for size. Replace laces. Store in dry place (bins or shelves).

Woolen garments—Clean thoroughly (dry cleaning rather than laundering recommended). Check with manufacturer or dealer regarding treatment of synthetic materials. Repair rips and mend holes. Tag for size. Store in airtight bins or trunks. Sprinkle naphthalene, paradichlorobenzene, or camphor crystals throughout woolen garments. Be certain that the container is airtight.

Cotton garments—Launder thoroughly. Inspect for places needing repairs. Renumber and indicate sizes. Store in dry place.

Silk garments—Launder or dry clean. Tag for size. Pack in boxes or bundles. Store in dry place.

Football pants—Launder thoroughly. Inspect for repairs. Renumber. Tag for size and grade. Save best of worn pants for mending. Store in dry place.

Wrestling mats—Launder cotton ones thoroughly, repair, and fold for storage in dry place. Clean plastic mats in accordance with manufacturer's directions.

Football linesman's markers, box, yard line markers—Repair, repaint, and store in dry place.

Football dummies and charging machines—Clean former and store in dry place. Repair and repaint charging machines and store inside, in dry place.

Baseball bats, balls, bases—Wipe off bats and store in dry place. Save used baseballs for practice. Clean bases and store in dry place.

Hurdles, benches, toeboards, and take-off boards—Repair, repaint, and store in dry place.

Javelins—Hang from a height with point downward to prevent warping. Store in dry place.

Vaulting poles—Lay in straight position to prevent warping. Store in moderately dry place.

Discus and shot—Store in a moderately dry place.

Tennis nets—Fold or roll around wooden pole. Store in dry place.

First-aid kit—Clean kit and bottles. Relabel bottles. Replenish stock as inventory indicates when season opens. Store kit in clean, dry place.

Ticket booths—Clean and repaint. Store in dry place if removable.

Scoreboards—Clean and repaint. Renumber and paint individual placards if necessary. Check mechanical device and wiring if electrical scoreboard is used. Store removable parts in dry place.

Public address system—Check transmitters, amplifiers, and wiring. Store in safe place.

An Important Responsibility

Careful, businesslike purchasing and care of athletic equipment is one of the major responsibilities of athletic directors. Not only must administrators practice good judgment, they must also develop and implement plans to ensure that coaches and players do likewise. This should be an item for discussion in staff meetings, and coaches should be instructed in their responsibilities for supervising the care of equipment issued to athletes. Frank discussions should be held on costs, possible savings, and the need for economizing without reducing the quality of equipment the school provides.

Teaching athletes the necessity of taking proper care of equipment can be educational as well as cost-saving. Coaches should impress upon players that it is a privilege to wear equipment provided by the school and that their cooperation is necessary in its care. Many football players graduate without knowing the cost of the uniforms and equipment they wore in games, which is the result of coaches not informing them. A clear understanding of cost values and learning to respect the property of the school can have important carryover value in building attitudes toward respecting other persons' property. Also, when the coach carries out his/her responsibilities of supervision in this matter, athletes will have a more lasting appreciation for their school.

Many individuals share in the responsibility for the proper care and maintenance of athletic equipment, but the athletic director must understand that the final responsibility is his or hers, and must try to meet that responsibility by making certain that all involved assume their appropriate duties in this regard.

SUMMARY

Safety-approved player equipment is a number one priority in purchasing athletic supplies.

Inventories of equipment taken at the close of sport seasons are important aids in determining which items need replacement.

Having coaches submit requisitions for all purchases helps the staff determine the quality of equipment desired, and a study of them provides a basis for the athletic director to keep within the athletic budget.

The three general procedures for purchasing include: (1) purchasing directly from an athletic goods salesperson or supplier, (2) purchasing by competitive bidding, and (3) centralized purchasing.

Purchase orders provide a way of checking and keeping records of all purchases.

Equipment issued to players should be identified by a marking system. Each athlete should be held responsible for the equipment issued to him/her. A card system is an efficient way to keep individual records.

Daily care is important in conserving equipment.

Reconditioning equipment and proper storage are significant in reducing equipment costs.

QUESTIONS AND TOPICS FOR STUDY AND DISCUSSION

1. Why is an official school policy concerning purchase of athletic equipment important?
2. Discuss the value of a complete equipment inventory. Who should take this inventory? Why?
3. What advantages and disadvantages can you give for each of the three general procedures for purchasing athletic equipment?
4. Why is a central purchase order system desirable for the buying of all athletic equipment?
5. Set up a plan for the issuing of athletic equipment to players, indicating forms and procedures to be used.
6. Why is daily care and checking of athletic equipment important?
7. Discuss methods of general care of equipment, including repair, cleaning, and storage. Set up an ideal plan or present features of one that has seemed especially good to you.
8. Evaluate plans suggested in this chapter for the conditioning and storage of

athletic equipment of all kinds. Do you agree with them? Can you suggest better methods?

9. In what ways can proper care of athletic equipment by athletes have an educational value?

NOTES

1. Lou Kaczmarek, "Unit Purchasing," *Interscholastic Athletic Administration,* 6, no. 4 (Summer 1980), 25–26.

2. Kenneth A. Penman, "Saving Money With An On-Premise Laundry," *Athletic Purchasing and Facilities,* 6, no. 3 (March 1982), 17–18 and 20.

3. Don Gleisner, "Reconditioning Athletic Equipment," *Interscholastic Athletic Administration,* 6, no. 1 (Fall 1979), 22–24.

BIBLIOGRAPHY

"Concern Grows Over Coaches Selling to Schools." *Athletic Purchasing and Facilities,* 5, no. 10 (October 1981), 30–31.

GALLON, ARTHUR J. *Coaching Ideas and Ideals,* Chap. 6. Boston, Mass.: Houghton Mifflin, 1974.

GLEISNER, DON. "Reconditioning Athletic Equipment." *Interscholastic Athletic Administration,* 6, no. 1 (Fall 1979), 22–24.

HODGSON, VOIGT R. "An Up-Date On NOCSAE Research." *Athletic Purchasing and Facilities,* 6, no. 11 (November 1981), 32, 34 and 36.

KACZMAREK, LOU. "Unit Purchasing." *Interscholastic Athletic Administration,* 6, no. 4 (Summer 1980), 25–26.

NATIONAL FEDERATION OF STATE HIGH SCHOOL ASSOCIATIONS. *1982–83 Handbook,* pp. 26–28. Kansas City, Mo.: National Federation, 1982.

PENMAN, KENNETH A. "Saving Money With An On-Premise Laundry." *Athletic Purchasing and Facilities,* 6, no. 3 (March 1982), 17–18 and 20.

"Purchasing Protective Football Equipment." *Athletic Purchasing and Facilities,* 8, no. 4 (April 1982), 11–13.

"Putting Inventory to Work for You." *Athletic Purchasing and Facilities,* 6, no. 1 (January 1982), 10, 12, and 14.

RESNICK, MATTHEW C., AND CARL E. ERICKSON. *Intercollegiate and Interscholastic Athletics For Men and Women,* pp. 100–103. Reading, Mass.: Addison-Wesley, 1975.

ROWLEY, ALLYN E. "A Coordinated System for Purchasing Athletic Equipment." *Athletic Purchasing and Facilities,* 5, no. 1 (November 1981), 20–22 and 24.

"Tips On Purchasing Inflated Athletic Balls." *Athletic Purchasing and Facilities,* 6, no. 3 (March 1982), 23–24, 26, and 28.

11

Athletic Finances and Budgets

GENERAL ATHLETIC FINANCE CONSIDERATIONS

Among the most serious problems athletic administrators will face during the next several years will be that of finances. There are at least seven significant reasons for this assumption:

Uncertain economic conditions.   If we have a prolonged period of recession, receipts from admissions will be reduced. The end of inflation is not yet in sight. The present tax rebellion on the part of the public leaves little hope that boards of education will be able to increase the subsidization of inter-scholastic programs. Reduced receipts resulting from recession and inflationary prices for athletic supplies and equipment will require careful financial management.

Expansion in girls' athletics.   Practically all states have had a tremendous increase in girls' interscholastic sports, which is creating additional expenses. Schools will be expected to offer girls' programs comparable to those for boys, and girls' participation will continue to grow for some time. At this time the receipts from admissions to girls' events are not comparable to those from boys' events. They may become so in the future, but until they do, financing them will create budget problems. How much additional subsidy funds can or will boards of education provide? If receipts from admissions and subsidies are not increased overall, what will be the effect upon both boys' and girls' programs?

Wider sports offerings.   Not considering the expansion of the girls' program, the number of sports offered boys has increased generally. A large number of schools in recent years have added such sports as golf, tennis, swimming, and wrestling. Previously, many offered only basketball, football, track, and one or two others. It was possible to expand the offerings as general school financing improved.

More levels of competition.   A good number of schools sponsor varsity, junior varsity, and freshman teams. Although on a more limited basis, junior high interschool competition is now common. This is very good in that more students are benefiting, but it has added to the total athletic costs for the school district.

Increased cost of game administration.   The day when each faculty member took his or her turn in "helping at the game" as part of the expected duties of teaching has practically disappeared. The fact that there are now so many more contests that require much more time of teachers is one cause. However, the theory of extra pay for extra duties seems to be the greatest factor. Additional expenses paid for ticket sellers, ticket takers, supervisors, and such add much to the overall costs of game administration for the total program.

Inflation.   There has been a steady increase in all school costs resulting from continuous inflation. Not only have costs of athletic equipment and supplies risen tremendously, but salaries paid are higher, energy costs have skyrocketed, transportation is more expensive, lodging and meals cost more, and other school expenses have risen proportionately. The fact that school financing has not kept pace with inflation, and in many instances has fallen behind, creates difficult problems for athletic administrators and boards of education, and declining budgets have resulted.[1]

Tendency to eliminate extracurricular activities.   Another problem posed for athletic directors arises when boards of education are faced with extreme financial crises and must consider reducing offerings; the elimination of extracurricular activities is one of the first considerations. In addition, threats to eliminate the athletic program are sometimes used as an attempt to influence the passage of school levies.

It is not the purpose of this discussion to paint a bleak picture for interscholastic athletics. Similar and even worse conditions prevailed during the Great Depression, and although athletics "felt the pinch," they survived, and following the depression emerged as a more significant phase of secondary education. It has been the authors' observation that extracurricular activities are not affected proportionately any more during financial crises than is the curricular program. Academic offerings, too, are reduced. Courses in which a limited number of students enroll are eliminated and class sizes are increased, which adversely influences the quality of education. Whether or not we achieve the educational and recreational objectives we proclaim for interscholastics will determine their status within the total school program more so than will financial conditions.

Hence, these statements have been made to cause athletic administrators and coaches to recognize that they will have to be realistic in coping with budget matters. They must understand the conditions that prevail and realize that the cost of their programs will have to be kept in proper perspective within the total school district financial situation. Good budgeting practices and sound financial management will be required.

FINANCING THE ATHLETIC PROGRAM

Budgeting is the process of estimating probable income and expenditures for a particular program or function. There are two general ways of approaching this task. One can first estimate the cost and then engage in seeking funds to meet the cost, or the procedure may be reversed by estimating the income and planning expenditures within that amount. The athletic director must do both, and in most cases will have to compromise to achieve a balance, but in most instances it is wise to begin with considering the finances available.

Interscholastic athletic financing has had an interesting history. When these activities were first initiated and administered by students, they arranged for what little financing was needed. The athletes themselves provided their own equipment and playing uniforms, which sometimes made them appear a motley lot. After school administrators resolved to tolerate rather than oppose schoolboy athletic games, faculty chaperones assigned to games gave some assistance in fund raising to secure the meager funds needed. "Passing the hat" to help defray expenses was not uncommon. Eventually, when conditions permitted, admissions were charged as schools began to exercise more control over the activities of student athletic associations, and this became the chief source of income. Following the recognition of educational values and athletics being accepted as a part of the total secondary school program, boards of education began to subsidize the interscholastic program by allocating some funds for it. It is interesting to note that most of these early methods of financing are still with us.

Sources of Athletic Funds

The methods of raising athletic funds are almost as numerous as are the schools that use them. No denial can be made of the fact that the easiest method of raising funds, except by board of education grant, is by having a successful team. Usually public and students alike will pay to see a winner. This seems to be an American tradition. In most schools, however, more than chance gate receipts are necessary to assure successful operation of the program for the year. Some of the methods followed in such schools will be presented. A word of qualification, however, is offered concerning them. Not all the plans mentioned here necessarily are recommended; the ones cited are those which apparently have been successful where they have been tried. They are offered only as suggestions.

Admission prices.   Keep admission prices to athletic contests at a minimum as far as high school students are concerned. They should be the first ones to have the opportunity to see their teams in action. Sometimes it is necessary to limit attendance at indoor contests because of limited seating capacity. In this case take care of students first, and make the admission charges as low as possible, consistent with assurance of reasonably sufficient funds to finance the program. Educationally, it is much more justifiable to fill gymnasiums and playing-field accommodations with students than with adults. Such a policy emphasizes to the public the real individuals for whom the program is maintained. In some instances, also, such a policy has been instrumental in awakening school patrons to the need for additional school facilities.

What admission should be charged adults? This is a question facing all athletic directors and school administrators. Differences in the size of school communities and their economic conditions cause some variance, but the admission fees charged by schools under similar circumstances can provide some guidance. Rates charged for public entertainment should also be studied. Although it would probably appear unreasonable to charge the same admission as movie theaters, for example, it would only be reasonable for athletic admissions to be raised as the price of public entertainment increases. In general, prices for high school games have not kept pace with inflation. When they are raised, it is wise to publicize the needs of the high school athletic program and the reasons for the increase. There are few places where comparable wholesome entertainment can be had as cheaply as in attendance at high school games.

Reserved seating offers a method of adding to admission receipts. Fans appreciate not having to arrive early to get desirable seats and are willing to pay more for reserved seats.

Season tickets.   The sale of season athletic tickets to students and adults is a recommended procedure. This accomplishes at least six things:

1. Prices for season tickets to students can be made much lower than the price of tickets purchased on a per game basis.
2. The plan assures the school of a definite minimum fund for program operations.
3. It obtains funds early in the season for use in getting the sport under way.
4. Season-ticket sales reduce the weather hazard that occurs when athletic funds depend entirely on game-day admissions.
5. In smaller communities, especially, season tickets are appreciated by inter-

ested adults. They offer a tangible way by which they may support the program. Such individuals are usually the more substantial citizens, and their presence at athletic contests lends a wholesome influence.

6. It helps to encourage regular attendance at games.

Two types of season tickets are recommended: the booklet form and that which has a detachable part to be removed when the ticket holder enters the gymnasium or field. The athletic booklet for students is numbered on the cover which has a space for the name of the owner. There is a separate slip with a number for each contest. Usually a space for the owner's signature is provided on each event slip. For identification purposes the signature may be compared with the cover signature, although some schools are not particular in this regard. The event slip must not be detached from the book prior to presentation at the gate or door. The entire book is then handed to the ticket taker, who tears out the appropriate slip and returns the book to the owner. A similar plan works out very well with adult season tickets and ensures that only one admission is obtained for each event on each ticket. This arrangement also is faster than ticket punching, in which a single ticket with designated punch spaces is used.

Student activity or general organization tickets. In schools in which student activity or general organization ticket plans are in effect it seems as though, generally, there is a better balance between athletics and other school activities. This is as it should be. Of course athletics appeal to many students, either as participants or as spectators. It is natural and proper to capitalize on this interest to aid in support of other school activities. The common practice in schools having general student tickets is to include some or all of the following, either entirely or partially, among the activities represented:

1. Admission to all home athletic contests
2. Admission to special school assemblies or programs
3. Admission, or part admission, to school plays, concerts, and operettas
4. Subscription to school paper
5. Part payment on the school annual
6. Admission to debates and other forensic contests
7. Admission, or part admission, to all-school parties

The plan definitely centers finances for all the activities of a school and, as in the case with season ticket sales in athletics, it establishes a working minimum for all school projects.

The division or proportioning of receipts from activity ticket sales will depend upon a number of different factors. A general board composed of representatives of all activities concerned should review the requests of each prospective recipient from the funds. Probable additional income to be realized by some of them during the year should be taken into consideration when making apportionments. When the total amount to be received has been estimated as nearly as possible and budgets for the activities of the year have been approved, it is a comparatively simple matter to apportion the percentages. Usually no single activity should be allowed to exceed its apportionment without the approval of the general activities board. Such a policy will ensure that all projects will have their allotted funds, and when balances from certain of them accrue, they may be placed in reserve for future use of all activities.

The student activity or general organization ticket plan in high schools seems to offer the following advantages as a method of financing athletics and other activities:

1. Unifies all school activities
2. Aids in keeping athletics in their relatively proper place in the school activities program
3. Capitalizes on student interest in athletics to aid in financing other justifiable school activities
4. Reduces ticket-selling campaigns to a minimum through regular organization plans.
5. Provides an early-season and known working capital for all activities
6. Provides accessible funds at the beginning of the school year
7. May be sponsored as a student activity project
8. Should result in considerable saving to students because prices may be reduced if sufficient tickets are sold

Participation fees.   Financial conditions have caused some school boards to initiate participant fees to help meet the costs of sports and other extracurricular activities. An ad hoc committee study in Minnesota revealed that an increasing number of schools in that state have established such fees.[2] These range from $5.00 to $15.00 per actvity, with the exception of football and hockey which extend as high as $50.00. Generally, a maximum charge is set for an individual student engaging in several activities and a maximum amount to be paid by a family. Schools considering this source should check their state laws. In some states such charges are permissible but in others they are illegal. Minnesota Statute 120.72 provides boards of education with this authority.[3]

There are arguments for and against participant fees. One can argue that interscholastic activities are a phase of the educational program and, therefore, no charge should be assessed for participation in them any more than for curricular courses. The principal counter-argument is that participation in extracurricular activities is a privilege from which benefits are received not available to all students, and a fee established for this extra privilege is not unreasonable. Some see no more wrong in charging participation fees than in charging admission fees to other students to see athletic contests. It appears evident, however, that the main reason for such fees is to help meet the costs of interscholastic activities and to avoid having to discontinue them.

Concessions.   Receipts from concessions at athletic contests can be a source of considerable income. Stands can be operated by students under the supervision of faculty members and can be planned to provide practical learning experiences. Parents and members of booster clubs often are happy to donate their services in operating concessions as a way of assisting in raising funds for the athletic program. Profits are also being realized from vending machines placed in gymnasium lobbies and about the school premises from which fruit and snacks can be purchased.

Contributions.   Occasionally some individual or organization will express to school officials an interest in making a contribution to help the athletic program. These may be in cash or in the form of athletic equipment of some type. Athletic booster clubs often are interested in providing such aid. Caution should be exercised in accepting contributions. If the donor is desirous of receiving advertising or recognition in return, the contribution should be rejected. Likewise, donations for a specific use or purpose should not be accepted. If they are accepted for a specified purpose, the school is allowing an outside group or individual to determine policy for the school. Any contributions that the school accepts should be with no strings attached, with the use of any moneys received to be determined by the school. This policy will help the school to retain full control of its program.

Special projects.   Some schools have allowed students to engage in special fund-raising projects to help finance the athletic program, such as candy sales, carnivals, popularity contests, and so on. Although there may be some educational value accruing from such projects, they generally take away valuable student time which could be better devoted to other educational activities.

Private funding.   When schools are faced with a financial crisis and boards of education must consider eliminating or reducing the athletic program, private organizations frequently offer to engage in fund-raising campaigns to save it. This happened in Rockford, Illinois; Detroit, Michigan; Buffalo, New York; and elsewhere.[4] The biggest pitfall in relying on private funding of an athletic program rests in the fact it does not represent a permanent solution. Generally, there is no guarantee the money will be raised from year to year. There is also the danger that pressure will be exerted on boards of education and athletic directors regarding use of the funds donated. Private funds should never be used to pay the salaries of coaches, as this could bias the hiring and firing of coaching personnel. Too often donors want a winning team at all costs.

However, private funding need not be inherently bad in emergencies if proper precautions are taken and appropriate policies are established. Many private and parochial schools have relied on contributions and private funding for years to assist in financing their athletic programs without loss of control. Some criteria which might be followed in accepting private funds are:

1. Can the source be considered temporary or permanent?
2. Will receipt of private funds affect future board of education allocations?
3. Will it affect the atttitude of school patrons toward district financing of the athletic program?
4. Will pressure to determine policy be brought on the board of education, the athletic director, and the coaching staff?
5. Will it cause loss of sight of the most worthwhile objectives of interscholastic athletics?

Although school administrators in general may be opposed to private funding, an increasing number of schools are finding the use of some private funds necessary to maintain their interscholastic programs. The National Federation recognizes both the dangers and the necessity and is attempting to aid schools experiencing financial difficulties in making agreements with reputable organizations to institute fund-raising projects.[5] It has recommended that criteria similar to those above be considered when contemplating the help of any of these organizations.

Board of education funds. It has been general practice in a large number of schools for the board of education to allocate some funds to supplement other sources of income for the interscholastic program. A few, which consider it an integral part of the total educational program, finance it entirely from school moneys and charge no admission for athletic events. Clayton and Ladue are two school systems in Missouri that follow this practice.

Actually, all school districts indirectly finance the interschool program in part from board of education funds. Capital outlays required to build gymnasiums and other athletic facilities are an example. Coaches' salaries are another. Most state associations will not permit an outside organization to pay any part of a coach's salary.

In some states receipts from school-sponsored activities are the property of the board of education and must be received and expended according to law. Missouri is one of these states. The athletic budget is, therefore, a matter to be considered and approved by the board of education. This presents no difficulty and encourages school board members to participate actively in financing interscholastics. Athletic directors work much more closely with boards of education under these conditions.

The Handling of Athletic Funds

The most important rule in handling athletic or any school activity finances is to have a simple, understandable system and then follow it. Nothing can cause more embarrassment or difficulty to a school administrator than inefficiency or carelessness in handling school or athletic funds. No transaction should be left unrecorded or unexplained. Be definite and brief, but be complete. At all times the entire records showing receipts, disbursements, balances, or deficits should be open to inspection.

Internal Accounting Records

In some school systems, board of education accounting divisions handle all financial transactions pertaining to high school athletics. Such a procedure relieves school officials entirely from keeping records of this type and centers financial matters in an agency that is expected by the public to have jurisdiction over them. In other schools, however, boards of education do not feel disposed to assume these duties. They think that athletic and other school activity funds should not be handled by them because they are not tax moneys and do not properly come within their scope of duties. Whether or not board of education officials have expressed themselves definitely on this matter, it is signifcant that in a great majority of large and small schools, high school activity funds are handled by the schools themselves. Most of them have their own internal accounting systems. Separate bank accounts are established, and funds are disbursed only on order of authorized school executives. In connection with such plans it is an excellent procedure to make regular reports of school activity funds to the finance officer or finance division of the board of education. These reports serve as an additional check on the accounting system of the school's athletic or activity program. Likewise, it is highly desirable to ask that board of education auditors annually examine and certify the recorded transactions of the activity fund accounts.

As far as athletic finances are concerned, it seems immaterial whether a school has a separate athletic association treasurer or a central internal accounting system in effect, with a general school treasurer. In order that each activity may be considered part of the entire school program, it is recommended that the latter plan be followed. A central accounting system for all high school activities presents the following advantages over the scheme of having separate systems for each activity:

1. Responsibility for disbursement of all school funds may be delegated to one individual.
2. It is in harmony with the plan of having all school activities under the general supervision of an all-school committee.
3. It enables the school administrator to have a composite picture of the general condition, financial and otherwise, of all the school activities.

4. It provides the possibility for a much more accurate audit of school activities funds than otherwise might be the case.

5. The purposes for which expenditures are to be made may be more easily checked to ascertain if they are in accordance with authorization.

6. Local banking institutions usually will prefer a single school deposit account rather than separate ones for each school activity fund.

7. By its nature, the plan appeals to students and school patrons as being more businesslike.

Schemes in local schools will vary with their plans of general organization and their size. Some of the most successful ones have a general faculty treasurer. It is recommended that the treasurer be someone other than the superintendent or principal. He/she should receive all funds from the proper officer of each activity organization on a regular form prepared for that purpose, enter them in the proper account, and make all payments from it by check to provide for adequate accounting. It is a good procedure to have all checks countersigned by the treasurer and an administrative officer designated by the board of education.

Publication of Financial Reports

At regular intervals—monthly, seasonal, term, or semester—statements should be prepared for submission to each activity organization and to the officials concerned. To illustrate a maximum policy in this respect, a list of statements which might be included in a seasonal report for football follows. Each of these could be prepared from the fund allocation heading in the bookkeeping procedure. Other sports would be comparable to this example.

1. Seasonal summary football statement of receipts and disbursements
2. Bar graph showing receipts and disbursements
3. Detailed statements of football gate receipts
4. Detailed statement of football guarantee income
5. Detailed statement of football equipment purchased
6. Detailed statement of food and lodging expense for football season
7. Detailed statement of laundry, cleaning, and reconditioning expense
8. Detailed statement of medical expense and medical supplies
9. Detailed statement of officials' expense
10. Detailed statement of office supplies expense
11. Detailed statement of opponents' guarantee expense
12. Detailed statement of printing expense
13. Detailed statement of scouting expense
14. Detailed statement of telephone expense
15. Detailed statement of towel service expense

16. Detailed statement of transportation expense
17. Bar graph showing profit or loss on each football game

It is advisable to see to it that records of finances are known to the public, especially if the public is partly responsible for some of the funds by which the athletic program is conducted. In dealing with this subject elsewhere, it was suggested that reports of receipts and disbursements for all athletic contests be placed in the hands of the superintendent or principal shortly after each game. Further, it is recommended that the school policy provide that such reports be placed on the school bulletin board and published frequently in the school or local newspaper. In this connection, however, be sure that reports of expenses for activities from which there is no income also are listed. These will show some of the expenses for activities that have to be supported out of income from other sources.

ATHLETIC BUDGETS

If projects, activities, or programs are to be successful, their approximate costs must be calculated in advance. Within schools, budgets are necessary not only for athletics but also for the operation of the entire school system. If several athletic activities are supported from a central source of funds, a budget is especially important because it gives each division reasonable assurance of the amount that will be available to it.

Purpose

A budget is merely an estimate of probable income and expenditures. Its preparation is of value to those in charge of high school athletic programs because it necessitates that they anticipate, as far as possible, all the probable factors involved. Thus, constructive planning is necessary. Many school administrators say that their athletic programs are so small that no budget is necessary. Some others assert that they have no time to prepare budgets. Usually these are not legitimate excuses. Although there may be some question about the amount of income to be realized from athletic contests, there can be no doubt as to the absolute minimum necessary to finance an activity or program. This matter should be discussed by all those concerned before the program is established for the year.

The school should attempt to make athletic experiences available to as many students as feasible. However, caution must be exercised in regard to the number of sports that can be adequately financed. Consideration must be given to the number for which adequate player and game equipment can be provided. Careful attention should be given to the funds available and whether they are sufficient to finance additional sports before any are added to the program. Because comparable programs must be offered both boys and girls, thorough study must be given to the extent of the total program the school can afford.

It is obvious that changes in budget allowances will have to be made in certain instances. Likewise, it is illogical to assume that a budget, once adopted, should be a hard-and-fast limit to which there must be blind adherence. In general, a budget should not be too specific or detailed. It should allow for flexibility within each activity. In the final analysis, then, an athletic budget simply is an attempt to balance receipts and expenditures, and its adoption should be the result of past experience in both of these matters. If accurate records of income and expenses for one year have been kept, it is a relatively simple matter to establish a budget for the program for the next year.

The athletic budget for one activity has more than the sport itself to take into consideration. The budget must be balanced in the sense that it takes all the activities of the athletic program into consideration and sees that funds for their operation are properly proportioned.

Planning

Planning of a proposed athletic budget must take both boys' and girls' sports into consideration. Although comparable activities must be provided both sexes, equal expenditures for each is not automatically necessary. Costs for different sports will vary considerably as will the number of students participating in them. Football, for example, is far more expensive than most other sports. Income from some sports will be far more than income from others, but this should not be a primary consideration in allocating budget items. It is important that the same general quality of equipment and supplies be provided.

There may be some differences of opinion, but it is generally best to have one athletic director responsible for recommending a budget for the total athletic program. All coaches, men and women, should be afforded the opportunity to submit budget requests with the understanding that the athletic director will compile a budget to be recommended to the school administration and board of education for their approval.

No general rule for the preparation of an athletic budget can be formulated that is applicable to schools of all sizes. General estimates of probable receipts from home games may be made from previous records. If there is a student or general organization ticket sales plan in effect, the probable amount forthcoming from that source may be estimated. Any amount to be received for athletics from the local board of education also may be included, and thus a probable total of all income may be determined. A suggested form for a composite report of estimated receipts to be used in preparation of an athletic budget appears in Fig. 11-1. It presents a simple method by which this information may be shown.

BUDGET SUMMARY OF ESTIMATED INCOME

School:_____   School Year: 19____-19____

| Sport | Home Games | | Away Games | | Total Estimate |
	No.	Receipts	No.	Guarantees	
Baseball.........		$		$	$
Basketball.......					
Football.........					
Hockey.........					
Swimming.......					
Track..........					
Other..........					
(1) Total estimated receipts........		$		$	$

(2) Estimated amount to be realized from student or general organization ticket sale................................ $_____

(3) Total amount, if any, to be received from the board of education for purchase of playing equipment........... $_____

(4) Grand total of estimated receipts for present year (Sum of 1, 2, 3)........ $_____

(5) Grand total of estimated expenditures for present year.................... $_____

(6) Estimated surplus for year (Difference between 4 and 5).................. $_____

or

(7) Estimated deficit for year (Difference between 5 and 4).................. $_____

FIGURE 11–1 Suggested form for budget summary of estimated income

Estimating details of probable expenditures may involve more time and effort than estimating probable receipts from athletic contests. A school must know what equipment it has on hand, its condition, and the amount of new equipment to be purchased. This information may be obtained from the seasonal inventories.[6] Also to be considered are such items as general administration; game officials; contract guarantees; expenses for games away from home; equipment repairs; new equipment; training, first aid, and medical supplies; awards; and incidentals, including pictures, meet and league fees, and the like (see Fig. 11–2). This suggested form will not show all the details necessary under each item; but if it is completely filled out for the sports sponsored by a school, it will disclose the general budget figures for each activity and the totals.

Obviously, one can devise other ways of preparing athletic budgets with possibly more successful application to individual school problems than the suggestions mentioned in this discussion. The purpose of the forms shown here is to present relatively general ones from which schools may select the parts that pertain to their situations. In some instances, no doubt, schools will add items to those suggested. As stated previously, it will be necessary to set up divisions under each heading. For example, the item "Cost of New Playing and Game Equipment" must be divided into various sports. Each sport then would be subdivided into different equipment items, with the estimated number of each that are needed and the cost price. In such a manner, total estimates may be obtained that would constitute the total as it appears on the budget summary blanks. Too much emphasis cannot be placed on the importance of correct inventories. Also, it is imperative that prices for sports equipment and material to be purchased be exact. These are items of the budget that can be estimated accurately, and their correctness makes the budget valuable. Budgets from year to year should be prserved for reference and statistical purposes.

PREPARATION OF A BUDGET
FOR BOARD OF EDUCATION APPROVAL

Each school will decide the form to be used for preparing and submitting a recommended budget. A few will budget a set amount for interscholastics and leave it to the activities or athletic director to determine how it will be expended. However, it is best that this individual be requested to prepare and submit a recommended budget in detail for approval. The advantage of this procedure is that it will show better the need for and use to be made of the money requested. It should be itemized in detail to explain clearly estimated receipts and expenditures, equipment to be purchased, administrative costs, and so on for each sport. Current prices and costs must be closely checked. A recapitulation summary of the total anticipated receipts and ex-

Sport	Administration: Cost of Bleachers, Guards, Tickets, Field, Printing, Postage, etc.	Cost of Officials for Home Contests	Home Game Contract Guarantees	Away-Game Expenses	Cost of Equipment, Repairs, and Maintenance	Cost of New Playing and Game Equipment	Cost of Training, First-Aid, and Medical Supplies	Cost of Awards	Incidentals: Team Pictures, Meet or League Fees, etc.	Total Estimate for Sport for Year
Baseball										
Basketball										
Boxing										
Cross-Country										
Football										
Golf										
Hockey										
Swimming										
Tennis										
Track										
Wrestling										
Others										
TOTAL ESTIMATE										

BUDGET SUMMARY OF ESTIMATED EXPENSES

School:_____   School Year: 19____-19____

FIGURE 11–2 Suggested form for budget summary of estimated expenses

penditures should be provided to facilitate consideration for approval. In most instances, it can be expected that the board of education will find it necessary to make some adjustments.

The abbreviated suggested form shown in Fig. 11–3 will provide an idea of a form to be used and the type of details to include.

In larger schools with several coaches the athletic director will want the coach of each sport to submit a detailed budget request including the number and cost of equipment and supply items needed for the ensuing year. These must be reviewed carefully, adjustments made if advisable, and then compiled in the budget to be presented to the superintendent and board of education (see Fig. 11–3).

PRESENTING THE BUDGET

Acceptance of a proposed budget will depend upon several factors, including available finances. However, careful preparation and presentation will enhance favorable consideration of it. The athletic director must realize other heads of departments will be making budget requests and there will be competition for board of education funds available. He/she must justify the requests, but also must understand that the athletic budget shall be kept in proper perspective within the total school budget. Considering a budget is tedious and time-consuming for the board, and the presentation should be concise but thorough.

The following suggestions may serve as helpful guidelines in preparing and presenting the athletic budget:

1. *Briefly state the philosophy and objectives for the interscholastic athletic program.* There is no better time to review the objectives and values of athletics as well as plans developed to implement them. It is important that members of the board understand that the money is being requested for educational purposes inherent in interschool competition and not merely to provide entertainment.

2. *Have a good knowledge of the total school budget.* A copy of the previous year's budget will provide worthwhile information and can be obtained from the superintendent of schools. These data will be helpful in justifying the athletic budget. A study from a random sampling of different size schools made by the National School Boards Association and reported in 1975 revealed that the total expended for interscholastic athletics ranged from six-tenths of one percent of the total budget in wealthy suburban districts to five percent in a small city.[7] Surveys made by the National Federation of State High School Associations indicate most schools expend about one percent of the total school budget for athletics.[8] Figuring the percent the re-

Budget Form

Estimated Income

Football   *Number*   *Unit Price*   *Total*

Season tickets	_____	@ $_____	$_____
Reserved seats	_____	@ $_____	$_____
General admissions	_____	@ $_____	$_____
J. V. admissions	_____	@ $_____	$_____

Total (Football) $_____

Basketball

Season tickets	_____	@ $_____	$_____
Reserved seats	_____	@ _____	_____
General admissions	_____	@ _____	_____
J. V. admissions	_____	@ _____	_____
Tournament receipts			

Total (Basketball) $_____

Girls' Volleyball

General admissions	_____	@ $_____	$_____
Tournament receipts			

Total (Girls' Volleyball) $_____

(Use same procedure for itemizing receipts for each additional sport)

Other Estimated Income

Student season tickets	_____	@ _____	$_____
Junior high admissions	_____	@ _____	_____
Board of Education			

Total (Other Income) $_____

Total Estimated Receipts $_____

Estimated Expenditures

Football   *Number*   *Unit Price*   *Total*

Equipment:

Footballs	_____	@ $_____	$_____
Game jerseys	_____	@ _____	_____
Game pants	_____	@ _____	_____
T-shirts	_____	@ _____	_____
Helmets	_____	@ _____	_____
Shoulder pads	_____	@ _____	_____
Hip pads	_____	@ _____	_____
Pad laces	_____	@ _____	_____
Shoes	_____	@ _____	_____
Shoe laces	_____	@ _____	_____
Audio visual aids	_____	@ _____	_____
Cleaning and repair of equipment	_____	@ _____	_____
Scouting			_____
Awards			_____

Total (Equipment) $_____

FIGURE 11-3 Suggested budget form *(continued on p. 272)*

Administration: Total
    Games officials $_____
    Sideline officials   _____
    Ticket sellers and takers   _____
    Ushers   _____
    Security   _____
    Extra custodial services   _____
    Scoreboard operators   _____
    Timer   _____
    Announcer   _____
    Supervisors   _____
    Field preparation and maintenance   _____
                               Total (Administration) $_____

Meals and Transportation:

Game Away	Meals	Trans.
_____	$_____	$_____ $_____
_____	_____	_____
_____	_____	_____
_____	_____	_____

                         Total (Meals/Transportation) $_____

(Use same procedure to itemize expenditures for each additional sport)

                               Total Estimated Expenditures $_____

Recapitulation of Estimated Income and Expenditures

Sport	Income	Expenditures	Balance
Football	$_____	$_____	$_____
Basketball	_____	_____	_____
Girls' Volleyball	_____	_____	_____
(Continue for each sport)			
Total	_____	_____	_____

    Estimated Balance or Deficit $_____

FIGURE 11–3 *(continued)*

quested athletic budget is of the individual school's total budget generally will help members of the board of education to understand its reasonableness.

3. *Cite the number of students participating in athletics.* This will vary with the size of the school, with a larger percent involved in smaller high schools. It is also important to emphasize the number of other students who participate in the pep club and other activities related to the athletic program.

4. *Compare the per athlete cost with per pupil costs in academic courses.* Such comparison should be made relative to funds requested from the board of education exclusive of receipts from admissions and other sources. (It should be remembered, however, that in most states all athletic funds are properties of the board of education.)

5. *Give careful estimate of expected receipts other than board of education funds.* Some might fear this may influence the board to reduce allocations for athletics, but it will have great value in convincing members that the request for additional funds is justifiable. It is unwise to request funds from the board of education which are not needed to adequately finance the athletic program. Explaining any plans to increase such revenues will also have a positive influence.

6. *Discuss steps being taken to reduce costs and to eliminate any unnecessary expenses.* Estimates of the amount of money that can be saved by having equipment repaired, for example, will convince the board of the reasonableness of the request and that good business practices are being followed.

7. *Always give sound reasons for the request of budget items.* The soundest reasons are those based on the needs of boys and girls.

8. *Be prepared to compromise and reduce requests if necessary.* It can be anticipated that the budget often will have to be "cut" by the board of education. Frequently, the athletic director will be asked to indicate where these cuts can be made without damaging the athletic program. If this situation arises, he or she must be prepared to give priorities and reasons for them.

9. *Do not seek support for more sports than the budget can properly finance.* In emergencies it is wiser to eliminate some sport(s) than to "spread allocations too thin," which often results in failure to provide quality protective equipment and supplies. Be ready to suggest what sport(s) may be eliminated if funds prove inadequate.

10. *Always express appreciation for the opportunity to present the budget and for the support received.*

When the budget is finalized, it should be made public along with the educational opportunities and values it offers high school students. Sound financial planning, careful budgeting, and giving the educational reasons for the expenditures will help to gain support for the interscholastic program.

SUMMARY

Expansion in boys' and girls' participation, inflation, and uncertain economic conditions have made the financing of interscholastic athletics increasingly difficult.

During school financial crises consideration may be given by boards of education to reducing or eliminating the interschool athletic program.

The principal sources of finances for the athletic program are allocations from board of education funds and receipts from admissions. The charging of participation fees has been adopted by a few boards of education to help meet athletic expenses and to avoid having to drop some sports or eliminate the program. Contributions and private funding may be accepted, but it is not wise to consider them as permanent sources of income. The board of education and school administration should always reserve the right to determine the specific use of such funds to avoid interference with policy considerations.

A central internal record-keeping system is the best procedure for the accounting of all athletic funds.

The best procedure for preparing a budget is first to estimate income and then to plan expenditures within that amount.

An athletic budget will receive more favorable consideration by the board of education if it is well presented by the athletic administrator.

QUESTIONS AND TOPICS FOR STUDY AND DISCUSSION

1. Discuss conditions which make financing of interscholastic athletics uncertain.

2. Discuss various methods of raising funds for interschool athletics. Which do you consider the most desirable? Why?

3. What are the values of using student activity or general organization tickets in financing athletics and other school activities?

4. Do you favor athletic participation fees? Why?

5. What are some of the precautions to be considered regarding private funding of interscholastic athletics?

6. Discuss the merits of a general internal accounting plan for handling athletic and all other activity funds.

7. Why is it important that published reports be made at regular intervals of the receipt and disbursement of athletic funds? Illustrate a good procedure for doing this.

8. What are the purposes and values of athletic budgets? By whom should they be prepared?

9. Should equal allocations be made for boys' and girls' athletic programs? What would be the determining factors in making this decision?

10. Assume you are the coach and your athletic director asks you to submit a tentative budget for the sport you are coaching. Explain what factors will be considered before you prepare it.

11. Assume that you have just been employed as high school athletic director and that one of your first responsibilities is to recommend an interscholastic budget for the consideration of your principal and the board of education. Outline the steps you would follow in determining the budget you would recommend.

12. Why must a proposed athletic budget be carefully presented to the board of education for approval? Explain what you would include in a budget presentation.

NOTES

1. "Survey by American Sports Education Institute Confirms Trend toward Declining Budgets," *National Federation Press,* 3, no. 3 (November 1982), 5.
2. Minnesota State High School League, "Study Report on the Cost Impact of Interscholastic Programs" (report of an ad hoc committee), 1979–81, p. 5.
3. Ibid., p. 5.
4. "The Role of Private Funding," *Interscholastic Athletic Administration,* 3, no. 2 (Spring 1977), 20–21.
5. "Fund Raising: The Next Interscholastic Activity?" *National Federation Press,* 1, no. 3 (November 1980), 1.
6. See suggested inventory form, p. 242.
7. National School Boards Association, *The American School Board Journal,* June 1975, p. 23.
8. "Interscholastic Athletics: Their Cost and Value," *Interscholastic Athletic Administration,* 3, no. 2 (Spring 1977), 17–19.

BIBLIOGRAPHY

"Cost-Saving Ideas from Atlanta." *Interscholastic Athletic Administration,* 7, no. 4 (Summer 1981), 29.

COTTON, JOHN K. "Tracking Sports Expenditures Provides Program Insight." *Interscholastic Athletic Administration,* 9, no. 1 (Fall 1982), 14–15.

DeLUCA, JOHN. "Austerity and School Athletics." *Interscholastic Athletic Administration,* 6, no. 4 (Summer 1980), 15–16.

"Fund Raising: The Next Interscholastic Activity?" *National Federation Press,* 1, no. 3 (November 1980), 1.

GALLON, ARTHUR J. *Coaching Ideas and Ideals,* pp. 141–73. Boston, Mass.: Houghton Mifflin, 1974.

"Interscholastic Athletics: Their Cost and Value." *Interscholastic Athletic Administration,* 3, no. 2 (Spring 1977), 17–19.

LONG, EDWIN. "Preparing Athletic Budgets Through Data Processing," in *Secondary School Athletic Administration—A New Look.* Washington, D.C.: American Association for Health, Physical Education, and Recreation, 1969, pp. 57–70.

"Michigan Association Outlines Methods For Saving Energy and Dollars in the 80s." *Interscholastic Athletic Administration,* 9, no. 2 (Winter 1982), 23–25.

MINNESOTA STATE HIGH SCHOOL LEAGUE. "Study Report on the Impact of Interscholastic Programs" (report of an ad hoc committee), 1979–81.

NATIONAL SCHOOL BOARDS ASSOCIATION. "All About the Real Cost of School Sports and How Not to Get Your Signals Crossed." *The American School Board Journal,* 162, no. 6 (June 1975), 23.

RESICK, MATTHEW C., AND CARL E. ERICKSON. *Intercollegiate and Interscholastic Athletics for Men and Women,* pp. 90–108. Reading, Mass.: Addison-Wesley, 1975.

SENNETT, OTIS. "Cooperative Venture Fund Raiser Utilized by New York District." *Interscholastic Athletic Administration,* 9, no. 2 (Winter 1982), 22–23.

"Survey by American Sports Education Institute Confirms Trend toward Declining Budgets." *National Federation Press,* 3, no. 3 (November 1982), 5.

"Teamwork Vital in Overcoming Battle of the Budget." *National Federation Press,* 2, no. 8 (April 1982), 5.

"The Budget—Its Importance Can't Be Overestimated" (a reprint through courtesy of *The Athletic Educator's Report*). *National Federation Press,* 2, no. 7 (March 1982), 4.

"The Role of Private Funding." *Interscholastic Athletic Administration,* 3, no. 2 (Spring 1977), 20–23.

YAFFE, ELAINE. "High School Athletics: A Colorado Story." *Phi Delta Kappan,* 64, no. 3 (November 1982), 177–81.

12

Providing for the Health and Safety of High School Athletes

Better health and safety of students is one of the important goals of secondary education. Each school should have a comprehensive program designed for the attainment of this objective. The interscholastic athletic program can and must contribute toward this end. Athletes and other students should be made cognizant of the fact that regularity in training habits, eating proper foods, sanitation, rigorous exercise, and getting sufficient sleep are as important in daily living as they are in conditioning for athletic contests. To be maximally effective, attention in the athletic program must be given to: (1) improving the health habits of the participants, and (2) safeguarding the physical welfare of students. These must be given careful consideration in the overall administrative planning, and definite steps and procedures must be developed to ensure their achievement.

THE SAFETY PROGRAM

School personnel, in their zeal to teach the game, must not be guilty of overlooking some of the common things that pertain to the health of participants. Safety in athletics and improved standards in sanitation, as well as health habits, are important. Today as never before, there is a health and safety consciousness among school students and adults. The athletic program provides a fine opportunity to emphasize these factors. Safety, probably more than anything else at the present time, catches the attention of the general public. Motivated largely by traffic accidents and fatalities, people are looking for safer ways of doing things. It behooves athletic administrators, therefore, to set up safety programs. Many schools, statewide organizations, and state departments of education have definite courses of study on safety that are available for the asking. Athletics in any school may be made an important phase of a program devoted to better and safer living. An athletic program conducted under the motto, "Safe, Sanitary, and Sane," will add immeasurably to high school education.

ATHLETIC SAFETY ESSENTIALS

Much has been written about the inculcation of safety habits in high school students and adults by various methods. In the discussion of such possibilities in athletics, we will consider several contributing factors and attempt to show their importance.

An Overall School Safety Program

Public concern regarding accidents and injuries and court decisions relative to them make it extremely important for each school to have a formalized school health and safety plan under the supervision of an individual or committee qualified to administer such a program. Incorporated in the plan should be academic courses such as health and physiology, the promotion of good health habits, instruction in safety techniques, provision for the prevention and care of injuries, and student accident insurance. Attention must be given to safety on the school premises, in transportation, and in all school-sponsored student activities off the premises. The discussions which follow will be limited to that part of the program which involves school athletics.

Responsibility for Health and Safety

Although the school is ultimately responsible for the health and safety of all students, it usually falls to the athletic administrator to oversee safety in athletics. It is obvious that he/she cannot personally see to all the numerous details and must, therefore, further delegate responsibilities. However, the athletic director can be expected to develop a plan to guide others in providing for adequate safety in athletic activities. Among the more important general details of the plan should be:

1. Establishment of safety guidelines to be followed by all coaches and athletes (with delegation to individual coaches of guidelines specific to his/her sport)
2. Formulation of safety and sanitation policies to be applied in the athletic program
3. Providing adequate protective player equipment
4. Keeping playing facilities safe and free of hazards
5. Establishment of a procedure, including a chain of command, for handling injuries
6. Arranging for proper medical supervision
7. Having a file of parents' telephone numbers available at all times for notification in case of serious injury

In addition to the above, it is an ultimate responsibility of the athletic director to ascertain that all coaches and others concerned are appropriately assuming their individual duties.

Coaches Dedicated to the Physical Welfare and Health of Athletes

The athletic director may be the captain of the athletic safety team, but it is the coaches upon whom he/she must rely to implement most of the safety policies. In addition to having a thorough knowledge of the sport he or she teaches, a coach must have training in the areas of first aid, the medical aspects of sports, physiological foundations of athletics, the kinesiology of movement, and drug abuse and the dangers therein. Coaches are also in a strategic position to influence good dietary attitudes and habits, which are important in maintaining and improving health.[1]

In supervising the athletic staff, an administrator must convince him/ herself that coaches are

1. Making certain no athlete begins practice in any sport without having had the required physical examination and parental permission

2. Providing a physical conditioning program to prepare athletes for strenuous activities, which includes acclimating players to heat in such sports as football

3. Having players always engage in purposeful warmup exercises before beginning rigorous practice or competition

4. Providing safety guidelines for athletes

5. Instructing players of the injury risks taken in the sport concerned and safety techniques to employ (see also Legal Aspects, pp. 365, 366)

6. Giving careful attention to the condition and care of protective equipment

7. Inspecting safety conditions of the playing field or gymnasium before all practices and contests

8. Being alert to any signs of drug abuse[2]

9. Properly supervising the dressing room and sanitary habits of athletes (see also pp. 293–295)

10. Adhering to established procedures for the prevention and treatment of injuries

11. Not allowing players who have been injured or ill to return to practice before they are beyond danger of reinjury or reoccurence of illness, which is upon advice of a physician in all serious cases

The coach who is dedicated to the health and physical welfare of athletes always puts the welfare of the player first and avoids risking injury in the desire to win games.

Adequate Protective Player Equipment

Equipment that meets accepted safety standards and fits properly is essential to the physical welfare of athletes. This is important in all sports and of particular significance in such sports as football and hockey. Headgear, shoulder, hip, and thigh pads, and shoes must provide for maximum safety. Coaches must exercise great care and effort to see that all athletes are appropriately fitted with safe playing equipment.

The National Federation has had the safety of participants as one of its chief concerns since its beginning. Primary attention has been given to this matter through its rules writing, game administration, and research activities. In 1970, in cooperation with the Athletic Goods Manufacturers Association, the American College Health Association, the National Athletic Trainers Association, the National Collegiate Athletic Association, and the National Junior College Athletic Association, the National Operating Committee on Standards for Athletic Equipment was formed. Arrangements have been made through NOCSAE for in-depth experimentation with protective equipment to be conducted by Wayne State University in Detroit, Michigan.

NOCSAE has stated its objectives as follows:

1. To promote, conduct, and foster research, and study and analyze the collection of data and statistics relating to athletic equipment with a view to encouraging the establishment of standards in the manufacture and use thereof for the benefit of amateur athletics.

2. To disseminate information and promote, conduct, and foster other activities designed to increase knowledge and understanding of the safety, comfort, utility, and legal aspects of athletic equipment.

3. To provide a forum in which individuals and organizations may consult and cooperate in considering problems relating to athletic equipment.

4. To do all of the foregoing exclusively for charitable, educational, and scientific purposes.[3]

It will carry on a continuous program of investigating all aspects of school sports in an attempt to provide for maximum safety of athletes. A standard has been established for evaluating the protective quality of football helmets. Helmets meeting this standard will carry a NOCSAE seal. The National Federation and the National Collegiate football rules committees require helmets bearing the NOCSAE seal be used in football contests played under their rules. Despite these safety precautions, injuries to the head and neck occasionally occur and court suits have resulted, primarily because players wearing the helmets have not been warned of possible danger of injury. To alleviate these problems, NOCSAE has provided *warning labels* to be placed on football helmets, which are supplied schools through their state associations. The costs of supplying the labels is borne by helmet manufacturers. Following is the wording in the warning:

WARNING

NO HELMET CAN PREVENT ALL HEAD OR NECK INJURIES A PLAYER MIGHT RECEIVE WHILE PARTICIPATING IN FOOTBALL.
Do not use this Helmet to butt, ram, or spear an opposing player. This is in violation of the football rules and as such can result in severe head or neck injuries, paralysis or death to you and possible injury to your opponent.[4]

Athletic directors should make certain coaches call this warning to the attention of all players.

NOCSAE has also published a Baseball Batter's Helmet Standard and is cooperating with the American Society for Testing and Materials to improve the safety of hockey face masks and other playing equipment.[5]

Statistics show that the efforts of NOCSAE and the National Federation's various rules committees have helped much to reduce injuries, and athletic directors and coaches should follow their recommendations in the purchase and use of player equipment.

The Need for Better Weight Control Policies in Wrestling

Wrestling is recognized as a fine high school sport when kept in proper perspective. Contestants are classified by weight, allowing individuals to compete in fair competition against others of essentially the same size. However, the desire to gain an advantage by qualifying for a lower weight classification by starvation diets, dehydration, and other questionable methods sometimes gives the sport a "black eye" and has been a cause for concern of the National Federation and state high school associations. Although there are no data available showing harmful effects upon the health of wrestlers, these organizations and many members of the medical profession do not believe that excessive weight reduction by questionable means can contribute to better health.

The National Federation has recommended that each state association consider the adoption of some type of certified weight plan to try to prevent abuses. Some of the plans tried include:

1. Establishing a minimum weight class for each wrestler early in the season below which he is not permitted to wrestle. Growth allowances permitting the individual a set number of additional pounds each month thereafter are allowed.

2. Requiring that a wrestler must have wrestled half or more of his regular season matches in a particular class to qualify for the minimum weight class in which he may wrestle in district and state tournament series. (The wrestling

rules allow him to wrestle only one weight class higher than the one for which he qualifies by weight.)

3. Minimum weight certification by a physician according to body composition. Costs of such physical examinations and the fact that inadequate guidelines are available for physicians to determine minimum weight certification have presented some problems in the administration of this method, but those who have used the plan think it has some merit.

None of these certified weight plans has solved all the problems of weight loss abuse, and concern about the possible ill effects upon the health of athletes continues. There is need for a good educational program for wrestlers and parents regarding acceptable weight control. The coach should assume the responsibility of providing information to both athletes and parents and trying to prevent excessive weight reduction. Athletic administrators should give the necessary supervision to see that this responsibility is assumed. Included in the educational program should be:

1. Consideration of body composition for determining proper weight goals
2. Knowledge related to defensible diets during the season
3. The role of weight training in maintaining a desirable weight
4. Self-discipline necessary to maintain an effective weight
5. Signs of excessive weight loss
6. The health dangers which may result from such practices as crash diets and sweating off weight, which may cause dehydration

The timing of weigh-ins can also contribute to health problems. Skipping meals to qualify at a certain weight means a loss of nutrition, and eating after weigh-ins but too soon before competition can cause nausea and other illnesses. Wrestlers should eat their last meal at least three hours before competition starts, and weigh-ins should be scheduled to allow for such.

Coaches should warn wrestlers and their parents of the dangers of excessive weight loss to gain a competitive advantage. They are in the most strategic position to provide the type of educational program needed to protect the physical welfare of wrestlers.

Proper Playing Facilities

Cross country running and golf are the only commonly sponsored high school athletic activities that do not require smooth surfaces. In cross country the path of the course, however, must be smooth for the runners. In golf the fairways should be free from ruts. Football and soccer are supposed to be played on a smooth, grassy playing area. Artificial turfs are being installed by a few schools that can afford them. Their safety features should be carefully examined. There is at present little conclusive evidence that they provide more or less protection against knee and ankle injuries. The baseball diamond should be smooth and generally level, outfield as well as infield. Tracks and tennis courts, of course, must be smooth. Runways and jumping pits must provide for safety against injuries. Discus, shot put, and javelin areas must be kept clear during warmups and competition. Under no circumstances should football fields have stones, hard surfaces, or ruts. Keep them smooth with a good turf. Obstructions should be well back from boundary lines. Gymnasium floors should be kept clean, not allowed to become slippery, and playing areas should be free for several feet from dangerous obstructions such as posts, stoves, walls, stairways, bleachers, drinking fountains, and tables. Be safety conscious as far as all playing facilities, both outdoor and indoor, are concerned. It is much easier to prevent an accident in athletics than it is to explain to parents that their child's misfortune was caused by someone's carelessness. All safety and sanitation precautions should be observed just as faithfully during practice sessions as during regular games, because generally there are between four or five times as many opportunities for accidents during practice as during games.

Adequate Physical Conditioning and Training

Strictly speaking, adequate training is a phase of athletic coaching. Good coaches always have insisted that members of their teams be in good physical condition. The necessity for state association regulations requiring minimum training periods in certain sports (see Chapter 6) apparently came about because some coaches were not particular about the training periods of their teams. The normal human body possesses a remarkable ability to withstand unusual demands made of it, and its ability to recuperate from strain is almost unbelievable at times. Athletic competition, however, should not rely or call upon this reserve unnecessarily. Coaches should set up training and conditioning schedules for participants in each sport that will ensure their being in proper condition to compete. After all, training is not difficult; it is simply getting into condition to play by means of commonsense living and intelligent hard work. The relation between injury and fatigue is more than an assumption. We know we are less able to perform normal functions when we are tired. It is only logical, then, that injuries are more apt to occur when we are fatigued. As a safety measure, therefore, it is essential that participants be in the best possible physical condition and go through an adequate training routine before they are allowed to compete in interscholastic athletic contests.

The following will aid in enhancing proper conditioning of players and in preventing injuries:

1. Provide players with instructions to follow in engaging in activities and exercises for pre-season conditioning
2. Require a physical examination before the athlete is permitted to begin practice

3. Hold abbreviated practices the first few days before graduating to strenuous activities, and have at least three weeks of practice before the first game

4. Exercise precaution against the possibility of heat exhaustion and heat stroke during hot weather (The first three to five days of football practice should be without pads and uniforms except shoes and helmets. Providing plenty of rest periods, wearing light clothing until athletes are acclimated, furnishing plenty of drinking water and some extra salt, and carefully noting the relative humidity index are wise precautions to take.)

5. Make certain that players warm up thoroughly before participating

The possibility of legal suits in cases of injuries resulting from negligence makes it extremely important for coaches to develop good conditioning programs, and athletic directors should ascertain that the staff is assuming this responsibility.

Sufficient Number of Reserve Players

It is difficult to set definite standards as to the number of reserve players necessary for each activity. Individual capacities and abilities of players vary, as do the policies of different coaches in the use of reserve players. There is a definite relation between fatigue and the possibility of injury. It is apparent, therefore, that there should be sufficient reserves on a squad to enable substitutes to be used when necessary from a safety standpoint as well as in consideration of the playing ability of the team. It is reasonable to assume that in general there should be at least two members on the squad for each position on the team. Coaches know that competition between players for team positions makes a better team. However, that is not the primary purpose in making this recommendation. It is made for the good of the athlete and to ensure safety in participation. A great many schools never enlist even this minimum number of players. When this is the case, grave doubt may be raised as to the advisability of conducting the activity, especially in football, basketball, and soccer.

If a player becomes injured, tired, has been ill, or is not in proper condition to play, he or she should not be in the game, as physical safety and health are endangered by competition under such circumstances. Be especially careful of athletes who, after serious or prolonged illnesses, require approval from doctors before they are allowed to return to practice or competition. Athletic coaches will be raising the standards of the coaching profession and their own reputations, as well as protecting the welfare of the participants entrusted to their care, if they maintain policies of frequent substitutions in athletic contests. It is an old adage that an athletic team is no stronger than its reserves. It is equally true that the best insurance against too much competition, which is likely to result in injuries or harm to an athlete, is to have a sufficient number of reserves available—and then not hesitating to make substitutions.

Proper Officiating

Great improvement has been made during the last few years in the standards of officiating in high school athletic contests. State athletic associations have had much to do with this through their rules-interpretation meetings and insistence that the protection of players receives the utmost consideration. Opinions of coaches vary as to what constitutes good officiating from a strictly rules-interpretation standpoint. Good coaches, however, usually are in agreement that an official should handle a game in football or basketball so that the physical welfare of contestants is protected. Officials must know the game rules, be alert physically and mentally, and, through their handling of the contest, keep it under control at all times. The day has gone when officials considered that they had properly discharged their duties when they had controlled a game simply by calling technical violations of the rules. While the play is in progress, players are actually under their care, especially in high school games. Good officials realize this, and that is an important reason why they are good officials.

Equitable Competition

A safety precaution of first importance is the policy of providing as nearly equitable competition as is possible in all athletic contests. Specifically, this means that the scheduling of games between large and small teams generally is undesirable. This observation applies especially in football. Schools invite criticism if those with large squads schedule games with others not comparable in size, and vice versa, especially if injuries occur in such games. Often these contests appeal to large schools as openers. Smaller schools, on the other hand, may be interested because of the financial guarantees. Some high schools also play college and independent teams in football, with decidedly unsatisfactory experiences. Although this criticism is not necessarily true in other sports of noncontact nature, in general it is a safe and wise procedure for a school to limit its athletic competition to other schools relatively comparable in size. It is one more safety precaution to which schools are beginning to give more attention than they did a few years ago, and the results will justify this attention.

Prompt Reporting and Attention to Injuries

As in many activities in which both older and younger people engage, injuries are a part of athletic competition, especially of the body-contact type. Although every possible precaution should be taken to prevent injuries, experience shows that they do happen. When they do, the school should have a definite policy for handling them. Students should be instructed to report injuries to their coaches immediately. This requirement should be as much a part of the training regulations as are the playing rules of the sport concerned.

It should be a "must" regardless of membership by a school in an athletic insurance or athletic protection or benefit plan. Participation by a school in any of these plans usually requires that all injuries must be reported officially within two to 20 days. In reality such a requirement is most beneficial to the student because he or she is the one who receives the necessary treatment. It also is important because, in most instances, rehabilitation is more rapid when there is prompt and proper treatment that enables the student to return to competition sooner. The old adage "A stitch in time saves nine" is applicable to athletic injuries. An ambulance should be at the site of football games or readily available.

Coping with the Problem of Drug Abuse

Drug abuse among high school students is recognized as a national problem. It is estimated that approximately 50 percent of our high school students will experiment with drugs and 30 percent will continue their use for social or recreational purposes.[6] The use of alcohol and tobacco is equally alarming. Athletes are not immune to drug abuse and can be influenced by the publicity surrounding the use of drugs by some professional athletes.[7]

No school can any longer feel itself free of the danger of drug abuse among its students. What was once considered typical of large city high schools is now just as prevalent in high schools in the smaller communities, and school administrators across the nation are seeking better ways of coping with the problem. A total school approach is considered the most effective.[8] A fundamental phase of a school appraoch should be a drug education program for both faculty and students.

The faculty should be taught how to recognize signs of drug abuse, and a procedure for reporting and handling cases should be established. The National Collegiate Athletic Association has published a pamphlet, *The Coach: Erogenic Aids and the Athlete,* which outlines symptoms to look for in detecting the abuse of drugs. Coaches and teachers cannot be expected to be experts, but they should be well informed about the symptoms of drug abuse and the dangers inherent in the use of alcohol and tobacco as well.[9] Since few teachers are aware of the kinds of drugs available and their effects, schools should consider an in-service training program in the form of workshops and seminars on drug education.

School administrators and faculty members should also have a basic understanding of the laws regarding reasonable search and seizure when students are suspected of possessing drugs in their clothing or lockers. The Fourth Amendment protects citizens from unreasonable searches and seizures, and a search warrant is required when a search is made by a governmental official. However, school searches are viewed somewhat differently by the courts and may be conducted under certain conditions without a warrant when official duties of school representatives are involved. The reasonableness of a search is weighed against the rights of an individual if protection of the majority of students is concerned.

Some guidelines to follow in deciding whether a search would be reasonable are

1. The duties and responsibilities of the school officials
2. The purpose of the search
3. The students' ages and records
4. The seriousness of the problem[10]

If a school is confronted with a major drug problem among its students, it may be advisable to establish definite policies and procedures for searches with the help and advice of an attorney.

The most effective drug education program for students incorporates units on the use and abuse of drugs into regular courses, such as health education. Separate drug courses are of questionable value. Students who refrain from using drugs may resent taking a special course, particularly if required, and it could have adverse effects. Incidental instruction by counselors and coaches should also be part of the program and can often be as effective as, or more so than, formalized instruction. Regardless of how taught, it is important for students to learn both the benefits of drugs prescribed by a physician and the possible harmful effects of illicit drugs. Much of the success of any type of drug education will depend upon the ability of the teacher to instill in students an attitude of respect toward their minds and bodies, which drugs should be used only to protect and not to harm!

The athletic administrator should be a leader in the drug education program. He/she should be alert to any possible abuse of drugs, not only by athletes but among the student body. What other students do can influence the health habits of athletes, and, conversely, it must be realized that proper attitudes shown by athletes toward the use of drugs can be a positive influence upon other students.

If a total school approach is in existence, the athletic director and staff will want to work actively in it. Coaches are frequently selected to teach health courses, including drug education, and the athletic director should assist them in obtaining the latest and best materials available on the subject.

If the school has no formalized approach, the athletic administrator should provide leadership in helping to establish one, or work with his/her staff in formulating one as part of the athletic program. This would involve primarily incidental teaching, but coaches would need an ample background on the use and abuse of drugs to be effective. Here the athletic director can help by securing resource materials and holding conferences with the staff on how to use them. An in-service training for coaches might be considered.

Some state high school associations have a statewide eligibility regulation requiring abstinence from alcohol, tobacco, and drugs (see page 114). In other states a number of individual schools have unilaterally established similar standards of eligibility, and several schools now prohibit smoking on school grounds as a result of public concern regarding the relation between the use of tobacco and cancer. The courts have upheld such eligibility rules when established for valid reasons (see page 376), and the athletic administrator might want to consider asking his or her school to adopt such standard if the state association does not have one.

SAFETY SUGGESTIONS

Safety Policies

In many instances safety suggestions are made too late. Great strides in safety education have been made in industry by making workers safety conscious. This same policy should be followed in athletics as well as in all other phases of the school program. Contestants as well as those administering athletic programs have many opportunities to make safety a tangible rather than a throretical part of athletics.

It is strongly recommended that definite policies be formulated cooperatively by the athletic director and coaches of the various sports. Such a practice is not only in the best interests of athletes but also is important for the protection of coaches when injuries or accidents do occur. There will be far less criticism and fewer charges of negligence if safety policies are in existence and enforced. Athletes should understand them and be expected to abide by them. The safety suggestions discussed in this chapter can provide many ideas to be considered in the formulation of policies.

General Suggestions

Prior to discussing a few safety suggestions that pertain to the sports more commonly sponsored in American high schools, it is well to consider the individual participant. There are many things the student may do to further the safety program in any school. In the final analysis much of the success of any safety campaign depends upon his or her contribution. Schools may well keep their student bodies and athletes safety conscious by means of safety posters, safety assemblies, and the like. The following list of personal safety habits, suggested by Lloyd, Deaver, and Eastwood some time ago, is still effective and should be learned by all individuals—students and adults:

1. Never continue playing a game when fatigued.
2. Do not attempt a hazardous new skill unless under the direction of a qualified person.
3. When jumping see that the landing surface is sufficiently soft for the height of the fall and that there are no obstructions or uneven surfaces.

4. Proper personal equipment should be worn for protection at all times.
5. Refuse to play the game if the equipment is improperly erected, the floor or field is slippery, rough, or has obstacles which may lead to injury.
6. When participating in an activity always keep in a position away from flying equipment, such as bats, discus, javelin, shot, etc.
7. Never enter the water unless supervisor is present.
8. See that all injuries are given immediate and adequte attention.
9. Never try any stunts beyond your range of ability.
10. Select activities which are within the range of your physical capabilities, e.g., cross-country running with an organic heart condition is dangerous.
11. Avoid partaking in activities in overcrowded space.
12. Never take advice or instruction from an unqualified person.
13. Warming up before participating in strenuous activities is a wise precaution in preventing strains and sprains.
14. Demand a physical examination before entering physical education activities and a recheck before going out for any arduous sport.
15. It is desirable that those participating in sports be protected against the cost of serious injuries.[11]

Safety Suggestions for Individual Sports

In the following enumeration of safety suggestions for high school sports, it will be assumed that methods dealing with safety in each sport, as far as techniques and skill of the game itself are concerned, have been properly covered by the coach. It is part of the coach's job to instruct players in proper safety methods in sliding, tackling, pivoting, serving, blocking, falling on the ball, and so on. Physical factors pertaining to personal and playing equipment will be the chief items of consideration in the suggestions offered. In all cases it is recommended that a physician be present at contests, and it is assumed that all participants have passed physical examinations.

Baseball. These also apply to other outdoor ball games.

1. Playing areas should be smooth and free from stones and ruts.
2. Spectators should be kept a reasonable distance from playing area.
3. Players' benches and extra equipment should be well away from the base lines.
4. Keep all substitutes seated on benches.
5. Have a first-aid kit on hand and someone who knows how to use it.
6. Be sure that catcher's protective equipment is adequate.
7. Immediate attention by a physician should be given to all injuries and infections.
8. Practice sessions should be well supervised.

9. Be sure of proper conditioning of all players.

10. Insist that all players wear helmets when at bat and on bases.

Basketball.   Many of these suggestions will apply to volleyball, badminton, indoor tennis, and other gymnasium activities.

1. Be sure of proper conditioning of all players.

2. Practice sessions should be well supervised and of not too great length.

3. Have a smooth, clean, but not slippery, floor.

4. Posts, players' benches, scoring tables, bleachers, and the like should be removed as far as possible from playing areas.

5. Give immediate attention to all injuries and infections. Report them immediately to a physician.

6. Keep all substitutes seated on benches.

7. Have ample space at end of court between end line and bleachers or wall.

8. Have first-aid kit on hand at all games and practice sessions.

9. Allow no injured players to participate in practice or games.

10. Check on proper equipment, especially shoes.

11. Keep players warm prior to participation.

12. Make frequent substitutions and instruct teams to take allowed rest periods.

Cross country and track.   These suggestions are also applicable to other running activities.

1. Proper conditioning in cross country and track is by far the most important safety consideration.

2. Be sure that contestants are thoroughly warmed up before they enter their events.

3. Limit the participation of each individual, as to number and type of events, in accordance with recommendations of the best authorities on the subject.

4. Have a first-aid kit on hand at practice sessions and meets.

5. Keep spectators a safe distance away from track and field events, both at practice sessions and at meets. Remember that the discus, javelin, and shot may cause serious injury to spectators. Keep discus and javelin areas roped off and allow no one in them. (Several state high school athletic associations have eliminated the discus or javelin events, or both, from their lists of field activities largely because of danger in conducting them.)

6. Be sure that vaulting and jumping pits are so constructed that they provide a soft landing place for vaulters and jumpers.

7. Give immediate attention to all injuries and infections. Report them to a physician.

Football.   The majority of these suggestions are also applicable to soccer and touch football.

1. Use only a noninjurious substance for field marking. Lime should not be used.

2. Insist on properly fitting equipment, especially pads, helmets, and shoes.
3. Keep field in good condition—sodded, level, and free from stones.
4. Be sure that substitutes are warmed up before they enter games.
5. Keep substitutes seated on benches.
6. Keep chairs, substitutes' benches, extra equipment, and band instruments a safe distance (5 to 10 yards) from side and end lines.
7. Place yard-line markers a safe distance from side lines.
8. Use flexible-staff goal-line flags.
9. Provide sweaters or jackets for substitutes.
10. Require that helmets be worn during all scrimmages and games.
11. Insist that a fitted, flexible mouth and tooth protector, as well as an approved face guard, be worn during scrimmages and games by each player.
12. Team members should be thoroughly warmed up before the start of each half.
13. Keep spectators off the field during practice sessions.
14. Immediate medical attention should be given to all injuries and infections. Instruct players to report injuries at once.
15. Do not allow a player who has been injured to return to practice or play until permission is received from the physician in charge of his case.
16. Remove fatigued and injured players from games.
17. Conduct well-organized and well-supervised practice sessions.
18. Check weights of squad members daily if possible.
19. Use tackling dummy instead of "live bait" in tackling practice as much as possible. Be sure that the mechanical release works properly.
20. Make certain of adequate conditioning for early practice sessions and give careful attention to the heat index on warm days. The first few practices should be held without pads and full dress player equipment, but helmets should generally be worn as protection against any possible head injuries.

Special attention should be given to the safety of athletes in early football practice sessions. Football practice in many states begins in August when the weather is often hot, and there are occasional cases of heat prostration during this period. Athletic directors must insist that their football coaches give particular note to both temperature and humidity and that they exercise extreme caution in conducting practices when either, or both, are high. They should follow such guidelines as *Hot Weather Hints* and other bulletins published jointly by the National Federation of State High School Associations and the Committee on Medical Aspects of Sports of the American Medical Association. They are reprinted in several state association journals and can be obtained from most state association offices.

Swimming. These suggestions apply to class as well as competitive swimming.

1. Have adequate supervision at all times.
2. Proper conditioning for speed and distance swimmers is most essential.

3. Limit the number of events contestants may enter to the number of events recommended by the best authorities in the field.

4. Give proper attention to diet.

5. Do not allow swimmers to swim alone.

6. An hour to two hours should elapse between eating and swimming times.

7. Surfaces at sides and end of pool should not be slippery.

8. Life preservers or "fish poles" should be available at all pools.

9. Bacteria counts in pools should be frequent and accurate.

10. Report all injuries immediately and refer them to a physician for medical attention.

11. Caution swimmers against the practice of deep breathing, known as hyperventilation, in which the individual ventilates an above normal amount of carbon dioxide, which is one of the chief causes of drowning.

SAFETY IN TRANSPORTATION

The subject of transportation has been discussed in Chapter 8. It seems advisable to consider it again, however, as an item to receive safety attention. The use of common carriers or school buses is recommended. In themselves they provide lessons in safety because of the excellent safety precautions of practically all drivers of such vehicles. Members of athletic teams should be cautioned regarding adherence to safety regulations and common courtesies while on the streets of cities or towns in which away games are played. Definite discipline rules, likewise, should be in effect while en route to and from schools for games.

A problem of considerable importance is that of impressing students with the need for following safety rules in traveling to and from practice sessions. Of course this is not a problem when practice and playing fields are adjacent to the school, but in many instances they are widely separated. If students travel from the school to the practice field in private cars, insist that the number of passengers carried is not in excess of the intended capacity of the car. For violation of this regulation, suspend the offenders from the squad for a definite period. Allow no fast driving or racing from the school to the practice field, and for any violation of this rule punish by the same penalty. Emphasize these regulations and enforce them if possible by an honor code. Insist that street parking be in accordance with city traffic regulations. Park cars in the practice field enclosure if possible. The ideal arrangement where a transportation problem of this kind exists is to use a common carrier bus to and from the school and field before and after practice sessions. Many schools follow such a procedure. Insistence on following the best-recognized safety traffic regulations in athletics is just another means of emphasizing safety throughout the entire school safety program.

It is highly important that coaches and athletic directors have a thorough understanding of state law in regard to legal liability of drivers and the so-called laws of negligence which might be applied to the school or coach. In many states the individual coach would be liable for negligence rather than the school. He or she should make certain that any car or bus in which athletes are transported is fully insured with the type of coverage needed in that state to protect him/herself and the school from any liability.

THE SANITATION PROGRAM

It was previously stated in this chapter that one of the purposes of inter-scholastic athletics is to develop health habits in participants. Lessons in sanitation also are important and certainly should become health habits. Ordinarily the athletes of a school are the finest of physical specimens. They come to coaches with almost perfect physiques. We must be sure that when they have finished their high school athletic competition they still are physically fine examples. They should have learned how to play; how to cooperate; how to give and take; what it is to be a good sportsman; and, above all, they should know more about how to live and take care of themselves physically. It is folly to think that an athlete will develop habits of health if these habits are not practiced by the athletic-team squad and those in charge of it. When rules of sanitation and safety are disregarded, some of the most valuable "carry-over" lessons of athletics are lost.

Experience in Sanitation

Probably all of us have shuddered on seeing at athletic contests things which flouted all the commonsense rules of health and sanitation. We have seen the single lemon that all the boys used, supposedly to quench their thirst. What about the common towel that all the members of the team used to wipe perspiration from their faces? Surely we remember how the towel went sliding across the floor and then was used to wipe everyone's face and neck. Then there was the common water bucket with its dipper or sponge that everybody used. Often, after the game was over, several boys used the same towel following the shower. Sometimes this towel was not laundered for several weeks. On occasions it was necessary (we thought) to exchange between team members items of personal playing equipment, such as socks, shirts, jerseys, and helmets, without sterilizing them, not to mention washing them.

There were times when cuts, infections, sprains, and bruises were laughed off and not reported because it was thought that an athlete should be able to take it. All these practices and probably many more could be cited. But suffice it to say that we do not want these to remain in the experiences of participants as some of the things they learned in high school athletics. They should remember that if at times the coach, director, or trainer seemed overscrupulous in enforcement of safety, sanitary, and cleanliness regulations, it was because the physical welfare of the players on the team meant more to the coach and to the school than did all the possible victories during a season.

Sanitation Suggestions

In addition to physical examinations, which it is assumed that all students have had prior to athletic competition, numerous other health and sanitation regulations are imperative. Sanitary habits are of such significance in the daily lives of citizens that the coach who fails to see that athletes develop proper attitudes toward sanitation standards and adhere to them daily is derelict in his or her responsibilities as a teacher. Athletics will be a greater educational force if desirable health practices are taught through them. Here are several common axioms for health and sanitation as they apply to the average high school athletic program:

1. Insist on properly fitting equipment. It lessens the chance of infection by irritation from apparel that is too loose or too tight.
2. Sterilize personal equipment prior to any interchange between players.
3. Provide sanitary drinking facilities. Use individual half-pint pop or milk bottles or paper cups on the field, and a fountain in the gymnasium.
4. Always have a first-aid kit on hand.
5. Keep personal equipment aired and dry between practice sessions.
6. Be sure players are cooled off and have thoroughly dried themselves before leaving locker rooms.
7. Inspect shoes regularly for nails and breaks that might cause infection.
8. Inspect showers frequently and keep them adjusted so that the possibilities of scalding and hot-water burns are reduced to a minimum.
9. Insist on the use of individual towels.
10. Provide or insist upon clean, dry towels every day.
11. Provide a separate towel for each member for use at time-outs or between halves of contests. Hand it to him/her or provide a sanitary receptacle for it. Don't allow it to touch the ground or floor.
12. Permit no exchange between players of personal equipment without coach's permission; the penalty for infraction of this regulation should be dismissal from squad.
13. Provide proper facilities in gymnasium for spitting.
14. Insist on a warm shower being followed by a cold one.
15. Keep players off wet ground between halves of football or soccer games.
16. Provide side-line sweaters or jackets for substitutes on rainy, cold days and during outdoor night contests.
17. Inspect players regularly for infections or injuries.
18. Insist that injuries, no matter how slight, be reported immediately after they are received.

19. Clean lockers, showers, and toilets frequently and scientifically.
20. Be sure that taping and bandaging are done correctly.
21. Do not allow ill or injured players to participate in practice or games.
22. Check weights of squad members frequently.
23. Launder uniforms and sweat clothes frequently.
24. Provide foot baths or other accepted treatment for the prevention of athlete's foot.
25. Provide a lemon or orange for each member of the squad.
26. Keep locker and gymnasium floors scientifically clean.

MEDICAL SUPERVISION OF ATHLETICS

Schools are treading on dangerous ground indeed if they have not made adequate preparation for medical supervision in connection with their athletic and physical education programs. This statement does not mean, necessarily, that a full-time school physician is required before an athletic program is launched. Rather, it implies that a qualified, licensed physician should be accessible in case of serious injuries. Likewise, he or she should be available for treatment of the less severe injuries that are incidental to athletic competition and physical education.

Methods in Effect

The foregoing discussion should not be construed as implying that any of the suggestions already mentioned are to take the place of adequate medical supervision of athletics. There are hazards in virtually everything we do. Participation in athletics, of course, is not an exception. The advantage that athletics offer is the ability to make some preparation for them before they occur. It should be a rule of first importance that arrangements for medical attention be available for all athletic practice and competition; that is, provision should be made for at least first-aid or emergency treatment in case of accident. Policies of schools vary in this particular. Boards of education in some states employ school physicians who are assigned to athletic teams, both for practice sessions and games. In certain instances school nurses also are available. In some schools the athletic association or athletic department of the high school employs a physician who takes care of all physical examinations of athletes and their injuries. The school athletic association usually pays the physician a flat fee plus the cost of medical supplies and hospitalization in such an arrangement. Other school systems operate on the theory that the physician of the student's family should take complete care of any injuries received. This does not mean that first-aid and emergency treatment should not be given an injured athlete at the direction of the school athletic authorities. Any professional services beyond first-aid and emergency treatment, however, should be at the expense and direction of the student's family.

Still another arrangement is that whereby the physician volunteers services. This plan is quite common, especially in small schools. Probably arrangements are not complete in many cases and are not ideal, but they exist because school athletic departments do not have the money to employ physicians at regular fees. Many state courts have decreed that public tax money raised for educational purposes may not be spent to defray cost of athletic or other school activity injuries. In hundreds of high schools throughout the nation public-spirited and interested physicians have given freely of their time and services in order that there might be at least a minimum of medical supervision of athletic programs.

Developing an Individual School Plan

Conditions regarding the availability of medical services will vary from community to community, but every high school should develop the best medical supervision it can under existing conditions. This generally becomes one of the major responsibilities of the athletic administrator. He or she should become familiar with the medical services prevalent and get well acquainted with the professionals in the community. These persons can offer counsel and assistance in establishing a medical supervision plan for the athletic program.

The following suggestions and possibilities are offered for consideration in developing a plan:

1. If the district has a school physician, or a team doctor, that person should be consulted and asked for assistance in formulating the plan. It is obvious that this person will not be available to attend all games and practice sessions, but he/she can play a supportive role and be contacted when needed.

2. Coaches should be trained to administer first aid, but they must understand that they are not to "practice medicine" and know when injuries should be referred to a physician.

3. Whenever possible and affordable, the school should have a qualified athletic trainer. Some schools have found a member of the faculty is willing to receive the professional training necessary and will serve in this capacity if paid for these extra services. Booster clubs frequently want to contribute to the athletic program, and providing funds for the training of a teacher-trainer is one project which will greatly benefit the athletic program and high school athletes. A National Athletic Trainers Association was formed in 1950 which has established standards for approving programs to train athletic trainers, and workshops and seminars are also available to prepare student athletic trainers.

4. A few schools have established their own student-trainer programs.[12] Student trainers can best serve as assistants to the athletic trainer, yet they

can also provide many services when that person is not available, or when the school cannot afford to employ a full-time trainer. Students serving as assistants should have specific preparation for their duties. Allowing untrained individuals to perform such services can be a source of serious problems and grounds for charges of negligence on the part of the athletic administrator who permits such a practice.

5. Many districts have a school nurse who, although no replacement for a doctor, often can help by treating minor injuries which frequently occur in practice.

6. Unfortunately, there are some small communities without a resident physician or nurse. In such instances county health officials can be consulted and asked to help formulate the best plan possible under the conditions and to offer what other services they can provide.

7. Names, addresses, and telephone numbers should always be available for immediately contacting parents when an athlete receives what could possibly be a serious injury. They should be asked whether they wish to have their family doctor treat the injury, and should be requested to officially grant permission to allow the team physician to handle the case if they do not.

8. An official command and channel of communications should be established to follow when medical emergencies arise.

9. It is desirable for high schools to have an ambulance present at all football and hockey games, but this is too expensive for most schools, and often arrangements cannot be made to have one at the site of competition. In that case, arrangements should be made with an ambulance service; the route to the playing field or gymnasium should be laid out in advance, and the service notified when games are scheduled.

10. It is advisable to maintain a file containing the medical history of each athlete, including a record of all injuries.

11. A set of policies and procedures should be established outlining the responsibilities of all parties involved in the medical supervision plan. They should be well publicized and a copy should be provided each person involved.

If a school has a formalized plan for medical supervision, it is less likely to face legal challenges, and above all else will be providing a service in the best interest of its athletes.

ATHLETIC ACCIDENT INSURANCE

Despite all safety measures, there will be accidents in athletic activities, and all athletes competing in interscholastic athletics should have accident insurance protection. It is unwise for a school to permit a student to begin practice for a sport without accident insurance in effect. To do otherwise could conceivably be considered negligence on the part of school representatives. There has been a trend during the past four decades for accident coverage to be made available to all students. Plans for basic coverage at school and while going and returning from school are now offered at relatively inexpensive group rates, but insurance against accidents occurring during practice and competition is becoming increasingly more expensive, primarily due to higher medical costs. School officials are in agreement that students participating in interscholastic athletics should have insurance protection, and the great majority now require it before an athlete is allowed to practice or compete. This is a wise policy for the protection of both athletes and school officials.

Sources of Athletic Accident Insurance

There are four general sources of accident protection for high school athletes: (1) family health and accident insurance, (2) commercial pupil and athletic accident insurance, (3) state high school association athletic accident and benefit plans, and (4) the National Federation Student Protection Trust. Schools in some states may purchase athletic accident insurance for which premiums are paid from the general athletic fund. This may be prohibited in other states by state law, in which case it is necessary for parents to pay the premium. This creates a problem for schools, because some families may be unable to pay such costs. Others object to paying an additional premium for school athletic insurance when they have family health and accident insurance. There is in some instances duplication in coverage. Conditions in the school community should be surveyed to determine what type of insurance plan would be most appropriate for the school's athletes.

Much has been said about athletic accident benefit and protection plans and the role they are playing in athletic safety. Their development is undoubtedly in keeping with the philosophy of the times, which claims that group provision should be made for the mishaps and eventual infirmities of individuals. Social Security, retirement plans, group hospitalization, and insurance are examples of this trend. Probably the development of benefit and protection plans on the part of state athletic and activity associations will be remembered as one of their greatest contributions to high school athletics. These plans represent an intelligent approach to, and attempt at solution of, the injury problem that is always present in athletic contests.

State Association-Sponsored Accident Coverage Plans

The Wisconsin Interscholastic Athletic Association is known as the "father" of association-operated benefit and protection plans for high school athletics. The first athletic accident benefit plan was established in Wisconsin in 1930 under the leadership of the late Paul F. Neverman, former Executive Secretary of the WIAA, who was a pioneer in this field. New York inaugurated a similar plan in 1931. The work done in these two states laid a pattern for programs developed in other states and by commercial companies. Today, virtually all athletes participating in interscholastic athletics are covered by some type of accident insurance.

Two general types of program are offered by the Wisconsin association. The Special Program will pay the cost of reasonable and necessary medical, hospital, and dental expenses incurred as a result of an accident sustained by a student while participating in a school-sponsored activity. The Scheduled Program of coverage will assist in meeting these costs but will not necessarily cover all costs. Both plans incorporate a nonduplication clause and become excess insurance for claims exceeding an established amount.

As the word *benefit* implies, the purpose of most state association benefit plans is to help defray the costs of accidents but not necessarily to cover all costs. Schedules are established which show the amounts to be paid for various injuries.

The statement of purpose in Michigan's plan makes this fact clear:

> The purpose of the Athletic Accident Benefit Plan is to assist member high schools having physical education, intramural, or interscholastic athletic programs to meet at least part of the costs of scheduled injuries incurred by registered students, provided the activities involved are conducted in accordance, and that there has been school compliance, with Benefit Plan regulations. The Benefit Plan is not injury insurance. No contract is entered into between the participating individual and the Michigan High School Athletic Association, Inc. or the Benefit Plan division of it. Neither the State Association nor the Benefit Plan guarantees the payment of costs of all or any injuries. It is expected that claims for scheduled benefits made by member schools will be paid in full, but it must be understood that it is impossible to distribute more money for injury claims than is paid in by schools in membership and registration fees. The experience of 37 years of operation of the Benefit Plan in Michigan, however, and that in other states, indicates that the schedule of membership and registration fees effective for 1979–80 will be adequate to meet the adopted benefit schedules for the activities included.[13]

The New York plan is administered as a corporation, New York State Athletic Protection Plan, Inc., under the Insurance Law of New York. Its purpose is stated as follows:

> To furnish medical and dental expense indemnity under the supervision of the New York State Public High School Athletic Association to bona fide students in elementary and high schools injured in intramural and interscholastic athletic games and sports activities, or while engaged in preparation for such games, sports, or contests, or in physical education classes, or in any other accidents which in the judgment of the Superintendent of Insurance, should be included;

however, the dental expense indemnity applies only in cases of dental expense caused by injury occurring in intramural and interscholastic games and sports activities, while engaged in preparation for such games, sports, or contests, or in physical education classes. The plan shall be open to the participation of every duly licensed physician and dentist in the territory to be served and there shall be free choice by subscribers of physicians and dentists admitted to such plan, subject to the acceptance of patients by the physicians and dentists.

    To do all and everything necessary and proper for the accomplishment of any or all of the objects herein enumerated or necessary or incidental thereto or to the protection and benefit of the corporation and in general to carry on any lawful business or understanding necessary to the attainment of the purposes of the corporation, subject, however, to all the provisions of the Insurance Law of the State of New York.[14]

These state associations and others offering benefit and protection plans provide a fine service to their member schools and high school athletes.

The National Federation Student Protection Trust

Through the leadership of the National Federation a National Federation Student Protection Trust was established in 1979 to assist high schools in providing accident insurance coverage at the lowest possible cost. It operates only in those states in which the Trust plan is endorsed by the state high school association.[15]

Alternative coverage plans are offered. A school can contract for one or more plans, including an all-school plan, all athletic and activities coverage, football only, voluntary student plan, catastrophic coverage, and others. The flexibility makes it possible for a school to select coverages it considers most advisable under existing circumstances. Coverage for teachers and administrators is also available, and insurance is offered to members of the National Federation Interscholastic Officials Association and the National Federation Interscholastic Coaches Association. All policies contain an excess provision, as do most other accident insurance policies, which avoids duplication of payments on claims and helps reduce premiums.

The broad base coverage offered through the National Federation Student Protection Trust has contributed to its phenomenal growth. Beginning with pilot projects in three states, it has expanded to include 36 participating state associations in 1982.[16] This accident insurance program sponsored by the National Federation represents another of its significant services to high schools and provides protection to millions of high school students. The processing of claims by computer is also resulting in a compilation of considerable accident data which will be a valuable basis for recommendations to rules committees and the development of still better player protective equipment, making interscholastic athletics safer for boys and girls.

Commercial Athletic Insurance

Commercial insurance companies now offer accident injury coverage similar to that of Wisconsin, New York, California, and other state associations. Data accumulated, much of which was originally through state association programs, have enabled them to provide acceptable group plans, and schools in several states obtain coverage through commercial companies. Their premiums have become sufficiently competitive and reasonable to cause some state associations to have discontinued their benefit plans. One of the factors in their offering reasonable premiums is the nonduplication clauses some have in their policies, commonly referred to as excess insurance. If other accident insurance was in prior effect, such as that carried under a family policy, only the amount not covered by that company's scheduled payment is paid under excess coverage provisions.

Catastrophe Insurance

Rising medical and hospital costs have resulted in some cases in which payments do not cover the total expenses of serious injuries under accident insurance offered by either state associations or commercial companies. The maximum basic coverage generally pays up to not more than $5,000 for any one injury. There are occasionally some serious injuries that cost much more. To meet this need some companies have group catastrophe policies available to state associations. Kansas was one of the first to initiate this type of plan in cooperation with a commercial company. Several others have followed suit.

These programs usually cover all students practicing for and participating in interscholastic activities sponsored by the association and provide for payments in cases of serious injuries beyond the amount paid under basic coverage in effect. Catastrophe policies do not provide basic coverage and contain an agreed-upon deductible amount, generally the amount provided under basic plans. Amounts beyond the deductible up to a set maximum, which in most instances is $50,000 or more, is paid. The deductible feature, nonduplication clauses, and broad group coverage have made it possible for companies to offer such insurance at reasonable rates as low as four to five cents per student enrolled collectively in the schools of the state, depending upon the maximum payment established.

This type of protection through state associations, which would otherwise be too expensive to afford, has been one of the outstanding contributions in protecting students and their families from great financial loss resulting from serious athletic injuries.

Considerations by the Athletic Administrator

As stated previously, athletes should not be permitted to practice for competition in contests without the protection of athletic injury insurance. It is one of the important responsibilities of the athletic administrator to determine and plan the type of insurance program to provide this protection. Following are some of the issues to be taken into consideration:

1. Decision must be made whether athletes shall secure individual coverage or whether the school shall provide a group insurance plan. The former is generally too costly for most athletes, and unless most of them have protection under family plans, the latter is the most economical.

2. The athletic administrator must have an adequate knowledge of the insurance laws of his/her state. It is necessary to know whether they allow the school to purchase from school athletic funds a group accident policy and whether students can be charged a fee to cover their share of the cost. This information is basic in determining the method of financing accident insurance.

3. The accident insurance needs of students must be analyzed. Knowing how many athletes already have protection through family policies will help to determine the type of coverage the school should select in regard to such matters as nonduplication or excess insurance provisions, deductibles, and so on.

4. Review the insurance available through the state association and commercial companies. If the state association offers accident benefits or insurance, it must be determined whether it is adequate to meet current medical costs or should be supplemented by additional insurance. Scheduled payments and premium rates should be studied.

5. The cost of providing the protection must be determined. Comparing premiums of policies with nonduplication and deductible clauses in relation to needs as discussed under "3" above will be helpful in selecting the insurance that will provide the protection desired at the most reasonable cost.

6. The method of financing that is in accord with state law must be ascertained. Payment of premiums from athletic funds is recommended if legal in that state. It is only reasonable that if athletes compete in games from which the school will collect receipts from admissions, they should be provided accident insurance protection by the school.

7. It is important that a statement be prepared for athletes and their parents giving full particulars regarding the type of insurance, amount of benefits, administrative procedures, and such, incuded in the program of accident insurance selected by the school. Because such statements will reflect school policies, they should have official approval of the board of education. This information is necessary to prevent misunderstandings and complaints from arising over payments of injury claims.

An adequate, well-planned, fully explained, and carefully administered program to provide athletic injury protection will contribute toward the success of the school's interscholastic program.

SUMMARY

In brief, a school may consider that its general athletic safety policy is consistent with good educational procedure if the following factors are considered:

1. A well-trained coach or coaches should be employed to have charge of the activities in the athletic program. Preferably, coaches should be members of the physical education staff.

2. Adequate, properly fitting equipment should be available for all players. If it cannot be provided, the activity should not be sponsored.

3. Playing facilities should meet commonsense standards. Athletes should not be expected to play under conditions and with facilities admittedly unsafe or dangerous. Playing areas should be free from hazards.

4. Adequate training is a requisite for all participants. They should not be allowed to play until they are in proper physical condition. Do not allow a student to practice or participate in a contest until he/she has had a physical examination by a qualified physician who has approved his/her participation.

5. Sufficient reserve material is an essential for good teams, but it is even more important as a safety factor. Generally, there should be at least twice as many members on a squad as there are playing positions on the team.

6. Competent officiating is an added means by which athletic contests may be made safer activities. Engage officials who are known to be strict in their enforcement of rules devised for the protection of participants.

7. Fair and equitable competition in all athletics is a safety essential. In general, schools should limit their athletic competition to schools of comparable size. By so doing there is greater assurance that squads will be more nearly equal in size, with the result that competition will be better and safer.

8. There should be insistence that all injuries be reported promptly by members of athletic squads. Frequently, an injury that appears to be inconsequential at the time it occurs later turns out to be serious. If possible, a physician should be present at all contact sport practice sessions and games, or at least on call at such times. Many coaches insist that there be at least a cursory inspection of squad members following each practice session and game in order to check on minor injuries that students might have failed to report.

Many serious infections as well as later injury developments may be prevented by this policy.

9. Drug abuse among high school students is recognized as a national problem, and a drug education program included in regular courses is considered the best approach toward a solution of it.

10. In the consideration of accident benefit and protection plans, several significant developments should be noted. Greater protection is being given to students before practice or playing of athletic contests through safety and sanitation precautions. Also, there is a definite trend toward the assumption of greater moral or social responsibility on the part of schools through the establishment of athletic accident benefit and protection plans. These developments should aid in raising the standards of physical education and athletic programs and at the same time provide valuable experiences in health education for high school students in general, as well as for members of athletic teams.

It is interesting to consider the attitude of state directors of health and physical education towards this matter some years ago. Considerable time was spent in discussing the development and growth of these plans at the twenty-first annual meeting of the Society of State Directors of Health and Physical Education, held in Seattle on April 19–22, 1947. It will be observed from the resolution adopted by this group that its members were interested not only in athletic accident coverage but also in the extension of such plans to include all school pupils.

WHEREAS, There is need for adequate insurance of all school children as well as athletes against accidents on playgrounds, athletic fields, and in the school building; and,

WHEREAS, Some states already have developed adequate and inexpensive coverage available to large numbers of students in the school; therefore,

BE IT RESOLVED, That the Society of State Directors of Health and Physical Education recommend consideration of such plans by the various states and encourage the state high school athletic associations that already have some coverage for athletes to consider a broader plan to include all children.

QUESTIONS AND TOPICS FOR STUDY AND DISCUSSION

1. What circumstances today make an overall school safety plan of increasing importance?

2. Discuss some of the major responsibilities of athletic administrators for the health and safety of athletes.

3. How are coaches in a strategic position to influence the health and safety habits of students?

4. Assuming you are coaching a sport of your choice, list ways you would provide for the safety of your athletes.

5. What are the purposes of NOCSAE?

6. Outline a good physical conditioning program for the athletes participating in a sport of your choice.

7. What is the best approach for coping with a problem of drug abuse among high school students?

8. Do you favor an eligibility regulation prohibiting the use of alchol, tobacco, and illicit drugs? Why?

9. Select a sport and outline a set of safety policies for the athletes participating in that sport.

10. List sanitation policies you would require athletes to follow in a sport you were coaching.

11. Outline what you think would be a desirable and practical athletic medical supervision plan for a school in which you coach or teach, or in which you would like to coach or be the athletic director.

12. Discuss the beginnings and growth of athletic accident benefit and protection plans.

13. Which of the sources of student accident protection do you prefer? Why?

14. Give your prediction for the future of the National Federation Student Protection Trust. Explain the reasons for your prediction.

15. Other than the amounts paid for accident expenses, what other values to the school can you give for providing accident insurance?

16. What factors must be taken into account by the athletic administrator in selecting an athletic accident insurance plan for his or her school?

NOTES

1. Irvin A. Keller, *The Interscholastic Coach* (Englewood Cliffs, N.J.: Prentice-Hall, Inc., 1982), pp. 141–44.

2. Ibid., pp. 162–63.

3. National Federation of State High School Associations, *1982–83 Handbook* (Kansas City, Mo.: National Federation, 1982), p. 26.

4. National Federation of State High School Associations, *Memorandum,* September 15, 1982.

5. Voigt R. Hodgson, "An Update on NOCSAE Research," *Athletic Purchasing and Facilities,* 5, no. 11 (November 1981), 34.

6. National Association of Secondary School Principals, "Dealing with Drug Abuse," *The Practitioner,* 8, no. 3 (April 1982), 1.

7. Keller, *The Interscholastic Coach,* p. 161.

8. Ibid., pp. 168–70.

9. Ibid., pp. 162–66.

10. *Search and Seizure in the Schools,* a legal memorandum (Reston, Va.: National Association of Secondary School Principals, February 1979), p. 7.

11. F. S. Lloyd, G. G. Deaver, and F. R. Eastwood, *Safety in Athletics* (Philadelphia, Pa.: W. B. Saunders Company, 1936), pp. 216–17.

12. Bill Beckman, "Organization of a Student Trainer Program," *Interscholastic Athletic Administration,* 1, no. 2 (Summer 1975), 9–10.

13. Michigan High School Athletic Association, Inc., *1979–80 Handbook,* p. 74.

14. New York State Public High School Athletic Association, *1980–82 Handbook,* p. 46.

15. Brice B. Durbin, "Evaluation of Student Protection Trust Exceeding Original National Objectives," *Interscholastic Athletic Administration,* 9, no. 2 (Winter 1982), 3.

16. Ibid., p. 5.

BIBLIOGRAPHY

BUTLER, PAUL S. "Administering the School's Athletic Training Program." *NASSP Bulletin,* 65, no. 446 (September 1981), 12–15.

CAREY, RICHARD J. "School Nurses Vis-a-Vis Athletic Trainers in Secondary School Sports Programs." *NASSP Bulletin,* 65, no. 446 (September 1981), 34–42.

CLANCY, WILLIAM "New Directions in Sports Medicine." *Athletic Purchasing and Facilities,* 6, no. 3 (March 1982), 30–36.

CLARKE, KENNETH S. "Expectations for Health Supervision of School Sports Programs." *NASSP Bulletin,* 65, no. 446 (September 1981), 1–3.

————. "The Health Supervision Loop in Sports." *National Federation Press,* 1, no. 4 (December 1980), 4–5.

DURBIN, BRICE B. "National Report: Evaluation of Student Protection Trust Exceeding Original National Objectives." *Interscholastic Athletic Administation,* 9, no. 2 (Winter 1982), 3–5.

GALLON, ARTHUR J. *Coaching Ideas and Ideals,* pp. 61–114. Boston: Houghton Mifflin, 1974.

HODGSON, VOIGHT R. "An Update on NOCSAE Research." *Athletic Purchasing and Facilities,* 5, no. 11 (November 1981), 32–36.

JOHNSON, PERRY B., and DONALD STALBERG. *Conditioning.* Englewood Cliffs, N.J.: Prentice-Hall, Inc., 1971.

KEELOR, RICHARD O. "The Realities of Drug Abuse in High School Athletics." *Journal of Physical Education and Recreation,* 43, no. 5 (May 1978), 48–49.

KELLER, IRVIN A. *The Interscholastic Coach,* Chap. 10. Englewood Cliffs, N.J.: Prentice-Hall, Inc., 1982.

LOURIA, DONALD B. *The Drug Scene.* New York: McGraw-Hill, 1968.

————. *Overcoming Drugs.* New York: McGraw-Hill, 1971.

MOUL, JAMIE. "Certified Athletic Trainers—Who Are They, and What Do They Do?" *NASSP Bulletin,* 64, no. 446 (September 1981), 27–29.

MUELLER FREDERICK O., and CARL S. BLYTH. "Research Indicates Reduction in Football Injuries." *National Federation Press,* 3, no. 2 (October 1982), 5–6.

NATIONAL ASSOCIATION OF SECONDARY SCHOOL PRINCIPALS. "Dealing With Drug Abuse." *The Practitioner,* 8, no. 3 (April 1982), 1–12.

NATIONAL FEDERATION OF STATE HIGH SCHOOL ASSOCIATIONS. "Athletic Safety and Protection," in *1982–83 Handbook,* pp. 26–28. Kansas City, Mo.: National Federation, 1982.

Nutrition for Athletes: A Handbook for Coaches. Washington, D.C.: American Alliance for Health, Physical Education, and Recreation, 1971.

RESICK, MATTHEW D., AND CARL E. ERICKSON. *Intercollegiate and Interscholastic Athletics for Men and Women,* pp. 217–27. Reading, Mass.: Addison-Wesley, 1975.

SCHWANK, WALTER C., and SAYERS, J. M. MILLER. "New Dimensions for the Athletic Training Profession." *Journal of Health, Physical Education and Recreation* (September 1971), 41–43.

Search and Seizure in the Schools, a legal memorandum. Reston, Va.: National Association of Secondary School Principals, February 1979.

SEATON, DON CASH. *Physical Education Handbook,* pp. 21–50. Englewood Cliffs, N.J.: Prentice-Hall, Inc., 1974.

SENDRE, RON, and GLEN SNOW. "Establishing a High School Training Program." *Interscholastic Athletics Administration,* 6, no. 3 (Spring 1980), 13–14.

TANNENBAUM, BEULAH, and MYRA STILLMAN. *Understand Food—The Chemistry of Nutrition,* pp. 173–74. New York: McGraw-Hill, 1962.

The Coach: Drugs, Erogenic Aids and the Athlete. Kansas City, Mo.: National Collegiate Athletic Association, 1976.

Tips on Athletic Training VIII. Chicago, Ill.: American Medical Association, 1966.

WEBER, DEAN. "Prevention of Toe, Ankle, and Knee Injuries in Football." *Athletic Purchasing and Facilities,* 6, no. 3 (March 1982), 40–41.

What Research Tells the Coach About Wrestling, pp. 41–50. Washington, D.C.: American Association for Health, Physical Education, and Recreation, 1964.

WHITESIDE, PATTI, and WILLIAM E. BUCKLEY. "How to Reduce Injury Incidence in High School Sports." *NASSP Bulletin,* 65, no. 446 (September 1981), 30–33.

13

Athletic Facilities—
Layout and Maintenance

In considering athletic facilities it will be assumed that the problems confronting those in charge of the athletic program deal chiefly with layout and maintenance rather than with construction. Separate treatment would be needed for the consideration of construction data and plans pertaining to the gymnasium, swimming pool, or stadium. Strictly speaking, these are engineering problems concerning which the physical education and athletic personnel in a school system should be sought for consultation. Experiences that they have had in teaching classes or in coaching teams, as well as observation of outstanding facilities in schools they have worked in or visited, are the best sources of information to be passed on to architects or engineers.

GENERAL AND INDOOR FACILITIES

Questions will be raised in schools with which physical education people are connected concerning the layout and dimensions of playing areas for different games. Current game rules books should always be examined for correct dimensions, markings, and such. Also, information should be available regarding the most efficient methods of maintenance and repair of common athletic facilities. The presentation of information of this general type is the purpose of this chapter.

Size of Playing Areas

The minimum amount of space required for various games is well defined in the official rules books. In most cases, however, certain sports may be played under better conditions if more than minimum requirements in space are available. For example, it is desirable to allow for extra field space in baseball and football. Indoor game areas, of course, must accommodate themselves to the gymnasium space available. In constructing gymnasiums, more than minimum rules-book recommendations should be allowed if possible in order that spectators may be accommodated. This extra space also will make play safe because it will allow the playing area to be laid out so that the out-of-bounds areas are at a safe distance from walls or other obstructions. The College Physical Education Association has compiled data concerning the areas needed for different sports as shown in Table 13–1.

TABLE 13–1 Comparative Areas Needed for Various Sports
(Ranked in ascending order of space required per player)

Game	Area per Player (Square Feet)	No. of Players	Minimum Size (Feet)	Total Area (Square Feet)
Volleyball	150	12	30 × 60	1,800
Handball (single wall)	170	4	20 × 34	680
Basketball (boys)	210	10	35 × 60	2,100
Badminton	220	4	20 × 44	880
Basketball (girls)	245	10	35 × 70	2,450
Softball (playground)	451	20	95 × 95	9,025
Soccer (girls)	1,309	22	120 × 240	28,800
Tennis	1,500	4	50 × 120	6,000
Field hockey	1,564	22	135 × 255	34,425
Soccer (boys)	2,250	22	165 × 300	49,500
Football	2,618	22	160 × 360	57,600
Baseball (hard)	5,000	18	300 × 300	90,000

Prepared by the College Physical Education Association.

Indoor Playing Facilities

However, once the gymnasium has been built, it is necessary to use the space as it is provided. Care should be taken to remove all possible hazards. Floors should not be allowed to become unsanitary or slippery. Special finishes for gymnasium floors are popular and some good ones are on the market. The floor should be thoroughly rinsed and dried before another coat of finish is applied. There is a trend toward installing synthetic gymnasium floors. They provide more resiliency and are easier to maintain. Regardless of the type of finish used on the floor, it should be one that may be washed with soap and water. Caustics should be avoided. Arrange and inspect temporary bleachers so that they are safe for spectators, and keep them as far away as possible from side and end lines. Cover unused bleachers at the end of basketball courts with gymnasium mats. Keep scoring tables off the playing court. Cover lights with wire guards, paint gymnasium ceilings a light color, and keep the windows clean. Figures 13–1 to 13–7 show diagrams and court dimensions for boys' and girls' basketball, volleyball, indoor baseball, badminton (singles and doubles), handball (four-wall and single-wall), and shuffleboard.

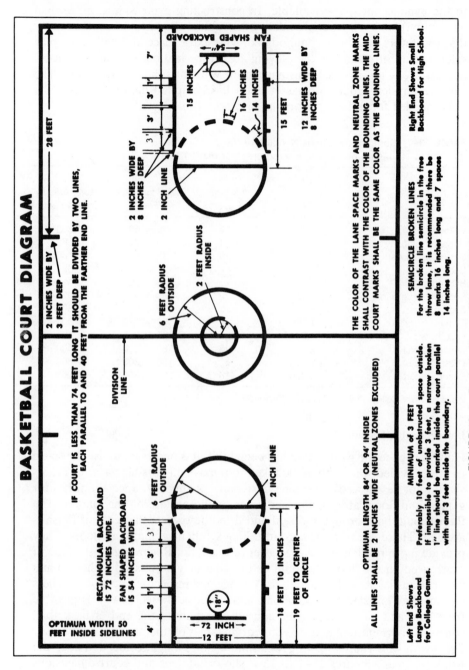

FIGURE 13–1 Basketball court (National Federation)

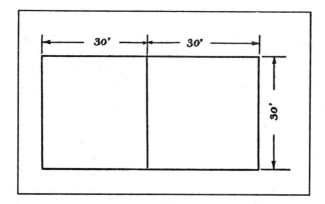

FIGURE 13-2   Volleyball court (National Federation)

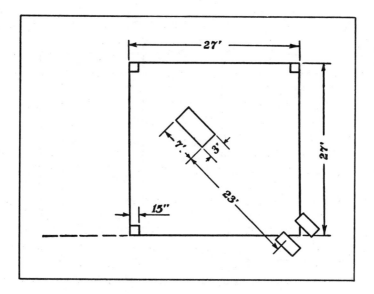

FIGURE 13-3   Indoor baseball diamond

OUTDOOR PLAYING FACILITIES

Many more athletic contests are conducted outdoors than indoors. Often it has been the case that when indoor athletic and physical education facilities have been constructed, outdoor facilities have been built improperly or laid out incorrectly. Generally accepted minimum space requirements for various sports are indicated in Table 13–1, together with dimensions and suggestions for construction of fields, diamonds, and track. (See also Figures 13–2 through 13–16.)

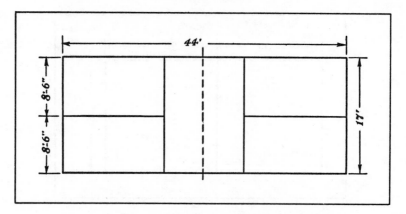

FIGURE 13–4   Badminton court (singles)

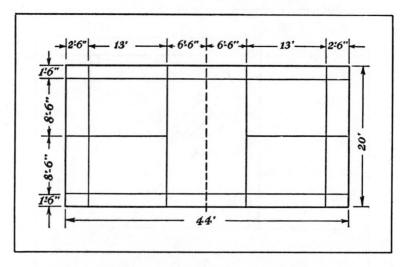

FIGURE 13–5   Badminton court (doubles)

Football Field

Generally it is desirable that a football field extend north and south so that punt and pass receivers do not have to face a late-afternoon sun. The extent to which night games are now played by high schools negates the importance of this suggestion considerably. Since drainage of the field is of most importance, a gravel subsoil is the best base. A slope of one-fourth inch per foot from the center to each sideline is recommended. Team boxes may be on opposite sides between the 35-yard lines, or on the same side between the two 45- and 20-yard lines. It is also recommended that the area between the team boxes and sidelines be solid white. Drainage tile, 4 or 5 inches in

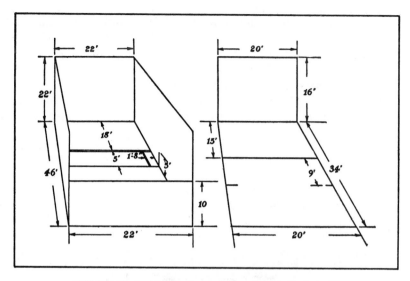

FIGURE 13–6   Handball court (4-wall and single-wall)

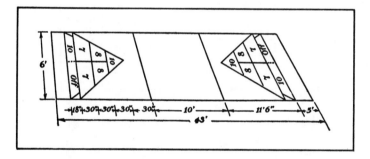

FIGURE 13–7   Shuffleboard court

diameter, should be laid diagonally across the field every 15 or 20 feet. Frequently these run into a drainage system encircling the gridiron and emptying into catch basins at each of the four corners of the field. The trenches holding the drain should be nearly filled with coarse stones so that water may quickly reach the tile. The field should have from 8 to 12 inches of loam topsoil and then should be sodded if possible.

If a track encircles the gridiron, the curb should be low enough so that it is not a hazard for football players who are thrown out of bounds. It is obvious, of course, that six-man football, soccer, field hockey, lacrosse, and speedball may be played on ordinary football gridirons with minimum changes in markings. Football fields should be kept mowed during the season, watered if necessary, and cut turf should be replaced. If possible, practice should not be held on game gridirons.

A small number of schools have installed artificial turfs. The safety features of this surface compared with grass turfs have not been fully determined. The initial cost is greater; however, the cost of maintenance is less, and they are superior in inclement weather. There is no indication at present that they will replace grass turf in the foreseeable future.

Figures 13–8 to 13–13 show diagrams and dimensions of playing areas for football (eleven-man and six-man), field hockey, lacrosse, speedball, and soccer.

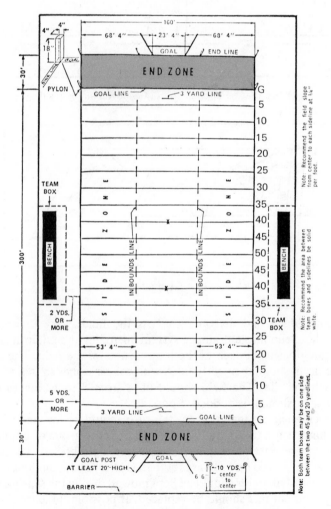

FIGURE 13–8   Football field (National Federation)

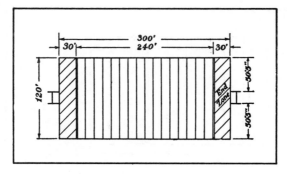

FIGURE 13–9   Football field (6-man)

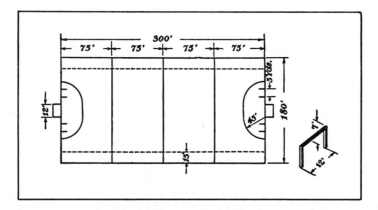

FIGURE 13–10   Field hockey

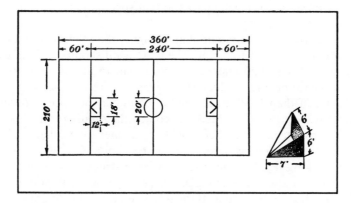

FIGURE 13–11   Lacrosse field

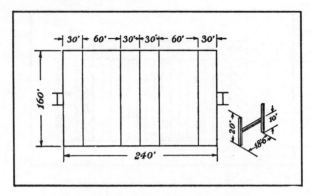

FIGURE 13-12   Speedball field

Baseball Field

Often it is necessary to locate the baseball diamond on part of the football gridiron because of lack of space for separate layouts. This practice is not recommended where it can be avoided, for the reason that a track often is built around the football field, which will lead to conflict because baseball and track both are spring sports. Also, the recommended grading of the baseball diamond and preparation of a "skinned" infield, if one is used, do not fit in well with gridiron construction. Drainage for the baseball field should be virtually the same as for the football playing area. Sometimes it is desirable that tile be placed directly under the base lines because they are used most and also because they may be a trifle lower than the remainder of the infield, especially if it is sodded. If the diamond is laid out so that the direction from home plate to first base is due west, a minimum number of players will have to face the sun. There is, however, a difference of opinion in the major leagues as to the general direction scheme for layout of baseball diamonds. Often the field is arranged in major league parks so that spectators rather than players do not have to face the sun.

Usually home plate should be slightly higher than the surrounding area, sloping to infield level in 6 to 8 feet. The plate itself should be flush with the ground. The pitcher's plate may be no more than 15 inches above the base-line levels and must be on a gradual, sloping mound. The pitcher's and batter's boxes, because of their hard usage, should be of clay mixture in order to be firmer than other parts of the field. Of course they must receive extra protection if it rains because they become sticky sooner than other parts of the infield. If the entire infield is bare, it should be kept absolutely smooth. Roll it every day, raking lightly if necessary. A large street brush or heavy wire-mesh screen may be used for grading purposes. Such care will "soften" ground balls and make them bound truer. If the infield is covered with grass, it should be watered daily and kept mowed. Grass should be removed from an area

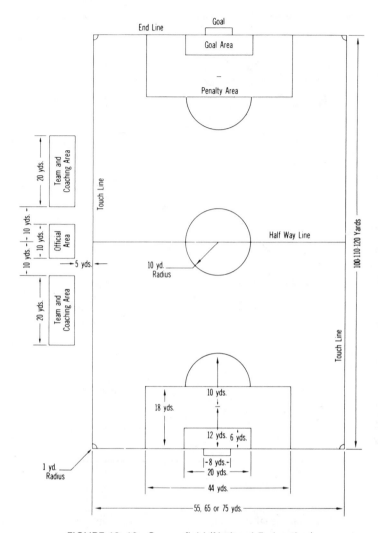

FIGURE 13–13 Soccer field (National Federation)

of 10-foot radius around home plate. Usually a comparatively small oval or circular area around the pitcher's plate is without grass. A path 2½ feet wide between home plate and first base and between home plate and third base should be devoid of grass. As much area as is desired, in addition to the base lines, between first and second base and between second and third base may be "skinned," but it is recommended that it be skinned back to a radius of 95 feet from the pitcher's plate. This includes the area on which the infielders usually play. Minimum distances of 300 feet from home plate to obstructions down the first- and third-base lines are recommended. Figure 13–14 shows

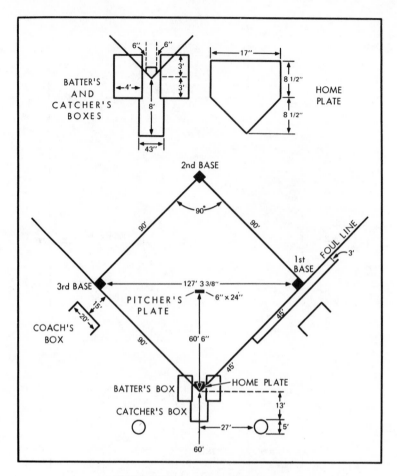

FIGURE 13-14 Baseball diamond

diagrams and dimensions of a baseball diamond, including the pitcher's plate, coacher's box, batter's and catcher's boxes, and home plate. Figure 13–15 shows the dimensions of a softball diamond.

The Track

As stated previously, the track often encircles the football field. In such cases drainage for the two is the same. Sometimes a string of tile is laid under the curb. In other instances tiles are laid under the center of the track itself below the so-called cushion layer. Crushed rock should form the bottom of the track, about 2 feet below the surface. A layer of coarse cinders, rolled on top of the rock, furnishes the next layer. Fine, hard cinders are next, with a top surface of equal parts of clay or loam and fine, hard, sieved cinders or

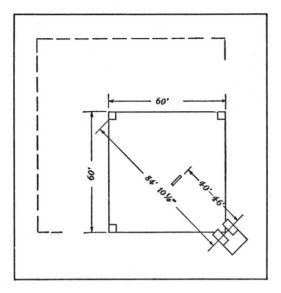

FIGURE 13–15   Softball diamond

brick dust. The track should be kept rolled and sprinkled regularly. A 25- to 35-foot width for the track is recommeded. If a new track is to be built, it would be well to investigate the new hard-surface, asphalt-combination type of track now on the market. It has the advantage of drying immediately after a rain and of taking on permanent markings for all lanes and finish lines.

Available space may determine the length of the track, but a quarter-mile track is standard and is recommended. The inner edge should be marked with a solid, rounded curb 2 inches above the track level. A painted 2-inch, or more, line may be substituted on all-weather tracks. Lanes should be at least 42 inches wide. Practically all state associations have available enlarged diagrams of the official quarter-mile furnished by the National Federation. It is an excellent guide in track construction and should be consulted when building a new track.

The running high jump landing pit must be at least 16 feet wide and 8 feet long, and the landing pit for the pole vault 16 feet wide by 12 feet long. Sand and sawdust are no longer approved under the track rules. The high jump pit should be filled with either 24 inches of foam rubber or other synthetic material, or should use an encased commercial rubber mattress no less than 18 inches thick. For the pole vault pit, a commercial mattress of at least 24 inches or loose, resilient synthetic no less than 36 inches is required.

In general, the shotput area needs no special construction, except that the event should not be conducted on the football playing field. Since the discus and javelin areas are generally located on the regular gridiron, they need no specific consideration.

The National Federation Track and Field Rules should always be consulted when constructing a new track or laying out space for events.

A track and field layout separate from the football gridiron was completed a few years ago at Michigan State University, East Lansing. Some special features of the arrangements are listed below, inasmuch as the arrangement is outstanding and, according to former Director Young, "was built according to the best information obtainable."[1]

1. The track is 35 feet wide at all points, permitting eight to twelve individual lanes.

2. Each of the two straightaways is 250 yards long. The oval part of the track is 440 yards.

3. It has "railroad" curves of 104-foot radius. Each curve and straightaway is approximately 110 yards.

4. Catch basins are staggered on both sides of the track every 35 feet, 3 feet from the curb.

5. All six field events are laid out with permanent runways, pits, rings, and the like, in the infield in such a way as to permit the holding of all field events simultaneously. Warm-up runways, pits, and rings are located between the two straightaway legs.

6. The broad-jump and pole-vault pits are approached by runways from two directions.

7. The high-jump pit is in the center of an 80-foot circle.

8. The javelin runway is built of cinders and is 75 feet by 25 feet.

9. The running track, field-event runways, circles, pits, and landing areas are 3 inches higher than the adjacent level of the field to provide drier conditions in wet weather.

10. The pole-vault landing pit has a false bottom of plank 2 feet below the ground level for extra "give."

11. Portland cement was mixed with the top dressing of cinders and clay for the field-event rings and runways in order to provide for better wear. (A hard-surface, asphalt-combination is now used.)

12. Portland cement was mixed with the top dressing for the shotput landing area in order to provide a hard landing area so the competitors may be given the maximum credit for their efforts.

13. There are two separate rings for meet competition in both the discus and shot.

14. The pole lane is used only for the distance events. The dash and hurdles races are held in the lanes farther away from the pole.

15. The top dressing for the running track is a mixture of two parts of fine cinders to one part of black soil. The soil is a loam containing about 15 percent organic matter. This type of soil has excellent resilient binding qualities and will not bake like clay.

16. The stands are placed 25 feet from the track at an angle to the straightaway.

Figures 13–16 to 13–18 are diagrams with detailed dimensions of a track,

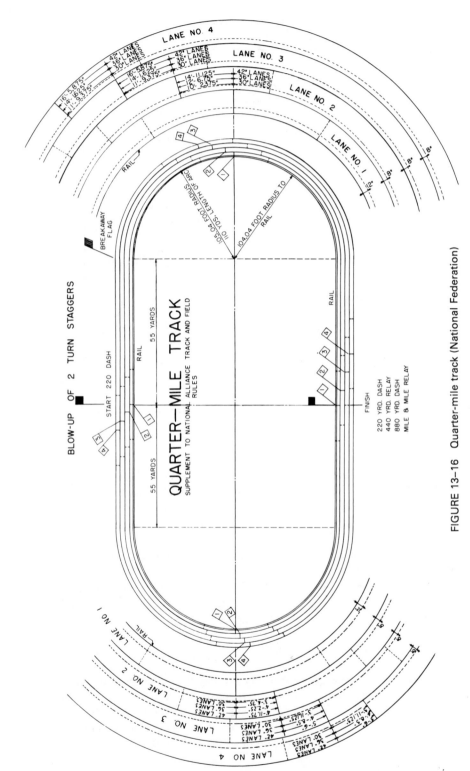

FIGURE 13–16 Quarter-mile track (National Federation)

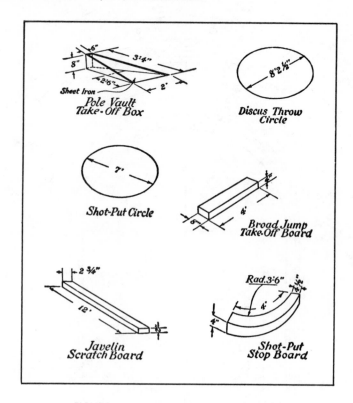

FIGURE 13-17 Track and field equipment

pole-vault take-off box, discus throw circle, shot-put circle, broad-jump take-off board, javelin scratch board, shot-put stop board, and an L-type hurdle, with details. Aluminum hurdles may be purchased which are lighter to handle, more durable, less prone to cause injuries, and cheaper to maintain in the long run. Modern-day construction of approaches for field events has employed the use of a type of asphalt material. This, however, requires the use of short spikes on shoes or flat-soled shoes exclusively.

Schools planning to build a new track will want to consider a track in metric measurements. Figure 13-16 is a diagram of a quarter-mile track. (See Appendix C for a diagram of a 400-meter track.)

Tennis Courts

Tennis courts with the greatest utility are made of concrete or asphalt composition. They are among the more expensive to install but least expensive to maintain. Some object that concrete is harder on the feet and there is more danger of falling. Clay courts are widely used by U.S.L.T.A. member clubs and cheaper to install than concrete or asphalt composition but require more

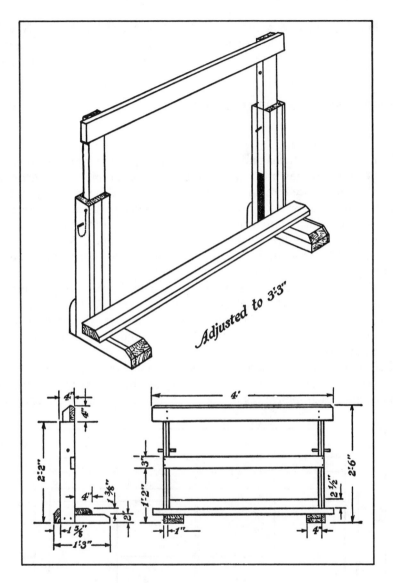

FIGURE 13–18   L-type hurdle and details

regular maintenance.[2] Grit courts are similar to clay and less expensive to build and maintain. "Patented Quick-Drying" courts are one of the best types, but they are the most expensive to construct and keep up.

A school planning to build tennis courts must consider which type best fits its needs, climatic conditions, and available financing. Approximate costs and valuable information regarding construction and upkeep of the types mentioned can be obtained from the U.S.L.T.A., 51 East 42 St., New York City. Experienced builders of tennis courts should be engaged for any construction. Figure 13–19 shows a diagram and dimensions of a tennis court.

MAINTENANCE OF ATHLETIC FIELDS

Seeding

Seeding of athletic fields and their care will depend upon the section of the country in which they are located. Soils also are an important factor in determining the procedure to be followed. It should be realized that more attention must be given to an athletic field than to an ordinary lawn or campus because of the much harder usage it receives. In general, athletic fields must be continually "built up" by the most approved methods. Wherever possible there should be separate practice and playing fields in order that the game field may be saved as much abuse as possible.

The development of a good turf is enhanced by proper preparation of the initial seed bed and the selection of the best grass for the type of soil and climatic conditions generally prevailing. It is always wise to have the soil tested to determine any nutrient deficiencies and for purchasing the most appropriate fertilizer for the grass chosen. Bermuda, bluegrass, ryegrass, fescue, and zoysia are among the most commonly used, and the advice of a lawn specialist can be helpful in selecting the best grass for the particular climatic and geographical region. Seeding should be done in the early spring

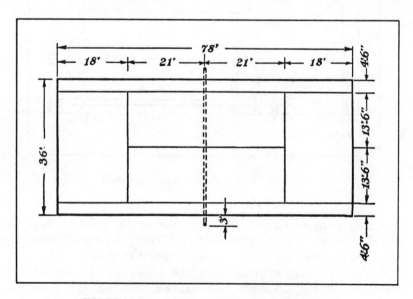

FIGURE 13–19   Tennis court (singles and doubles)

(or fall if the field is not to be in use), and the grass allowed to develop sod before being subjected to play, which can be stimulated by a regular mowing schedule.

Maintenance

Once the turf is established and use begins, maintenance then becomes the primary concern. A professional lawn care company would be the preferred option; however, the budget of many schools may prohibit this added expense. The school's own maintenance staff can do an excellent job under the supervision of the athletic administrator or football coach. Some of the essentials of a good maintenance program include:

1. A regular mowing schedule which will keep the grass from 2 to 3 inches in height.
2. The application of turf fertilizer in early spring and fall. It may be advisable to include crabgrass and weed preventative in the spring application.
3. Regulating the amount of irrigation. Automatic sprinklers are available and tend to be one of the most satisfactory systems, and traveling sprinklers are used by a number of schools. Care should be taken not to overwater. During the playing season more water can be applied to keep the ground moist, which will promote growth as well as providing a softer surface which offers greater safety for players. When the field is not in use, only enough water is needed to prevent wilting.
4. Cultivating with a tine harrow in the spring or early summer to lightly loosen the soil, which helps to produce sod and prevents compacting. If the equipment is available, aerating followed by light harrowing is a good practice.
5. Reseeding in the fall and spring when necessary. Bare and sparse areas can be "overseeded" by first cultivating with a harrow, or by "dormant seeding" after the playing season which allows seeds to get well covered while dormant during the winter for early spring sprouting. Another method is to overseed before home games and allow the cleats to work the seeds into the ground, which is particularly practical with ryegrass which requires a few warm days for germination.

It is important that the field turf be maintained regularly. Periods of neglect are one of the principal sources of problems in keeping a field in condition from year to year.

Lighted Outdoor Areas

When schools began to play outdoor games on lighted fields, opinions were divided about the advisability of this practice. However, evening games caught on as more lighted fields were constructed. General observations about this development are that

1. Gate receipts are increased
2. It is more difficult to control the actions of spectators, particularly following the contest

3. Better community relations are promoted
4. The educational values are the same for night games as they are for daytime contests
5. There is less conflict with the classwork of students

Purposes for which lighted fields are used now include (1) football games, (2) band concerts and festivals, (3) softball games, (4) baseball games, (5) track meets, (6) physical education demonstrations, (7) soccer games, and (8) various community activities.

The common construction practices followed in lighting fields are: (1) from 4 to 8 poles are used on each side of the field, with 5 or 6 being the most common number (towers are used in some instances); (2) poles run from 40 feet to 85 feet high, with 60- to 70-foot poles used most; (3) the most recent practice seems to be that of using single lights in single reflectors, with several reflectors (6 to 12) on each pole; (4) the better lighted fields seem to have from 10–12 to 15–18 foot-candles on the playing field; (5) attention is given to lighting fences, entrances, exits, and spectator stands.

Parking lots should also be well lighted to help prevent vandalism and misconduct following games.

LONG-RANGE PLANNING

Whether a school is contemplating new facilities or planning to improve existing facilities, long-range planning is needed. Here are some factors that should be taken into consideration:

1. Survey the needs of the school and school community. Knowing the approximate number of students (boys and girls) to be served in physical education classes, intramurals, and interscholastic athletics is basic. Possible community use is another factor that should be studied. Some communities desire to use school facilities during the summer and off-seasons for programs sponsored by local organizations.

2. Plans must take into account how much financing can be made available. They must be kept within financial reality. All possible sources should be explored. Whether it must be derived entirely from school moneys or whether some might be derived from other sources should be determined. Cooperative use of facilities may stimulate the city council or some other organizations to give financial support, particularly for such facilities as baseball diamonds and swimming pools. The Columbia, Missouri Public Schools, in cooperation with the City of Columbia, built an indoor-outdoor swimming pool on the Hickman High School campus with each sharing in the building costs. The pool is used during the school day for high school swimming classes

and for interscholastic swimming practice and competition after school and some evenings during the swim season. The City of Columbia Parks and Recreation Department uses it other evenings, on Saturdays when not in use, and during the summer for a community swimming program. The plan has been very successful and mutually beneficial to all concerned. Another productive approach was demonstrated in Missoula, Montana, where the cooperation of three booster clubs resulted in the building of a football stadium for the school district's three high schools which previously had had to rent football facilities.[3] The high cost of facilities and the fact that taxpayers have a financial interest in them makes it advisable to get as much as possible from them without interfering with the school program. School-community cooperation and planning makes maximum use possible and financing more justifiable.

3. Facilities should be planned to serve physical education, intramural, and interschool athletic programs. Roll-out bleachers may be more desirable than permanent seating in a gymnasium if they allow space for more activities in physical education.

4. Future enrollments should be considered. If increases can be expected, planning should take this into account. Many schools have found what were adequate facilities became inadequate as enrollments increased. Possible community population growth must be taken into consideration.

5. In any event, there should be a carefully planned public relations program in conjunction with the program to improve facilities. Providing full information regarding the philosophy and objectives of the school's total physical education and interscholastic program, the facilities necessary to accommodate such program, approximate costs, extent of use to be made of the facilities, and so on will help to create interest and gain support.

There are many architects, engineers, and builders who specialize in the design and construction of institutional facilities. Their professional knowledge, services, and advice should be sought when a school is planning to build new facilities or improve existing ones. Their help can be used best when school officials provide them with full information regarding the type and scope of the program for which the facilities are needed. The latest game rules books will contain up-to-date dimensions for playing areas. This is one of the most important responsibilities of athletic administrators in the layout and maintenance of athletic facilities. Buildings alone will not make a program, but if they are planned and used to help achieve the most worthwhile objectives of physical education, intramural activities, and interscholastic athletics, the education of the high school students will be enhanced.

METRIC SYSTEM

No exact date has been set for conversion to the metric system in athletics, but it is likely to occur in the not-too-distant future. When it does, it will affect planning of school facilities. Terminology in game rules, dimensions of courts and fields, and more will be converted to metric measures. There will probably be some changes in game rules, such as track and field. Athletic administrators and coaches must keep informed of these developments. Appendix B provides a table that will be helpful in understanding conversion to the metric system.

SUMMARY

Rules books contain the minimum measurements for playing fields and floors, but more space is advisable to meet local conditions when constructing new facilities.

All outdoor fields should be well drained. Football fields should extend from south to north if games are to be played in the daytime. Baseball fields are best when laid out so that batters are facing west or northwest. Tracks are generally constructed around football fields to save space and reduce expenses in providing for seating. The track and field rules should be consulted to determine the dimensions for individual events.

The football field can be best maintained by contracting with a professional lawn service. The turf should be kept well watered, mowed regularly, cultivated occasionally, and fertilized in fall and spring.

Outdoor lighted areas have proved satisfactory and have several advantages, except for crowd control.

School districts might well consider school-community cooperation in the construction of new facilities to reduce costs for the district and to allow for wider use.

All new facilities should be planned to allow for conversion to the metric system of measurement in the future.

QUESTIONS AND TOPICS FOR STUDY AND DISCUSSION

1. What square footage is recommended as the minimum requirement for: (a) softball; (b) volleyball; (c) basketball; (d) football; (e) baseball?
2. Discuss essentials to be considered in layouts for indoor playing facilities.
3. What main factors should receive attention in building a football field?
4. Discuss the layout and construction of a baseball field. In what direction should the batter face? Why?

5. A track is one of the most difficult athletic facilities to build. List important items to be considered in its construction.
6. List the essentials for good athletic field maintenance.
7. What are some of the advantages of playing contests on lighted fields?
7. Why is long-rage planning important in planning athletic facilities?
8. Assume that you are the athletic administrator in a school of 1,000 students planning to build a new high school campus. List and briefly describe the facilities you would want for the total boys' and girls' physical education and athletic programs.
9. Enumerate the effects you think conversion to the metric system will have upon athletics.

NOTES

1. General information regarding Michigan State University track and field facilities was provided by Ralph H. Young, former Director of Athletics.
2. United States Lawn Tennis Association, *Service Bulletin No. 17* (New York: The Association).
3. Lander J. Fred, "Facilities: Unique Approach Builds Community Football Stadium, *Interscholastic Athletic Administration,* 8, no. 3 (Spring 1982), 18–21.

BIBLIOGRAPHY

DANIEL, WILLIAM. "Preparing and Maintaining Your Grass Athletic Fields." *Athletic Purchasing and Facilities,* 6, no. 4 (April 1982), 29–44.

FRED, LANDER J. "Facilities: Unique Approach Builds Community Football Stadium." *Interscholastic Athletic Administration,* 8, no. 3 (Spring 1982), 18–21.

HILL, WENDELL. "Facilities: Fulfilling a Promise." *Interscholastic Athletic Administration,* 8, no. 4 (Summer 1982), 16–17.

LUTZ, LEROY. "Maintenance Tips for Natural Turf." *Athletic Purchasing and Facilities,* 6, no. 1 (January 1982), 24–26.

PAZIK, CAROL S. "Schroeder Center: The All-Purpose Pool." *Athletic Purchasing and Facilities,* 6, no. 4 (April 1982), 36–38.

RESICK, MATTHEW C., AND CARL E. ERICKSON. *Intercollegiate and Interscholastic Athletics for Men and Women,* Chap. 11. Reading, Mass.: Addison-Wesley, 1975.

SACK, THOMAS F. *A Complete Guide to Building and Plant Maintenance.* Englewood Cliffs, N. J.: Prentice-Hall, Inc., 1965.

UNITED STATES LAWN TENNIS ASSOCIATION, 51 East 42nd Street, New York: *Service Bulletin No. 17.*

14

Intramural Activities

This chapter will concern itself with the place of intramural activities in our schools, consideration of some of the objectives to be realized from the intramural program, and presentation of the major policies involved in it. Attempts will be made to point out suggestions to be kept in mind in the administration of intramurals in high schools.

PLACE IN THE PROGRAM

Intramural versus Interschool Athletics

The word "intramural" means "within the walls"; therefore, intramural athletics are athletic activities conducted within a school itself, as contrasted with athletic contests played between two or more schools. There is no conflict between properly conducted programs of intramural and interscholastic athletics; in fact, they are both a part of the same overall athletic program. Each group of activities should be complementary to the other. Each has a place in the school prgram; each may be defended educationally; and each offers opportunities not necessarily possessed by the other.

Intramural activities should form the basis of all athletics. All students should have the opportunity to compete regardless of their degree of skill. They have an inherent right to play or to attain self-expression through intramural games. As part of the physical education program of a school, intramurals should receive the major attention of those in charge of the department. They should be the laboratory for the physical education program. Primarily, intramural competition is for the contestants themselves. Of course, this purpose also is the major objective of interschool athletic competition; yet there are school, student spectator, and community interests that must be given consideration as well. The intramural program should be set up so that the boys and girls themselves may play the games in which they are interested individually. They also should have the opportunity to learn new games and, as a result of having learned them, to acquire new skills and new interests.

Interschool athletics by their very nature are more selective than intramurals. This is not an indictment against the former if all the facts are kept in mind. They provide additional experiences for the more talented athletes, whose potential abilities may not be challenged in intramural competition. Under no circumstances should a school consider that its interscholastic athletic program is a legitimate substitute for intramural games. As stated previously, each serves different purposes and achieves different ends. Intramural athletics may be likened to the general courses that are taken because, by so doing, students lay the groundwork for other activities and interests. So it is with intramurals.

The intramural athletic program may be viewed in another way. When a student engages in intramurals, which should be under the direction of the physical education department of a school, such participation may be likened to taking part in general activities such as music, debating, public speaking, and dramatics. Out of these general groups the more proficient students are selected to make up the bands, orchestras, and choruses of the school, as well as the debaters, public speakers, and the actors in school plays. They all have been grounded in general fundamentals through the courses they have taken. Then, those who show greater skills than others or who possess greater aptitudes or natural abilities are selected for further training and often become their school's representatives if competition in any of these activities is a part of the school program or policy. Ideally, that is the way the athletic program should work. The interscholastic athletic program should represent the training program for those individuals in a school who are most proficient in particular sports. It should be the outgrowth, not the antecedent, of the intramural program, which should have as its objective the teaching of and participation in many games whereby new skills are learned by all the boys and girls in a school. In both instances students will have had the chance to play, which is the most important consideration.

World War II showed us conclusively that physical education and intramural programs in our high schools and colleges had failed miserably in teaching a variety of games and skills. True, we found many men who came into the armed forces who knew how to play, and could intelligently watch, football, basketball, and baseball games. However, many more could watch than could play these games. As far as other athletic activities were concerned, even mass games of low organization were generally unknown. During periods of basic or recruit training in the armed forces many opportunities were offered to men and women to engage in athletic competition. Those who had had intercollegiate or interscholastic competition usually did. But this number was small compared to the number who did not play. Why? Because they did not know the games or failed to possess the elementary skills necessary to play them. It was indeed sad to see several hundred men at a training center participating in organized games and then to observe that there were several times this number standing idly around *because they did not know how to play.* In most cases these men and women could have learned something about games and their attendant skills if our schools, colleges, and recreation programs had been organized and administered correctly and had included broad physical education and intramural activities. As a result of intramurals it is possible to prepare more and better participants as well as better informed spectators.

The President's Council on Physical Fitness has made good use of the news media to emphasize the importance of all citizens' keeping physically fit and has stimulated many students and adults to realize the wisdom of regular participation in various types of individual activities and athletic games.

The values of athletic participation have been widely recognized. It is claimed that athletic competition helps to prevent dropouts and that some students who are not academically talented can derive educational benefits from competition. School administrators of larger cities have expressed the desire to have more educationally deprived and ghetto youth compete in interscholastics to stimulate greater interest in education. The number of students that can be afforded athletic experiences through interschool contests is limited. Because of the fact that only those with superior athletic abilities are permitted to compete on interscholastic teams, a much larger percentage will have little opportunity to participate in athletic games unless the school has a broad intramural program. If more youths are to be accommodated, more emphasis must be placed on intramurals. Practically all high schools have well organized interscholastic programs, but many give insufficient attention to providing intramural athletics for the vast number who do not get to compete in interschool athletics. Among the reasons for this situation are:

1. Many schools lack adequate facilities for both.
2. There is greater public interest in interscholastic contests, which results in their getting more attention.
3. Interscholastic coaches who are often also responsible for intramurals are evaluated in many communities more by their win-loss record than for their work in intramurals; consequently, they neglect the latter for the former.
4. Many athletic directors, likewise, give more support and attention to the interscholastic phase.
5. Too little recognition is given for individual and team accomplishments in intramurals by the school and news media, which affects the attitudes and interests of students.
6. Insufficient coaching is provided those participating in intramurals to help them to improve their athletic skills and to gain a feeling of satisfaction from more skillful playing.
7. There is inadequate planning and supervision for the best potential intramural program.

8. The tremendous increase in the number of interscholastic contests during the past decade, and particularly in girls' interschool competition, has required greater use of facilities and made scheduling more difficult for both interscholastics and intramurals. Too often the intramural program suffers under these conditions.

9. Intramurals do not receive sufficient administrative and board of education support. Despite the fact that educational administrators proclaim the values of athletic activities for all youth, many have failed to show sustained interest in intramurals to implement these values for those who do not get the opportunity to compete in interscholastic competition.

Small high schools in which a larger proportion of the student body competes in interscholastics often provide athletic experiences to a greater percentage of their students than do larger schools. Although there is general agreement that participation in school athletics has value for all students and should be offered to as many as possible, the general practice in a large number of schools is not fully compatible with this philosophy, and physical education class is the only opportunity for athletics offered a large segment of high school students. The popularity of the boys' interscholastic program often results in a neglect of any significant program of intramurals. Until boards of education, school administrators, and athletic directors give more attention and support to the intramural program, this condition will persist.

For many years the girls' intramural program has been superior to that for boys in most schools. This has been due in large part to the philosophy of girls' athletics that prevailed among women physical educators, most of whom were members of the Division for Girls' and Women's Sports of the American Association for Health, Physical Education and Recreation (now the National Alliance for Girls' and Women's Sports). Intramural and extramural competition received more attention by that organization and by girls' physical education teachers than did girls' interscholastic competition. Broad participation has been one of the primary objectives. The following policy statement has given direction to the girls' intramural program.

STATEMENT OF POLICIES FOR COMPETITION IN GIRLS' AND WOMEN'S SPORTS

The division for Girls' and Women's Sports of the American Association for Health, Physical Education, and Recreation believes the competitive element in sports activities can be used constructively for achievement of desirable educational and recreational objectives. When favorable conditions are present, competitive experiences may be wholesome and beneficial and result in acceptable conduct and attitudes. Competition in and of itself does not automatically result in desirable or undesirable outcomes.

The adoption of practices best suited for the attainment of desirable outcomes is the responsibility of all associated with competitive events. Sponsoring agencies, players, teachers, coaches, officials, and spectators must share responsibility for valid practices in competitive sports.

DGWS believes participation in sports competition is the privilege of all girls and women. Sound, instructional and well-organized intramural programs will answer the needs and desires of the majority of young women. For the college woman and high school girl who seeks and needs additional challenges in competition and skills, a sound, carefully planned and well-directed program of extramural sports is recommended. The provisions for extramural sports opportunities should be broad, including such events as sports days, leagues, meets, and tournaments. Development of all participants toward higher competencies and advanced skills should be a major objective in all sports programs.

DGWS advocates the following policies through which desirable outcomes in competition may be achieved.

Definition of Competition

Competition is defined as the participation in a sport activity by two or more persons, in which a winner can result. The educational values of competition are determined by the quality of leadership and of the participation. For the best results, there should be comprehensive physical education, intramural, and extramural programs. The organized competitive programs should offer opportunities in terms of individual ability and should be adapted to the needs and interests of the participants.

Forms of Competition

Intramural competition is sports competition in which all participants are identified with the same school, community center, club, organization, institution, or industry, or are residents of a designated small neighborhood or community. This form of competition stresses the participation of "the many." A good intramural program which offers a variety of activities, at various skill levels, including corecreational activities, frequently is sufficient to meet the needs and desires of the majority of girls and women.

It is the responsibility of the school or agency sponsoring the intramural program to provide the time, facilities, and competent leadership, with preference given to professional, qualified women. Intramural programs should be an outgrowth of and a complement to the school physical education program or the organized community recreation program.

Extramural competition is a plan of sports competition in which participants from two or more schools, community centers, clubs, organizations, institutions, industries, or neighborhoods compete. The forms of extramural competition include:

1. Sport days—school or sport group participates as a unit.
2. Telegraphic meets—results are compared by wire or mail.
3. Invitational events—symposiums, games, or matches, for which a school or sport group invites one or more teams to participate.
4. Interscholastic, intercollegiate, or interagency programs—groups which are trained and coached play a series of scheduled games and/or tournaments with teams from other schools, cities, or organizations.

The extramural program is planned and carried out to complement the intramural and instructional programs. For the best welfare of the participants, it is essential that the program be conducted by qualified leaders, be supported by budgeted funds, and be representative of approved objectives and standards for girls' and women's sports, including acceptable conditions of travel, protective insurance, appropriate facilities, proper equipment, and desirable practices in the conduct of events. When the program affords group participation as a team in a series of games on appropriate tournament or schedule basis, additional coaching by qualified staff members must be provided.

It is assumed that the sponsoring organization recognizes its obligation to delegate responsibility for this program to the supervisor or specialist in charge of the girls' and women's sports programs. When admission charges are made, the proceeds should be used for furthering the sports programs for girls (instructional, intramural, and extramural).[1]

It is noted that this official statement of policies provides for a well-rounded program for all girls. Interscholastic athletics are afforded highly skilled girls whose abilities are not sufficiently challenged by intramural competition. Considerably more emphasis has been placed upon girls' interscholastic competition since the early 1970s, and the number participating has increased tremendously, while there has been a decrease in sports days and other types of extramural activities. We are not yet able to gauge the ultimate effect on girls' intramural athletic activities; however, athletic administrators should be concerned that ample opportunities remain for those boys and girls to participate in intramural activities who do not compete in interscholastic athletics. No school should discriminate against students who are not capable of being on the school's athletic squads by denying them the educational experiences of intramural athletics.

GENERAL INTRAMURAL OBJECTIVES

The development of intramurals began when educators came to realize that interscholastics did not fulfill all the educational objectives of athletics. Intramural activities have also been given great impetus as a result of the attention they have received comparatively recently in our teacher training institutions. Recent graduates of these schools have been prepared for the handling of intramurals and the establishment of necessary objectives. It is obvious that play for the masses will not be on as high a level of skills in intramurals as in interscholastics. The games and activities to be included should be selected carefully. They should be ones that are interesting and may be learned easily, and both team and individual sports should be included.

The intramural program must appeal to students, and the opportunity to play must be the objective most obvious to them. Among other objectives usually advanced for intramurals are the following:

Health and physical fitness.   The objective of any activity should be consistent with the first of the Cardinal Principles of Education and contribute toward its realization. Proper attitudes must be instilled in regard to the importance of physical fitness. The same general principles regarding safety and sanitation should obtain for the intramural program as apply to interscholastic athletics. Since there should be many more students participating in intramurals than in interscholastic athletics, the opportunity exists for teaching much more both in immediate and long-range health education programs. Insist on compliance with commonsense safety and sanitation standards (see Chapter 12).

Leisure time and recreation.   Physical activity should consume a part of one's leisure time. The opportunity to participate in sports and games in school may stimulate interest and open an avenue to wise selection of leisure-time and recreation activities both during school days and afterward.

Development of citizenship.   In athletic games, interscholastic and intramural, life situations develop that may aid in helping students adjust themselves to the social order in which they live. The realization of a group spirit which results from team competition is a valuable experience to participants. It teaches responsibility as well as cooperation. Sportsmanship, fair play, truthfulness, and courage are attributes of citizenship that may be realized from intramural competition.

Social contacts.   In both large and small schools, friendships are inevitable and invaluable. A broad friendship list is desirable during the adolescent and pre-adult periods. Intramurals offer an additional opportunity for realization of this objective.

There are socializing values derived from participation in intramural athletic sports which are not always recognized by school people. Generally, varsity athletes develop companionships with fellow teammates and perhaps with opponents in rival schools, but the number involved in the socializing experience is comparatively small. Intramural players, however, engage in many sports, participate in various contests, and establish friendships with large numbers of fellow players and opponents in their own schools. In intramural sports the establishment of cordial social relations among opponents, officials, and the few interested spectators is most valuable.

Development of interest and skills.   We usually enjoy most doing those things we do well. This is especially true in athletics and recreational activities. The intramural program gives students the chance to discover and develop their skills. With these discoveries and developments there is bound to be a more permanent interest in many more activities than otherwise could be the case.

Pleasure in playing. The intramural program has little or no value if there is not genuine pleasure in the competition it affords. Games and activities should be of varied types so that different interests of students may be served. Make the program afford joyous participation. Special attention should be paid to the inclusion of as many individual sports as possible in the intramural program. This feature is important because it will give the student who is not especially team-minded an opportunity to participate. In this connection, it should be kept in mind that many of us have the time and chance to engage in activities or hobbies only when we are alone or with comparatively few others present. Emphasis should be placed upon the so-called lifetime sports, which will motivate some students to continue them as adults. Most highly organized team games offer little chance for participation after high school or college.

Academic standing. There is no definite proof of high correlation between athletic prowess and academic or scholastic standing. In fact, the opposite sometimes is claimed to be more obvious. Neither premise is entirely correct. It is safe to say, however, that wholesome, well-directed athletic activity is a contributing factor to good health. It is also reasonable to presume that an alert body and mind will make for better academic work. Intramurals, therefore, can have a part in this general situation and at the same time provide enjoyable experiences for participants. Schools generally do not have prerequisites for participation in extracurricular activities. Conversely, many educators feel that intramurals will stimulate interest in school and thereby be a factor in better academic success.

Physical education supplement. Intramurals should be a part of the physical education program. There should be a definite correlation between the skills taught in physical education classes and participation in intramural games and contests. It is important, however, that intramural athletics be elective, because the student should want to participate in the activity instead of being forced to do so. The physical educator's problem is to make the intramural program one of such varied and interesting activities that students are attracted to it because they want to play. In reality, the learning may be incidental but the playing should be basic.

Aid to interschool program. As stated previously, the interschool program should be an outgrowth of the intramural program. When this ideal is realized, each is a contributing factor to the success of the other. Inevitably, varsity players will be discovered through their intramural competition. Thus, varsity competition may be the goal of some who take part in intramural play, but it should not be the dominant one.

The junior high school program should not be considered a "farm system" for senior high school interscholastics. Yet, it is a fact that all senior high varsity players will have attended junior high school. It is at this level that intramural participation should be emphasized and interschool competition kept in proper perspective. There is sometimes a tendency for senior high school coaches to look almost exclusively at junior high interscholastic teams as the source of prospective players for their varsity teams. This can be a serious mistake. Growth patterns and physical maturity vary widely among junior high school students. Ample opportunities to participate in a broad junior high intramural program will enable more youth to gain athletic knowledge and skills. Some of the less physically mature junior high school students may become better varsity players if afforded the chance. Hence, good junior and senior high intramural programs will help students develop their skills and open the door to the senior high interscholastic program as well.

ADMINISTRATION OF INTRAMURAL ACTIVITIES

Some of the major problems involved in the administration of an intramural athletic program are discussed briefly below. Naturally, the administrative details will vary according to the size and plan of organization of the school itself. They will be quite different in a school of a hundred students or less as against a school with several hundred to a few thousand. Further, available facilities and faculty personnel will be most important factors.

Responsibility

Preferably, whoever is in charge of the intramural program should not have the major responsibility of coaching an interscholastic team. In a small school in which this policy may not be feasible, the faculty member in charge should be impressed with the fact that the intramural program is of equal educational importance with the interscholastic competition. The purpose in recommending that the person in charge of intramurals not be a major interscholastic coach is to ensure that interscholastic interests will not overshadow intramurals. It is advisable to have an intramural athletic council in a school, with a substantial number of its membership composed of students. The principal and the director of intramural athletics should be permanent council members, with one or two additional faculty members who serve for annual or staggered two-year terms. The intramural director should be the executive in active charge of the program. This person should be a member of the physical education staff, if possible. Above all else, he or she must be genuinely enthusiastic and knowledgeable about intramurals. The success or failure of many programs often can be attributed to one individual, who more than anyone else will determine the quality of the school's intramural program.

Organization

Units of organization will vary with individual schools. Class, homeroom, gymnasium class squads, clubs, color groups, study groups, and the like are possible units to serve as a basis for competition. Whenever possible, competition should be based on other than class teams, to ensure greater equity in competition. Often it is desirable to select teams using a coefficient involving an age, weight, height, or grade combination, or some one of them. Equal strength of teams is almost essential to the success of intramurals just as it is in other types of competition. As far as possible the intramural program should be a part of the regular school day. Many times an activity period during the day can be utilized for the playing of intramural contests. Noon-hour periods may be used for the less strenuous activities, and in some cases the school day may be lengthened by the addition of an extra class period. Evening, Saturday, and late-afternoon periods usually are not satisfactory.

Student Involvement in the Administration of Intramurals

In the typical high school, the intramural director and physical education instructors will find it impossible to attend to all of the details of administering an intramural program involving a high percentage of the students. This need not be a disadvantage. Students should be involved in the administration of intramurals under established policies defining their responsibilities. Many worthwhile learning experiences can be afforded them by this method. Carefully selected team managers, captains, record keepers and so on can assist in the administration of intramurals. Policies should make clear their authority over other students, and procedures must be established to handle cases when players fail to respect the authority delegated to the holders of these positions. The intramural director should hold meetings with these individuals for the purpose of instructing them in their responsibilities and the policies which are to guide them. They should be provided outlines of their duties and the procedures they are to follow.

An important phase of a good intramural program is a student officials training plan. Student officials should be provided rules books, and conferences should be held regularly to instruct them in the mechanics of officiating. Some schools have policies which provide that varsity athletes are not permitted to compete on intramural teams in the sport in which they compete interscholastically, but they are encouraged to serve as team managers and officials. Providing these experiences offers several benefits. It helps to provide a better administered intramural program and may also contribute to the development of officials for interscholastics. Maintaining an adequate supply of well-qualified varsity officials is a continuous problem of schools and their state associations. Teaching officiating through intramurals can be an important means of helping to resolve this problem.

Intramurals should be both recreational and educational. Establishing definite objectives, planning properly, adhering to good administrative policies, involving students to the level of their capabilities, and supervising them adequately will make intramurals an important part of the total school program.

Program of Activities

One development in intramurals in recent years is a broadened scope in some schools, which does not limit them to just athletic activities. It has been found that more students are inclined to participate in the total program when competition is offered in chess, checkers, bridge, and other activities. Although all students should be encouraged to participate in athletic games because of the benefits they offer, those interested in other types of activities should not be neglected. The wise activities director will survey the interests of the student body before planning the program. The interests and needs of students should be basic in planning. This does not mean that attempts should not be made to stimulate both interest and a feeling of need. This is just as important to success in intramurals as it is in the classroom. The results of the survey will help to select activities and establish seasons for them, which will offer students a variety of experiences.

Following are lists of seasonal athletic activities from which selections may be made:

Junior High School Boys

Fall

Archery	Softball	Touch football
Golf	Speedball	Volleyball
Horsehoes	Swimming	
Soccer	Tennis	

Winter

Basketball	Handball	Swimming
Boxing	Ice hockey	Table tennis
Foul shooting	Shuffleboard	Twenty-one
Gymnastics	Skating	Wrestling

Spring

Archery	Horseshoes or quoits	Tennis
Fieldball	Newcomb	Track activities
Golf	Softball	Volleyball
Hit-pin ball	Swimming	

Junior High School Girls

Fall

Archery	Kickball	Swimming
Fieldball	Kick-pin ball	Tennis
Golf	Newcomb	Track activities
Hit-pin ball	Paddle tennis	Volleyball
Horseshoes or quoits	Schlagball	

Winter

Archery	Quoits	Table tennis
Basketball	Shuffleboard	Twenty-one
Foul shooting	Skating	Volleyball
Gymnastics	Skiing	
Newcomb	Swimming	

Spring

Archery	Kickball	Swimming
Fieldball	Kick-pin ball	Tennis
Golf	Newcomb	Track activities
Hit-pin ball	Paddle tennis	Volleyball
Horseshoes or quoits	Schlagball	

Senior High School Boys

Fall

Archery	Horseshoes	Tennis
Bicycling	Playground ball	Touch football
Cross country	Soccer	Volleyball
Football field meet	Speedball	Walking races
Golf	Swimming	

Winter

Badminton	Ice hockey	Table tennis
Basketball	Relay carnivals	Track activities
Bowling	Shuffleboard	Twenty-one
Foul shooting	Skating	Water polo
Gymnastics	Skiing	Wrestling
Handball	Swimming	

Spring

Archery	Horseshoes	Tennis
Baseball	Softball	Track activities
Golf	Swimming	Volleyball

Senior High School Girls

Fall

Archery	Golf	Speedball
Bicycling	Handball	Swimming
Cross country	Horseshoes or quoits	Tennis
Deck tennis	Newcomb	Track activities
Fieldball	Softball	Volleyball
Field hockey	Soccer	Walking races

Winter

Archery	Foul shooting	Skiing
Badminton	Gymnastics	Stunts
Basketball	Handball	Swimming
Bowling	Quoits	Table tennis
Deck tennis	Shuffleboard	Twenty-one
Fencing	Skating	

Spring

Archery	Horseshoes or quoits	Swimming
Deck tennis	Newcomb	Tennis
Fieldball	Sixty-yard dash	Track activities
Field hockey	Soccer	Volleyball
Golf	Softball	
Handball	Speedball	

Eligibility

In general, there should be as few as possible eligibility regulations in effect for participation in intramural athletic activities. The only exceptions might be those pertaining to violations of discipline rules of the school and the requirement that all contestants must have successfully passed physical examinations. In no sense of the word should rules of scholastic eligibility, as they apply to interschool games, be effective for intramurals. Such a policy would defeat the aim of having as nearly 100 percent participation as possible. Individuals who are varsity letter winners in one sport should not be allowed to compete in intramurals in the activity unless their participation does not prevent any other high school student from taking part in that sport. At the same time, intramural competition should be equitable.

Awards

Some feel that, because of the pleasure of playing, it is not necessary to give awards for intramural participation, while others are of the opinion that some type of symbolic awards is important in recognition of team and individual achievement to stimulate interest and participation. If awards are offered only for competing in interscholastic activities, students may well interpret this to mean that the school does not really believe intramurals to be significant. Some schools have established point systems as the basis for making awards for participation in intramurals. The accumulation of a certain number of points earns an intramural letter or certificate of recognition. Attractive certificates can be offered at little expense. The honor of receiving the award is more important to the athlete than the award itself. It is recommended that all awards be symbolic only. If it is desired to have students consider intramurals worthwhile, some type of recognition is important.

Intramural Competition

Most intramural competition is arranged so that round-robin schedules may be played. These allow for a maximum amount of competition. In such cases, generally, it is desirable to set up leagues of not more than eight teams each, because with more teams than this number, competition is likely to be quite drawn out, with consequent loss of interest. If additional competition is necessary, another round may be played, and so on in order to provide as much competition as desirable. With a large number of teams it usually works out well to arrange for play-offs between league winners, and often runners-up are included in the post-league competition. Table 14–1 is a schedule for round-robin competition for up to eight teams.

Another type of competition is single or straight elimination. In this scheme of play the number of byes must be known before competition starts, in order that all of them may occur in the first round. Entries should first be numbered. The bracket must be arranged for 4, 8, 16, and so on in geometric progression, the byes being arranged to fill out the bracket to the next greater number in the progression. To illustrate, suppose there were 11 entries. The bracket would be for 16 teams, the next greater member in the progression above 11. There will be 5 byes, 2 at the top and 3 at the bottom of the bracket. If the number of byes is even, there is an equal number of them at the top and bottom of the bracket. If not, the extra bye is placed at the bottom. An illustrative 11-team single-elimination bracket is shown in Table 14–2.

A double-elimination or double-"knockout" schedule is seldom used unless the number of teams or individuals is small, usually eight or less. This arrangement provides a maximum amount of tournament play because two defeats are necessary before a team is eliminated. With an eight-team entry the schedule as included in Table 14–3 is operative. If there are only seven teams there is a bye in game 4, and this bye is carried into game 6 or 8. If there are only six teams, byes obtain in games 1 and 4 and then are carried into games 5, 6, 7, and 8. Teams should be given letters A to H. Draw them from the hat and follow the schedule listed in the table. This procedure will bring the two winners into the finals, all losers having been defeated twice.

In addition to the types of competition discussed here, there are the ladder and pyramid tournaments as well as consolation series of eliminations.

TABLE 14–1 Round-Robin Schedule

	3 Teams	4 Teams	5 Teams	6 Teams	7 Teams	8 Teams
First-date games	1 plays 2 3 bye	1 plays 2 3 plays 4	1 plays 2 3 plays 4 5 bye	1 plays 2 3 plays 4 5 plays 6	1 plays 2 3 plays 4 5 plays 6 7 bye	1 plays 2 3 plays 4 5 plays 6 7 plays 8
Second-date games	1 plays 3 2 bye	1 plays 3 2 plays 4	1 plays 3 4 plays 5 2 bye	1 plays 3 2 plays 5 4 plays 6	1 plays 3 2 plays 5 4 plays 7 6 bye	1 plays 3 2 plays 4 5 plays 7 6 plays 8
Third-date games	2 plays 3 1 bye	1 plays 4 2 plays 3	1 plays 4 2 plays 5 3 bye	1 plays 4 2 plays 6 3 plays 5	1 plays 4 2 plays 6 3 plays 7 5 bye	1 plays 4 2 plays 3 5 plays 8 6 plays 7
Fourth-date games			1 plays 5 2 plays 3 4 bye	1 plays 5 2 plays 4 3 plays 6	1 plays 5 2 plays 7 3 plays 6 4 bye	1 plays 5 2 plays 8 3 plays 7 4 plays 6
Fifth-date games			2 plays 4 3 plays 5 1 bye	1 plays 6 2 plays 3 4 plays 5	1 plays 6 2 plays 4 5 plays 7 3 bye	1 plays 6 2 plays 5 3 plays 8 4 plays 7
Sixth-date games					1 plays 7 3 plays 5 4 plays 6 2 bye	1 plays 7 2 plays 6 3 plays 5 4 plays 8
Seventh-date games					2 plays 3 4 plays 5 6 plays 7 1 bye	1 plays 8 2 plays 7 3 plays 6 4 plays 5

Ladder and pyramid tournaments work better with individual competition (see Figs. 14–1 and 14–2). Players challenge those directly above them on the ladder after drawings have been made. In order to advance, a player must defeat the one above him/her, in which case their names change places on the ladder. In a pyramid tournament players may challenge anyone in the same horizontal row. The successful one in the match may challenge anyone in the row above. Almost unlimited competition is provided in the ladder and pyramid arrangements—sometimes so much that interest is lost because of inability to conclude. A consolation tournament simply is matching first-round losers in a straight or single-elimination bracket; then a procedure identical with that shown in Table 14–3 is followed.

TABLE 14–2   Single-Elimination Bracket

First round	Second round	Third round	Fourth round	Championship

TABLE 14–3   Double-Elimination Schedule (8 Teams)

1—A plays B
2—C plays D   } To start
3—E plays F
4—G plays H
5—loser of game 1 plays loser of game 2
6—loser of game 3 plays loser of game 4
7—winner of game 1 plays winner of game 2
8—winner of game 3 plays loser of game 4
9—winner of game 5 plays loser of game 7
10—loser of game 8 plays winner of game 6
11—winner of game 7 plays winner of game 8
12—winner of game 9 plays winner of game 10
13—winner of game 11 plays winner of game 12 (winner is champion; loser is runner-up)
14—loser of game 11 plays loser of game 12 (winner wins 3rd place; loser wins 4th place)

Extramurals

Much interest can be added to intramural competition if it is supplemented by a limited number of extramural competitions in the form of sports days. Intramural teams from one school competing against those of another appeal to students and help to stimulate intramural play (see pp. 334–335 for description).

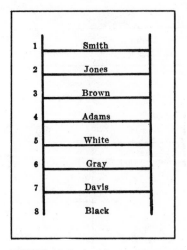

FIGURE 14–1   Ladder tournament

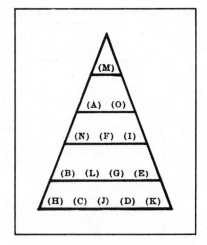

FIGURE 14–2   Pyramid tournament

SUGGESTED INTRAMURAL POLICIES AND PRACTICES

As a checklist for the conduct of the intramural athletic program, the following suggested policies and practices are included. It may not be possible to realize them in all schools or under all circumstances, but at least they may provoke thought or provide policy stimulation.

1. The intramural program should be an integral part of the physical education program.
2. There should be a director of intramural athletics whose chief interest is the development and administration of these activities.
3. The intramural program should be dignified by its regularity, completeness of schedules, and definiteness of policy.
4. An intramural athletic council should exist in the school.
5. The cost of intramural athletic supplies should be met by the board of education.
6. The local school paper should give an appropriate amount of space to intramural activities.
7. Constant emphasis should be placed on the parity of intramural and interscholastic activities.
8. Keep the school-patron public informed concerning the scope, size, and objectives of the intramural program.
9. No matter how small the school, there is a place for intramural athletic competition in it.
10. Combine the intramural and physical education activities as far as possible but maintain intramurals on an elective or voluntary basis.
11. Use the intramural program as a method of fixing health, safety, and sanitation habits in the lives of participants.
12. Broaden the program to include individual activities as well as team sports.
13. Provide awards and hold dignified awards ceremonies to provide satisfying recognition for accomplishment in intramurals.
14. Hold one or more sports days to climax the intramural season.

FINANCING INTRAMURALS

It has been common practice for boards of education to subsidize interscholastic athletics from general school funds, but some have been reluctant to allocate sufficient funds for intramurals although they are an outgrowth of the physical education program. The fact that intramurals comprise a recognized program within the school is sufficient reason for them to be financed by the board of education and included in the school budget. It is just as logical to provide funds to supplement the salaries of coaches, or to purchase intramural equipment, as it is to purchase equipment for interscholastics.

Some students and parents are beginning to raise questions of discrimination regarding the amount of school moneys spent per student engaging in interscholastic athletics as compared to the amount spent per student participating in intramural activities. After considering the results of a committee study on discrimination in the Palm Beach County Schools in Florida in 1973–74, the Board of Education made a special allocation of 90 cents per student enrolled to support intramurals, or a total of $32,000.[2] Other schools have provided support from general school funds with intramural directors receiving a salary supplement on much the same basis as athletic coaches.[3]

Some schools charge a small intramural fee for such intramural activities as golf, tennis, ice skating, bowling, and swimming when local community facilities are used. A part of student activities fees is used by other schools to help finance intramurals in states in which it is legal to charge an activity fee. Special fund-raising projects have been used, but this procedure generally is not recommended. Charging a small admissions fee for championship intramural games held on selected evenings also has been tried with some success when the program has been properly publicized and advertised.

In summary, the best and most logical source of financing is from general school funds. All taxpayers then support it for the benefit of all students who desire to participate in it.

SUMMARY

Intramural athletics should be an extension of physical education to provide supplementary competitive experiences to all students not currently participating in interscholastic athletics.

Many schools give insufficient attention to intramurals because of a lack of facilities, inadequate funding, or low priority, among other reasons.

Girls' intramural activities have been superior to boys', but the emphasis on girls' interscholastic athletics may have an adverse effect upon them.

A school should establish definite objectives for its intramural program just as it does for any other educational program.

The administration of the intramural program should be well planned and organized to involve students under the supervision of a director of intramurals.

There is a wide variety of sports activities which may be included in an intramural program.

Eligibilitiy rules for interscholastic athletics should not be applied to intramurals, except that participants should be good school citizens and shall have passed a physical examination.

Appropriate awards should be given for achievement in intramurals to add to their significance for students.

Policies and procedures should be established to guide the intramural program.

It is best to have intramurals financed from board of education funds, but other methods are also used.

QUESTIONS AND TOPICS FOR STUDY AND DISCUSSION

1. Discuss intramural versus interscholastic athletics. Are these programs in opposition to each other?
2. How may the interscholastic athletic program be likened to bands, orchestras, school plays? To what can the intramural program be compared?
3. What is meant by extramural athletic competition? How can it make intramurals more interesting?
4. What were some of the findings among soldiers in World War II regarding intramurals?
5. Prepare a statement of general objectives for an intramural program. Discuss.
6. Assume that you are the intramural director of a school of 500 students. Outline an administrative plan for conducting intramurals in this school.
7. Explain in detail how you would involve students in the administration of intramural activities.
8. List and explain the types of competition common in intramural athletics.
9. Assuming that you are the intramural director of a school of your choice, outline the procedures you would employ to develop the program of intramural activities you would recommend to your school administrators and board of education.
10. Give reasons why intramural activities should be financed from general school funds.

NOTES

1. Division for Girls' and Women's Sports of the American Association for Health, Physical Education, and Recreation, *Philosophy and Standards for Girls' and Women's Sports* (Washington, D.C.: The Association, 1970), pp. 32–34.

2. *Journal of Physical Education and Recreation* (Washington, D.C.: American Association for Recreation, March 1975), 23.

3. Ibid., 23.

BIBLIOGRAPHY

COBB, ROBERT A., AND PAUL M. LEPLEY, eds. *Contemporary Philosophies of Physical Education and Athletics*, pp. 245–60. Columbus, Ohio: Charles E. Merrill Co.

Intramurals for the Senior High School—A Survey. Washington, D.C.: The Athletic Institute, 1958.

MUELLER, P., AND E. D. MITCHELL. *Intramural Sports*. New York: Ronald Press, 1960.

SEATON, DON CASH, et al. *Physical Education Handbook*. Englewood Cliffs, N.J.: Prentice-Hall, Inc., 1974.

TEFF, JIM. "Scheduling Intramural Programs." *Interscholastic Athletic Administration*, 6, no. 3 (Spring 1980), 28–29.

15

Junior High School Athletics

The development of junior high school athletics has had its greatest impetus during the last half century. It has come about largely as the result of: (1) attempts to find a solution to administrative problems caused by the rapid growth in high school attendance, and (2) the desire to provide a broader program better adapted to the needs of all junior high school students. The curriculum has been enriched, a limited number of terminal courses have been introduced, and exploratory courses have been added. In more recent years special education classes have been introduced for those with limited academic aptitude. The junior high school is now an established administrative unit in many school systems across the nation.

DEVELOPMENT OF ATHLETICS IN JUNIOR HIGH SCHOOLS

Just as the senior high school imitated intercollegiate athletic programs, the junior high schools began to pattern their athletic programs after those found in the senior high schools. Rules for games were modified so they more nearly met the level of competition for students in grades seven, eight, and nine. The interscholastic program was simply stepped down from the ninth-to-twelfth grade level to the seventh-to-ninth grade level.

The type of program most appropriate for junior high school has been a matter of controversy for many years. High school coaches often look upon it as a *farm system* for high school varsity squads. An opposite position has been taken by several professional education organizations. The Joint Committee on Athletic Competition for Children of Elementary and Junior High School Age (representatives from the National Education Association; the National Council of State Consultants in Elementary Education; the Department of Elementary School Principals; the Society of State Directors of Health, Physical Education, and Recreation; and the American Association

for Health, Physical Education, and Recreation) issued the following statement in 1952:

> A few *invitational* contests in certain sports between schools (or natural neigh-
> borhood groups) on an *informal* basis might be carried on—but only as a sup-
> plement to good instruction in physical education, recreational opportunities
> for all children within the school, and additional informal recreational oppor-
> tunities during out-of-school hours. . . .
>
> Interscholastic competition of a varsity pattern and similarly organized
> competition under auspices of other community agencies are *definitely dis-
> approved* for children below the ninth grade.[1]

In 1954 the Educational Policies Commission of the National Education
Association and the American Association of School Administrators, after
three years of investigation and study, published a report containing the
following statements:

> The core of the athletic program in junior high school, as elsewhere, should
> be instruction in sports that takes place in the required classes in physical
> education. What is learned in such classes is applied in after-school and noon-
> hour games. . . .
>
> Junior high school pupils, with their increased social interests and more
> highly developed athletic skills, can profit from informal games with children
> of other schools. . . .
>
> Sports days and invitational games with nearby schools should be re-
> garded as an occasional extension of the intramural program to extramural
> dimensions rather than as a restricted form of interscholastic competition. . . .
>
> No junior high school should have a "school" team that competes with
> school teams of other junior high schools in organized leagues or tournaments.
> Varsity-type interscholastics for junior high boys and girls should not be per-
> mitted.[2]

The fact that the recommendations of these groups and others had little
effect upon junior high school athletics can be seen by noting that approximately 85 percent of the junior high schools had programs of interscholastics
in 1957–58.[3] This development has resulted more from outside influences than
from any fundamental change in philosophy on the part of educational leaders.
There has been a significant increase since World War II in the number of
organized competitive athletic programs sponsored by nonschool organizations and individual promoters. Leagues have been formed in baseball, basketball, and football. Age group competition has been organized in golf,
tennis, track, and swimming. Realizing that junior high school pupils were
going to play on teams outside the school if they did not have the opportunity
to participate in interschool competition, junior high schools have extended
their athletic programs to include more interscholastic competition. The history of junior high athletics is similar to that of senior high interscholastics

as discussed in Chapter 2. Despite initial resistance from school administrators and educational organizations, it was considered better to have students compete on teams supervised by school representatives than on teams with no such supervision. Thus it came about that interschool competition has been tolerated and given a certain amount of support.

Unable individually to cope with the problems of nonschool promotions, which resulted in interference and overemphasis on competition in the junior high program, junior high school representatives began to look to the state high school associations for help. In 1958 a group of Missouri junior high school principals requested that consideration be given to amending the Missouri State High School Activities Association Constitution to allow junior high schools to become members. The primary reason given was that such a move was necessary to establish standards and controls for junior high school athletics like those applicable to senior high interscholastics. A survey conducted by a committee of junior high school principals appointed by the Board of Control of the Missouri State High School Activities Association revealed that some junior high teams were playing more basketball games per season than senior high schools were permitted to play, and in some instances they were playing two tournament games on the same day. An amendment was adopted in 1959 admitting junior high schools to membership. Special regulations for junior high teams and players were included. According to these regulations interschool competition is allowed but is restricted. The maximum number of football games is 4, 5, and 6 and the maximum number of basketball games is 8, 10, and 12 for grades 7, 8, and 9, respectively. No district or state tournaments are permitted. The fact that some 500 junior high schools are included in the membership of the Association is evidence that standards and controls are considered necessary and desirable.

What occurred in junior high school athletics in Missouri is typical of the trend found in other states. Junior high interscholastics have increased, but efforts have been made to keep them in proper perspective by regulations adopted through junior high school conferences and state high school associations.

The New York association has a well-organized modified interscholastic sports program for its junior high schools.[4] It has the approval of the Medical Society of the State of New York, requires a set number of practice sessions with a maximum time limit for the length of a practice, provides for limitations on the number of games, encourages the inclusion of lifetime sports, and has modified game rules for contact sports. Adapting the program to the maturity level of junior high school students is important and has been a major objective of the New York and other state associations.

However, athletic programs for elementary school pupils have had considerable influence upon junior high school athletic competition. During the summer months nonschool organizations sponsor and promote competitive athletics for children this age, culminating in district, state, and national tournaments, particularly in baseball, basketball, track, and swimming, and some attempts have been made to conduct these activities during the school year. Because of interference with the academic and athletic programs of the junior high school, administrators began to take some steps to cope with the inherent problems. First, junior high schools began to seek membership in state high school associations for the purpose of establishing collective controls similar to those of senior high schools; and, second, interscholastic athletic competition in junior high schools was increased to satisfy the interests of junior high school students and their parents. This resulted primarily from the conclusion that junior high school boys and girls were going to compete in outside programs if the schools did not provide sufficient opportunities for interscholastic athletics.

Although as late as 1960 interscholastic athletics in junior high schools were condemned by James B. Conant in a report to school boards,[5] it also became clear by 1963 that outside pressures had influenced the philosophy guiding junior high school athletics as revealed in a report of the Junior High School Athletics Subcommittee of the Joint Committee on Standards for Interscholastic Athletics (see pages 354–355).

Interschool competition is now a part of the junior high school athletic program, and the problem facing athletic administrators and junior high school principals is how to best provide guidance and direction to ensure that it will contribute to the overall educational program and not detract from it.

GUIDING PRINCIPLES FOR JUNIOR HIGH SCHOOL ATHLETICS

Experience in athletic competition is desirable for all youth. Athletic participation for junior high school pupils will provide educational benefits and contribute toward desirable behavior only if it is based on sound principles consistent with the educational objectives of junior high schools. School officials should plan their programs in accordance with these principles.

Primary emphasis should be on providing educational experiences. Junior high school athletics should not exist merely to develop a "farm system" for the senior high school or to offer entertainment.

Physical education should receive first consideration in the athletic program. The program of physical activities required of all students should include instruction and the opportunity to play in a variety of games.

A well planned and well administered *program of intramurals* should complement the physical education program. Although not mandatory, all students should be encouraged to participate. They should be made to realize that intramural competition can be *fun* and will contribute further to the development of athletic skills.

The junior high athletic program should include a few *extramural contests* involving teams selected from among the intramural teams to compete against similar teams from other schools. These contests may occur on sports days and play days which will provide the more athletically skilled some additional opportunities for competition. If students can be given a good understanding of the fact that the extramural phase is a culmination of the physical education and intramural phases, this will serve as a stimulus for increased interest.

If a junior high school provides adequately for physical education, intramural, and extramural activities, it may offer additional opportunities for those pupils with superior athletic abilities to compete in a limited number of *interschool contests* with teams representing other junior high schools.

A report of the Junior High School Athletics Subcommittee of the Joint Committee on Standards for Interscholastic Athletics, sponsored by the American Association for Health, Physical Education and Recreation, the National Association of Secondary School Principals, and the National Federation of State High School Athletic Associations, issued in 1962, contains some significant guidelines for consideration in regard to junior high interscholastic competition. The following excerpts are drawn from the recommendations found in that report.

RECOMMENDATIONS OF THE COMMITTEE

Values of Participation

The Committee also reaffirms the belief that junior high school boys can profit educationally, as well as physically, from participation in well-planned and well-conducted programs of athletic activities of a competitive nature. Participation in such programs provides wholesome recreation and contributes materially to the development of (a) strength, endurance, and organic vigor; (b) proficiency in physical skills; and (c) the ability to compete ethically and to cooperate effectively.

The Committee wishes to emphasize that participation in athletic activities of a competitive nature does not automatically result in the benefits listed above. Participation in poorly planned or poorly conducted programs can harm the student physically and can contribute materially to the development of undesirable habits of behavior. Also, the Committee recognizes that in most junior high schools the benefits that may be derived from participation in competitive athletics can be realized as readily through intramural athletics as through interscholastic athletics. A well organized and properly administered interscholastics program requires additional money from the educational budget. The ever-increasing demands on the educational dollar make mandatory the justification of such a program. The Committee believes that an interscholastic athletic program in junior high school can be justified only if:

1. The school officials and the community greatly desire to offer the students the experience of participation in interscholastic athletics.

2. The programs can be controlled to the extent that the entertainment features of the program do not detract from its educational aspects.

3. Sufficient funds are available to support a program that offers the highest type of educational experience without jeopardizing the other phases of the physical education program.

Program of Interscholastic Athletics

In those junior high schools in which adequate programs of required physical education, intramurals, and physical recreation are provided for all students, a limited program of interscholastic athletics provides for boys with superior ability additional opportunities to fully develop and utilize this talent. Such programs of interscholastic athletics should be organized and conducted in accordance with the principles outlined below.

1. The interscholastic athletics program for boys in the junior high school should make definite contributions toward the accomplishment of the educational objectives of the school.

2. The interscholastic athletics program for boys in the junior high school should supplement—rather than serve as a substitute for—an adequate program of required physical education, intramurals, and physical recreation for all students.

3. The interscholastic athletics program for boys in the junior high school should, under the administration and the supervision of the appropriate school officials, be conducted by men with adequate professional preparation in physical education.

4. The interscholastic athletic program for boys in the junior high school should be so conducted that the physical welfare of the participants is protected and fostered.[6]

Consider factors in selecting sports for junior high school interscholastic competition. Several factors must be considered in selecting sports in which the junior high school will offer interscholastic participation. Interests and needs of students, staff, facilities, finances, scheduling limitations, opportunities to compete with other junior high schools, and community competitive programs are among the most important.

It is generally impossible for a school to provide adequately for all students to engage in interscholastic athletics. The fact that there are often several community organizations that offer competitive opportunities in some sports, particularly during the summer, makes it advisable to coordinate the school and community programs as much as possible. A wider offering including a greater variety of sports opportunities is thereby feasible. For example, if there is a good community baseball program in the summer, the school may not want to offer baseball in its spring interscholastic program, but may offer track, tennis, golf, or another sport. Whenever possible, school representatives should be involved with community organizations in giving direction to and in planning their programs. Junior and senior high school coaches are frequently sought to direct summer recreation programs. They should use this opportunity to better coordinate school and community programs in an attempt to offer broad sports opportunities to as many young people as realistically practical and to avoid unnecessary duplications and conflicts.

Provisions should be made for all students. Junior high school athletics should provide for all students through physical education, intramural, and inter-scholastic activities. The needs of and benefits to the less talented must be given attention. Intramural competition should not be limited to the talented, and interscholastics should include as many who desire to participate as possible. Some junior high schools have adopted a "no-cut" policy, which enables larger numbers to receive instruction, enjoy being "a member of the squad," and to take part in intrasquad scrimmage games. It is impossible to ascertain at this age with any high degree of reliability which individuals will have the most athletic ability by the time they are seniors in high school, or which will have the most interest in athletic participation in later life. Hence, basic instruction and experiences in a variety of sports should be widely extended.

The junior high school athletic program should be under the supervision of an administrator professionally prepared in physical education. In practically all states coaches must be certified teachers, but they are not required to have a major or minor in physical education and some are appointed junior high school athletic directors without this training. The person in charge of the junior high programs should have a good background in the philosophy and objectives of physical education and of junior high school interscholastic athletics.

Avoid specialization. Specialization is an integral part of today's society. However, it is unwise for any individual to decide to specialize until it can be determined in which field he or she has the most abiding interest, potential, and likelihood for success. Early specialization in athletics is no guarantee of producing a champion or of excellence in varsity competition in senior high school or college. Those who specialize too early may miss opportunities to develop themselves in other sports that might prove better suited for them. Definite seasons should be established in junior high school, which, among other advantages, will encourage participation in a variety of sports. Specialization at this age should be discouraged.

Teach the purposes and values of school athletics. There is no better place to teach the most worthwhile objectives of school athletics than in junior high school. These objectives are essentially the same as for senior high school (see Chapter 2). Personal values should be emphasized. The reasons why the school offers athletic experiences as a part of the educational program should be made clear. Too often athletes who play in junior and senior high school and intercollegiate athletics fail to understand the difference between school athletics and professional athletics. The primary purpose of athletics in a school setting is to provide individuals with experiences that are educational in nature, while professionals operate to sell entertainment as a business enterprise. Teaching the most important values of high school athletics is one of the principal responsibilities of physical education teachers and coaches.

Avoid overemphasis on winning.   Anyone who plays a competitive game should want to win. However, if winning is the only purpose the individual under-stands for playing the game, winning is being overemphasized. Students must be taught how to accept defeats without being emotionally upset and must come to understand that this will be of value in later life when they are confronted with failure in other endeavors. Parents of junior high athletes, too, should be helped to understand that athletics have values for their chil-dren even when games are lost. They may be prone to overemphasize winning unless this is done. Valuable lessons can be learned from realizing that mis-takes are a primary cause of losses, but it must be realized that half of those competing in a game will lose—there will be a winner and a loser. It is important to teach those who win that this achievement in itself may not be a significant accomplishment if other more important values do not accrue to the winners. There is less likelihood of overemphasis on winning when there is no neglect of attention given to the most important values of athletic participation.

Playing and practice schedules should be adapted to the emotional and physical maturity levels of the students.   The number of contests should be limited according to guidelines similar to those established in Missouri and New York (see page 352), and practice sessions should not exceed 90 minutes.

Proper medical supervision should be provided.   This is as important, and for the same reasons, in the junior high program as for senior high school athletics.

Prevent exploitation of junior high school programs and athletes.   All junior high school games should be sponsored by the school. Nonschool organiza-tions and individuals must not be permitted to use them to gain recognition, advertise, or for any other vested interests. All-star games should not be allowed. Athletes should be protected from overparticipation by regulations prohibiting them from competing on school and nonschool teams during the same season. This type of regulation also generally gives another student a chance to participate. Unless there are regulations and steps taken to prevent them, there will be attempts to exploit popular school programs and those athletes who have gained some degree of recognition.

MAJOR CONCERNS OF JUNIOR HIGH SCHOOL ATHLETIC ADMINISTRATORS

There may be one athletic administrator for both the junior and senior high athletic programs, or there may be a separate athletic director for the junior high school. In either case there will be some major concerns this person will have regarding the administration of the junior high athletic program.

Finances

Although the expenses are less, it is often more difficult to secure adequate financing for the junior high than for the senior high athletic program. Gate receipts are inevitably less and other sources must be sought. It is usually best that the financing be separate from the senior high program. Board of education funds are the most desirable source, but they are often insufficient and special fund-raising projects are conducted. Some which have proved successful for various schools include:

1. *Door-to-door sales by athletes and other students.* It is important that these involve useful and quality products from dependable companies. Some school administrators are opposed to selling campaigns, but if properly planned and conducted, they can be educational. If such a plan is adopted, students should be taught how to be courteous in selling, how to graciously accept refusals, and how to express appreciation for the time of the person contacted and for any support received. We generally appreciate more those things we earn ourselves, and students may appreciate school athletics more if they share in the responsibility of securing adequate financing. A list of reputable companies which have products available for school fund raising can be obtained from the National Federation. Students receive a commission from sales with the receipts to be used to finance school activities.

2. *Concession and vending machines.* (See page 261.)

3. *Booster club donations.* Booster clubs sometimes provide financial support in the form of funds or in purchasing equipment. In either case the school should determine the use of any money received and specify any equipment which may be purchased to help avoid that organization's determining or interfering with school policy.

4. *School carnivals, fairs, or bazaars.* In some instances considerable amounts have been raised from such projects. Parents and booster club members are usually glad to cooperate by donating their services in the administration of these events.

Fund-raising projects conducted by students are legitimate if they involve real learning experiences; of course they must not conflict with the study and academic responsibilities of students.

How to Reduce Expenses

Along with fund raising comes the necessity of reducing expenditures as much as possible without damaging the athletic program. Possibilities of accomplishing this include:

1. *Buying on bids.* (See page 244.)

2. *Proper care and repair of equipment.* Junior high school athletic equipment that receives proper care and repair will generally last longer than comparable senior high equipment because of fewer contests and shorter practice periods.

3. *Using "hand-me-down" equipment from senior high school.* Equipment unsuitable for use in senior high school should not be accepted for junior high school athletics, but the senior high school occasionally has player equipment which is too small for senior high school athletes and which will properly fit those in junior high school.

4. *Making use of volunteer help.* Services of a number of individuals are required in operating concession stands and in the management of contests. Parents and booster club members are generally happy to assist in these matters, and the faculty and students should assume their fair share in them.

It is important for the athletic administrator to pursue these and other possibilities of reducing expenses which will not adversely affect the physical welfare of students and the educational values of junior high school athletics.

Difficulties in Adequate Staffing

Due to a personnel shortage, it has become increasingly difficult to employ a sufficient number of qualified coaches for senior high school sports, and the problem is still more serious at the junior high level. Many coaches are of the opinion that to secure advancement it is better to start as an assistant coach in a senior high school than as a head coach in a junior high school. The retention of junior high coaches is another concern. Equal salary schedules help somewhat, but the greater recognition and publicity received by senior high coaches tend to offset this. The fact that a number of coaches begin their careers in junior high school and then graduate to senior high school results in a lack of experiential background and less competent coaching in junior high school. Several athletic directors have found that in-service programs will help to alleviate this problem.

The National Federation's Annual Conference of High School Directors of Athletics includes a session in which athletic administrators can pool their concerns regarding junior high school athletics and share methods of solving or alleviating them. Recommendations offered can be found in the proceedings published after each conference.

GUIDELINES FOR LEVELS OF ATHLETIC COMPETITION

It was mentioned earlier in this chapter that junior high schools were looking to state high school associations for help in resolving their interscholastic problems. Evidence of this fact is a resolution adopted in 1966 by the National Federation of State High School Athletic Associations. No discussion of appropriate types of athletics for junior high school would be complete without giving this resolution careful attention (see pages 58–60).

SUMMARY

Interscholastic athletics are now a part of the athletic program of the typical junior high school. Although there was opposition to this development, the tremendous increase since World War II in organized athletic competition sponsored by nonschool organizations for pre-high school age students convinced school officials that junior high boys were going to compete. It was realized that it would be better for them to participate during the school year on teams under the supervision of the school than on outside teams in programs patterned after professional athletics, with championships and all-star games. Standards and limitations have been established and are being enforced through state high school associations in several states. Athletics administrators and school officials are attempting to keep them in proper perspective within the junior high school educational program.

NOTES

1. American Association for Health, Physical Education and Recreation, *Desirable Athletic Competition for Children* (Washington, D. C.: The Association, 1952), p. 4.
2. Educational Policies Commission, *School Athletics—Problems and Policies* (Washington, D. C.: The Commission, National Education Association, 1954), pp. 35–36.
3. American Association for Health, Physical Education and Recreation, *Standards for Junior High School Athletics* (Washington, D.C.: The Association, 1963), pp. 7–8.
4. New York State Public High School Athletic Association, *1980–82 Handbook,* pp. 89–120.
5. J. B. Conant, *A Memorandum to School Boards: Recommendations for Education in the Junior High School Years* (Princeton, N.J.: Educational Testing Service, 1960).
6. American Association for Health, Physical Education and Recreation, *Standards for Junior High School Athletics,* pp. 14–19.

BIBLIOGRAPHY

ALLEY, LOUIS E. "Junior High Interscholastic Athletics?" *NEA Journal,* 50, no. 5 (May 1961), 10–13.

AMERICAN ASSOCIATION FOR HEALTH, PHYSICAL EDUCATION AND RECREATION. *Desirable Athletic Competition for Children.* Washington D. C.: The Association, 1952.

———. *Standards for Junior High School Athletics*. Washington, D.C.: The Association, 1963.

BIGGERS, JULIAN. "Alternative Sources to Funding a Junior High Program." *Proceedings,* National Federation's Twelfth Annual National Conference of High School Directors of Athletics, pp. 72–74. Kansas City, Mo.: National Federation, 1981.

BOOKER, TED. "Junior High Program—Financing and Fund Raising." *Proceedings,* National Federation's Eleventh Annual National Conference of High School Directors of Athletics, pp. 72–74. Kansas City, Mo.: National Federation, 1980.

COBB, ROBERT A., AND PAUL M. LEPLEY, eds. *Contemporary Philosophies of Physical Education and Athletics,* pp. 92–110. Columbus, Ohio: Charles E. Merrill Publishing Co., 1973.

CONANT, JAMES B. *A Memorandum to School Boards: Recommendations for Education in the Junior High School Years.* Princeton, N.J.: Educational Testing Service, 1960.

EDUCATIONAL POLICIES COMMISSION. *School Athletics—Problems and Policies,* pp. 35–36. Washington, D. C.: The Commission, National Education Association, 1963.

NEW YORK STATE PUBLIC HIGH SCHOOL ATHLETIC ASSOCIATION. *1980–82 Handbook.* pp. 89–120.

O'CONNOR, DONALD K. "Special Concerns of the Junior High Athletic Director." *Proceedings,* National Federation's Tenth Annual National Conference of High School Directors of Athletics, pp. 34–36. Kansas City, Mo.: National Federation, 1979.

16

Legal Aspects
of Interscholastic Activities

As in many areas of current societal affairs, there is an increasing tendency across the nation to take matters relating to interscholastic activities to court. No longer can the individual school or state high school association adopt standards and regulations without giving consideration to whether they will be upheld if legally challenged. Rules are no longer accepted without being questioned. Of particular significance is that more attention is being given by legal bodies to the protection of *individual* rights and freedoms, including those of students. This is evident from decisions pertaining to freedom of speech, dress, grooming, and so on.

Judicial decisions sometimes cause it to appear that *individual rights* are given more favorable consideration than *individuals' rights*. Rules and regulations established by *individuals* through an organization are prone to be challenged by an *individual* who does not want to comply with them although they may have been adopted from the basic belief that they were in the best interests of the majority. So it is with schools and their state high school associations whose representatives have adopted standards and regulations believed to be in the best interests of the great majority of students. Some are beginning to think that individual challenging of standards is eroding the rights of *individuals* to make reasonable regulations. The so-called permissiveness in society may well be the result of this situation.

NECESSITY OF BASIC LEGAL UNDERSTANDING

It is important for school officials to be aware of the trend to seek relief through the courts. Over 200,000 civil suits of various types were filed in federal courts in 1982, and the last year, 1977, for which the National Center for State Courts compiled a complete record, more than 12,000,000 cases were filed in state courts.[1] In earlier suits involving interscholastic athletics, the legal authority of schools and state associations was challenged by charging that rules and regulations established by them violated constitutional rights of athletes; more recently, however, the most serious charges have been in the areas of liability for negligence and product liability. Today's school administrators, directors of athletics, and coaches must understand how legal issues may arise in these areas and how best to cope with them. They must be familiar with the fundamental requirements of *due process* and the general position taken by the courts in various types of cases. It is well to consider a few of the more significant areas in which legal problems may occur.

Negligence

Athletic directors, coaches, and school administrators should understand the basic elements of *torts,* which are all damages except those that result from breaking a contract or committing a crime. Negligence torts present the greatest danger for those responsible for athletic activities. Liability for negligence is established in a law suit by proving the defendant guilty of the following:

1. A breach of the duty of due care to protect a person from unreasonable risk of injury or damages.
2. Failure to see that the danger of risk or injury was proximate.
3. An act, or the omission of an act, that resulted in injury or damages.
4. The act, or omission of the act, that was the actual cause of the injury.

There is a tendency in litigation to name as codefendants all parties directly or indirectly involved in cases involving injuries. These include the coach, the athletic director, school administrators, and members of the board of education or school district committee. The best protection against suits is to establish policies and procedures which will help prevent injuries. A well organized and administered safety program is in itself important in defending against any charge of negligence.

Such a program begins with the board of education. Of immediate importance is the employment of only those coaches who meet accepted certification standards. Each coach must have a functional knowledge in the following areas:

1. First aid
2. Care and treatment of injuries
3. The necessary and proper fitting of protective equipment
4. Physiological foundations of athletics
5. Safety rules contained in the official playing rules for the particular sport
6. Appropriate drills for conditioning athletes for the sport concerned
7. Methods of teaching safety techniques for practice and competition

8. The health and nutritional needs of athletes

9. Essential supervision necessary in the dressing room, on the practice and playing field or floor, and in transportation

10. Safety guidelines to provide athletes and parents

11. The risks of injury the athlete will be taking in the sport involved.

In times of a shortage of coaches, boards of education are sometimes prone to employ nonfaculty persons or paraprofessionals to coach particular sports. Great care must be exercised in these instances to make certain such individuals have an adequate background and training essential in the care and treatment of injuries in order to avoid any grounds for claims of negligence in their employment.

Providing proper medical supervision is another important responsibility of the board of education. It should make certain its administrative representatives make arrangements for a team physician, and it is wise to have a certified athletic trainer for the athletic program.

An official statement of safety policies and procedures for use by the athletic staff, developed by the staff and high school principal and officially approved by the board of education, can be significant in both preventing and defending against charges of liability for negligence against the district.

The board of education must either provide athletic accident insurance or adopt a policy requiring athletes and parents to provide it before a student can become a member of an athletic squad.

The superintendent and/or high school principal are often named codefendants in negligence suits. Because the laws in several states provide some degree of sovereign immunity for school districts, charges in these states are commonly brought against individuals, including the superintendent and principal. Anyone in a supervisory position can be held liable for the negligence of individuals under his/her supervision. For example, in *Vargo* v. *Svitchan,* 301 N.W. 2d 1 (Mich. App. 1981) the principal was held responsible for the actions of a coach who required a student to lift weights which resulted in an injury.

It is important for both the superindendent and the principal to make certain a broad safety program is formulated, effective policies and procedures are established, and that each person, including athletes, connected with the athletic activities of the school assumes his or her responsibility in implementing the safety measures involved. Further, they must be aware that if any coach is found to be negligent and is not fully qualified, they can be liable for negligence in recommending that individual for employment. All persons in supervisory positions can be held liable for the actions of those responsible to them, which makes it vital for superintendents and principals to exercise proper supervision over athletic directors and coaches.

The athletic director may be a defendant or codefendant in a suit based on charges of negligence. Because of his/her supervisory position, the athletic administrator may be held responsible for the actions of coaches as well as for any negligence on their part. He or she should give careful attention to ways of helping to avoid litigation, including:

1. The purchase of recognized quality protective player equipment
2. Making sure the athletic field or floor is kept free of any hazards
3. Providing for ample supervision in implementing safety measures in all phases of the athletic program, including transportation
4. Sponsoring in-service programs to keep coaches and athletic trainers up to date in providing for the health and safety of athletes
5. Supervising the distribution of safety guidelines and policies to athletes and their parents
6. Making certain all coaches properly instruct players in the fundamental and particular playing techniques for the sports concerned and warn them of the risks involved
7. Keeping complete records of all athletic injuries
8. Recommending only fully qualified coaches for employment
9. Arranging for adequate medical supervision
10. Contracting competent game officials

State laws differ regarding liability for negligence of school districts and their agents. The Washington Supreme Court ruled in *Carabba* v. *Anacortes School District*, (1967) No. 38188 72 Wn. 2d 939 Pac 2d 936 that the assumption of risk doctrine was inapplicable to action against school districts for injuries due to negligence of districts acting through their agent, the referee. In various states the individual employing an incompetent referee could be held liable. In either situation the athletic administrator must excerise great care in selecting game officials and others who assume responsibility in contest management.

The coach is in the most strategic position to both prevent charges of negligence and to be sued for liability for such. In two cases involving heat prostration and the death of one athlete, the Michigan Court of Appeals, Division 2, in *Lovitt* v. *Concord School District* and *Cecil* v. *Concord School District*, (1975) Nos. 19657 and 19658 58 Mich. App. 593, 228 N.W. 2d 479 ruled that the doctrine of governmental immunity could be applied to protect the school district and its employees executing functions of the school; but that individual teachers must account for their personal acts of negligence.

The Appellate Court of Illinois, First District, Third Division held in essence in *Thomas* v. *Chicago Board of Education*, (1978) No. 77–117 377 N.E. 2d 55 that coaches and school districts are liable for negligence when players are not warned of the hazards of football.

These and similar cases make it imperative for the coach to exercise every precaution to avoid any grounds for negligence charges. Some of the most important precautionary measures include:

1. Keeping abreast of the latest knowledge and techniques in the cause and prevention of injuries
2. Regularly inspecting all player and game equipment to make certain they meet required safety standards
3. Properly fitting all athletes with protective equipment for the sport involved
4. Carefully instructing players in the use of all safety equipment
5. Making certain all practice and playing fields and floors are free of hazards
6. Thoroughly acquainting players with the rules of safety contained in the game rules, including special points of emphasis
7. Carefully instructing players in all safety playing techniques and requiring their use in practice and competition
8. Issuing clear warnings of the risks taken in the sport and of possible injuries from failure to apply all safety measures, particularly of such acts as using the head in butt blocking, spearing, and so on
9. Preparing a statement of safety policies and risks involved for distribution to players and parents. (It is wise to require verification that these have been read and understood and that they will be applied.)
10. Providing sufficient appropriate drills to properly condition athletes for the sport concerned
11. Allowing no athlete to start practice for a sport without a certificate of fitness from a physician
12. Making certain all athletes are covered with athletic accident insurance prior to reporting for their first practice
13. Always acclimating athletes to heat and humidity factors
14. Making certain all vehicles transporting athletes are fully insured
15. Requiring parental permission for out-of-town trips
16. Providing proper supervision at all times and making sure any faculty members assisting in supervision are properly instructed
17. Checking to see that proper medical supervision is provided for both practices and games
18. Being prepared to administer first aid, but *careful not to practice medicine*
19. Keeping careful and complete records of all injuries, including the circumstances
20. *Exercising at all times the best judgment a reasonable person would under the circumstances*

Centralia High School in the state of Washington has developed a Safety List for football players, which they are required to read and sign as a way of reducing the risk of liability for negligence of coaches.[2] Similar statements can be prepared for other sports and are worthy of consideration.

Negligence is defined as the failure to excerise that degree of caution and good judgment necessary to avoid exposing others to unreasonable danger or risk of injury. Following the above suggestions will help to avoid circumstances in which a coach might be guilty of neglect, and because school administrators and athletic directors may be named as codefendants in litigation, it is important that they make certain coaches assume these precautionary responsibilities.

In defending against charges of negligence, the defendant seeks to prove contributory negligence on the part of the plaintiff. Was there an assumption of a known risk on the part of the plantiff? This is why it is extremely important that he/she be properly informed of the risk prior to the injury.

The frequency of legal suits and their costs have influenced many school districts to purchase liability insurance for the faculty, administrative staff, and members of the board of education for protection against tort liability. It is strongly recommended that the school district provide this coverage, but if it does not, the individual should purchase liability insurance.

Principles for Formulating Rules and Regulations

Rules and regulations will be challenged by some who do not want to conform to them and who will claim they are arbitrary and unreasonable. Standards established by the school and coaches' training rules are the most likely to be defied. Applying some basic principles in the formulation of rules will help to avoid or to minimize difficulties arising from the enforcement of them and lessen the likelihood of an unfavorable decision should there be court action. These guiding principles are suggested to coaches and all school officials involved in the establishing of rules and regulations:

1. Develop the need and reasons for the standard or regulation before it is adopted. The need and reasons should be well publicized.

2. Reasons must be related to the health and welfare of participants, performance of the individual or team, moral effect upon students, and educational factors.

3. Involve representatives of all groups or individuals, as far as practical, who will be affected. The level of involvement should be compatible with the level of the individuals' abilities and experiences.

4. Provide copies of the rules and regulations to all individuals to whom the standards will apply. It should be made certain that they understand them. Every coach should thoroughly teach athletes the standards of eligibility and training rules at the beginning of each sports season. It is recommended that each athlete be required to sign a statement verifying that he or she has studied these standards, understands them, and agrees to abide by them (see Chapter 5).

5. Outline the policies for enforcing standards and regulations. They must be enforced fairly and consistently, and the policies should be well publicized.

The importance of applying these principles can be seen by examining a few court decisions. A student in Tamalpais Union High School in California was not permitted to compete in track because of the length of his hair. The rule had been established in accord with principles essentially the same as the above. The court upheld the school's rule because the purposes for it were considered reasonable and were known by the athlete. *Jay Neuhaus* v. *Tamalpais Union High School,* California (1970),   No. C-70   304 GBH.

In New Jersey a court ruled that the standard length of hair was an essential part of the sport of wrestling, again because the rule had been established for valid reasons related to health, welfare, and performance. *Craig S. Willer* v. *Freehold Regional High School Board of Education,* No. C-1210-71, New Jersey (1972). On the other hand, students were reinstated to interscholastics when a Vermont court found that grooming regulations were applied only to athletes and, therefore, were not consistently applied. *Steven Dunham, Prentiss Smith, Paul B. Weber,* v. *Vermont Superintendent of Schools,* No. 5862, Vermont (1970), 312 F. Supp. 411.

DUE PROCESS

U. S. Supreme Court decisions have made it clear that students must be provided due process in the application of rules and regulations. If one analyzes the decisions handed down, it will be noted that they require that students be treated fairly by being permitted to present their side and that they understand the reasons for any action taken. The Civil Rights Act of 1971 brought any interference with constitutional rights into focus, including the right of due process. There is reason to believe that courts will continue to give close consideration to procedures of due process in the future. It is, therefore, wise for any school to have and to follow a procedure that will meet the requirements of due process in handling disciplinary and eligibility cases in interscholastics.

Elements of Due Process

There are five basic elements generally required in due process procedures applied to disciplinary and eligibility cases:

1. Athletes must have ample opportunity to know the standards and/or regulations they are to meet.
2. When there is evidence that a violation has occurred, there must be adequate notice of the charges.
3. Adequate time must be allowed for the athlete to prepare an answer to the charges and evidence in his or her behalf.
4. There must be an appropriate hearing to consider evidence against and in behalf of the athlete.

5. A fair and impartial decision must be made, and the decision should be put in writing.

Recommended Due Process Procedure

These basic elements will satisfy the rudimentary requirements of due process required by the courts. It is strongly suggested that each school formulate a statement of the due process procedure it will follow in handling eligibility and disciplinary cases. This should be done before there is a case. The steps outlined below are offered as guidelines for establishing a due process procedure:

1. The athlete will be informed of the charges against him or her. (It is best to put them in writing.)
2. The athlete will be allowed an appropriate time to prepare an answer to the charges and evidence in his or her behalf.
3. The school administrator will hold a hearing within seven days to allow the athlete to answer the charges and present evidence in his or her behalf. (The athlete may be asked to show reason why action should not be taken.)
4. A summary of the findings and the action taken will be put in writing, and the athlete will be provided a copy. (It is also recommended that coaches provide the athlete an opportunity to tell his or her side of the case before suspending or dismissing the athlete from the squad for breaking training rules.)
5. An appeals committee will hear an appeal if requested by the athlete or parents within seven days following notice of the action taken by the administrator. The following steps will be applied in an appeal hearing:
   a. The school administrator will present a written statement of findings and action taken under (4) above.
   b. Opportunity will be provided for the athlete and/or parents to present any additional evidence having a bearing on the case.
   c. A summary of the proceedings of the hearing and the committee's decision will be put in writing and mailed to the athlete and parents.
6. If the student and/or parents are not satisfied with the decision of the appeals committee, a hearing may be requested before the board of education. The principal or superintendent must receive a request for such hearing within seven days after the mailing of the appeals committee's findings and decision. The steps followed under (5) above will be applied in the board of education hearing.

State High School Association Due Process Procedures

The state high school association, likewise, should have an established procedure of due process under which appeals may be made from the decision of a board of education, or for handling the other appeals from a member school. It is best to have a policy providing that all appeals to the state association must be made through a member school. This school should place such an appeal when requested by an athlete or parents following a board of education decision. Unless this is done, complete due process may not be provided, which could be a factor should there be legal action. Steps suggested for a state association due process procedure are:

1. The school must present in writing the findings and decision of the board of education to the executive secretary of the association for an opinion. (In matters that do not involve appeals heard by the local board of education, full information shall be provided in writing.) The executive secretary will provide a hearing within seven days, summarize the findings, and mail the opinion to the school as soon as practical.

2. If not satisfied with the findings and opinion of the executive secretary, an appeal may be made by the school administrator for a hearing before the board of control or executive committee. (Some associations may have established a special appeals committee for this purpose.)

3. A hearing will be provided no later than the next regularly scheduled meeting of the board or executive committee. The following procedure will be applied:

   a. An administrator of the school shall provide in advance, with his/her letter requesting an appeal, a written statement of the findings and decision of the board of education and review it at the hearing.

   b. Opportunity will be given to present any additional information having a bearing on the case.

   c. A summary of the findings and decision of the state association board will be mailed within seven days to the school administrator and athlete or parents.

   d. If additional information which has a bearing on the case is obtained, the school may ask for a review hearing of the decision of the association. The procedures outlined above will again be applied.

Special Appeals Board

A few state associations have given some consideration to the formation of a special appeals board to review, upon request, decisions of its executive board. The Kansas Association has an appeals board elected from its board of directors, its legislative body, for such a purpose. Care must be taken in the election of a special appeals board or committee. Its members must be thoroughly knowledgeable of the standards and regulations adopted by the schools through the state association and of the philosophy and objectives of interscholastics.

In an appeal at any level, it should be made clear that the function of those hearing the appeal is to determine whether the existing rules were applied fairly and to see that justice has been provided. It must be understood that it is not a legislative body with authority to change a rule to which there is objection. Due process is the providing of a procedure to guarantee fairness and justice in the application of rules, and the primary purpose of an appeals body is to assist in seeing that this is done.

DEALING WITH UNRULY FANS

Providing for good sportsmanship is one of the important objectives of interscholastic athletics. However, there will be some acts of poor sportsmanship that will need attention. Unsportsmanlike conduct of coaches, players, and student spectators usually can be handled through proper school channels. Unruly fans can cause more serious problems, and occasionally there are some cases that are difficult to handle. How to cope properly with them has been a matter of concern to many school administrators.

Some Missouri schools have successfully applied a procedure recommended by their state association for dealing with individual fans guilty of serious infractions. If a gross act of unsportsmanlike conduct occurs, such as abusiveness toward officials or drinking intoxicating beverages, the fan is informed that because of those actions, he or she is being asked to appear before the board of education to show reason why admission to future games should not be refused. The individual is thereby being afforded due process. In all cases reported, the fan appeared and guaranteed support of the standards of good sportsmanship and conduct in accordance with those standards at all times in the future. If the fan should fail to appear, the board of education could assume that it would not receive his or her cooperation and would notify the individual that he or she is being barred until such time as good conduct is assured. Although not tested in any court case in Missouri, it is believed that the board of education would be acting within its legal authority, as in the ruling on a similar case, *Tamelleo* v. *New Hampshire Jockey Club, Inc.,* 102 N.H. 547. 163 A.2d 10 (1960). It would have reason to conclude that the fan might be prone to repeat acts of misconduct or poor sportsmanship, which would further embarrass the school, have an adverse effect upon other adult spectators and students, and be detrimental to the attainment of the most worthwhile objectives of interscholastics.

A fan may be ejected by an official from the vicinity of a game for flagrant or persistent acts of unsportsmanlike conduct. Rule 10–9 of the National Federation *Basketball Rule Book* includes a penalty providing that for flagrant or persistent infraction "he shall go to the locker room or leave the building until the game is ended." The official is further authorized to forfeit the game for failure to comply.

When there is just cause, the school may have a fan removed from the gymnasium or field. The person must be afforded civil treatment, physically and verbally, but may be removed by force if the offender becomes abusive or violent. Any force used, however, must not be excessive, and it is best to have an officer of the law carry out the ejection. It is generally a wise policy to refund the admission when a fan is evicted.

Any fan guilty of deliberately striking an official, or any person for that matter, should be promptly charged and prosecuted.

State association action can be taken. Virtually all state high school associations have standards authorizing them to take action against a member school for the unsportsmanlike conduct of coaches, players, or team followers. Action is generally taken only when the school does not, or cannot, take proper action. Some have questioned the authority of a state association to take action against or to bar an individual fan from attending games. However, the association does have the authority to discipline its schools and may consider prohibiting a school team from competing in the presence of a fan who has committed a gross act of misconduct. In *Watkins* v. *Louisiana High School Athletic Association* (1974), Louisiana Court of Appeals, Third Circuit, No. 4706 301 So. 2d 695 the court ruled that if there is a right to be a spectator at athletic events, it is subject to reasonable nondiscriminatory limitations of the LHSAA with which courts will not interfere.

DISCRIMINATION

Any standards adopted by schools or state associations must be devoid of any discrimination on the basis of race, religion, or sex. Many schools and some associations in the past have had regulations that prohibited interscholastic athletic competition for girls. The civil rights and women's liberation movements have been influential in reversing this situation, and girls' interscholastic competition is now being promoted.

Court cases have made it clear that discrimination on the basis of sex is prohibited and that schools must provide comparable opportunities for girls and boys or permit girls to compete on boys' teams. *Cynthia Morris* v. *Michigan State Board of Eucation*, No. 38169, Michigan (1972); *Debbie Reed* v. *Nebraska School Activities Association*, CV-72-L-145, Nebraska (1972).

The U.S. Department of Health, Education and Welfare Guidelines for Federal Enforcement of Title IX of the Education Amendments of 1972 have had a profound influence on eliminating discrimination between the sexes in interscholastic athletics. *Subsection 86.41 Athletics* contains the following provisions:

(a) *General.* No person shall, on the basis of sex, be excluded from participation in, be denied the benefits of, be treated differently from another person or otherwise be discriminated against in any interscholastic, intercollegiate, club or intramural athletics offered by a recipient, and no recipient shall provide any such athletics separately on such basis.

(b) *Separate teams.* Notwithstanding the requirements of paragraph (a) of this section, a recipient may operate or sponsor separate teams for members of each sex where selection for such teams is based upon competitive skill or the activity involved is a contact sport. However, where a recipient operates or sponsors a team in a particular sport for members of one sex but operates or sponsors no such team for members of the other sex, and athletic opportunities for members of that sex have previously been limited, members of the excluded sex must be allowed to try out for the team offered unless the sport involved is a contact sport. For the purposes of this part, contact sports include boxing, wrestlng, rugby, ice hockey, football, basketball, and other sports the purpose or major activity of which involves bodily contact.

(c) *Equal opportunity.* A recipient which operates or sponsors interscholastic, intercollegate, club, or intramural athletics shall provide equal opportunity for members of both sexes. In determining whether equal opportunities are available the director will consider, among other factors:

  (i) whether the selection of sports and levels of competition effectively accommodate the interests and abilities of members of both sexes;
  (ii) the provision of equipment and supplies;
  (iii) scheduling of games and practice time;
  (iv) travel and per diem allowance;
  (v) opportunity to receive coaching and academic tutoring;
  (vi) assignment and compensation of coaches and tutors;
  (vii) provision of locker rooms, practice and competitive facilities;
  (viii) provision of medical and training facilities and services;
  (ix) provision of housing and dining facilities and services;
  (x) publicity.

  Unequal aggregate expenditures for members of each sex or unequal expenditures for male and female teams if a recipient operates or sponsors separate teams will not constitute noncompliance wth this section, but the director may consider the failure to provide necessary funds for teams for one sex in assessing equality of opportunity for members of each sex.

(d) *Adjustment period.* A recipent which operates or sponsors interscholastic, intercollegiate, club or intramural athletics at the elementary level shall comply fully with this section as expeditiously as possible but in no event later than one year from the effective date of this regulation. A recipient which operates or sponsors interscholastic, intercollegiate, club or intramural athletics at the secondary or post-secondary level shall comply fully with this section as expeditiously as possible but in no event later than three years from the effective date of this regulation.[3]

In brief, Title IX guidelines require comparable opportunities for both sexes. Except for contact sports, if a school offers a sport for one sex but not the other, both sexes must be permitted to try out for the same team. If the sport is offered separately for both sexes, team membership may be restricted by sex. To provide opportunities for a greater number of boys and girls, schools should provide separate teams for each sex. Otherwise, the number of girls competing in interscholastic athletics at the senior high school level would be limited.

Each superintendent should have received from the U.S. Department of Health, Education and Welfare a copy of the *Memorandum to Chief State School Officers, Superintendents of Local Educational Agencies, and College and University Presidents, Subject: Elimination of Sex Discrimination in Athletic Programs,* September, 1975. This publication contains valuable information for taking affirmative action in providing comparable opportunities for both sexes.

Of greater concern to schools than Title IX itself has been the number of legal suits brought under the Fourteenth Amendment, many of which have been prompted by Title IX guidelines. Although the decisions are generally based on whether comparable opportunities for boys and girls exist and petitions are denied if they do, the decisions are mixed. As previously stated, courts generally have ruled in favor of girls when they were not afforded comparable opportunities and sought to play on boys' teams. However, in *Clark* v. *Arizona Interscholastic Association, U.S. District Court* (Arizona 1981) No. CIV81-42-TUC-RMB, in which an injunction was sought against the Arizona association's rule prohibiting boys from playing on the girls' volleyball team, the court held the rule was reasonably related to increasing opportunities for girls to participate.

Although Title IX makes an exception for contact sports, court decisions are not always analogous. In *Darrin* v. *Gould* (1975), Washington Supreme Court, No. 43276 85 Wn. 2d 859 540 P. 2d 882, the court ruled in favor of two girls who sought to play on their schools' football team.

State high school association rules regarding athletes playing on teams of the opposite sex vary. Except for contact sports, several allow teams of mixed sexes if comparable opportunities are not afforded. A few have no restrictions but require a mixed team to compete in the boys' division in any state association tournament series.

The most significant result of Title IX and court rulings on sex discrimination in athletics is that they have operated to increase opportunities for girls in interscholastic athletics.

STANDARDS OF ELIGIBILITY AND THE LAW

Practically all standards of eligibility have been challenged in court at some time, and all schools and state associations face this possibility. To reduce this possibility and to be in a more favorable position should there be legal action, the following are strongly recommended:

1. Eligibility should be clearly defined. The definition should be included in the state association's constitution and in the school's athletic handbook. It is best if the two are the same. It should be clear that participation in interscholastics is a privilege and not an inherent right of an individual. Missouri has such a definition, which is also included in a number of handbooks or policy statements of its member schools (see Chapter 5).

2. The reasons and necessity for the rule must be well established. It must be proved in court hearings that the rule in question is not arbitrary or capricious and that it was adopted for valid reasons that made it necessary. The reasons should be related to the objectives of interscholastics and to the best interests of the great majority of boys and girls.

3. It must meet the test of reasonableness. When there is room for two opinions regarding the rule, although reasonable minds may differ, courts will accept

it as meeting this test. *Brown* v. *Wells*, 288 Minn. 468, 181 N.W. 2d 708 (1970).

4. The rule must be applied consistently.

Eligibility Standards Challenged by Court Action

Age.   Reasonable age standards have been upheld consistently by the courts. They are necessary to prevent danger to the health and safety of athletes at the lower end of the age scale from competing against older ones, to provide equity among competing players and teams, and to prevent "laying out of school" to gain maturity, thus resulting in inequity in competition. The age rules of state associations were discussed in Chapter 5. Although most state associations have a "hardship" rule, which authorizes its executive board to waive a regulation in emergency situations, the age standard is one that is not waived. *State of Missouri, ex rel. Missouri State High School Activities Association* v. *The Honorable Fred E. Schoenlaub*, No. 58.477. 507 S.W. 2d 354 Supreme Court of Missouri (1974).

All-star rule.   Most states have an all-star rule patterned after the National Federation recommended rule (see Chapter 3). One of the earliest cases involving an all-star rule was in Texas. *University Interscholastic League* v. *Midwestern University*, No. A-3802, 255 S.W. 2d 177, Supreme Court of Texas (1952). The court's decision was based on the "fact that a voluntary organization has the right to enact and enforce rules." One of the chief purposes of all-star rules is to prevent exploitation of high school athletes and the interscholastic program, which is considered reasonable.

Attendance rules.   Attendance rules of schools and state associations will be upheld by the courts if applied consistently. In *Edward S. Voelker* v. *Louisiana High School Association*, No. 14,985 (1971), the court held that the LHSAA was the recognized body to fix definite standards of eligibility and to enforce strict and impartial adherence. The fact that the rule had been applied uniformly in other situations was important in this case.

Award standards.   *Morrison* v. *Roberts*, 82 P.2d 1023, Oklahoma (1938) is an historic case, not only because it held that the courts should not interfere with the enforcement of the Oklahoma rule, but because it established the precedent that participation in interscholastic athletics competition is a privilege rather than an inherent constitutional right. It has been cited in numerous other cases and has been helpful to state high school associations in developing better definitions of eligibility.

Outside competition.   All state associations have limited team membership regulations prohibiting a player from engaging in nonschool competition during the high school season in the same sport (some even prohibit post-season contests). The courts have consistently upheld the reasonableness of such regulations in most cases. An example is *Reisdorff* v. *Nebraska School Activities Association* (1977), U.S. District Court, District of Nebraska No. 77-0-3. The plaintiff was ruled ineligible for competing in a meet sponsored by a private gymnastics club during the high school season. The court found the association's rule reasonable and the enforcement by the association not unconstitutional.

Sportsmanship and good conduct standards. Several cases involving standards of good conduct have been tried in court. In all instances these rules have been supported. In *John C. Stock* v. *Texas Catholic League, et al.*, CA 3-7577 B, Texas (1973), the plaintiff contended that he was deprived of a constitutional right after he had been ruled ineligible for misconduct during a football game. The court ruled in favor of the defendant by refusing to assume jurisdiction.

Training rules. Coaches have always assumed the right to set training rules for their athletes, and this right has been recognized by the courts. It is recommended, however, that the rules be reasonable and that the principles suggested earlier in this chapter be applied in formulating them. An injunction was sought after a cocaptain was expelled from the team for breaking the no-smoking rule, but it was denied and the school's decision upheld. *James McMillen* v. *Doctor Alfred Jacques*, Pennsylvania (1974) No. 3912.

Scholarship standards. Minimum academic eligibility standards are applied in all states but New York. Few have challenged these standards. One interesting case was tried in Louisiana. Nineteen boys in St. Augustine High School were ruled ineligible by the Lousiana Association for failure to pass the required number of subjects. The school was fined $100 for using them in two games while they were ineligible. A temporary injunction against the LHSAA was obtained, a permanent injunction sought, and the school continued to use them in two subsequent games. The association filed a motion to dismiss. Both the permanent injunction and the motion to dismiss were denied, but the Federal District Court ruled that the LHSAA had the authority to discipline its schools. *St. Augustine* v. *Louisiana High School Athletic Association*, No. 67-1620, Louisiana (1967).

Semester rule. Athletes are limited to eight semesters of eligibility in virtually all states. This standard was upheld in three separate cases in Florida. *Timothy Murray* v. *Florida High School Activities Association* (1968); *Michael E. Ryan* v. *Florida High School Activities Association* (1968); *Dennis Arthur Lee* v. *Florida High School Activities Association*, No. 73-22569, Florida (1973).

These and other cases indicate that the courts recognize that without semester limitations gross inequity in competition could result.

Transfer rules. Transfers of enrollment are a source of many eligibility problems. All states allow a transfer student to be eligible immediately if there is a simultaneous change of residence of parents. Hardship situations complicate enforcement of this particular rule. In virtually all states, when there is no change of residence of parents and no hardship circumstances, the student who transfers is ineligible for a semester or for a year from the date of transfer.

A misinterpretation of transfer rules occurs when they are construed to be for the purpose of preventing recruiting of high school athletes for high school teams. The primary purpose of a transfer rule is to discourage "school hopping" by students who for one reason or another, such as becoming disgruntled with a coach or because of disciplinary action, decide to transfer enrollment to another school. All state associations have a specfic *recruiting rule* to prevent recruiting. Attorneys defending a school or high school association should be made aware of this fact.

There have been several court decisions involving transfer standards. When there were no extenuating or hardship conditions, rulings were favorable to the schools and state associations. *Tennessee Secondary School Athletic Association* v. *Cox*, 425 S.W. 2d 597, Tennessee (1968); *Bobby W. Kilpatrick* v. *Alabama High School Athletic Association*, No. 3359, Alabama (1970); *James Brashears and Marked Tree School District No. 28* v. *Arkansas Activities Association*, No. LR–72–C–255, Arkansas (1972). The rulings in these cases are typical to those in others involving similar circumstances.

It is wise for associations to have a hardship clause under which certain emergency transfers can be considered. These have to be carefully administered to prevent abuse, but there are some circumstances that occasionally make it necessary for a student to transfer schools without a change of residence of parents. If a court should consider the application of a rule unreasonable or arbitrary, a transfer athlete may obtain a favorable decision. *Warren B. Sturrup* v. *Robt. Nahan, Phil Eskew, Indiana High School Athletic Association*, No. 174 S 14, 305 N.E. 2d 877, Indiana Supreme Court.

Recruiting rules. A precedent was set by the Supreme Court of Ohio in *Canton-McKinley* v. *Ohio High School Athletics Association*, No. 37342, Supreme Court of Ohio (1961). The school was suspended when an assistant football coach used undue influence in transfers of students from a neighboring school. A restraining order against the Ohio association was granted by the County Judge of Common Pleas. On appeal, the Supreme Court ruled that "A court has no jurisdiction to enjoin a voluntary association or its members from enforcing a penalty."

The courts recognize that recruiting rules are necessary in high school athletics to maintain fairness and equity in competition, prevent "raiding" of good athletes, and to avoid ill feeling among schools.

Dress and grooming standards. Court decisions have not been completely consistent in cases involving dress and grooming regulations. Reasons for establishing these standards must be educationally sound and cannot be arbitrary or capricious. Courts will generally uphold a dress or haircut rule if it is reasonable, contributes to the health and welfare of athletes, is necessary to prevent demoralizing others, is related to performance, and is applied consistently without discrimination. Three court decisions concerning haircut rules have been cited previously in this chapter (see page 368).

Married students. Very few state associations have had a rule prohibiting married students from participating in interscholastics. However, prior to 1971 many local school districts had such rules, and the courts upheld these regulations. In 1971, a married woman student challenged the rule of the Iowa Girls' High School Athletic Union and won a favorable decision in the United States District Court for the Southern District of Iowa. It was established in court that the prohibition against married students applied only to girls and not to boys in Iowa, which was considered discriminatory. The court ruled, therefore, that she could not be deprived of equal protection under the Iowa Constitution. *Jane Rubel* v. *Iowa Girls' High School Athletic Union*, No. 11–412–C–2, United States District Court for the Southern District of Iowa (1971).

Since 1971 there has been a trend toward courts reversing their former position, and they have invalidated "married student" rules. Although some local school boards still have regulations prohibiting married students from participating in extracurricular activities, it is becoming increasingly difficult to enforce them.

NATIONAL FEDERATION LEGAL AID PACT

We have cited only a few of the many cases decided in the area of interscholastic athletics in order to illustrate specific points. Several years ago the National Federation began providing state associations with its Legal Aid Pact, a compilation of court cases involving interscholastics arranged alphabetically according to the subjects of the cases. This project has now been taken over by Doug Ruedlinger, Inc., P. O. Box 2159, Topeka, Kansas 66601, as the Mutual Legal Aid Pact Summary of Cases. It is brought up to date annually and distributed to subscribers and members of the Fund Administrators Association. It contains a table of contents by subject classification of cases and an alphabetical listing of cases with summary decisions. It is an invaluable resource for attorneys representing schools and state high school associations. Any school confronted with legal action should have its attorney contact its state association, which will have a copy of the Mutual Aid Pact, briefs of many cases, and other valuable information.

LEGAL STATUS OF STATE HIGH SCHOOL ASSOCIATIONS

An excellent statement concerning the legal status of state associations is included in the National Federation of State High School Associations 1976–77 *Official Handbook.*

LEGAL STATUS OF STATE ASSOCIATIONS[4]

The legal status of state high school associations varies. In certain states, the organization is considered an instrument of the state and in others a completely independent body. The majority are designated as independent but quasigovernmental organizations responsible to the schools. The legal aspect of state associations is of increasing concern because of the frequency of court action. At one time, standards adopted by state associations were accepted without question. When they were not followed, or if they were ignored, the resulting disciplinary action was expected. Recently, however, nearly every rule and regulation is questioned. The attitude that "rules are for others but do not apply to me" is prevalent. When standards are applied and an individual or school is aggrieved, court action often follows.

The first recorded court action questioning the authority of a state high school association involved the Ohio High School Athletic Association. In 1924, the OHSAA declared some students of Scott High School in Toledo ineligible. An injunction was sought by Scott High School but was denied on the grounds that: (a) Scott High School, through the acts of its principal, became a bona fide member of the Ohio High School Athletic Association and thus became voluntarily subject to its rules and regulations; (b) the board of control in refusing to reinstate the boys of Scott High School, upon petition, was acting in good faith and was within its rights as provided by the rules and regulations of the association; and (c) under these conditions, the board of control did not transcend its authority nor violate any state law. Therefore, its action was legal and binding on the members involved.

There was a lull of 14 years before the next case involving a state association. This was the landmark case of 1938 of *Morrison* v. *Roberts of the Oklahoma High School Association.* In this case, a high school football player violated the award rule of the Oklahoma High School Athletic Association and the board of control declared him ineligible to play football for a one-year period. Court action was brought against the Oklahoma High School Association. The Supreme Court of Oklahoma, in ordering dismissal of the suit stated:

> The Plaintiff has many rights as a citizen and as a high school student, but he has no vested right in "eligibility" as dealt with at such great length in the rules of the Oklahoma High School Athletic Association. There is nothing unlawful or evil in either of those rules or in provision vesting final authority in the board of control.

This case established the authority for state high school associations to formulate and enforce rules of eligibility. It also established the principle that participation on an interscholastic athletic team was a privilege to be earned by meeting certain criteria.

Courts have held that those who are trained in education and administration are charged with the responsibility of developing reasonable rules of participation. In the *Brown* v. *Minnesota State High School League* case in 1970, the court, in upholding the state high school league, explicitly recognized the delegation of authority to school officials when it stated:

> In considering the validity of the rules in question we must at the outset view them in context with the total educational process, the responsibility for which rests with officials of our educational institutions. Those officials are apparently of the view that high schools are not obligated to prepare or train students for a career in professional athletics. We gather that they conceive their obligation to be the development of the whole person and to avoid an overemphasis in extracurricular athletic activity, which may detract from the student's interest in and contribution to the total educational process. They have determined that such overemphasis on athletic activities interferes with academic goals as well as the goals and responsibilities of life for which the education system seeks to prepare our citizens.

> We cannot say that this policy is clearly wrong, and accordingly hold there is no basis for substituting our judgment for that of league authorities upon a question which is authorized by law to determine.

The authority of state associations to formulate and enforce rules is fundamental in nearly all litigation involving state high school associations and is repeatedly upheld by the courts where the rule in question is reasonable. This is clearly stated in *Art Gaines Baseball Camp* v. *Clair Houston* (1973), Missouri Court of Appeals, St. Louis District, N. 34,693 500 S.W. 2d 735. The Court of Appeals decision, affirming the lower court decision dismissing the suit, reads in part:

> Along with entrusting the education of our children to teachers and administrators, we also entrust the control and supervision of the extracurricular activities incident to that education. Implicit in the responsibility for these activities is the power to make reasonable rules and regulations. We are dealing here with numerous schools who have voluntarily joined an association. As members of this association, they may, by majority vote, enact rules to govern their interaction. It is obvious that chaos would result without such rules. It is also obvious that the members are in the most advantageous position to appreciate the regulations under which they must act to achieve desired goals. The court should not interfere with the enactment of those regulations as long as they are reasonable and do not infringe on public policy or law.

That extracurricular participation is a privilege was reinforced by three cases during 1973. First, the Kentucky High School Athletic Association prohibited one of its member schools from participating in regional tournament competition because the school had exceeded the maximum number of games permitted by the KHSAA Constitution and By-Laws. When this ruling was challenged in court, claiming the school was denied the right to participate in tournament play, the judge in *Watt* v. *Kentucky High School Athletic Association* (1973), U.S. District Court, Western District of Columbia at Bowling Green, No. 1618, dismissed the case, stating it is a privilege, not a property right, to participate in athletics. Second, an Iowa student who began school at the age of seven was ruled ineligible for athletics by the Iowa High School Athletic Association because he had reached his twentieth birthday. He claimed his rights were denied him. In *Miller* v. *Iowa* (1973), Polk County District Court, Iowa, No. 76459, the court ruled interscholastic athletics is a privilege, not a fundamental interest, and it upheld the IHSAA rule. Finally, the U.S. Supreme Court in *San Antonio* v. *Rodrigues* (1973), U. S. Supreme Court No. 71–1332, gave support to the same contention. The Chief Justice concluded the majority opinion by stating: "Although education is one of the most important services performed by the state, it is not within the limited category of rights recognized by this court as guaranteed by the Constitution." By implication, then, educational athletics do not fall in the category of rights either.

It is recommended that each state association periodically review its rules to be certain they have educational purposes, are based on the welfare of students, and the rationale for each is either stated explicitly in the rules or is documented in a covering statement of the association. Each state association should be certain it is reflecting the point of view of its member schools and is responsive to and representative of these views. In addition, it should carefully define all terms used in its rules and regulations. Building a file of factual illustrations to support and illustrate various terms is recommended. There is a need to keep crystal clear that participation in interscholastic activities is voluntary, that it is extracurricular and a highly coveted privilege which can be afforded only to those who are willing to pay a high price of self-discipline and strict obedience to necessary rules. Each state association should investigate the statutory authority for its existence.

There are several tests which rules and regulations governing participation in interscholastic activities must meet. These criteria were suggested by Bernhard W. LeVander, attorney for the Minnesota State High School League during the December 1970 mid-winter meeting as follows: (a) rules should be so clearly stated a layman can easily understand them; (b) the structure establishing and governing state associations should be clearly separated from the rules, and means to alter the structure should not necessarily be the same as for altering the rules; (c) state associations should move toward standards which accord due process on eligibility cases; (d) the state association staff must keep abreast of what is developing in the legal field as it relates to eligibility rules.

It has been stated that state high school associations are *extrapolitical* but not *extralegal* organizations. Court decisions, in essence, have supported this contention.

SUMMARY

Court decisions have made it clear that high schools can form state associations through which they can work cooperatively. Reasonable standards of eligibility and regulations governing membership can be established and will be upheld by the courts. They must not be arbitrary or capricious. Reasons for them should be publicized before their adoption. It is important to involve those parties who will be affected by a rule in the formulation of that rule. Regulations must be applied impartially and consistently. Due process shall be provided and negligence avoided.

In the event of legal action, few statutes, if any, will be found that apply directly to standards of eligibility. Therefore, it is important that the reasons for an eligibility rule be carefully and thoroughly established. It must be proved that it is reasonable to the extent that reasonable minds may differ regarding it. The reasons for the rule must be used to substantiate that it was not adopted arbitrarily or capriciously.

In this current era in which there is a tendency to challenge existing standards and regulations in court, a major responsibility of school activities administrators is to find ways of coping with this situation; that is, to meet legal challenges so that reasonable and necessary interscholastic standards will prevail. Unless they do, the status of interscholastics will be in jeopardy.

QUESTIONS AND TOPICS FOR STUDY AND DISCUSSION

1. Why do you think interscholastic standards and regulations are being challenged more today than formerly?

2. Why must athletic administrators have a basic understanding of state law and precedent-setting court cases?

3. Assume that you are the athletic director of a high school; outline policies you would want to apply to reduce the possibility of any charge of negligence being brought against you or members of your coaching staff.

4. Explain the importance of each principle discussed for formulating rules and regulations.

5. Why is it important to make certain that due process is provided in the enforcement of rules? If you were to consider expelling an athlete from a squad, explain the due process procedures you would follow.

6. What steps would you recommend in dealing with unruly fans?

7. Explain how the issue of sex discrimination in sports has affected interscholastic athletics.
8. Which eligibility rules do you think are most likely to be challenged in legal suits? Why?
9. From the brief references to certain court cases in this chapter select some that you think were particularly significant and explain why.
10. What is the general position taken by the courts in regard to the authority of state high school associations?
11. Of what value is the National Federation Legal Aid Pact?
12. When may a rule be considered unreasonable? Arbitrary? Capricious?

NOTES

1. Ted Gest and others, "See You In Court—Our Suing Society," *U. S. News & World Report,* December 20, 1982, p. 58.
2. Samuel H. Adams, "Court Decision Hits Hard with New Liability Twists," *Athletic Purchasing and Facilities,* 6, no. 5 (May 1982), 14.
3. U.S. Department of Health, Education and Welfare/Office of Civil Rights, "Final Title IX Regulations Implementing Education Amendments of 1972," *Federal Register*, 40, no. 108, pt. II, 24142–43.
4. National Federation of State High School Associations, *1976–77 Official Handbook* (Kansas City, Mo.: National Federation, 1976), pp. 60–61.

BIBLIOGRAPHY

ADAMS, SAMUEL H. "Court Decision Hits Hard with New Liability Twists." *Athletic Purchasing and Facilities,* 6, no. 5 (May 1982), 12–16.

ARNOLD, DON E. "Staffing Interscholastic Athletic Programs." *NASSP Bulletin,* 62, no. 419 (September 1978), 75–87. This article deals with the legal aspects of staffing.

BALL, RICHARD T. "Litigation: Establishment of Foundation Could Bring Viable Solution." *Interscholastic Athletic Administration,* 8, no. 2 (Winter 1981), 12–13.

———. "Athletic Injury Litigation—You Are the Solution." *Interscholastic Athletic Administration,* 7, no. 3 (Spring 1981), 7–10.

———. "Lessons Learned from Litigation." *Interscholastic Athletic Administration,* 7, no. 4 (Summer 1981), 18–20.

CLEAR, DELBERT K. "Participation in Interscholastic Athletic Athletics: They Fight-Fight-Fight for the Right-Right-Right." *Phi Delta Kappan,* 64, no. 3 (November 1982), 166–71.

DOUGHERTY, NEIL J. "Are You an Effective Risk Manager?" *Athletic Purchasing and Facilities,* 5, no. 10 (October 1981), 18–21.

ECKER, TOM. "Liability—A Major Concern for All Directors of Athletics." *Proceedings,* National Federation's Eighth Annual National Conference of High School Directors of Athletics, 1977, pp. 22–23. Kansas City, Mo.: National Federation.

FLYGARE, THOMAS J. "Supreme Court Says Title IX Covers Employment but Raises a Serious

Question About the Future Impact of the Law." *Phi Delta Kappan,* 64, no. 2 (October 1982), 134–36.

GALLON, ARTHUR J. *Coaching Ideas and Ideals,* Chap. 9. Boston Mass.: Houghton Mifflin Co., 1974.

GRADWOHL, JOHN M. "Reducing the Risk of Personal Liability." *Proceedings,* National Federation's Eighth Annual National Conference of High School Directors of Athletics, 1977, pp. 24–29. Kansas City, Mo.: National Federation.

KELLER, IRVIN A. *The Interscholastic Coach,* Chap. 11. Englewood Cliffs, N. J.: Prentice-Hall, Inc., 1982.

ROBERTS, JOHN E. "Title IX—Putting It in Perspective." *Proceedings,* National Federation's Eleventh Annual National Conference of High School Directors of Athletics, 1980, pp. 34–37. Kansas City, Mo.: National Federation.

THURSTON, PAUL. "Judicial Dismemberment of Title IX." *Phi Delta Kappan,* 60, no. 8 (April 1979), 594–96.

17

Interscholastic Activities
and the Future

Although it is difficult to predict with a great deal of certainty the future of interscholastic athletics, we can note some prevalent conditions which may affect them in the 1980s. If economic conditions worsen and inflation and the costs of energy continue to rise, these factors alone may have an adverse impact. There are also the problems of staffing and litigation, among others, which can influence the direction of the school athletics program during the next several years. It is important for athletic administrators to keep abreast of developments and seek ways of best coping with them. Several issues that impinge on interscholastics have been discussed elsewhere in this book but are referred to again in this chapter in terms of their impact on the future of interscholastic activities.

THREE MAJOR PROBLEMS FACING
ATHLETIC ADMINISTRATORS

Among the many problems facing athletic directors are three that are of major concern.

Finances

The economic conditions facing schools are not bright. Although inflation has slowed down, there is no sign of its totally abating, and expenses for both adequate protective equipment and maintenance of athletic facilities continue to increase. Taxpayers' attitudes are making it increasingly difficult to vote district levies needed to finance the educational program. Federal aid to education will in all probability be less in the future. Many boards of education are faced with the problem of considering reducing educational offerings or eliminating some programs, and extracurricular activities are often one of the first areas to be affected. As we discussed in Chapter 11, it may become necessary for many schools to look for additional sources for financing the athletic program. It is not the purpose of this section to paint a dismal picture for the future, but it is important that we be realistic and look for ways of coping with the situation confronting us.

Staffing the Athletic Program

An expanding interscholastic program in the 1970s, influenced greatly by the tremendous increase in girls' interscholastics, created a greater demand for high school coaches with which the supply did not keep pace. As the scope of both boys' and girls' programs swelled, it became increasingly difficult to find qualified coaches for various sports. This problem was aggravated by a number of coaches leaving the profession for one reason or another, including undue pressure to win, insufficient pay for extra services, threats of litigation, conflicting family responsibilities, and so on. These same reasons have operated to deter others from a career in coaching. Simultaneously, there has been a move to require higher certification standards for coaches, and many who are not physical education majors are unwilling to take the extra course work essential to become certified. A declining college enrollment is also resulting in fewer teachers and coaches being graduated.

All of these conditions have created a shortage of qualified coaches about which athletic administrators and high school principals are seriously concerned, and the solution is not an easy one. Because properly trained coaches are not available, some administrators are employing part-time coaches, and a few are allowing volunteer coaches to assist. However, this practice leaves a school open to charges of negligence should a serious injury occur under the supervision of a coach who is not properly trained. On the other hand, if a sport must be dropped because no coach is available, the athletic director and the board of education come under fire from athletes and their parents.

The most serious long-range question is how seriously this shortage may affect the educational quality of interscholastic athletics.

Litigation

As we observed in the previous chapter, rules and regulations governing interscholastic athletics are being widely challenged in courts throughout the nation. Athletic directors, school administrators, and coaches are frequently named codefendants in such cases. More serious in magnitude are the suits involving liability for negligence and product liability. From November 1977 through July 1981 there were 12 such cases in which half of the defendants received favorable verdicts, while in the other six the plaintiffs were awarded over 15 million dollars in damages.[1]

The trend in litigation is mandating professional liability coverage. An increasing number of school districts are purchasing liability insurance for the district and its employees. The athletic director and coaches should be very careful to make certain the policy covers them in their responsibilities. Also, they must be familiar enough with their state laws to ascertain whether the school enjoys some degree of sovereign immunity, which would cause a suit to be brought against the individual coach and/or athletic director and school administrators. It is of extreme importance to realize that an insurance carrier who pays a claim under a school policy for proven negligence can file suit against the individuals responsible for the negligence to recover the loss.[2] The only protection in such instances is personal liability coverage. Under these conditions the ways of avoiding legal liability discussed in Chapter 16 are of added significance.

ANTICIPATED DEVELOPMENTS AND TRENDS

Because of the issues just raised and for other reasons, there are some developments and trends that we can anticipate will affect the future of interscholastic activities.

Fund Raising

With dwindling board of education financing available, athletic directors are beginning to utilize methods of raising additional funds to support the athletic program (see Chapter 11).

Participation Fees

Several school boards are establishing participation fees for extracurricular activities, and the number applying this procedure for helping to finance the athletic program will in all probability increase (see Chapter 11).

In-Service Training Programs for Coaches

Those schools employing nonfaculty coaches and paraprofessionals to avoid eliminating sports are finding it wise to provide in-service training programs for their own protection against liability for negligence. Athletic directors are becoming more and more aware of the importance of conducting workshops and seminars for their entire coaching staff to improve their professional competencies and to keep them informed about procedures to avoid charges of negligence.

Evaluation and Supervision of Athletic Programs

When financial resources are strained to support educational programs, the public and boards of education exercise greater scrutiny about educational outcomes, including those accruing from extracurricular activities. We can no longer feel satisfied with just proclaiming the educational values of inter-scholastic athletics—we will have to "practice what we preach." Coaches must be held accountable for teaching students attitudes and ideals in addition to athletic skills. Athletic directors must give more attention to evaluating the athletic program and to the supervision necessary to enhance the educational significance of athletics. Better methods and techniques of evaluation must be explored and applied.[3]

Greater Cooperation Between Schools and Communities

Differences in the philosophies of school athletics and nonschool sports in the past have resulted in a lack of cooperation between schools and community organizations. It is now being recognized that neither the schools nor the nonschool groups alone can accommodate the athletic interests of all students, and a more cooperative attitude on the part of both is developing. More and more coaches are participating during the summer months in coaching and supervising sports sponsored by community organizations. In turn, an in-creasing number of booster and service club members are donating services in assisting in some phases of contest management, which helps reduce ex-penses for schools.

A better mutual understanding is developing concerning the importance of regulations regarding limited team membership. For many years high schools and state associations have had rules under which athletes who participated on nonschool teams during the same school sports season were ineligible for the school team. We are now finding community organizations adopting sim-ilar regulations, which provide that no member of a high school sport squad shall be eligible for the nonschool competition they sponsor in that sport. In this way athletic opportunities are being extended to greater numbers of students.

Various community organizations are assisting in fund-raising activities to help finance the interscholastic program and are accepting the policies of the schools to determine the use of such funds.

In some communities there has been joint cooperation in the financing and construction of athletic facilities (see Chapter 13). Careful planning allows greater shared use of the facilities without conflict. We can expect to see more of such projects in the future.

Junior High School Athletics

Difficulties in school finances and in staffing the athletic program may cause more changes in junior high athletic programs than in senior high school athletics. If boards of education are forced to consider reducing or eliminating programs, there is a strong probability they will act first at the junior high school level. This could result in more attention being given to intramural athletics, which could cost less and conceivably benefit more students. On the other hand, more athletes may decide to join nonschool athletic teams, which could detract from the junior high athletic program and conflict with students' academic responsibilities.

Each athletic administrator should study carefully the conditions and possibilities in his/her school and community and assume leadership in helping provide the best program possible for junior high school students under the conditions which may develop.

Nonschool Athletic Competition

There has been a growth in highly organized competition for youth promoted by individuals and organizations outside the schools. These contests involve children of ages seven and upward. Most are administered during the summer, but some are conducted during the school year. Several include state and national championships and are organized more in accord with the interests and maturity level of adults than of children. There is a growing amount of criticism of the overemphasis on winning on the part of the adults coaching and managing these teams. Children want the opportunity to play for the fun of playing and do not need the same kinds of rewards as adults to get them to participate. There are some programs that have worthwhile objectives appropriate to the levels of the participants, while others appear to be more for the benefit of the sponsors, who are capitalizing on public interest and the desire of youngsters to play. Because of conflicts with the philosophy, principles, and standards of school athletics, these programs are frequently criticized by school administrators and professional physical educators. A few popular magazines and newspapers have carried articles questioning their values.

International athletic competition sponsored and promoted by various agencies is on the increase. Cultural exchange programs involve high school teams touring foreign countries and engaging in competiton with teams in those countries. Several of the programs are during the school year and conflict with the athletic and academic programs of high schools. Various sports-governing bodies sponsor international games as a phase of their developmental programs. The International School Sport Federation (ISF) centered in Europe holds World School Games for the purpose of developing the "sporting activity of boys and girls going to school."[4] Participants cannot be over 17 years of age. These events must be sanctioned by the National Federation, and some high school teams have competed in them.[5] The number of organizations in this country seeking to send teams of high school age abroad is growing, and athletic administrators should keep abreast of developments and any possible effects they may have on the interscholastic athletic program.

There is a need for better cooperation between school officials and nonschool athletic program sponsors. Some of the programs could be greatly improved through some leadership and assistance from school representatives. In communities where this exists, parks and recreation departments and other organizations offer many fine athletic activities for young people during the summer. If there is a decrease in junior high interscholastics, will nonschool groups promote more athletic activities for junior high age youth? Will this cause conflicts with academic and intramural programs? Or will school officials cooperate and provide the leadership that will keep nonschool athletics in proper perspective and appropriate for the youth participating in them? These are questions to which athletic administrators should be alert and prepared to provide leadership in arriving at decisions in the best interests of students.

Sex Discrimination in Athletics

The issue of sex discrimination has subsided to a considerable extent as a result of the expansion in girls' interscholastic athletics offered by the high schools. Most schools have either separate teams for boys and girls or mixed teams, except in contact sports. By state association rules mixed teams must compete in the boys' division in state association-sponsored district and state tournaments. Although Title IX guidelines do not mandate schools' allowing girls to compete on boys' teams in contact sports, a few girls have been successful in getting relief through the courts to permit them to play on boys' football teams. This has complicated the matter for schools. For example, if a girl is allowed to compete on the boys' football team, can a school deny boys the privilege of playing on the girls' volleyball team? Such a situation could present numerous problems. The matter could be resolved by permitting students of either sex to try out for any sport team, but what effect would this have on girls' interscholastic competition? It is hoped that providing comparable athletic opportunities for both sexes will alleviate the problem, but it is difficult to predict what effect court rulings may have in the future.

Decline in Participation

An analysis of the National Federation's annual sports participation surveys shows an increase in both boys' and girls' participation which peaked in 1977–78 and then a decline, with boys' participation decreasing more than girls'. Changes in the data collection system make it impossible to make accurate comparisons and tend to magnify the decline. However, the total combined number of participants of both sexes reported reached 6,450,482 in 1977–78 compared to 5,219,752 in 1981–82.

In the absence of any comprehensive study, one can only speculate as to the causes of the decline in participation. Financial conditions have resulted in a few schools' dropping interscholastic athletics altogether, and several schools have dropped some sports. Because of a declining high school enrollment, some districts with multiple high school units have closed some of them. Reorganization of high school districts into larger units has also been a factor. In the early 1970s there were about 20,00 high schools in the membership of state associations, while this number diminished to approximately 18,000 by 1982. Both the closing of schools and the reorganization of districts result in fewer high school teams.

In terms of preparing for the future, it is important for each athletic administrator to study participation trends in his/her school district to ascertain whether a decline is taking place and, if so, why. Some causes for the decline may be beyond his/her control, while there may be others which could be reversed or eliminated.

Pressure to Raise Academic Standards

Because of the difficulty some collegiate athletes have had in maintaining their eligibility because of academic deficiencies—with some grade-fixing scandals being publicized—criticism is beginning to develop regarding academic standards of eligibility in high school programs. We may see pressure from college administrators and coaches to raise these standards. It should be understood that state association standards are a suggested minimum, and a number of individual schools have established higher requirements.

Television

The sale of television rights is an increasingly lucrative source of revenue for professional sports organizations and "big time" collegiate athletics, involving long-term contracts running into millions of dollars. Some contests are telecast at times adversely affecting attendance at high school games and district and state tournaments sponsored by state associations.

Professional athletic organizations enjoy immunity from antitrust regulations under federal law. The fact that there has been encroachment on times that have been set aside for high school games may make it necessary for athletic administrators to consider seeking relief through federal legislation by working with their National Interscholastic Athletic Administrators Association in cooperation with the National Federation of State High School Associations and professional secondary school administrators' and coaches' associations.

SUMMARY

Although athletic administrators and their high schools are faced with numerous problems and developments which may cause concern, it should be realized that interscholastics have faced difficulties in the past and survived. They weathered the Great Depression and were continued on a limited basis during World War II, emerging in both instances to become more significant in the educational program than they had ever been before.

It is said that successful administrators are those who anticipate and prepare for major administrative tasks and problems. In this book we have discussed most of the tasks and responsibilities faced by athletic administrators, and in this last chapter we have considered problems which may be anticipated from ongoing trends. What the future holds for interscholastic athletics will depend greatly on how well athletic directors, school administrators, and coaches meet the challenges faced in the years ahead.

QUESTIONS AND TOPICS FOR STUDY AND DISCUSSION

1. What effects may the three major problems facing athletic administrators have on interscholastic athletics?
2. Do you favor participation fees as a means of helping to finance athletic programs? Why?
3. Why should in-service programs for coaches be provided?
4. Why will evaluation and supervision of athletic programs be more important in the future?
5. Explain ways you think schools and community organizations should cooperate in providing for the athletic interests of youth.
6. Do you think junior high athletic programs will change more than senior high programs in the future? If so, how?
7. Discuss different types of nonschool athletic programs and explain the position you as an athletic administrator would take regarding them.
8. Do you agree that the issue of sex discrimination in athletics is subsiding? Why?
9. What reason can you give for the decline in high school athletic participation? Will it continue?
10. Do you think the academic standard for high school eligibility should be raised? Why?
11. Should professional athletic organizations continue to enjoy the privilege of immunity from antitrust regulations? Explain your position.
12. Discuss any changes in interscholastic athletics we may expect to see in the future.

NOTES

1. Richard Ball, "Litigation Trends Now Dictate Professional Liability Coverage," *National Interscholastic Coach*, 1, no. 2 (October 1981), 4.
2. Ibid.
3. Glenn Potter and Thomas Wandzilak, "Athletic Evaluation: Assessment for Survival," *Interscholastic Athletic Administration*, 8, no. 4 (Summer 1982), 8.

4. Federation Internationale Du Sport Scolaire et Association Du Sport Scolaire et Universitaire, *Bulletin,* no. 2 (Paris), January 1976, p. 3.

5. "Frankfort High School Participates in ISF Basketball Competition," *National Federation Press,* 1, no. 10 (June 1981), 1.

BIBLIOGRAPHY

ADAMS, SAM. "Assessment of an Athletic Program." *Interscholastic Athletic Administration,* 6, no. 11 (Fall 1979), 7–8.

———. "A Look at Athletics in the Eighties." *Interscholastic Athletic Administration,* 7, no. 4 (Summer 1981), 16–17.

ARNOLD, DON E. "Staffing the Interscholastic Athletic Program." *NASSP Bulletin,* 62, no. 419 (September 1978), 75–87.

BACHMAN, DALE R. "Surviving the Elimination of Extracurricular Activities." *National Federation Press,* 2, no. 6 (February 1982), 3.

BALL, RICHARD. "Litigation Trends Now Dictate Professional Liability Coverage." *National Federation Interscholastic Coach,* 1, no. 2 (October 1981), 4.

BOWLUS, WARREN C. "Should Athletic Administrators Hire Non-Teaching Coaches?" *Interscholastic Athletic Administration,* 6, no. 1 (Fall 1979), 11.

CHILES, BARBARA. "Jogathons Answer Fund-Raising Challenge." *Interscholastic Athletic Administration,* 9, no. 1 (Fall 1981), 19–21.

DELUCA, JOHN. "Austerity and School Athletics." *Interscholastic Athletic Administration,* 6, no. 4 (Summer 1980), 15–16.

"From the 1970s into the 1980s." *Interscholastic Athletic Administration,* 6, no. 4 (Summer 1980), 5–12.

GHOLSON, RONALD E., AND ROBERT L. BUSER. "Student Activities: Guide for Determining Who Is Participating in What." *NASSP Bulletin,* 65, no. 445 (May 1981), 43–47.

HILL, WENDELL. "Facilities: Fulfilling a Promise." *Interscholastic Athletic Administration,* 8, no. 4 (Summer 1982), 16–17.

"ISF Membership to be Emphasized." *National Federation Press,* 1, no. 5 (January 1981), 1.

KELLER, IRVIN A. *The Interscholastic Coach,* Chap. 13. Englewood Cliffs, N. J.: Prentice-Hall, Inc., 1982.

LIEDTKE, CAROL. "Can Gymnastics Survive the 1980s?" *Interscholastic Athletic Administration,* 7, no. 4 (Summer 1981), 9–10.

POTTER, GLENN, AND THOMAS WANDZILAK. "Athletic Evaluation: Assessment for Survival." *Interscholastic Athletic Administration,* 8, no. 4 (Summer 1982), 6–9.

SENNETT, OTIS. "Coaches Evaluation." *Interscholastic Athletic Administration,* 6, no. 4 (Summer 1980), 21–23.

THOMAS, M. DONALD. "Surviving the 1980s." *Interscholastic Athletic Administration,* 7, no. 3 (Spring 1981), 5–6 and 14.

WEISS, ALAN. "Coaching Shortage." *Interscholastic Athletic Administration,* 6, no. 1 (Fall 1979), 9.

Appendix A

DIRECTORY OF STATE HIGH SCHOOL ASSOCIATIONS*

ALABAMA HIGH SCHOOL ATHLETIC ASSOCIATION (1924)
> Secretary-Treasurer: HERMAN L. SCOTT, 926 Pelham Street, Montgomery 36101

ALASKA HIGH SCHOOL ACTIVITIES ASSOCIATION (1954)
> Executive Secretary: ED NASH, 650 International Airport Road, Anchorage 99502

ARIZONA INTERSCHOLASTIC ASSOCIATION, INC. (1925)
> Executive Secretary: TONY KOMADINA, 2606 West Osborn Rd., Phoenix 85017

ARKANSAS ACTIVITIES ASSOCIATION (1924)
> Executive Director: LEE CASSADY, 1500 West 4th St., Little Rock 72201

CALIFORNIA INTERSCHOLASTIC FEDERATION (1940)
> Commissioner: THOMAS E. BYRNES, 2282 Rosecrans, Fullerton 92633

COLORADO HIGH SCHOOL ACTIVITIES ASSOCIATION (1924)
> Commissioner: RAY C. BALL, 11351 Montview Blvd., Aurora 80010

CONNECTICUT INTERSCHOLASTIC ATHLETIC CONFERENCE, INC. (1926)
> Executive Secretary: JOHN T. DALY, 60 Connolly Parkway, Hamden 06514

DELAWARE SECONDARY SCHOOL ATHLETIC ASSOCIATION (1945)
> Executive Secretary: DALE C. FARMER, John G. Townsend Bldg., Dover 19901

DISTRICT OF COLUMBIA (1958)
> Supervising Director of Athletics: OTTO T. JORDAN, D.C. Public Schools—
> Lovejoy School, 12th & D Streets, N.E., Washington 20002

FLORIDA HIGH SCHOOL ACTIVITIES ASSOCIATION (1926)
> Executive Secretary: FRED E. ROZELLE, 240 S.W. First St., Gainesville 32602

GEORGIA HIGH SCHOOL ASSOCIATION (1929)
> Executive Secretary: W. C. FORDHAM (Box 71), 151 So. Bethel St., Thomaston 30286

HAWAII HIGH SCHOOL ATHLETIC ASSOCIATION (1957)
> Executive Secretary: EDWARD S. KIYUNA, 941 Hind Luka Drive, Honolulu 96821

* National Federation of State High School Associations, 1982–83 *Handbook* (Kansas City, Mo.: National Federation, 1982), pp. 104–113.

IDAHO HIGH SCHOOL ACTIVITIES ASSOCIATION (1928)

Executive Secretary: RICHARD STICKLE (P.O. Box 1400), Boise 83701

ILLINOIS HIGH SCHOOL ASSOCIATION (1920)

Executive Secretary: LAVERE L. ASTROTH (P.O. Box 2715), 2715 McGraw Dr., Bloomington 61701

INDIANA HIGH SCHOOL ATHLETIC ASSOCIATION (1924)

Commissioner: WARD E. BROWN, 9150 No. Meridan St., Indianapolis 46204

IOWA HIGH SCHOOL ATHLETIC ASSOCIATION (1920)

Executive Secretary: BERNIE SAGGAU (P. O. Box 10), Boone 50036

KANSAS STATE HIGH SCHOOL ACTIVITIES ASSOCIATION, INC. (1923)

Executive Secretary: NELSON HARTMAN (Box 495), 520 West 27th St., Topeka 66601

KENTUCKY HIGH SCHOOL ATHLETIC ASSOCIATION (1941)

Commissioner: TOM MILLS (Box 7502), 560 E. Cooper Dr., Lexington 40502

LOUISIANA HIGH SCHOOL ATHLETIC ASSOCIATION (1925)

Commissioner: FRANK SPRUIELL (P. O. Box 52778), 7370 Airline Hwy., Bellemont Motor Hotel, Baton Rouge 70805

MAINE ASSOCIATION OF PRINCIPALS OF SECONDARY SCHOOLS (1939)

Executive Secretary: HORACE O. McGOWAN, 15 Western Ave., Augusta 04330

MARYLAND PUBLIC SECONDARY SCHOOLS ATHLETIC ASSOCIATION (1946)

Executive Secretary: EDWARD F. SPARKS, 200 W. Baltimore St., Baltimore 21201

MASSACHUSETTS SECONDARY SCHOOL PRINCIPAL'S ASSOCIATION, INC. (1944)

Executive Secretary-Treasurer: RICHARD F. NEAL, 75 Central St., Ashland 01721

MICHIGAN HIGH SCHOOL ATHLETIC ASSOCIATION (1920)

State Director: VERN L. NORRIS, 1019 Trowbridge Road, East Lansing 48823

MINNESOTA STATE HIGH SCHOOL LEAGUE (1923)

Executive Director: MURRAE FRENG (P. O. Box 672), 2621 Fairoak Ave., Anoka 55303

MISSISSIPPI HIGH SCHOOL ACTIVITIES ASSOCIATION, INC. (1924)

Director of Activities: WOODROW MARSH (Box 4521), 152 Millsaps Ave., Jackson 39216

MISSOURI STATE HIGH SCHOOL ACTIVITIES ASSOCIATION (1926)

Executive Secretary: JACK W. MILES (Box 1328), 1808 I–70 Dr., S. W., Columbia 65201

MONTANA HIGH SCHOOL ASSOCIATION (1934)

Executive Secretary: DAN L. FREUND, 1 South Dakota Ave., Helena 59601

NEBRASKA SCHOOL ACTIVITIES ASSOCIATION (1924)

Executive Secretary: JAMES RILEY, 8230 Beechwood Dr., Lincoln 68508

NEVADA INTERSCHOLASTIC ACTIVITIES ASSOCIATION (1939)

Executive Secretary: BERT L. COOPER, 400 W. King St., Capitol Complex, Carson City 89701

NEW HAMPSHIRE INTERSCHOLASTIC ATHLETIC ASSOCIATION INC. (1945)

Executive Secretary: WALTER A. SMITH (P. O. Box 1215), 121 North State St., Concord 03301

NEW JERSEY STATE INTERSCHOLASTIC ATHLETIC ASSOCIATION (1942)

Executive Secretary: ROBERT F. KANABY, Route 130, Robbinsville 08691

NEW MEXICO ACTIVITIES ASSOCIATION (1932)

Executive Secretary: JAMES ODLE (P. O. Box 8407), 3620 Thaxton St., S. E., Albuquerque 87198

NEW YORK STATE PUBLIC HIGH SCHOOL ATHLETIC ASSOCIATION (1926)

Secretary-Treasurer: ALTON B. DOYLE, Executive Park S., Albany 12203

NORTH CAROLINA HIGH SCHOOL ATHLETIC ASSOCIATION (1949)

Executive Secretary: SIMON F. TERRELL (Box 3216), Finley Golf Course Road, UNC Campus, Chapel Hill 27514

NORTH DAKOTA HIGH SCHOOL ACTIVITIES ASSOCIATION (1923)

Executive Secretary: BRUCE ANDERSON (P. O. Box 817), 134 N. E. Third St., Valley City 58072

OHIO HIGH SCHOOL ATHLETIC ASSOCIATION (1924)

Commissioner: RICHARD L. ARMSTRONG, 4080 Roselea Place, Columbus 43214

OKLAHOMA SECONDARY SCHOOL ACTIVITIES ASSOCIATION (1924)

Executive Secretary: CLAUD E. WHITE (Box 53464), 222 N. E. 27th St., Oklahoma City 73105

OREGON SCHOOL ACTIVITIES ASSOCIATION (1931)

Executive Secretary: DR. EDWARD J. RYAN, No. 1 Plaza Southwest, 6900 S. W. Haines Rd., Tigard 79223

PENNSYLVANIA INTERSCHOLASTIC ATHLETIC ASSOCIATION (1925)

Executive Director: DR. ROSSELL T. WERNER, 550 Gettysburg Road, Mechanicsburg 17055

RHODE ISLAND INTERSCHOLASTIC LEAGUE, INC. (1952)

Executive Secretary: REV. ROBERT C. NEWBOLD (P. O. Box 6367), 20 Regent Ave., Providence 02908

SOUTH CAROLINA HIGH SCHOOL LEAGUE (1947)

Executive Secretary-Treasurer: JIM PINKERTON, Rm. 408, Carolina Coliseum, University of South Carolina, Columbia 29208

SOUTH DAKOTA HIGH SCHOOL ACTIVITIES ASSOCIATION (1923)

Executive Secretary: MARLYN GOLDHAMER, 204 N. Euclid, Pierre 57501

TENNESSEE SECONDARY SCHOOL ATHLETIC ASSOCIATION (1925)

Executive Secretary: GILL GIDEON, 3333 Lebanon Rd., Hermitage 37076

TEXAS UNIVERSITY INTERSCHOLASTIC LEAGUE (1974)

Director General: BAILEY M. MARSHALL (Box 8028), University Station, 2622 Wichita St., Austin 78712

UTAH HIGH SCHOOL ACTIVITIES ASSOCIATION (1927)

Executive Secretary: J. MARION TREE, 199 East 700 South Midvale 84047

VERMONT HEADMASTERS' ASSOCIATION, INC. (1945)

Executive Secretary: DR. RICHARD H. BREEN (P. O. Box 128), 148 State Street, Montpelier 05602

VIRGINIA HIGH SCHOOL LEAGUE (1948)

Executive Secretary: WILLIAM C. PACE (Box 3697), University Station, Zehmer Bldg., 104 Midmont Lane, Charlottesville 22903

WASHINGTON INTERSCHOLASTIC ACTIVITIES ASSOCIATION (1936)

Executive Secretary: CLIFF A. GILLIES, 4211 W. Lake Sammamish Blvd. S. E., Bellevue 98008

WEST VIRGINIA SECONDARY SCHOOL ACTIVITIES COMMISSION (1925)

Executive Secretary: SAM WILLIAMS, Rt. 9, Box 76, Parkersburg 26101

WISCONSIN INTERSCHOLASTIC ATHLETIC ASSOCIATION (1920)

Executive Director: JOHN E. ROBERTS, 41 Park Ridge Dr., Stevens Point 54481

WYOMING HIGH SCHOOL ACTIVITIES ASSOCIATION (1936)

Executive Secretary: WILLIAM SULLINS, 218 W. 9th, Casper 82601

Affiliated Members (Canada)

CANADIAN SPORTS FEDERATION (1967)

Executive Director: DAVE FISHMAN. 333 River Rd., Ottawa, Ontario, KIL 8B9

ALBERTA SCHOOLS' ATHLETIC ASSOCIATION (affiliated 1968)

Secretary-Treasurer: LORNE WOOD, Percy Page Centre, 13 Mission Ave., Alberta T8N IH6

BRITISH COLUMBIA FEDERATION OF SCHOOL ATHLETIC ASSOCIATIONS (1969)

Executive Secretary: DONALD A. STEEN, 1200 Hornby Street, Vancouver, British Columbia V6Z 2E2

MANITOBA HIGH SCHOOLS ATHLETIC ASSOCIATION, INC. (affiliated 1962)

Executive Secretary: MORRIS GLIMCHER, 1700 Ellice Ave., Winnipeg, Manitoba R3H 0B1

NEW BRUNSWICK INTERSCHOLASTIC ATHLETIC ASSOCIATION (affiliated 1943)

Secretary-Treasurer: W. S. RITCHIE, Department of Education (Box 804), Fredericton, New Brunswick E3B 5B4

NEWFOUNDLAND-LABRADOR HIGH SCHOOL ATHLETIC FEDERATION (affiliated 1972)

Executive Secretary: WALTER CROTTY, Bldg. 25, Torbay Airport, St. John's, Newfoundland A7C 5T7

NOVA SCOTIA SCHOOL ATHLETIC FEDERATION (affiliated 1952)

Executive Director: RON O'FLAHERTY (P. O. Box 3010–s), 5516 Spring Garden Rd., Halifax, Nova Scotia B3J 3G6

ONTARIO FEDERATION OF SCHOOL ATHLETIC ASSOCIATIONS (affiliated 1953)

Executive Secretary: ANDY GIBSON, 111 Railside Rd., Don Mills, Ontario M3A 1B2

PRINCE EDWARD ISLAND INTERSCHOLASTIC ATHLETIC ASSOCIATION (affiliated 1964)

Executive Secretary: JANE CUSHING, Physical Education Consultant, Department of Education, Charlottetown, Prince Edward Island C1A 7N8

SASKATCHEWAN HIGH SCHOOLS ATHLETIC ASSOCIATION (affiliated 1953)

Executive Secretary: R. BARRY STINSON, Parkview Place, 423–2220 College Ave., Regina, Saskatchewan S4P 3V7

OKINAWA SECONDARY SCHOOL ATHLETIC ASSOCIATION (1978)

Executive Director: EDWARD F. WAGGONER, Kadena High School, APO San Francisco, California 96651

PHILIPPINE SECONDARY SCHOOLS ATHLETIC ASSOCIATION (1974)

Executive Secretary: JOHN J. STAUFFER, George Dewey High School, USNS Box 70, FPO San Francisco, California 96651

GUAM INTERSCHOLASTIC ACTIVITIES ASSOCIATION

Contact: CARLIAN SMITH, SPS-Interscholastic Activities, Department of Guam, P. O. Box DE, Guam 96910

ST. THOMAS-ST. JOHN INTERSCHOLASTIC ATHLETIC ASSOCIATION

President: HARRY BISKE, P. O. Box 11102, St. Thomas, U. S. Virgin Islands 00801

Appendix B

METRIC CONVERSION TABLE

This table provides an approximate conversion to metric measures.

If You Know Length	Multiply by	To Find	Symbol
inches	2.54	centimeters	cm
feet	30	centimeters	cm
yards	0.9	meters	m
miles	1.6	kilometers	km
Area			
sq. inches	6.5	sq. centimeters	cm^2
sq. feet	0.09	sq. meters	m^2
sq. yards	0.8	sq. meters	m^2
sq. miles	2.6	sq. kilometers	km^2
acres	0.4	hectares	ha
Weight or Mass			
ounces	28	grams	g
pounds	0.45	kilograms	kg
short tons (2000 lb.)	0.9	tonnes (metric tons)	t

METRIC AND ENGLISH DISTANCE EQUIVALENTS

Feet	Meters	Feet	Meters	Yards	Meters	Miles	Meters
1	0.305	20	6.096	40	36.58	1	1,609.3
2	.610	30	9.144	50	45.72	2	3,218.7
3	.914	40	12.192	60	54.86	3	4,828.0
4	1.219	50	15.240	70	64.01	4	‣ 6,437.4
5	1.524	60	18.288	75	68.58	5	8,046.7
6	1.829	70	21.336	100	91.44	6	9,656.1
7	2.134	80	24.384	110	100.58	7	11,265.4
8	2.438	90	27.432	120	109.73	8	12,874.8
9	2.743	100	30.480	220	201.17	9	14,484.1
10	3.048	200	60.960	300	274.32	10	16,093.5
				440	402.34		
				600	548.64		
				800	804.67		
				1000	914.40		
				1320	1207.01		

Appendix C

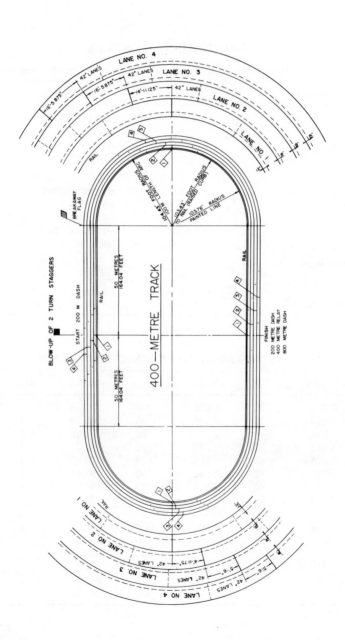

Index

A

Accident insurance (*see* Athletic accident insurance)
Administration, athletic program (*see also* Athletic conferences; Athletic policies; Contest management):
  activities director, 198
  administrative organization, 200–212
  athletic council, 201, 202, 203–4, 213–15
  athletic director, responsibilities of, 5–6, 197–98 (*see also* Athletic administrator)
  coach's responsibilities in, 198–99
  evaluation (*see* Evaluation of athletic program)
  involvement of students, 200
  organizational plan for large high schools, 203–4
    for medium size schools, 201–2
    for multiple high school districts, 204–12
    for small high schools, 201–2
  policies, establishing of, 215–17 (*see also* Athletic policies)
  principal, responsibilities in, 196–97 (*see also* High school principal)
  responsibility for, 194–200
  superintendent, responsibilities in, 195–96
Alabama High School Athletic Association:
  coach, regulation of conduct, 145
  penalty for violation of rules, 144
  unsportsmanlike conduct rule, 117
Alumni clubs, 182–83
Amateur:
  award standards, 30
  definition, 110–11
  philosophy, 12–13
Amateurism, 110–13
  difference in standards, 237
  problems in, 237–38
American Association for Health, Physical Education and Recreation, 57–58
Athletic accident insurance:
  catastrophe insurance, 301

Athletic accident insurance (*cont.*):
  considerations for obtaining, 301–3
  National Federation Student Protection Trust, 300
  plans, 76–77, 297–303
  sources, 298
  state association plans, 298–300
Athletic administrator (*see also* Athletic director):
  developments facing, 387–91
  evolution of position of, 1–2
  problems faced, 385–87
  professional status, 2–4
  qualifications of, 4–5
  responsibilities, 5–6
  staffing, difficulties faced in, 386
Athletic awards (*see* Awards)
Athletic banquets, 183, 236–37
Athletic camps (*see* Specialized athletic camps)
Athletic conferences:
  early purposes, 212
  obligations to, 183
  optimum size, 213
  origin, 11
  services of, 213
  St. Louis Public High School League, 205–12
Athletic council (*see* Administration, athletic program)
Athletic director (*see also* Athletic administrator):
  administrative responsibilities, 197–98
  changes in position of, 198
  code for, 82–83
  early athletic directors, 2
  enforcement of policies, 218–19
  responsibilities, 5–6, 197–98
Athletic equipment:
  cleaning and repairing, 250–51
  daily care of, 247, 249
  inventory, 241–42
    form for, 242
  issuance of, 245
  marking of, 246–47
  purchase order (form), 246

Athletic equipment (*cont.*):
purchasing of, 245–46
record cards, 247, 248, 249
requisition for purchase (form), 243
responsibility for, 252–53
storage, 251–52
Athletic facilities (*see* Facilities, athletic)
Athletic finances and budgets:
accounting, 263–64
admission prices, 258
board of education funds, 262
budget, 265–73
considerations in, 255–57
definition of, 257
forms, 267, 271, 272
planning, 266–68
preparation of, 268–70, 271, 272
presentation to board of education, 270–73
purpose, 265–66
contributions, 261
finance sources, 257–62
participation fees, 260–61
private funding, 261–62
publication of reports, 264–65
season tickets, 258–59
student activity tickets, 259–60
Athletic leagues (*see* Athletic conferences)
Athletic policies:
board of education authority in, 194–95
coach's share in, 198–99
director of physical education, consultation with, 199
enforcement of, 224
establishment of, 215–17
faculty representation in, 199–200
implementation of, 217–25
issues for consideration, 217
principal, responsibility in, 196–97, 218
relations with outside groups, 216–17
responsibility for, 216
superintendent, responsibility of, 195–96, 218
Athletic scholarships, college, 237–38
Awards:
athletic banquets, 183, 236–37
basis for granting, 234–36
cost of, 233
elimination of material awards, 232
general policies for, 231–32
importance of maintaining standards for, 238
methods of granting, 234
origin, 231–32
philosophy for high school, 232
problems in, 232, 237–38
regulations for, 235–36
school practices in, 233–34
state association regulations, 109–110, 232
types, 232–33

Awards (*cont.*):
St. Louis Public High School League regulations, 235–36

B

Badminton court, diagram, 312
Baseball:
agreement with professional baseball, 53–55
diamond, 318
field, 316–18
indoor diamond, 311
Basketball, court diagram, 310
Board of education:
authority of, 194–95
responsibilities for athletic policies, 216
Boxing:
elimination of high school boxing, 146
resolution, Society of State Directors of Physical and Health Education, 147
Budgets (*see* Athletic finances and budgets)

C

Cardinal Athletic Principles, 57–58
Centralized purchasing, 244
Certification of coaches, 132, 135–36
Civil Rights Act of 1972, effect on eligibility, 147
Coaches:
administrative responsibilities, 198–99
certification of, 132, 135–36
code for, 83–84
conduct of, 145, 185
manual for, 219–23
negligence, avoiding of, 363–64, 366
non-faculty, 134–36
policies, share in establishing, 198–99
responsibility to teach, 219–23
safety responsibilities, 279
selection of, 219
shortage of, 386
Codes for administration of athletics, 81–85
College recruiting:
coping with, 51–53
Guide for College-Bound Athlete, 53
influences on athletes and parents, 237–38
Colorado High School Activities Association, antifraternity rule, 115
Competitive bidding, 244
Concessions, 161, 170
Conduct (*see also* Contest regulations; Crowd control):
coaches, 145
players, 145
team followers, 145
Connecticut Interscholastic Athletic Conference, Inc., purposes, 70

Contest management (*see also* Contest regulations; Meet and tournament management):
after-game responsibilities, 170–71
application to participate, 157
  form, 104
arrangement for field or court, 158
awards, 184 (*see also* Awards)
before-game preparation, 156–65
care of facilities, 163
checklist for home contests, 165–71
concessions, 161–62
contracts for contests, 156
courtesies to visiting school, 159
courtesy information (form), 160
crowd control, 184–85 (*see also* Crowd control)
dressing rooms, 180
eligibility certificate, 130
eligibility records, 157–58
equipment, 158, 176
filing of contest data, 171–72
game manager, 165
general duties and policies, 177–86
half-time activities, 163–64
importance of, 154–55
officials, contracting of, 156–57, 179–80
organizing for school staff cooperation, 165
out-of-town games, preparation for, 171, 174–77
parents' permissions, 157, 174–75
payment of officials, 170
permanent records, 177–79
phases of, 156
physical examination, 157
physician's services, 164
police protection, 162–63
programs, 161
public address system, 164
publicity, 158–59
records, 170–71, 173, 177–79
reserve games, 159–61
reserved seats and areas, 163
responsibility for, 155–56
scoreboards, 163
scores, timers, officials, 165
state association regulations, 186
student managers, 184
supplies and equipment, 166–67
tickets, 161
transportation, 174–76
trip finances, 176
ushers, 162
Contest regulations (*see also* Contest management):
agreement to violate state association rules prohibited, 144
approval of meets and tournaments, 142
conduct of coaches, 145
conduct of players, 144

Contest regulations (*cont.*):
contracts for contests, 125–28
  form, 126
eligibility list procedures, 128–32
faculty managers, 140
game contract provisions, 127
modifications for junior high school, 148–49
National Federation rules, to be used, 144
number of contests, 142–43
official's contract, 137–39
  form, 139
officials for contests, 136–40
protests and forfeitures, 140–42
purposes, 124
responsibility for team followers, 145
sports seasons, 142–43
transfer students' records, 132
  form, 133
Contracts:
athletic contests, 125–28, 156
officials', 156–57, 178–79
Court cases (*see also* Legal aspects):
age rule, 375
all-star competition, 375
attendance rules, 375
award standards, 375
conduct and sportsmanship, 376
discrimination, 372, 374
dress and grooming, 368
interscholastics a privilege, 380–81
liability for injuries, 364, 365
married students, 378
Morrison v. Roberts, precedent, 95
negligence, 365
nonschool competition, 375–76
recruiting rules, 377–78
scholarship standards, 376
semester limitations on competition, 376–77
specialized athletic camp, 380
training rules, 376
transfer rules, 377
unruly fan, 371, 372
Crowd control:
enforcement procedures, 185
phases of, 184
plan for, 185
police protection, 162–63
strategic position of coach in, 185

D

Director of athletics (*see* Athletic administrator; Athletic director)
Director of physical education, 199
Drugs (*see* Health and safety program)
Due process:
elements of, 368–69

Due process (*cont.*):
  in handling ineligibility cases, 141–42
  procedures recommended, 369–70
  state high school association procedures,
    369–70

E

Educational Policies Commission of the Na-
    tional Education Association and the
    American Association of School Ad-
    ministrators, statement on junior high
    school athletics, 351
Eligibility requirements:
  academic, 31
  age, 29, 97–98
  all-star competition, 116
  amateur and award standards, 30, 109–10
  amateurism, 110–13
  antifraternity rule, 115–16
  assumed name, 32
  certification of, 130
  conduct and character, 113–15
  definition, 95
  development of standards of, 94–95
  enforcement of, 114–15
  enrollment and attendance, 30
  girls' eligibility for boys' teams, 147
  hardship cases, 116–17
  limited team membership, 99–101
  married students, 116
  maximum participation, 30
  medical examination, 31, 101–4
  military service, 116
  nonschool competition, 31
  parental consent, 32, 101–4
  penalty for ineligible players, 141
  pressure to raise standards, 391
  purposes of eligibility regulations, 95–97
  records of, 157–58
  recruiting and undue influence, 32
  residence, transfer of, 31
  scholarship, 104–7
  seasons of competition, 98
  semesters of attendance, 99
  special education students, 106
  special eligibility regulations, 113–19
  specialized camp rule, 117–19
  time of enrollment, 98
  tobacco and liquor rule, 114
  transfer and undue influence rule, 107–8
  transfer record (form), 133
  unsportsmanlike conduct, 117
Eligibility rules (*see* Eligibility requirements)
Equipment (*see* Athletic equipment)
Evaluation of athletic program:
  coach (form), 227
  methods and techniques, 225–28
  program (form), 226

Evaluation of athletic program (*cont.*):
  uses of, 228
Extracurricular activities, tendency to elim-
    inate, 256–57

F

Facilities, athletic:
  badminton court, 312
  baseball field, 316–18
  basketball court, 310
  field hockey diagram, 315
  football field, 312–14
  football, 6-man field, 315
  handball court, 313
  indoor playing facilities, 309–11
  lacrosse field, 315
  lighted outdoor fields, 325–26
  long range planning for, 326–28
  metric measurements, 328
  Michigan State University, track and field
    layout, 320
  playing areas, size of, 309
  seeding of fields, 324
  shuffleboard court, 313
  soccer field, 317
  softball diamond, 319
  speedball field, 316
  tennis courts, 322–24
  track and field, 318–22
    equipment, 322–23
  turf, maintenance of, 325
  volleyball court, 311
Finances (*see* Athletic finances and budgets)
Florida High School Activities Association:
  hardship clause, 117
  unsportsmanlike conduct rule, 144
Football:
  field diagram, 314
  6-man field, 315

G

Georgia High School Association, award
    standard, 109
Girls' interscholastic athletics:
  increase in, 15
  philosophy of, 14–16
  separate but equal program, 16
  Title IX, effects on, 15, 372–74
Guide for the College-Bound Athlete, 53
Guidelines for Levels of Athletic Competi-
    tion, 58–60

H

Handball court, 313
Hardship cases, 117

Health and safety program (*see also* Athletic accident insurance):
accident insurance, 297–303
alcohol and drugs, abuse of, 286–88
coach's position in, 279
drug education, 287–88
injuries, reporting of, 285–86
medical supervision, school plan for, 296–97
NOCSAE, objectives of, 280–81
physical conditioning, 283–84
proper playing facilities, 282–83
protective equipment, 280–81
responsibility for, 278–79
safety essentials, 278–88
safety policies, importance of, 288
safety suggestions, 288–92
sanitation program, 293–95
school safety program, 278
transportation, safety in, 292–93
wrestling, weight control in, 281–82
High school athletics (*see also* Interscholastic athletics):
anticipated developments, 387–91
decline in participation, 390–91
development of controls, 10–11
history, 8–10
philosophy, 12–13
High school principal:
code for, 82
enforcement of policies, 218
responsibility for policies, 196–97

I

Idaho High School Activities Association, amateur rule, 112–13
Illinois High School Association:
all-star participation rule, 116
military service rule, 116
protest and forfeiture procedure, 141
provision for emergency coaches, 135
Indiana High School Athletic Association, undue influence rule, 107
Injuries (*see* Health and safety program)
Insurance (*see* Athletic accident insurance)
International competition (*see also* National Federation, international competition):
political prestige of, 41
types, 42–43, 389
International School Sport Federation (ISF), 389
Interscholastic athletics (*see also* High school athletics):
developments presenting challenges in, 18–20, 387–91
objectives of, 16–18
records, 33–34

Interstate meets and tournaments:
application for sanction, 40
sanctioning procedure, 39
Intramural athletics:
administration of, 338–47
awards, 342–43
definition, 330, 334
DGWS policies for competition, 333–35
director, responsibility of, 338–39
double elimination schedule, 345
eligibility for, 342
extramural competition, 334–35
financing, 347
lack of attention to, 332–33
ladder tournament, 346
objectives of, 335–38
organization for, 339
policies and practices, 346
pyramid tournament, 346
relationship to interschool athletics, 330–31
round-robin schedule, 344
seasonal programs of activities, 340–42
single-elimination bracket, 345
types of competition in, 343–45
Iowa High School Athletic Association:
award standard, 109
undue influence rule, 107

J

Junior high school athletics:
age group competition, 351–52
development of, 350–53
Education Policies Commission, report on, 351
excesses in competition, 352–53
financing, 358–59
Guidelines for Levels of Athletic Competition, 58–60, 360
guiding principles for, 353–57
Joint Committee on Athletic Competition for Children of Elementary and Junior High School Age, statement, 351
Junior High School Athletic Subcommittee of the Joint Committee on Standards for Interscholastic Athletics, 354–55
modification in contest regulations, 148–49
New York Public High School Athletic Association, modified program, 352
selection of sports for, 355–56
staffing, difficulties in, 359

K

Kansas State High School Activities Association:
athletic eligibility certificate, 130

Kansas State High School Activities Association (*cont.*):
purposes of, 70
Kentucky High School Athletic Association, officials' registration procedures, 136–37

L

Lacrosse field, 315
Legal Aid Pact, 378–79
Legal aspects of interscholastic athletics (*see also* Court cases; Due process; Legal Aid Pact):
board of education, responsibilities of, 364
discrimination, 372–74
due process, 368–72
eligibility and the law, 374–78
individual rights, 362
liability for negligence, 363, 365
negligence, definition of, 367
negligence, precautionary measures against, 366
principles for formulating rules and regulations, 367–68
search and seizure guidelines, 287
state associations, legal status of, 379–82
tests for rules and regulations, 381
Title IX Guidelines, 372–74
trends in litigation, 362–63, 386–87
unruly fans, dealing with, 371–72

M

Maintenance (*see* Facilities, athletic)
Married student rule, 116
Medical supervision (*see* Health and safety program)
Meet and tournament management:
administration of, 190–91
approval of, 142
considerations in hosting, 187–88
district and state, 78–80
pre-tournament organization, 188–90
purposes of, 80
types, 186–87
Metric system, 328, 400
Michigan High School Athletic Association:
affiliation with State Department of Education, 72–73
codes for administration of athletics, 81–85
eligibility list exchange provisions, 131
Michigan State University, track and field layout, 320
Missouri State High School Activities Association:
application to participate (form), 104

Missouri State High School Activities Association (*cont.*):
coaches' manual, 219–23
definition of, 69
form for agreement on officials, 128
physical examination form, 103
purposes of state tournaments, 80
regulations for junior high school athletics, 352
removal of team from play, procedure, 145
report to athletic official, 87
report to principal, 86
specialized camp rule, 117–18
transfer of eligibility (form), 133
worksheet for rating officials, 138

N

National Alliance for Girls' and Women's Sports, policies for girls' athletic competition, 333–35
National Athletic Reconditioners Association, 251
National Athletic Trainers Association, program for athletic trainers, 296
National Collegiate Athletic Association (NCAA):
all-star eligibility rule, 56–57
drug pamphlet, 286
Guide for College-Bound Athlete, 53
National Council of Secondary School Athletic Directors, 3
National Federation Interscholastic Coaches Association (NFICA):
formation, 37
objectives, 37
National Federation Interscholastic Officials Association (NFIOC):
formation, 37
objectives, 37
National Federation of State High School Associations:
accomplishments of, 29–33
administration of, 27–28
agreement with professional baseball, 53–55
application for sanction of international competition (form), 44–45
athletic accident insurance, 35–36, 300
athletic philosophy, 13–15
athletic safety and protection, 36
audio-visual aids, 35
awards standard, 60–61
bowl, charity, and all-star games, position on, 55–57
Cardinal Athletic Principles, 57–58
criteria for evaluating international competition, 43, 45–46
definition and nature of, 27

National Federation of State High School Associations (*cont.*):
executive secretaries of, 27
expansion in scope, 24–25
experimental studies, 35
Guidelines for Levels of Athletic Competition, 58–60
high schools and students represented, 29
international competition, position on, 41–42
Legal Aid Pact, 62
membership, 26
National High School Activities Week, 61
National High School Hall of Fame, 61
national interscholastic records, 33–34
national teams, policy on, 42
national tournaments, elimination of, 39
nonschool sponsored activities, position on, 46, 49–50
criteria to evaluate, 50
officials' code, 180
origin and growth, 23–24
philosophy, 28
press service, 33
protection of eligibility of high school athletes, 51
recommended eligibility requirements, 29–32
report for international competition (form), 47–48
rules interpretation meetings, 60
rules to be observed, 144
rules writing program, 34–35
sanctioning policies and procedures, 38–46
services of, 32–38
sports participation surveys, 60
Student Protection Trust, 300
territorial sections, 25
National High School Activities Week, 61
National high school championships, elimination of, 39
National High School Sports Hall of Fame, 61
National Interscholastic Athletic Administrators Association (NIAAA):
objectives, 3–4
organization, 3
National Operating Committee for Standards of Athletic Equipment (NOCSAE), 36
activities of, 280–81
objectives, 280
National teams (*see* National Federation, national teams)
New Brunswick Interscholastic Athletic Association, purposes, 70–71
New York Public High School Athletic Association:
affiliation with State Department of Education, 72

New York Public High School Athletic Association (*cont.*):
elimination of academic requirements, 105
junior high school modified program, 352
protection plan, 299–300
Nonschool athletic competition, growth in, 389–90
North Dakota High School Activities Association, tobacco and liquor rule, 114

O

Officials:
classification of, 137
code for, 84, 180
contract with, 137–38
contracting of, 156–57
evaluation of, 137–38
fees paid, 138–39
form for agreement on, 128
registration, 77, 136–38
report to, 87
responsibility in safety, 285
Ohio High School Athletic Association:
academic eligibility standard, 105–6
contract for athletic contests (form), 126
officials' contract (form), 139
requirements for coaches, 132, 134
responsibility at contests (by-law), 40
Oklahoma Secondary School Activities Association:
conduct rule, 113
individual participation record (form), 172

P

Parents' permission, 157, 174–75
Parkway School District, athletic philosophy, 13
Pennsylvania Interscholastic Athletic Association:
amateur rule, 111–12
eligibility exchange provision, 131
purposes of, 69–70
Pep club sponsor, 223
Physical examinations (form), 103, 157
Policies (*see* Athletic policies)
Practices, athletic, length of, 181–82
Principal (*see* High school principal)
Professional athletic philosophy, 12
Protests and forfeiture, 140–42
Publications, state associations', 77–78
Publicity:
for athletic contests, 158–59
media for disseminating athletic information, 223–24
Purchase orders (form), 245, 246

R

Recruiting (*see* College recruiting; Eligibility requirements, recruiting and undue influence)
Reserve games, 159–60

S

Safety (*see* Health and safety program)
Sanctioning (*see* National Federation, sanctioning policies and procedures)
Schedules:
planning, 180–81
practice, 181–82
responsibility for, 180–81
Seasons (*see* Sports seasons)
Shuffleboard court, 313
Soccer field, 317
Society of State Directors of Physical and Health Education, 147, 304
Softball diamond, 319
Specialized athletic camps, limitation on attendance, 117–19, 380
Speedball field diagram, 316
Sportsmanship (*see* Conduct)
Sports seasons, 142–43
Standards of eligibility (*see* Eligibility requirements)
State high school associations (*see also* Appendix A):
activity associations, 68
athletic accident insurance plans, 76–77
district and state competition sponsored, 78–80
early associations, 67
establishment of athletic standards, 80–81
functions of, 75–89
interpretation of playing rules, 76
judicial function, 85, 88
legal authority of, 380–82
publication of, 77–78
purposes of, 68–71
registration of officials by, 77
support of, 89–90
types, 71–74
St. Louis Public High School League:
constitution, 205–12
regulation for awards, 235–36
Student managers, 184
Sunday or Christmas Day games, prohibition of, 146
Superintendents:
delegation of responsibilities, 195
responsibility for athletic program, 195–96

T

Television, encroachment on high school playing time, 391
Tennessee Secondary School Athletic Association:
married student rule, 116
requirements for coaches, 134
team follower regulations, 145
Tennis courts, 322–24
Texas University Interscholastic League:
contests sponsored, 75–76
organization of, 74–75
specialized camp rule, 117
Tickets for contests, 161
Title IX:
Guidelines for Federal Enforcement of the Education Acts of 1972, 372–74
impact on girls' athletics, 15
Tournaments (*see* Meet and tournament management)
Track and field (*see also* Facilities, athletic; Appendix C):
equipment, 322
L-type hurdles, 323
layout, 318–22
quarter-mile track diagram, 321
Transportation:
arrangement for, 174–76
safety in, 292–93

U

Unit purchasing, 244
U.S. Lawn Tennis Association, 322, 324
United States Olympic Committee:
developmental programs, 41–42
sports festivals, 42

V

Varsity clubs, 182–83
Virginia High School League:
special education eligibility standard, 106
sport seasons, 143
Volleyball court diagram, 311

W

Wisconsin Interscholastic Athletic Association:
athletic accident benefit plans, 299
provision for non-faculty coaches, 135
Wrestling, weight control policies, 281–82